TRANSPACIFIC, UNDISCIPLINED

Edited by Lily Wong | Christopher B. Patterson | Chien-ting Lin

TRANSPACIFIC

UNDISCIPLINED

University of Washington Press | Seattle

Transpacific, Undisciplined was made possible in part by a grant from the Samuel and Althea Stroum Endowed Book Fund.

Photographs by the author unless otherwise noted.

UNIVERSITY OF WASHINGTON PRESS | uwapress.uw.edu

LIBRARY OF CONGRESS CATALOGING-IN-PUBLICATION DATA
Names: Wong, Lily, editor. | Patterson, Christopher B., editor. | Lin, Chien-ting, editor.
Title: Transpacific, undisciplined / [edited by] Lily Wong, Christopher B. Patterson, Chien-ting Lin.
Description: Seattle : University of Washington Press, [2024] | Includes bibliographical references and index.
Identifiers: LCCN 2024014452 (print) | LCCN 2024014453 (ebook) |
     ISBN 9780295752747 (hardcover ; alk. paper) |
     ISBN 9780295752754 (paperback ; alk. paper) |
     ISBN 9780295752761 (ebook)
Subjects: LCSH: Pacific Area—History. | Pacific Area—Civilization. | Transnational history—Pacific Area.
Classification: LCC DU28.3 .T728 2024 (print) | LCC DU28.3 (ebook) |
     DDC 909/.09823—dc23/eng/20240515
LC record available at https://lccn.loc.gov/2024014452
LC ebook record available at https://lccn.loc.gov/2024014453

∞ This paper meets the requirements of ANSI/NISO Z39.48-1992 (Permanence of Paper).

CONTENTS

PART THREE UNSETTLING THE PACIFIC

ACKNOWLEDGMENTS

The ideas for this collection first sparked at conferences across Asia, Oceania, and North America, from Taipei to Manila to Honolulu to Atlanta to Vancouver to Seoul to Hong Kong. As we inhabited these geographic spaces—all of which felt marginal to both Asian American studies and Asia studies—our discussions gravitated toward our own transnational lives and how, like our lives, the works we produced did not seem to fit into any recognizable paradigm. "Transpacific studies," we had to admit, was not an accurate description either, though it was the closest term we could find at the time. Full of doubt about "the transpacific," we never accepted this moniker as our identity or our discipline. But as we searched for jobs, publications, and communities, we continued to rely on it.

The transpacific helped us gain the recognition for our work that other terms could not give and that other disciplines did not recognize. Yet, we continued to see "transpacific studies" as a term only meant to hold space, until a better term came along. Over time, as we met and read more scholars in this growing field, we found that most everyone who used the term "transpacific studies" shared the same doubts. Like us, they too were planning to jettison "the transpacific" term once the keyword outgrew its use. And yet, the more "transpacific studies" scholars we encountered, and the more we critiqued and sought to disabuse ourselves of the term, the more we realized that the term had already helped create the very thing we had been seeking: a community of scholars who shared our feelings, our critiques, and our doubts. We began to ponder: what if this community was not brought together *despite* the doubts we shared about "the transpacific," but precisely *because* of these doubts. Perhaps we felt tethered to this keyword precisely because of its ability to *un*tether us from other disciplines, in the collective hope that the future will provide us with something more.

We acknowledge this community of transpacific studies scholars whose mentorship and whose passion for the field have given us the energy and encouragement to produce this work: Aimee Bahng, Andrea Bachner, Brian Bernards, Tina Chen, Howard Chiang, Yu-fang Cho, Adrian De Leon, John Erni, Yến Lê Espiritu, Tara Fickle, Thy Fu, Donald Goellnicht, Vernadette Gonzalez, Grace Hyungwon Hong, Janet Hoskins, Clara Iwasaki, Joseph Jonghyun Jeon, Christine Kim, Jodi Kim, Christopher Lee, James Lee, Russel C. Leong, Helen Hok-Sze Leung, Shirley Geok-lin Lim, Lisa Lowe, Tan Jia, Viet Thanh Nguyen, Vinh Nguyen, erin Khuê Ninh, Jan Padios, Shuang Shen, Shu-mei Shih, E. K. Tan, Andy Chih-ming Wang, Alvin Wong, and Danielle Wong. Like transpacific studies itself, this list of names is incomplete, and always growing. Through this volume we hope to pass on their generosity to others.

We also thank all the contributors of this anthology: I-ting Chen, Leanne Day, Josen Masangkay Diaz, Evyn Lê Espiritu Gandhi, Kyung Hee Ha, Tzu-hui Celina Hung, Simeon Man, Y-Dang Troeung, and Quynh H. Vo. The project started before the COVID pandemic and evolved as our contributors and collaborators worked through childbirths, illnesses, and losses. Thank you for entrusting us with your words, labor, and contemplations. Special thanks to Mike Baccam and the team at the University of Washington Press, for believing in this project from day one and supporting it through the years. We are grateful for the two anonymous referees who offered astute suggestions that took the project that extra mile, and to Shyama Kuver, whose incredible artwork graces the cover of this book.

Lily thanks her fellow editors—Chris and Chien-ting—for envisioning, building, and collaborating on this project for over half a decade. Thank you for being such a generative intellectual home. Deep appreciation to Chrissy Lau and Nhu Le for their encouragement of interdisciplinarity and the trans-pacific-as-analytic, beginning in graduate school back at UCSB. Lily thanks her thought-partners and co-conspirators in and out of American University: Kirstie Dorr, Rae Jereza, Sara Clarke Kaplan, Taemin Kim, Keith Leonard, Alexis Lothian, Manissa Maharawal, Kamryn Olds, Amanda Phillips, Malini Ranganathan, Theresa Runstedtler, Eric Tang, and Connie Wun. She thanks her family, who also spans the Pacific, for their never-ending care, inspiration, and support. To Yan Zheng, Rae Wong Zheng (who arrived while this project was still in formation), and Roary (who we miss every day): none of this would be possible without you.

Chris thanks Lily and Chien-ting for never being shy to share their doubts and for their trust that our shared distrust could align across the seas and find greater purpose. Thanks to his committee members who, after he had faced the stone walls of many disciplinary mechanisms, suggested thinking of his dissertation as a transpacific project. Thank you Alys Weinbaum, Chandan Reddy, Gillian Harkins, and Francisco Benitez. Thanks also to his family, the Pattersons, the Guillermos, and the Troeungs, as well as his Vancouver coven: Ayasha and Uli, Ayesha and Rumee, David and Sophie, Maddie and Rawi, Jasbir and Jordy, Becca and Ollie, Mila and Will, Vinh and Thy, Kim, Logan, Justin, Alifa, and the many caretakers and friends whose kindness has remained abundant. Most of all, thank you Kai, for the love and joy you give every day.

Chien-ting thanks Lily and Chris for cultivating the space of collective thinking and acting in solidarity, for indulging with trust and care his belatedness and at times obstinacy, for reckoning with unsettling moments of debate and dis/agreement, and for coming to terms with yet remaining unsettled for the transpacific, undisciplined. Chien-ting feels forever connected with and grateful to their UCSD diasporic community, including Lisa Lowe, Lisa Yoneyama, Takashi Fujitani, Josen Diaz, Ash Kini, Victor Betts, Joo Ok Kim, Chris Perreira, Yumi Pak, Kyung Hee Ha, Davorn Sisavath, Angie Chau, Amie Parry, and Ari Heinrich, among others. Also, he is deeply appreciative of his queer and inter-Asia comraderies, especially Josephine Ho, Ding Naifei, Hans Huang, Liu Jen-peng, Grace Wu, Jonathan Yeh, Dai Peng-yi, Laura Pérez, Chen Kuan-Hsing, Tejaswini Niranjana, Chang Hsing-wen, Wong Wing-kwong, Eno Chen, Wu Pin-hsien, Daren Leung, Feng Pin-chia, Michelle Huang, Selta Lu, Glory Ho, Wendy Li, Amber Xiao, and Sony Coranez Bolton. His writing and thinking in this book are dedicated to his *family*, for more than he can express his gratitude in words, and beyond.

This collection is dedicated to the memory of Y-Dang Troeung, who passed away in November 2022 during the final stages of editing this manuscript. Her work appears here as a coauthor alongside her frequent collaborator, husband, and soulmate, Chris Patterson. Y-Dang lived and wrote with patience and care. Her works, like her coauthored chapter in this volume, are not compelled by argument and persuasion, but on the desire to teach, to share, to express, to reflect, and to hold onto hope. Her works are gifts, models of trust and restraint, and built upon the prevailing belief that our future holds something more.

TRANSPACIFIC, UNDISCIPLINED

INTRODUCTION INTIMATING CURRENT(S) OF THE TRANSPACIFIC

LILY WONG, CHRISTOPHER B. PATTERSON,

AND CHIEN-TING LIN

We write this introduction amid a global COVID-19 pandemic; a pandemic in which uneven effects have exposed and exacerbated imperial and colonial structures around the world. The viral outbreak has given rise to Sinophobic racism and anti-Asian violence in North America, Europe, the South Pacific, and South/East Asia.[1] In addition to the worldwide spread of xenophobic and anti-immigrant rhetoric, the sense of crisis has also worked to legitimize authoritarian repression and state-led militarization. As African residents in Guangzhou China are evicted from their homes and barred from restaurants, the detainment of Uighur Muslims in Xinjiang raises concerns of ethnic genocide by viral spread. Migrant workers continue to risk being infected living in tight lodgings, many of whom are undocumented and risk deportation from places that rely heavily on their essential labor, such as Singapore and Hawaiʻi.[2] While Pacific Islanders suffer disproportionately high rates of infection in areas like Los Angeles, viral outbreaks on US military bases in the Pacific Islands intensified the already unbalanced political relationship between the US federal government and its colonized territories.[3] The crowded conditions aboard the USS *Theodore Roosevelt*, for instance, led to the housing of US sailors quarantining in civilian areas of Guåhan despite expressed concerns from local residents. On March 16, 2021, eight women — six of whom were Asian — were killed in Asian-owned spas near Atlanta by a white man who was reported to be having "a bad day." The murders laid bare a long history of Asian sexualized racialization and of Asian sex work and care work, as well as its convergence with empire and state-sanctioned violence in a global context, including but not limited to the United States. These events highlight the fault lines of a long and broad history of biopolitical control and economic extraction and urge us to reckon with these evolving historical attachments in, across, and beyond the Pacific.

As an analytic, the "transpacific" allows for interdisciplinary examinations of imperial relations and unequal exchanges in and across Asia, the Pacific, and the Americas, as it is formed through historical complexities of war, militarism, racial capitalism, and settler colonialisms. Lisa Yoneyama argues that the transpacific framework—developing along the interstices of area studies, ethnic studies, and postcolonial studies—can "illuminate the predicaments that such disciplinary divides have concealed through their management of knowledge."[4] Lisa Lowe maintains that such interdisciplinarity exposes the way fields such as Asian studies, American studies, and Asian American studies are linked to US nationalist epistemologies that have "traditionally produced knowledge for the established centrality of the United States."[5]

Collective efforts to challenge such epistemological centrality continue to inspire critical knowledge formations that examine inter- and intra-imperial workings of power in relation to and beyond the structuring forces of US empire. This includes emergent frameworks such as Global Asia studies, Sinophone studies, and inter-Asia cultural studies, all of which contribute to the envisioning of a transpacific paradigm. In forging creative convergences across fields, the transpacific interrogates the connection between domestic race-based exploitation in imperial centers (e.g., the United States, China, Japan, and others) and their expansions abroad, exposing their inter- and intra-imperial entanglements.

Since the transpacific formulates in relation to geohistorical currents of colonial and imperial power dynamics, its emergence across disciplines also unevenly mediates the material conditions of political, economic, and epistemological asymmetries operating in a global Anglophone and inter-Asia context. To analyze the transpacific in relation to the ongoing logic of empire warns us against theorizing the transpacific as simply a descriptive form of migrancy and exchange across the Pacific Ocean. It prompts us to contend with the entanglements among ongoing settler-colonial practices, inter-Asia modernization, militarized global capitalism, and migrant and Indigenous navigations that challenge the disciplinization of knowledge.

Transpacific, Undisciplined approaches the transpacific not as a stable discipline or descriptor, but as an activating and problematizing analytic that continually reconfigures itself in relation to, even against, epistemological pulls across disciplines. We use "undisciplined" here to reconsider the multidisciplinary and interdisciplinary turn that has in some instances resulted in the sedimentation and institutionalization of particular fields like Asian studies, Asian American studies, and Indigenous studies, among others. Such field-building within the neoliberal institution, as Kandice Chuh has argued, can result in the existing disciplines remaining "at least at a radical level, relatively untouched by difference," in a form of "multidisciplinarity" that does not challenge existing disciplines and only serves to manage and "domesticate" forms of radicality and disciplinary critique.[6] Undisciplined, on the other hand, unsettles the liberalizing management of power by accounting for how various fields—and the methods they use for study—have historically affirmed the liberal discourses of multiculturalism and exceptionalism that value socioeconomic success.

We instead seek to understand the "undisciplined" in methods already in practice, from Lowe's methods of "intimacy" to the "transpacific entanglements" of Lowe, Espiritu, and Yoneyama, to Chuh's "deliberate promiscuity."[7] By putting into relation key approaches to the transpacific—as an *analytic* rather than the study of a given place—this collection intimates generative, if unexpected, connections and mobilizations of the concept against the fixation on national, disciplinary, or methodological boundaries. It holds space for a "messiness" of relations, projections, and bodies for study that perhaps approximates Martin Manalansan's rethinking of mess as "plentitude—as abundance and as opportunity."[8] For while Janet Hoskins and Viet Thanh Nguyen caution against the institutionalization of transpacific studies as an emerging field, they also stress the potential for the transpacific to emerge as a set of theories and methods that could both link and activate unorthodox intellectual currents.[9]

By placing a comma in the title—*Transpacific, Undisciplined*—we aim to denaturalize the grammatical relationship between the two concepts it both links and disrupts. In such an unsettled formation, the transpacific is not a fixed noun that is passively or inherently undisciplined; its undisciplinarity requires the reader's active interaction with the dynamism punctuated by the disruptive space the comma points to: an intermediary pause, an incoherence, and discomfort. It also compels a view of both concepts as unstable signifiers that at times work as nouns, as verbs, and as adjectives in relation to each other and dependent on context. The title's destabilizing formation is reflected in the way it puts into dialogue scholars with various specializations but whose critical work undercuts institutionalized divides of knowledge, thought, and practice (e.g., North American studies about Asia, American studies in Asia, Asian area studies in North America, Global Indigenous studies in relation to the Pacific Islands and Asian America, and inter-Asia studies in English).

We ask: How are we to grapple with the uneven material conditions that make the study of the transpacific legible and urgent? How do we unsettle the transpacific from imperialist frameworks that have obscured not only histories of the Pacific Islands but also the *historical interconnections* between ongoing militarized colonization of the Pacific Islands, legacies of inter-Asia Cold War formations, and the linkages between bodies of water in and beyond the Pacific Ocean? How might an undisciplined approach to the transpacific, grounded in historical relations among peoples, regions, and epistemologies, highlight the affective routes of peoples and populations who, despite being often rendered unintelligible through disciplinary frameworks, have long navigated imperial binds?

TRANSPACIFIC, UNDISCIPLINED

The transpacific formulates in relation to varied, and at times converging material histories and power dynamics. As Erin Suzuki notes, "There is not just one transpacific, but multiple transpacifics that conflict, intersect, and overlap."[10] While previous work on the region often furthered the militarized and economic expansion across Asia, the Americas, and the Pacific—through examination of treaties, trade agreements, and formal alliances—some scholars and activists have also reconceptualized the Pacific in a multitude of ways that challenge the very power structures that fashion its legibility.[11] It might be precisely these conceptual complexities, even incommensurabilities, that generate the framework's potential to "undiscipline" the very systems of knowledge that render the transpacific legible across fields of thought.

To rethink the transpacific framework entails both a remapping of scope and a reconstitution of methods. In questioning the frameworks "Pacific Rim" or "Asia-Pacific," some scholars have focused on how such frames hide US militarization as an extension of colonialism and its gendered and racialized processes, linking the effects of British, Japanese, and US imperialisms and their relation to the rise of China's political, economic, and military power in recent decades.[12] Suzuki and Aimee Bahng caution against formulating the transpacific through settler-colonial taxonomies that might rebrand comparative analysis between nation-based settler units and only serve to pass over or even obfuscate Indigenous place-based relations.[13] They argue, instead, for decolonial reworkings of the transpacific that engage more directly with Oceanic, Indigenous-centered epistemologies "that not only emphasize passage through or across the oceans, but are intimately engaged with the complexities of the local cultural, historical, and environmental specificities of the many spaces and places that comprise the region as a whole."[14] Similarly, work on the "Black Pacific" examines racial formations, Indigenous movements, and coalition politics, as scholars index geographies of Blackness across Oceania and between the Americas and Asia.[15]

As these scholars have shown, the task of transpacific studies today is not merely to expand previous terms to include others that have been exploited and obscured by its frameworks, but rather to reformulate such systems of knowledge altogether. Tina Chen stresses that to remap the transpacific critically is to not just create new maps, but also to question the methods and functions of the mapping itself.[16] It prompts us to rethink discourses of civilizational development (democracy vs. authoritarianism), moral hierarchy (human rights discourse), and nation-states (competing hegemonic views) that sustain Euro-American–centered Cold War ideological frameworks.[17] It cautions against mining the people, land, or goods of a region as extractable content or as resources to sustain the viability, or "coverage" of ongoing imperial epistemologies and practices.[18] Such a rethinking necessitates a restructuring of knowledge across and against disciplines.

Scholars working at the intersections of fields have stressed the potential for the transpacific to formulate epistemological reimagining. With the idea of "transpacific entanglements," Espiritu, Lowe, and Yoneyama offer methods for tracing "related, yet often illegible, struggles" against the foreclosure of imperial narratives.[19] Focusing on epistemological "entanglements," they call upon us to "link apparently separate subjects, contexts, and issues whose connections have been rendered unavailable by existing geographical, political, and disciplinary boundaries."[20] By juxtaposing seemingly disparate objects of study to reveal relational dynamics that would otherwise remain invisible, the authors refocus attention onto the openings and excesses of imperial knowledge formations and find potential in what "we cannot entirely know or anticipate."[21] "Critical juxtaposition," as Espiritu defines it, questions a politics of comparison that presumes two or more "already-constituted and discrete entities," to instead see such entities as "fluid rather than static and [that thus] need to be understood in *relation* to each other and within the context of a flexible field of political discourses."[22] To reconceptualize the transpacific analytic through Espiritu's model of critical juxtaposition allows us to examine the relations between militarism in Asia and the Pacific Islands, global formations of racial capitalism, and ongoing settler-colonial practices.

In mobilizing a critical juxtaposition and entanglement approach to the transpacific, this collection aims to trace seemingly unrelated, even conflicting intellectual fields across empires, local struggles, and interimperial intimacies. Formulating beyond simple Asia and America dyads, the transpacific framework offers critical pathways across comparative imperial and settler-colonial problematics.[23] At the center of our efforts to "undiscipline," is a rethinking of racialized regimes of knowledge that comfortably rest upon colonial-imperialist compartmentalization of areas, nations, peoples, and disciplines. Our political investment in this project lies in both the potential for the transpacific to destabilize disciplinary regimes of power *as well as* the risk of its collusion with neoliberal knowledge forms (that is, the institutionalization of disciplinary fields and reification of anthropological differences of areas and peoples). In understanding this problematic in view of the increasing currency bestowed upon transpacific studies as an emerging field, this collection's contributors explore the potentials of decolonial imaginaries enabled by the transpacific's political and affective *infidelity* to any discipline.

This intellectual move is in part a response to Hoskins and Nguyen's reminder to not privilege the United States as the primary or sole site for critical interrogations of imperialist formations in the Pacific.[24] They suggest that to provincialize the US empire and its transpacific imperialist design in Asia and the Pacific requires a simultaneous departure from East-Asian centrism.[25] In turn, *Transpacific, Undisciplined* aims to unsettle epistemic (b)orders informed by colonial-imperialist and Cold War formations of Asia and the Pacific that reify the demarcations of the West and the East; the universal and the particular; the developed and the underdeveloped. We stress that anti–East Asian centrism requires a de-Cold War disarticulation of epistemologies that cohered through a colonial investment in additive forms of academic fields. The categorization of "East Asia," "Southeast Asia," and "the Pacific," for instance, needs to be interrogated as a transpacific *problem of knowledge* rather than an object of study that invites an oppositional critique.

Cast in this light, inter-Asia cultural studies has shared the problems of knowledge that concern the "epistemic asymmetries" in transpacific discourses vis-à-vis "the rise of China" by critically engaging with the ongoing interimperialist formations and the Cold War's lingering effects in the Pacific.[26] As Yoneyama observes, these renewed meanings of the transpacific may be understood "as a symptom of growing North American preoccupations with China's military, financial, political, and cultural power in recent decades."[27] That is, China's economic ascendence since the 1980s and its growing impact on the military and diplomatic landscapes of global politics have urged us to constantly renew the transpacific analytic to attend to the shifting geopolitical tensions in the South China and East China Seas; regarding the One Belt, One Road initiatives in Africa, Central Asia, South Asia, Southeast Asia, the Middle East, Latin America and the Caribbean; the Chinese capital flow into Asia and the Pacific Islands; and developments in the US-China trade war, which has been referred to as the "new Cold War" of political, military, and economic transformation; not to mention the global racialization of the COVID-19 pandemic regarding China and beyond.[28]

The transpacific geopolitical asymmetries about China—perceived as a new challenge to US hegemony—have made it crucial to attend to issues such as the Hong Kong protests, the pro-Trump stance in Taiwanese and Vietnamese nationalisms, and the anti-China alliance in Japan.[29] How do we account for the global "rise of China" discourses that often position China as a new empire contributing to the precarity of neighboring nations on the one hand, and reckon with the lingering colonial unconscious and the disavowal of racism central to nationalistic historical narratives on the other?[30] The transpacific analytic allows us to reexamine the longer histories of imperial formations and Cold War entanglements, not only through national lines but also through the nationalistic logics at work in sovereign state formations in transwar and postwar development.

Transpacific, Undisciplined aims to understand these entangled yet obscured histories of violence, subjugation, and loss. The imperial and colonial conditions that the Japanese and US empires kept intact in Asia and the Pacific have very much informed postcolonial state formation and the ways knowledge is produced in the region. These conditions prevent us from arriving at a transregional and transnational understanding of our position within longer genealogies of power and reveal the importance of a transpacific critique that is geohistorically grounded in analysis of the colonial and imperial violence of nationalism, racial capitalism, and settler militarism. The transpacific is cautiously contingent on the geohistorical re/dis/articulations of power-in-shift that unevenly mediate the political economy of emerging knowledge paradigms. Taking together these transpacific insights and inter-Asia inter-referencing helps us understand how "marginality" is produced and how it impacts the historical understanding of changes taking place in geopolitical arrangements on a global scale. We analyze ongoing imperialist formations in the historical conjuncture of the "new cold war" developments in and between China and the United States and their triangulation with Asia and the Pacific.

Thus by tracing the varied and at times overlapping discourses of the transpacific, this collection situates transpacific studies not as another merging of disciplines, but as a set of tools to trouble logics embedded in disciplinization, through its consideration of multiple interdisciplinary fields, their relation to geopolitical spaces and state interests, and the positionalities of many of their leading scholars. *Transpacific, Undisciplined* resists the neoliberal management of regional marginality, which simply incorporates understudied areas of Asia and the Pacific Islands. In our intellectual praxis, as demonstrated in each individual chapter and in the collection as a whole, we challenge the Cold War logics and colonial legacies that demarcate differentiated areas of concern by addressing the interconnected histories of imperialism, settler colonialism, and racial capitalism in the seemingly unrelated "areas" of Asia, the Pacific, and the Americas.

One way we can begin to undiscipline transpacific studies would be to see its sliding back and forth among imagined geographies and discourses as similar to the slash in the term "Asia/America" that David Palumbo-Liu coined in 1999 as signifying "a dynamic, unsettled, and inclusive movement."[31] We see a similar gesture made in Tina Chen's 2020 essay "(The) Transpacific Turns," which we find generative for sketching out the blurred boundaries of geographies as well as understanding the bodily, artistic, and affective knots that entangle these discourses within global capital. For Chen, transpacific studies carries varied possibilities through its "inherent incoherence," where ideas and methods are subjected to "turns and turning" and are in "rotation, revolution, repression, relation, and recursivity."[32] To think through "turns" as both thing and action is also to build frameworks that allow for multiple ways of seeing: the trans-epistemologies that do not put sharp focus on particular spaces and peoples but rather note how each "turn" can reveal alternative political investments and different dynamics of power. And here we hear the inquiring reader: How does one invest in a field made up of turns—of inconsistencies, uncertainties, and blurs? How long can one continue to turn before spinning off balance?

To give a brief example of the ways transpacific studies might find momentum in turning among discourses—or, the "turn" as an undisciplined method—we consider the imagined geography of the transpacific itself among the turns of Asia / Pacific \ America. In their introduction to the edited special issue of *positions: asia critique*, titled "The End of Area," Gavin Walker and Naoki Sakai ask how a relational focus on race and ethnicity between Asian studies scholars and the areas they study can expose the desires, commitments, and privileges of the scholars themselves, whose role can exhibit "an imperialist will to sovereignty" and "does not conceal the manifestation of colonial cartography according to which the surface of the earth is divided into multiple segments for remote control."[33] The consistent disavowal of race that Walker and Sakai find intrinsic to Asian studies presumes an ideal scholar to be an objective evaluator whose epistemologies rely upon a concealed imperial gaze. Through this logic, scholars of Asian racial backgrounds can be habitually dismissed in Asian studies as people "deemed to be lacking the requisite distance from the object of study."[34] At the same time, this dismissal itself can be read as an affective response to conceal the Asian studies scholar's own nonbelonging as an outsider and presumed producer of imperial knowledge. This claiming of *objectivity* by dismissing Asian/American *subjectivity* has become a recognizable tactic that legitimates the whiteness of Asian studies and detracts from its imperial formations and US state investments.

These affective motivators, when it comes to academic studies of Asia, have had a grave impact on how geographies of "the Pacific" are imagined as a binary between Asia and America and how it has remained trenchant, less through an orientalist logic of opposed (and self-productive) difference but more through a presumed logic of epistemological (and therefore political) *distance*. While in Asian studies this distance is often incorporated as the objectivity of "non-Asian" (often white) scholars to "their area," in Asian American studies it frequently recurs through discourses of trauma, war, homophobia, and multiculturalism, wherein Asia is situated within a political spectrum as a place — often a homeland — of regression, destruction, and traumatic memory. Rather than reinforce a scholar's *objectivity*, this form of epistemological distancing reinforces the Asian American scholar's (and thus America's) perceived *progressivity*. For instance, in her 2020 book *Traffic in Asian Women*, Laura Kang argues that the discourse of Asian sex slavery by Asian American academics shifted ways of viewing race from "Asian difference and unknowability" to discourses of trauma and memory that frame Asian women as "bodies in pain" (or, as Sara Ahmed describes, "the other as the one who 'has' pain").[35] Asia itself has become framed as a space of regressive distance in its vulnerability to state-sanctioned violence, thus displacing relational concerns for labor exploitation, US military bases, and the varied impacts of knowledge production from the United States (even from US minoritized subjects) to Asia. We can use Kang's reading of the "much-touted transnational turn" in Asian American studies to assess the affective motives of Asian American studies scholars who have sought to marshal empathy and support for Asian "bodies in pain" yet want to simultaneously "confirm and affirm a range of other 'American' identity categories," such as the category "Asian American" itself.[36]

In turn (or, to continue our turn), we could also explore this affective racial hinge of Asian distance in the work of Pacific Island scholars who have understood the scholarship of many settler scholars of Hawai'i and other Pacific Islands as an attempt to "self-indigenize" and "possess" the islands — to claim the islands as American rather than Asian. Maile Arvin's 2019 book, *Possessing Polynesians*, sees the intellectual projects on racializing Polynesian populations as indicative of a "settler colonialism in Hawai'i and Polynesia more broadly" that is fueled by "a logic of possession through whiteness."[37] In Pacific Island studies this logic of possession has sometimes taken the form of repeatedly positioning Polynesians "as almost white (even literally as descendants of the Aryan race), in a way that allows white settlers to claim indigeneity in Polynesia."[38] Working among the fields of Pacific Island studies, Asian American studies, and Black studies, Arvin's work follows Indigenous critiques of settler colonialism directed at both white and Asian diasporic scholars in Hawai'i. Haunani-Kay Trask's critiques of Asian settler colonialism since the 1980s has coincided with studies by Ronald Takiki, Gary Okihiro, and the early work of many others who sought to frame Asians in Hawai'i as "builders" who earned civil belonging in Hawai'i's multicultural state.[39] As Candace Fujikane wrote in the 2008 anthology she coedited with Jonathan Y. Okamura, *Asian Settler Colonialism*, "ethnic histories written about Asians in Hawai'i demonstrate an investment in the ideal of American democracy that is ideologically at odds with Indigenous critiques of US colonialism."[40] Asian academics in Hawai'i, as Trask pointed out in the late 1990s, claimed "Hawai'i as their own, denying Indigenous history, their long collaboration in our continued dispossession, and the benefits therefrom."[41] The Indigenous critique of Asian settlers and self-described "locals" in Hawai'i has traced the deep fidelity of many Asian/American scholars to American belonging even in their critiques of US imperial violence, where the injustices of Japanese American incarceration and anti-Chinese racism are remembered not as part of the long history of US racial atrocities that began with the violences of Black slavery and Indigenous dispossession but as the failure of the US state to recognize Asian Americans' belonging as Americans.

To (re)turn to Arvin's critique of settler-colonial possession of Polynesian bodies, we may also note how an account of settler colonialism on Kanaka Maoli (Native Hawaiians) can also risk transposing logics of distance not merely to Asian settlers but toward Indigenous peoples across Oceania and Asia, where Polynesians have often been framed as "almost white" in comparison to Micronesians and other "darker" groups in the Philippines and Indonesia as well as to Black and South Asian settlers.[42] At the same time, Oceanic discourses across the South Pacific have envisioned Oceanic connections as an Indigenous world-making praxis where, as Epeli Hau'ofa wrote, "there are no national boundaries drawn across the sea between our countries."[43] The many authors across Oceania extending this tradition have remained conscious of the ways that state-condoned and academically sedimented Indigenous identities have been continuous of colonial race-making and separative tactics, and in so doing have sought to disrupt binaries of land/water, Indigenous/Asian, "good native"/"bad colonizer."[44]

To be clear, these examples are not meant to sum up, canonize, historicize, nor even make comparisons among the arguments in these fields in a way that might propose a single transpacific, where "distance" plays a privileged role and scholars can be psychoanalyzed for their affective or political motivations. The point is to consider the "turn" as an undisciplined method that can produce far more questions than it can answer, whose characteristics of a field or a place are always (and explicitly) interdependent—such is their relation—to other fields and places. It is also meant to call attention to ways of understanding that might follow J. Kēhaulani Kauanui's ask of American studies scholars to seek not "better 'coverage' within the field" but the "multidimensions of US domination."[45] Our attention to the tethering of a scholar's identity as white "objective" scholar, Asian American scholar, Asian settler scholar, and the like, are meant to question the consistent flattening (rather than disavowal) of one's own standpoint in relation to the way Asia \ Oceania / America are conceived: as objective, as resistant, as traumatized, as belonging within a multicultural nation. Following Lowe's *The Intimacies of Four Continents*, we desire to "focus on relation across differences rather than equivalence, on the convergence of asymmetries rather than the imperatives of identity."[46] How, then, can transpacific studies focus on "relation across difference"? What methods or relations can we understand as undisciplined by the consistent and sometimes incoherent movement of turns?

INTIMATING TRANSPACIFIC CURRENT(S)

We might begin to consider transpacific relations with a simple dialectical antithesis taken from Lowe: "intimate" rather than "distant." Lowe instructs her use of intimacy as "a heuristic, and a means to observe the historical division of world processes into those that develop modern liberal subjects and modern spheres of social life."[47] Expanding on Lowe, we read intimate less as a noun and more as a verb: to intimate, to make familiar, to impress, to imply, or to hint. While in scholarly practice "to state" or "to argue" clarifies one's particular episteme—*one* object of analysis and *one* conclusive series of recommendations—to intimate contains multiple interpretations, multiple epistemes, multiple objects of analysis and functions through hint, tease, allusion, suggestion, implication, and clue. "To state" insists on a state of things and relies on "state"-condoned institutional power; "to intimate" leaves crumb trails that might suggest various aims and can invite multiple readings (reading queerly, reading against the grain).[48]

Many scholars writing within emerging fields of transpacific studies, Oceanic studies, inter-Asia cultural studies, and others have sought ways of intimating the distance between Asia and America without overriding their differences and power imbalances. Transpacific studies scholars in particular have shown how the separations of Asia and America are entangled with anti-immigrant racial formations that were violently equipped and remade during the Philippine-American War, World War II, and the Cold War, including the Korean War and the Vietnam War (which secretly and illegally included the bombings of Laos and Cambodia). They have also understood America as *in* Asia in multiple ways: as fiftieth state (Hawaiʻi), as colonized territory (Guam/Guåhan), as military bases that scatter the Philippines, Japan, and South Korea, as hegemonic global media, as the ubiquity of American capital and the English language, and as the American "sub-empires" of Taiwan, South Korea, the Philippines, and others that establish imperial routes and buttress an American Pacific "transnational garrison state."[49]

Since the emergence of transpacific studies in the early 2010s, many scholars have conceived methods for intimating the transpacific:

- Lisa Lowe's "intimacy" as heuristic
- Denise Cruz's use of *trans* in *trans*pacific as "states of transition and change"
- Yến Lê Espiritu's notion of "grafting" across maps
- Eng-Beng Lim's "brown boy–rice queen" dyad to read colonial erotics
- Simeon Man's use of "soldiering" to understand the multitude of war-related labor
- Long Bui's framing of "The Pacific Theater" as the Vietnamization of war
- Lily Wong's concept of "transpacific attachments" to read Chinese-ness as a deterritorialized affective product
- Lowe, Espiritu, and Lisa Yoneyama's use of "transpacific entanglements"
- Chris Patterson's use of "transitive cultures" to understand diasporic practices of racial shifting
- Chien-ting Lin's framing of "transpacific medical modernity" to account for nationalist discourses of disability
- Christine Kim and Helen Leung's use of "minor transpacifics" to explore the interdependences and lateral relations among "minor histories and minor locations"[50]
- Chua Beng-Huat's attempts to relate "inter-Asia beyond Asia"
- Tan Jia's "transpacific inter-referencing" to problematize "the existing epistemic structures that rest on the binary of West/non-West or West/Asia"[51]
- Craig Santos Perez's use of the "transterritorial turn" to foreground "the territorial and maladjust the national," as well as his use of "terripelago"[52]
- Jinah Kim's formulation of "Postcolonial grief" to describe "a structure of feeling across the Pacific Arena"[53]
- Tina Chen's characterization of transpacific "incoherence" through "turns" and "imaginative ageography"

This is an admittedly narrow, reductive, and incomplete list based on scholars whose work has direct use of the term "transpacific studies" or has the term in the title of the book or article that features their referenced ideas.[54] In listing these methodological interventions, we observe shared intellectual efforts to "intimate" transpacific relations through (1) languages of *affect and erotics* ("intimacy," "entanglement," "attachments," "grief," "brown boy/rice queen"); (2) languages of *unsettlement and movement* ("turns," "trans," "soldiering," "transitive"), and (3) languages that find new relations among transpacific spaces without reference to national borders ("grafting," "interreferencing," "minor," "medical modernity"). Intimated knowledges may not seek direct arguments or impacts but rather allow different perspectives and discourses to dwell beside each other. Such ways of "unthinking mastery" are, in Julietta Singh's words, "not anticipatable, and thus are vitally antimasterful and lead us toward our vulnerabilities."[55] The contributors to this anthology expand on many of the methods outlined here to intimate space across Asia / Pacific \ America and the disciplinization of knowledge.

Such undisciplined potentials are reflected in the contributors' work that, together, intimate convergences that are frequently concealed by epistemological divides. While each chapter enacts its own transpacific turns, we as editors critically juxtapose their work to show how they intimate transpacific entanglements relationally across multiple scales: from minor-to-minor subject formations, to epistemological intersections, to coalitional movement building. Part 1, "Figuring the Pacific," analyzes figures who are often flattened out through cross-Pacific forms of commodified extraction and attempts to intimate these figures' relations to narratives of national progress, capital, and militarism. Leanne Day's chapter, "'This Is Paradise': Transpacific Labor, Indigeneity, and 'Undocumented' in Hawaiʻi's Hospitality Industry," examines the intersection of settler colonialism and diasporic migration by exploring how the narrative erasure of the "undocumented immigrant" figure reveals the mutual exploitation of migrant labor and Kanaka ʻŌiwi culture in Hawaiʻi's hospitality industry. Also utilizing a relational paradigm, I-ting Chen's chapter, "Paradoxical Affect: Cross-Strait Intimacy in the Taiwan Teahouse," investigates how the legacy of the Cold War and the Chinese Civil War shape understandings of cross-strait relations. In particular, Chen focuses on the figure of mainland Chinese hostesses who entertain Taiwanese clients in Taiwan teahouses, analyzing the potentials of the erotic and intimate. While both Day's and Chen's chapters complicate concepts of "illegal" and "illegible" subjectivity within the liberal security state, Y-Dang Troeung and Christopher Patterson's chapter, "The Arts of Emotional Automation: Empathy Machines and Asian 'Victims' in Virtual Reality," details the affective politics of rendering the refugee figure "legible" through virtual reality. They argue that virtual reality automates the process of empathy meant to provide humanity not to the refugee but to the viewer, an argument that emerges through the conjunctive pull among critical refugee studies, transpacific studies, and critical game studies.

Part 2, "Grafting the Pacific," expands the interdisciplinary focus to show how an undisciplined approach to the transpacific allows us to not only analyze figures whose livelihoods are easily obscured, but also to trace—or graft—linkages across such obscurity. As Yến Lê Espiritu maintains, such a grafting connects the dots to critically juxtapose colonial histories in various spaces (such as in the Philippines, Guam, and Vietnam) and "offers the promise that even deliberately discarded histories will continue to be told as they bump against, intersect with, and route through the lives of kin communities."[56] Josen Masangkay Diaz's chapter, "Apprehending Filipino America," troubles the epistemological category of Filipino America, arguing that it is an unstable formation that reveals transpacific relations of overlapping empires, authoritarian governmentality, and multidirectional circuits of capitalist exchange. Diaz employs the transpacific as an analytic to apprehend the ways nations and peoples who were once deemed the object of colonial governance become subjects of global remaking. That is, rather than employ the transpacific to recover unfound knowledges, the transpacific for Diaz helps disentangle the objects and subjects from the practice of knowledge. Evyn Lê Espiritu Gandhi's chapter, "Transpacific Archipelagic Poetics: Connecting Antibase Activism in Okinawa with Military Buildup Protests in Guåhan," stresses the need for archipelagic analyses of transpacific American military empire as well as tactics of island-based solidarities and resistance. As an example, she locates resonances between Okinawa and Guåhan in relation to Japanese and American settler colonialism, imperialism, and militarism. Extending Gandhi's call to trace decolonizing solidarities, Tzu-hui Celina Hung's contribution, "Fishers, Captives, and Storytellers in Taiwan's Transnational Fishing Industry," analyzes the entanglement of Asia's multinational seafarers in Taiwan's controversial offshore fisheries. Hung argues that the trans in transpacific studies signals both the necessity and challenge of cultural translation—the affix functions first and foremost as a critical action-word for scrutinizing the specific manners of intercommunity exchange, as well as the ensuant epistemological ruptures between Taiwan's local storytellers and the often-ineffable migrant life spent in the rarely seen spaces of boat, harbor, prison, and tropical home.

The epistemological intersections grafted in part 2 leads into part 3, "Unsettling the Pacific," which explores the decolonizing practices that both enable and are enabled by transpacific knowledges, asking how more intimate knowledges might generate and reimagine decolonial methods. Kyung Hee Ha's chapter, "Transpacific Feminist Movement: Challenging Japan's Military Sexual Slavery System," examines the collaborative campaigns carried out by the Comfort Women Justice Coalition in San Francisco and the Kansai Network in Osaka, Japan. Ha argues that this transpacific coalition formulates a unique mode of collective action and community-building based on a shared feminist critique of sexual violence under Japanese colonialism and ongoing historical denialism. Similarly, Simeon Man's piece, "Pacific Internationalism: Movements for a Nuclear-Free and Independent Pacific," traces the history of another transpacific coalition: the Nuclear Free and Independent Pacific movement in the 1970s and 1980s that coalesced interlinked geographies, including Micronesia, Okinawa, and the Black Hills of North Dakota, as well as Chamorro, Micronesian, Okinawan, and Indigenous peoples of North America. The movement, Man shows, forged a radical alliance that broadened the call for "safety" advocated by mainstream antinuclear activists. Also analyzing transpacific mobilizations, Quynh H. Vo's chapter, "Transpacific Rupture: Neoliberal Relationalities and Economic Violence in the COVID Era," traces an asymmetrical form of solidarity between Vietnamese nationals and Vietnamese Americans in the era of COVID-19 and rising Sinophobia. To Vo this partnership is grounded in historical erasures of militarized cooperation across empires, in unjust geopolitical interventions, and in neoliberal economic violence; a hostile political assemblage she terms "transpacific rupture." By scrutinizing the deep historical entanglements that mobilize current-day transpacific ruptures, Vo argues for the urgency of (re) imagining decolonial futurities.

Together the chapters here interrogate the cross-disciplinary entanglements involved in the emergence of transpacific studies. Foregrounding shifting relations among minor-to-minor figuring (part 1), epistemological intersections (part 2), and historical mobilizations (part 3), the collection grapples with the affective, spatial, and temporal encounters that undisciplined approaches to the transpacific activate across and against national, cultural, and historical (il)legibility. Capacious, if not definitive, the works included here aim to convene and catalyze ongoing conversations around the transpacific in the hope that others will continue to turn it in different directions. As such, we approach the transpacific as less a cohesive paradigm and more as epistemological "current(s)" that are urgently and unevenly felt as tensions in the psyche and as debilitations of the bodymind. We use the Oceanic metaphor of current(s) to invoke the *spatial currents* activated through conjunctive pulls among divergent bodies, epistemologies, and geopolitical relations, as well as the *temporal* current of our historical moment imbricated in ongoing transformations of colonialism, empire, and militarization. To conceptualize the transpacific in light of such current(s) is to engage with the geohistorical relations that give rise to what Keith Camacho and Setsu Shigematsu call the "current desirability of the Pacific": a region that is at present heavily exploited for its "visible militarist and tourist value yet ultimately made invisible in its human diversity and complexity."[57]

Our desire to see the undisciplining of transpacific studies as a method of intimated knowledge inevitably must function as self-critique, as any method of turn must eventually turn against the self. We thus gesture too to how we might read ourselves against the grain, to consider how our positionalities as diasporic, US-trained, and well-traveled Asian/American academics has led us to resist the "disciplining" of transpacific studies, or to enclose the "distance" of Asia and America. One may notice in our choice of references a revisiting of the difficult problem of theorizing from a top-down, center-periphery mode, where the West *theorizes* while the rest *analyzes*, or as Kuan-Hsing Chen puts it, "the West is equipped with universalist theory; the rest of us have particularist empirical data; and eventually our writings become a footnote that either validates or invalidates Western theoretical propositions."[58] From the purview of Oceania, the Māori/Pacific and Indigenous scholar Alice Te Punga Somerville similarly states that the Pacific "suffers from being understood as a region in which research 'content' may be found, whereas research 'practice,' including critical or theoretical work, happen elsewhere."[59] We thus question to what extent thinking toward turn could presume a particular "Western-facing" direction as a starting point. Following Somerville, we use "turn" to push for a transpacific studies that also takes into account how many intellectuals and writers "have not needed a 'turn to the sea' because we were already there."[60]

Another important self-critical gap we have come across as editors of this collection is the centering of the Pacific Ocean itself within a somewhat globalizing discourse that is in conversation with, but also not seeking to incorporate, studies of Oceania. In other words, perhaps what we've unsettled in this collection is the very "Pacific" of trans*pacific*, a large ocean that resignifies the value of spatial proximity (and, in fact, can have many oceans). Even as we may seek to move away from "us" to the "larger us" or to the spaces and peoples "beside(s) us" (the spaces and histories in between), this imaginary geographical limitation makes it difficult to understand current movements across lands and bodies of water that remain of crucial importance. China's colonial projects in Africa, its One Belt, One Road initiative projecting through western Asia, and its inner-colonial enterprises in Xinjiang and Tibet, are all far from the Pacific Ocean. We also leave out attention onto the United States' antipodal space (its global opposite) of the Indian Ocean, which continues to remain an area of imperial traffic, less of consumer goods and more of extracted materials (mined ore), food (rice, tea), and other resources that have yet to be manufactured into commodities for Western markets.

We titled this introduction "Intimating Current(s) of the Transpacific" to offer a metaphoric conjoining that can delineate the ontological blur between continents and oceans. We invoke both Lowe's "intimacies of four continents" and Shigematsu's and Camacho's notion of "currents" as both geohistorical and temporal metaphors that offer an affective grammar that challenges the boundaries of sea and land, that is, the many Pacifics and the many continents. We follow those in Native Pacific studies who have offered critical frameworks for making visible the histories and ongoing impacts of American empire by troubling distinctions of land and sea, as well as public and private, commons and non-commons. As Susan Y. Najita writes in her essay on "public lands" in Hawai'i, the segmentation of sacred lands into public commons and terra nullius "justified a new boundary of (colonial) 'public' domain from which private entrepreneurs stood to gain substantially."[61] Troubling such categories, the Chamoru (Chamorro) poet and scholar Craig Santos Perez builds off of Shelley Fishkin's call to blend boundaries of imperial and nonimperial zones to call instead for a "transterritorial turn" that explores the boundaries of incorporated and unincorporated territories (rather than national borders).[62] For Perez these boundaries frequently invoke divisions of land and sea and obscure the territorializing efforts of US empire that seek to capture Pacific peoples and lands. In turn Perez offers the term "terripelago," which "combines territorium and pélago" to foreground how territoriality (or envisioned claims to territory) conjoin "land and sea, islands and continents." Terripelago contrasts the view of territoriality as a claim to land rather than to ocean and broadens the terms of settlement toward cartographic logics of possession and elimination. Similarly, Somerville metaphorizes the relations of Pacific peoples and continental powers through the great Pacific garbage patch, which, as Somerville notes, challenges distinctions like plastic/water, trash/people, health/pollution, as well as the presumed dynamics of America, Asia, and the Pacific, through its visibility as aggregation but invisibility as discard, and through its reversal of ocean to land relations (where ocean is threatened by land rather than the inverse). The invisibility of the patch that renders it "out of sight" from both Asia and North America depends partially on its blurring of land and sea, as affected by "currents and tides" but also as an active and mobile archipelagic network.[63] The great garbage patch thus analogizes the need to think outside of empire to understand the global impact and accumulation of "debris," but also the remaining importance of imperial critique, as Somerville writes: "Like the Pacific region, the garbage patch is both under the control and beyond the control of several nations—not just one—but the dominant supplier of plastic to the patch is America and American-controlled industry, and the dominant language used to talk about the patch—the dominant referent—is American."[64] Centered within the Pacific, the great Pacific garbage patch might operate as a metaphor here too for transpacific studies, as an undisciplined potentiality and a field of seas and lands "made up of constituent parts whose medium both of connection and disconnection is the ocean."[65]

"Intimating current(s)" compels us to understand how an undisciplined transpacific studies blends Pacific studies with Asian and Asian American studies without needing to encompass or speak for any particular field or region. We see such blending in Rob Wilson's readings of Chinese militarism in the South China Seas through Pacific and oceanic discourses;[66] in the ways that trans-Indigenous organizing has emerged in militarized zones of Okinawa, Jeju island, and Taiwan; and in the ways that subempires like the Philippines have been read as part of an American archipelagic colonial network. Part of our project is not only to understand how transpacific methods can unsettle other prominent discourses, but also to see what gets obscured by these prominent methods and what remains unaccounted for when we center "the transpacific." Our use of intimacy as a verb, "to intimate," hopes to keep these terms animated toward unseen possibilities. As Mel Chen writes, intimacy can be reframed "so that it might not be restricted to operating between only human or animate entities," and can rather operate "as a temporalized notion insofar as it might provide a hint or prediction of the future."[67] The future orientation of "to intimate" urges us to both remain "current" and follow the currents where they may lead, even if they flow away from the transpacific and the term itself becomes less capable of animating our respective methods and political commitments. Put another way: if the undisciplining of transpacific studies can reveal new wayward histories, methods, and relations, can we also imagine a post-transpacific-studies forum that seeks to understand how transpacific studies can mis-recognize imperial power today? Even in this attention to peripheries, what delimits the transpacific itself? In our turn to "turn," can we see our risk of falling off balance not as a failure but as the very goal of the transpacific project itself?

NOTES

1. Lauren Aratani, "'Coughing while Asian': Living in Fear as Racism Feeds Off Coronavirus Panic," *The Guardian*, March 24, 2020, https://www.theguardian.com /world/2020/mar/24/coronavirus-us-asian-americans-racism; Paula Larsson, "Coronavirus: How Language of Disease Produces Anti-Asian Racism, Hate and Violence," *The Conversation*, March 31, 2020, https://theconversation.com/anti-asian-racism-during -coronavirus-how-the-language-of-disease-produces-hate-and-violence-134496; Seashia Vang, "Trump Adds to Asian-Americans' Fears: We Already Have an Epic Health

Crisis; We Don't Need a Racialized Social Crisis as Well," *The Diplomat*, April 1, 2020, https://thediplomat.com/2020/04/trump-adds-to-asian-americans-fears/; Society of Sinophone Studies, "Anti-Racism Solidarity Statement," June 14, 2020, https://www .sinophonestudies.org/antiracism-solidarity-statement.

2. Phoebe Zhang and Guo Rui, "Coronavirus: Crackdowns, Racism and Forced Quarantine Heighten Tension for Africans in Guangzhou," *South China Morning Post*, May 2, 2020, https://www.scmp.com/news/china/society/article/3082186/coronavirus -crackdowns-racism-and-forced-quarantine-heighten; April Zhu, "A Lost 'Little Africa': How China, Too, Blames Foreigners for the Virus," *New York Review*, May 5, 2020, https://www.nybooks.com/contributors/april-zhu/; Prakhar Raghuvanshi, "The Persecution of the Uighur Minority Amidst COVID-19," *Jurist*, May 21, 2020, https:// www.jurist.org/commentary/2020/05/prakhar-raghuvanshi-uighur-muslims-covid19/; "China Plans to Send Uygur Muslims from Xinjiang Re-Education Camps to Work in Other Parts of Country," *South China Morning Post*, May 2, 2020, https://www.scmp .com/news/china/politics/article/3082602/china-plans-send-ugyur-muslims-xinjiang -re-education-camps-work; Dominique Mosbergen, "COVID-19 Surge Exposes Ugly Truth About Singapore's Treatment of Migrant Workers," *Huffington Post*, April 24, 2020, https://www.huffpost.com/entry/singapore-coronavirus-migrant-worker _n_5ea15e27c5b69150246df77f; Saket Soni and Marielena Hincapie, "What We Owe Undocumented Workers during COVID-19," *CNN*, May 6, 2020, https://www.cnn .com/2020/05/06/opinions/undocumented-immigrant-resilience-workers-covid -19-soni-hincapie/index.html.

3. Tony Barboza and Ben Poston, "Pacific Islanders Hit Hard by the Coronavirus," *Los Angeles Times*, July 19, 2020, https://www.latimes.com/california/story/2020-07-19 /california-pacific-islander-native-hawaiian-communities-hit-hard-by-coronavirus; Kevin Escudero, "An Indigenous Futurity Approach to Decolonization: Navigating Imperial Borders and Indigenous Sovereignty during the Emergence of the COVID-19 Pandemic in Guåhan," *Journal of Asian American Studies* 23, no. 3 (October 2020): 459–74.

4. Lisa Yoneyama, *Cold War Ruins: Transpacific Critique of American Justice and Japanese War Crimes* (Durham, NC: Duke University Press, 2016), 99.

5. Lisa Lowe, "The Trans-Pacific Migrant and Area Studies," in *The Trans-Pacific Imagination: Rethinking Boundary, Culture and Society*, ed. Naoki Sakai and Hyon Joo Yoo (Hackensack, NJ: World Scientific, 2012), 65.

6. Kandice Chuh, *The Difference Aesthetics Makes: On the Humanities "After Man"* (Durham, NC: Duke University Press, 2019), 13.

7. Lisa Lowe, *The Intimacies of Four Continents* (Durham, NC: Duke University Press, 2015); Yến Lê Espiritu, Lisa Lowe, and Lisa Yoneyama, "Transpacific Entanglements," in *Flashpoints for Asian American Studies*, ed. Cathy J. Schlund-Vials (New York: Fordham University Press, 2018); Chuh, *The Difference Aesthetics Makes*.

8. Martin F. Manalansan IV, "Messy Mismeasures: Exploring the Wilderness of Queer Migrant Lives," *South Atlantic Quarterly* 117, no. 3 (July 2018): 496.

9. Viet Thanh Nguyen and Janet Hoskins, "Transpacific Studies: Critical Perspectives on an Emerging Field," in *Transpacific Studies: Framing an Emergent Field*, ed. Janet Hoskins and Viet Thanh Nguyen (Honolulu: University of Hawai'i Press, 2014), 23–24.

10. Erin Suzuki, "Transpacific," in *Routledge Companion to Asian American and Pacific Island Literatures*, ed. Rachel Lee (New York: Routledge, 2014), 352.

11. The framework, adopted by scholars studying the movements of people, goods, and capital across and within a region, has been variously conceptualized as "Asia-Pacific," "Pacific Rim," and "Pacific Basin." As Tina Chen maintains, the transpacific is an asymmetrical and incoherent concept and "such epistemic asymmetry should be considered not simply as a description of the massive inequalities undergirding the geopolitical arrangements of the transpacific world, but also as a catalyst through which transpacific knowledge and critical orientations of the transpacific are produced." See Tina Chen, "(The)Transpacific Turns," in *The Oxford Encyclopedia of Asian American Literature and Culture*, ed. Josephine Lee (London: Oxford University Press, 2020), 2, https://doi.org/10.1093/acrefore/9780190201098.013.782.

12. Setsu Shigematsu and Keith Camacho, eds., *Militarized Currents: Toward a Decolonized Future in Asian and the Pacific* (Minneapolis: University of Minnesota Press, 2010); Jodi Kim, *Ends of Empire: Asian American Critique and the Cold War* (Minneapolis: University of Minnesota Press, 2010); Lon Kurashige, ed., *Pacific America: Histories of Transoceanic Crossings* (Honolulu: University of Hawai'i Press, 2014); Yoneyama, *Cold War Ruins*; Jinah Kim, *Postcolonial Grief: The Afterlives of the Pacific Wars in the Americas* (Durham, NC: Duke University Press, 2019).

13. Suzuki and Bahng, "The Transpacific Subject in Asian American Culture," 1–4.

14. Suzuki and Bahng, 11.

15. See the report of the symposium "Pacific Worlds: Indigeneity, Blackness, and Resistance" hosted by the School of Humanities at the University of California, Irvine, January 22, 2021; Nitasha Tamar Sharma, *Hawai'i Is My Haven: Race and Indigeneity in the Black Pacific* (Durham, NC: Duke University Press, 2021); Anaïs Duong-Pedica and Zoé Samudzi, "On Solidarity's Blindspots: Thinking with Bla(c)k Oceanian Indigeneity," *Funambulist* 46 (March-April 2023), https://thefunambulist.net/magazine/questioning -our-solidarities/on-solidarys-blindspots-thinking-with-black-oceanian-indigeneity; and Vincent Schleitwiler, *Strange Fruit of the Black Pacific: Imperialism's Racial Justice and Its Fugitives* (New York: New York University Press, 2017).

16. Chen, "(The) Transpacific Turns," 5.

17. Chih-ming Wang and Yu-fang Cho, "Introduction: The Chinese Factor and American Studies, Here and Now," in *The Chinese Factor: Reorienting Global Imaginaries in American Studies*, ed. Chih-ming Wang and Yu-fang Cho, special issue of *American Quarterly* 69, no. 3 (September 2017): 455.

18. Chen, "(The) Transpacific Turns," 5; J. Kēhaulani Kauanui, "Imperial Ocean: The Pacific as a Critical Site for American Studies," *American Quarterly* 67, no. 3 (2015): 625.

19. Espiritu, Lowe, and Yoneyama, "Transpacific Entanglements," 187.

20. Espiritu, Lowe, and Yoneyama, 183.

21. Espiritu, Lowe, and Yoneyama, 187.

22. Yến Lê Espiritu, *Body Counts: The Vietnam War and Militarized Refuge(es)* (Berkeley: University of California Press, 2014), 21, emphasis in original.

23. See Hoskins and Nguyen, *Transpacific Studies*; Chih-ming Wang and Yu-fang Cho, eds., *The Chinese Factor*.

24. Nguyen and Hoskins, "Transpacific Studies," 23–24.

25. Nguyen and Hoskins, 20–23.

26. In Asia, "inter-Asia cultural studies" has, since the 2000s, emerged as a critical discourse of methods and tactics for cultural studies scholars in Asia to cite and collaborate with each other and with those in the Global South (known as "inter-referencing"), rather than to by default seek collaborations and collusions with Western (typically white) scholars of Asia. In one of the formation's key texts, Kuan-Hsing Chen argues that "Asia as method" warns against literally taking Asia as a geographical site of fixation and intrinsic (disciplinary, cultural, and historical) identity. See Kuan-Hsing Chen, *Asia as Method: Toward Deimperialization* (Durham, NC: Duke University Press, 2016).

27. Lisa Yoneyama, "Toward a Decolonial Genealogy of the Transpacific," *American Quarterly* 69, no. 3 (Fall 2017): 471–82.

28. Sit Tsui, Erebus Wong, Lau Kin Chi, and Wen Tiejun, "Toward Delinking: An Alternative Chinese Path Amid the New Cold War," *Monthly Review*, October 1, 2020, https://monthlyreview.org/author/wentiejun/.

29. Chien-ting Lin, "In Times of Love and War," *Inter-Asia Cultural Studies* 21, no. 4 (2020): 576–77.

30. Such unresolved colonial relations of race and imperialism is apparent in the example of Taiwan's pro-Trump nationalism and the debate over US military protection in popular discourse. As Chien-ting Lin argues in "In Times of Love and War," such sentiments—of nationalism and militarism—continue to reproduce uneven effects of neocolonial violence that differentially affect and subjugate various racialized groups and populations.

31. David Palumbo-Liu, *Asian/American: Historical Crossings of a Racial Frontier* (Stanford, CA: Stanford University Press, 1999), 1.

32. Chen, "(The) Transpacific Turns," 2.

33. Gavin Walker and Naoki Sakai, "The End of Area," *positions: asia critique* 27, no. 1 (2019): 3.

34. Shu-mei Shih, "Racializing Area Studies, Defetishizing China," *positions: asia critique* 27, no. 1 (2019): 42.

35. Laura Hyun Yi Kang, *Traffic in Asian Women* (Durham, NC: Duke University

Press, 2020), 15; Sara Ahmed, *Cultural Politics of Emotion* (Edinburgh: Edinburgh University Press, 2014), 22.

36. Kang, *Traffic in Asian Women*, 35, 43.

37. Maile Renee Arvin, *Possessing Polynesians: The Science of Settler Colonial Whiteness in Hawai'i and Oceania* (Durham, NC: Duke University Press, 2019), 3.

38. Arvin, *Possessing Polynesians*.

39. One of these writers, Joshua Agsalud, coauthor of *The Filipinos in Hawai'i: The First 75 Years (1906–1981)*, is editor Chris Patterson's great-uncle.

40. Candace Fujikane and Jonathan Y. Okamura, *Asian Settler Colonialism: From Local Governance to the Habits of Everyday Life in Hawai'i* (Honolulu: University of Hawai'i Press, 2008), 2.

41. Haunani-Kay Trask, "Settlers of Color and 'Immigrant' Hegemony: 'Locals' in Hawai'i," *Amerasia Journal* 26, no. 2 (2000): 2.

42. Arvin, *Possessing Polynesians*, 3.

43. Epeli Hau'ofa, "The Ocean in Us," *Contemporary Pacific* 10, no. 2 (1998): 392–410.

44. A cursory list would include Hawaiian writer Ty P. Kāwika Tengan; Samoan artist and writer Albert Wendt; Tongan writer and scholar Epeli Hau'ofa; Fijian writer Subramani; Black and I-Kiribati writer Teresia Teaiwa; Māori writer Alice A Te Punga Somerville; and Chamorro writer Craig Santos Perez. On disrupting the "good native–bad colonizer" binary, Camacho writes that in Guam, "some members of the navy utilized native labor, racism, and violence to develop their intelligence and police units, just as some Guamanians appropriated the military's logics to their own ends." See Keith L. Camacho, *Sacred Men: Law, Torture, and Retribution in Guam* (Durham, NC: Duke University Press, 2019), 41.

45. J. Kēhaulani Kauanui, "Imperial Ocean: The Pacific as a Critical Site for American Studies," *American Quarterly* 67, no. 3 (2015): 625.

46. Lowe, *The Intimacies of Four Continents*, ii.

47. Lowe, 17.

48. See further discussion of "intimate" in Christopher B. Patterson, "Brown Theory: A Storied Manifest of Our World," *positions: asia critique* 31, no. 1 (2023): 91–116.

49. Walden Bello, "Conclusion: From American Lake to a People's Pacific in the Twenty-First Century," in *Militarized Currents: Toward a Decolonized Future in Asia and the Pacific*, ed. Setsu Shigematsu and Keith L. Camacho (Minneapolis: University of Minnesota Press, 2010), 311.

50. Phanuel Antwi, Nadine Attewell, Beng Huat Chua, John Nguyet Erni, Christine Kim, Joanne Leow, Helen Hok-Sze Leung, Jia Tan, Chih-ming Wang, and Audrey Yue, "The Minor Transpacific: A Roundtable Discussion," *BC Studies: The British Columbian Quarterly* 198 (2018): 1.

51. Antwi et al., 6.

52. Craig Santos Perez, "'Thank God for the Maladjusted': The Transterritorial Turn towards the Chamorro Poetry of Guåhan (Guam)," in *Oceanic Archives, Indigenous Epistemologies, and Transpacific American Studies*, ed. Yuan Shu, Otto Heim, and Kendall Johnson (Hong Kong: Hong Kong University Press, 2019), 95.

53. Kim, *Postcolonial Grief*, 17.

54. In reference to our own positionality, and so as not to claim or decontextualize a method from a scholar's own position or intention, we do not include methods that could be perceived as "intimate" such as "De-Cold War" (Chen), "the tilde" (Perez), and others that emerged from inter-Asia cultural studies, Oceania studies, blue humanities, archipelagic studies, and others.

55. Juliette Singh, *Unthinking Mastery: Dehumanism and Decolonial Entanglements* (Durham, NC: Duke University Press, 2017), 22.

56. Espiritu, *Body Counts*, 181.

57. Shigematsu and Camacho, *Militarized Currents*, xxx.

58. Chen, *Asia as Method*, 226.

59. Alice Te Punga Somerville, "Unpacking our Libraries: Landlocked, Waterlogged, and Expansive Bookshelves," *American Quarterly* 67, no. 3 (2015): 650.

60. Alice Te Punga Somerville, "Where Oceans Come From," *Comparative Literature* 69 (2017): 28, quoted in Craig Santos Perez, "'The Ocean in Us': Navigating the Blue Humanities and Diasporic Chamoru Poetry," *Humanities (Basel)* 9, no. 3 (2020): 66.

61. Susan Y. Najita, "Land, History, and the Law: Constituting the "Public" through Environmentalism and Annexation," in *Oceanic Archives, Indigenous Epistemologies, and Transpacific American Studies*, ed. Yuan Shu, Otto Heim, and Kendall L. Johnson (Hong Kong: Hong Kong University Press, 2019), 113.

62. Perez, "'Thank God for the Malajusted," 95.

63. Alice Te Punga Somerville, "The Great Pacific Garbage Patch as Metaphor," in *Archipelagic American Studies*, ed. Brian Russell Roberts and Michelle Ann Stephens (Durham, NC: Duke University Press, 2020), 322.

64. Te Punga Somerville, 321.

65. Te Punga Somerville, 322.

66. Rob Wilson, "Oceania as Peril and Promise: Towards Theorizing a Worlded Vision of Transpacific Ecopoetics," in *Oceanic Archives, Indigenous Epistemologies, and Transpacific American Studies*, ed. Yuan Shu, Otto Heim, and Kendall Johnson (Hong Kong: Hong Kong University Press, 2019), 261–82.

67. Mel Chen, *Animacies: Biopolitics, Racial Mattering, and Queer Affect* (Durham, NC: Duke University Press, 2012), 218.

PART ONE FIGURING THE PACIFIC

1 "THIS IS PARADISE"

Transpacific Labor, Indigeneity,
and "Undocumented" in Hawai'i's
Hospitality Industry

LEANNE DAY

On April 17, 2018, in penthouse 1038 of the trendy Waikīkī hotel The Surfjack, visitors stepped into a typical a hotel room that had been transformed into an interactive art installation called *Dahil Sa'yo* by local Hawai'i-based Filipinx artists Ara and AJ Feducia. Greeted with a looped video projected on an oversized screen above the bed, visitors watched Ara performing the hospitality staff's daily cleaning obligations like making the bed, vacuuming, scrubbing the toilet, and taking out the trash. The penthouse's walls, typically decorated with macramé hangings, local artwork, and dreamy landscapes, were covered in portrait photographs featuring the Surfjack's Filipinx staff of mixed genders, close-ups of cleaning supplies, and snaps of areas of hotel rooms that require cleaning; in addition, some images included Ara completing the tasks and others centered on simply the objects of housekeeping, such as the supply cart. On the other side of the room by the couch, at least five of the Surfjack's Filipinx hospitality staff sang karaoke, ate food, and were hanging out with voluntary audience members. Visitors were invited to join in singing, dancing, and eating. The penthouse juxtaposes the karaoke's neon lights, loud music, and singing with snacks littered on the coffee table and the constant loop of Ara performing daily labor tasks. *Dahil Sa'yo* invites audience members to participate by both observing the routine tasks of the hotel service industry and playfully interacting with the predominantly Filipinx workers. As the exhibit ran for two nights only, this immersive and ephemeral experience of hotel workers, the artists, and the audience reveals both the quotidian daily routine of service workers as well as the possibilities of pleasure, albeit unexceptional and fleeting, in a live karaoke session. *Dahil Sa'yo* celebrates and complicates the commonly overlooked and dismissed Filipinx labor of the settler state's $2.07 billion-dollar tourism industry that supports 216,000 jobs.[1]

In considering the centrality of Filipinix labor in the hospitality industry, I turn to the legal categorization of "undocumented," which classifies almost a quarter of hospitality labor as being from the Philippines and Micronesia. The term undocumented thus indexes a complicated legal and political terrain made visible through labor, which the exhibit begins to make legible. Through the concept and heuristic of undocumented, my goal is to reveal the institutional illegibility of peoples residing within the United States without legal documentation, which include lawful permanent residents who arrived under the Compact of Free Association (COFA) for the Federated States of Micronesia, the Republic of the Marshal Islands, and Palau. By juxtaposing the dual invisibilization of Micronesians, miscategorized as undocumented, with undocumented Filipinx, I explore the illegibility of immigrant categories within the liberal settler state's conceptions of citizenship to destabilize accepted imperial relations of migration and labor. Undocumented thus destabilizes and "undisciplines" the liberal legal structure of categorizing racialized labor embedded in historical imperialist logics of the Pacific. By reading the figure of undocumented through the analytic of the transpacific, I attend to the affective and cultural movements of both Micronesians and Filipinx labor to Hawai'i ,whose presence and militarized relationships to the United States continuously are rendered illegible within mainstream multicultural liberal legal discourses. I suggest that the transpacific animates and navigates the perplexing ongoing elision of settler-colonial, imperial, and militarized relations inherent in both the misnaming of COFA residents as undocumented and the continued dismissal of Filipinix undocumented labor.

In order to concretely demonstrate the connections of Filipinx and Micronesian undocumented and documented labor in the tourism industry, I juxtapose the Feducias' *Dahil Sa'yo*, which stages a performance of quotidian life in Filipinx service workers, with the short story by Kanaka 'Ōiwi writer Kristina Kahakauwila, "This Is Paradise," which appeared in her debut 2013 collection *This Is Paradise*. "This Is Paradise" threads together the troubled and uneven gendered relations produced by settler colonialism by highlighting three different socioeconomic and racial groups of women connected through the sexualized murder of Susan, a haole (foreign tourist) woman. One of the groups of women Kahakauwila focuses on is the collective Micronesian housekeepers, who bear witness to Susan's murder and offer care for her body. Read together, the text of the art installation and the short story illuminate the invisible hospitality labor of Filipinx and COFA migrants, whose existence is politically precarious as undocumented subjects. The quotidian social acts in *Dahil Sa'yo* via the immersive group karaoke experience and the story's portrayal of the Micronesian housekeepers' maternal care evoking Kanaka 'Ōiwi conceptions of "aloha" as reciprocal care, animate the collective political survival within the tourism industry.[2] Framed as a collective mode of existence—through Kahakauwila's use of the plural "we" and Ara and AJ Feducia's shifting participants, between viewers and workers—I demonstrate how both texts simultaneously acknowledge the racialized and gendered logics of institutional obscurity that perpetuate the subjects' existence by making their routine labor visible, if only momentarily. Framed perhaps more cogently as a necessary absent presence for a system of tourism predicated on the extraction of Indigenous lifeways for capitalist profits and to fulfill the fantasies of consumer visitors, the Filipinx and Pacific COFA migrants activate joy, intimacy, and collectivity that reckon with the multiple nuanced forms of transpacific labor extraction required to perpetuate the tourist industry.

HOSPITALITY, COMPACTS OF FREE ASSOCIATION, AND LABOR

According to a 2018 US Census Bureau survey, immigrant workers in Hawai'i comprise 23 percent of the state's labor force, with the majority involved in the accommodation and food services industry, the second largest industry.[3] More specifically, a May 2019 US Bureau of Labor Statistics report identified that Hawai'i's domestic, housekeeping, and janitorial work constitute 4.2 percent, or 13,230 people doing building and grounds cleaning and maintenance occupations.[4] In order to consider the demographics of hospitality labor embedded in *Dahil Sa'yo*, I turn to the statistics around undocumented immigrants and their often-obscured participation in Hawai'i's hotel industry.

A March 2019 State of Hawai'i survey identified that 45,000 of the 253,000 immigrants in Hawai'i are undocumented.[5] This number is higher than the national Migration Policy Institute's (MPI) estimate of 36,000 undocumented in Hawai'i.[6] Still, the MPI breaks down the top countries of birth as the Philippines, with 48 percent or 17,000 people, and similar numbers from Japan and Micronesia, with 11 percent and 10 percent, respectively (although it is not clear if the MPI total includes Marshallese and Palauans, who are often grouped under the label "Micronesian"). These demographics demonstrate how 23 percent of Hawai'i's immigrant labor actually is comprised of undocumented and documented immigrants from the Philippines and Micronesia. Furthermore, this multiracial labor force, with differing relationships to liberal citizenship, is contingent upon the continued exploitation of Kanaka 'Ōiwi, the Indigenous peoples of Hawai'i.

COFA by its name alone indexes the United States' agreement to open migration as compensation for the numerous nuclear weapons tests conducted by the United States from 1946 to 1958. As noncitizens but legal residents, COFA migrants often obscure the legal distinctions around citizenship, where even the MPI's statistics on undocumented peoples in Hawai'i are unclear about how COFA recipients are categorized. This conflation of undocumented and COFA migrants highlight the institutional obscurity bound up in the settler-colonial state's adjudication of immigrant subjects as either "legal" or "illegal." What becomes clear is how the hospitality industry and specifically hotel housekeeping labor is predominantly comprised of Filipinx and Micronesian labor. This is upheld through the 2020 Hawai'i state report on COFA migrants and labor, which indicates that "building/grounds, cleaning, and maintenance accounted for 15.3 percent of jobs."[7] As such, Filipinx and COFA migrants working in hospitality become visible through the problematic notion of undocumented, which allows for the misnaming of COFA migrants as noncitizens who are illegally residing in the country; this directly misunderstands the conditions of US militarism and colonialism that produce COFA migrants in the first place.

By showing how undocumented Filipinx communities and COFA recipients have been accounted for and represented in Hawai'i's service industry, I challenge how the category of undocumented is calculated in national statistics, as it misnames COFA recipients whose militarized and political relationship to the United States differs from what is typically understood as nonlegal residence. This leads to a constellation of labor relations that reframe immigrants' matrices of legality simply to account for militarized engagement in the Pacific. As Vernadette Gonzalez explains: "Paradise . . . is conjured through imaginative labor, sustained by such economic apparatuses as plantation and tourism economies and the hierarchized societies they engender, secured through the threat and reality of violence or the promise of rescue, and continually contested by the people who live there."[8] Undocumented service work further names the imaginative labor required to uphold tourism, where the possibility of liberal citizenship is foreclosed; instead, the housekeeping staffs featured in *Dahil Sa'yo* and "This Is Paradise" must negotiate alternative forms of daily solidarity and redemption. As embodied subjects of imaginative labor, COFA migrants and Filipinx immigrants secure the success of the tourist industry even as their very presence haunts the exploitative conditions of settler colonialism and militarism. "This Is Paradise" and *Dahil Sa'yo* generate a critique on the explicit precarity and the isolating ramifications of exploitative labor conditions that are embedded in the tourist industry complex. While the material effects produced by undocumented communities and anti-Micronesian sentiments in Hawai'i require further analysis, the Feducias' and Kahakauwila's cultural production imagine the possibilities for daily acts of social cohesion that challenge the complexity and necessity of transpacific migrant labor.[9]

By analyzing two texts, a multisensory art experience and a short story, I emphasize the role of cultural representation when making visible the ongoing extraction of the tourist industry's gendered and racialized labor. In line with how Lisa Lowe questions whether the fundamental construction of historical narrative can make visible the mechanisms that bring the (colonial or imperial) past into the present, this multigenre representation makes legible the illegible intersection of hospitality labor and undocumented migrants who live under the ongoing US militarism and settler colonialism in Hawai'i and the Pacific.[10] Cultural representation not only reminds us of the history of US imperialism in the Pacific, nuclear testing in Micronesia, and the colonization of the Philippines, but also "unsettle[s] and recast[s] the dominant histories we receive of liberal modernity."[11] Both *Dahil Sa'yo* and "This Is Paradise" navigate the context of Hawai'i's tourism, dependent as it is on exploiting and capitalizing on Kanaka ʻŌiwi culture while also positing the complexity of a multiracial immigrant labor force required for the perpetuation of the hotel industry. Still, the imaginative possibilities of cultural production to represent and innovate undocumented labor is how Grace Hong renders racialized immigrant women's culture that "seize[s] the imaginative function of literature and culture for different ends, revealing and intervening in the dynamics of power that subtends the production of knowledge."[12] Both the Feducias and Kahakauwila use cultural mediums to destabilize the power dynamics that produce the ongoing precarities of immigrant labor required for the settler-colonial state's extraction of Indigenous culture.

SETTLERS OF COLOR, TOURISM, AND UNDOCUMENTED LABOR

The long-documented discussions over Hawaiʻi as a site of settler-colonial exploitation and tourist commodification are well-established through the marketing of "paradise," from Pan American Airways' pre-statehood flights, to the latest "Go Hawaiʻi" marketing campaign, which features options like eco-tourism and cultural experiences, to the use of the Kanaka ʻŌiwi concept of aloha as a sellable package of the "aloha state of" Hawaiʻi.[13] As Haunani-Kay Trask explains, "the utter degradation of our culture and our people under corporate tourism" can be understood as the prostitution of not only the concept of aloha, but also of Hawaiian culture.[14] Aloha, as Stephanie Nohelani Teves elaborates, is "an ideology—to promote and reinforce the image of Hawaiʻi as a paradise in every sense."[15] Within the framework of the tourist industry that is being upheld by the settler state, undocumented labor further complicates the vexed relations between settlers and Kanaka ʻŌiwi: undocumented migrants, as illegal and illegible to the state, make visible the imperial conditions of their existence. Still, settler colonialism, as Patrick Wolfe reminds, is an ongoing structure and process that destroys Indigenous peoples and replaces them with settlers.[16] For Hawaiʻi, the massive influx during the nineteenth and twentieth centuries of predominantly Asian immigrants that fueled plantation labor changes the dynamics of the perception of how settlers operate in a post-statehood in 1959 period.[17] As Candace Fujikane and Jonathan Okamura have theorized extensively, Asian settler colonialism involves the "political capacity to colonize Hawaiians" and historically shifts with the rise to economic power of Japanese Americans and East Asian Americans in the second half of the twentieth century.[18] This raises the specter of how undocumented migrants, both Filipinx and Micronesian, complicate what is often delineated through Jodi Byrd's use of Kamau Brathwaite's term "arrivant" within the category of Indigenous people and settlers. Byrd suggests how the horizontal scope of settler-arrivant colonialism interrogates the "competing claims to historical oppressions" as a zero-sum struggle that "distract from the complicities of colonialism."[19] To read the figure of an undocumented person performing hospitality labor is to undo the conception of "Asian settler" hegemony, as service labor does not equally exploit Indigenous culture even as migrant labor upholds tourism. Therefore, while Trask names local Asians as beneficiaries of settler dominance over Kanaka ʻŌiwi, undocumented Filipinx and COFA migrants fall out of the binary of native and settler. While all non-Indigenous peoples participate in settler-colonial relations of dominance, migrant service workers of Filipinx and Micronesian descent upend the typical settler-native dynamic of "local"; Asian settlers transform what Dean Saranillio offers as "the intricate relationality of power [which] shows how multiple binaries organize and layer differences within the settler state."[20] Undocumented labor thus destabilizes and reveals settler colonialism's power demands to flatten settler-native dynamics, where the incongruities and intimacies of militarized imperial relations are often obscured.

The ongoing conflation of undocumented COFA migrants with undocumented Filipinx migrants allows for a critical reexamination of how precisely the tourist industry extracts, exploits, and forgets the imperial and militarized imaginative labor that upholds its success. The pervasive history of nuclearism and militarism in the Pacific informs the context of migration for Micronesians to the United States under COFA. Given the historical and ongoing context of US access to Pacific Ocean and airspace as a perceived trade-off for "open" migration, transpacific migrant labor is thus explicitly militarized and then utilized to support tourism and the hospitality industry. As noted by multiple Pacific scholars and activists such as Kēhaulani Kauanui, Vince Diaz, Teresia Teaiwa, Barbara Rose Johnson, Holly Barker, and Kathy Jetñil-Kijiner, the use of the Marshall Islands at Bikini and Enewetak Atolls as well as fallout exposure on Rongelap and Utirik from the sixty-seven nuclear tests occurred from 1946 to 1958 by the US military. Teresia Teaiwa emphasizes the effects of the twenty-five tests on Bikini Atoll alone, including catastrophic long-term radiation exposure and entire population displacement, both of which explicitly embody the legacies of nuclearism and colonialism in the Pacific.[21] This history of nuclearism continues to affect current and future generations of Marshallese, who often become COFA migrants seeking opportunities for education, health care, and employment in Hawaiʻi. Keola Davis clarifies how "the Compact with the Marshall Islands established routes for compensation to the people of the Marshall Islands for the loss of life, health, land and resources due to the 67 nuclear tests."[22] This explicitly reveals what Rebecca Hogue describes as "forced migration from nuclearism" that indexes "the erasing impulses of nuclear imperialism and settler colonialism, which often seek to hide, obfuscate, or excuse their environmental and embodied impact."[23] Thus, the suggested exchange of military access for perceived civil protections produces a desirability for migration, even as it is embedded in the continued "erasing impulses of nuclear imperialism and settler colonialism" once someone is working in Hawaiʻi's tourism industry.

While the Philippines have their own colonial and militaristic relations with the United States, which began in 1898 with the "acquisition" of the Philippines after the Spanish-American War, the emphasis on predominantly Filipina domestic labor as transpacific migrants emerged by the 1980s, as "74% of the labor force . . . [and] they constituted more than half of international migrants (55 percent) by the early 1990s."[24] Constituted by global economic changes, Filipina migrants work in more than 160 countries and "are the domestic workers *par excellence* of globalization."[25] While the focus of migrant domestic workers often considers in-house labor and sponsoring families, the role of the hospitality industry and tourism simultaneously operate as a site of "conditional membership of migrant domestic workers in host societies [that] reflect[s] the culture of benevolent paternalism."[26] Even further, the concept of partial citizenship as gendered and racialized weaves worker vulnerability into the context of migration for domestic Filipina laborers. The liminal or partial access to citizenship available to domestic transpacific migrants correlates to how Hawaiʻi's hospitality industry replicates the precarity of legal belonging and undocumented status haunts the workforce. This is not to undermine the materiality of partial access to citizenship, but to emphasize the often-erased conversation of undocumented

Filipinx migrants within the service industry in Hawai'i. As such, the history of US militarism, imperialism, and continued economic investments in the Philippines and Micronesia together illustrate the complex conditions for labor migration to Hawai'i. The figure of the undocumented migrant serves to both haunt the service industry and make legible the necessary institutional obscurity of labor extraction required for tourism to continue to operate.

DAHIL SA'YO (BECAUSE OF YOU) THIS TOURISM INDUSTRY SURVIVES

Dahil Sa'yo was part of Contact Hawai'i and the Pu'uhonua Society's fifth annual multi-site art exhibition titled *Contact Zone*, which highlights contemporary art made in Hawai'i and whose 2018 theme focused on "spaces of cultural exchange and migration in Hawai'i."[27] Located on O'ahu at Waikīkī, Kaka'ako, Kalihi, and Chinatown, *Contact Zone* exhibits were open to the public and featured locally based artists. Self-titled as an "immersive experience," *Dahil Sa'yo* invites public engagement with the material realities of predominantly Filipinx service work in the hotel industry. The Feducias center the Filipinx subjects of imaginative labor in a ritzy penthouse, singing karaoke and engaging with audience members as part of their daily tasks under the conditions of settler colonialism. Through photographs of mixed genders, objects, and Ara herself, paradise's infrastructure is no longer invisible; it is embodied, material, and belting out song lyrics collectively with the audience.

As stated on Ara Feducia's website, *Dahil Sa'yo* is a "commentary on the tourism industry's relationship with Filipino immigrant workers" where they constitute 14 percent of Hawai'i's population and 46.4 percent of the state's foreign-born population."[28] While the census numbers do not necessarily account for undocumented persons, *Dahil Sa'yo* incorporates the presence of undocumented Filipinx migrants because of its central emphasis on the invisibility of service labor. This is amplified through the changing participation in karaoke by both audience and service workers, the latter of which is captured in limited video footage and whose permanence is fleeting; unlike the photographs and prerecorded video, the variation adds further complexity to the exhibit. Even further, the dissolution of boundaries between audience and performer echoes Josephine Machon's framing of how "immersive theaters can establish links across sensation, perception, emotion, and moral reasoning in form and content."[29] *Dahil Sa'yo*'s disruption of space, audience, and participants elicits a form of performance that leads to social engagement. The literal placement of *Dahil Sa'yo* occurs in the penthouse of a 2016 remodeled Waikiki hotel; the objective is "to pay homage to the true soul of Waikiki, not the prefabricated version peddled to the masses" from the midcentury.[30] Consequently, *Dahil Sa'yo* disrupts the established nostalgic version of a 1960s Hawai'i as well, post-statehood in 1959. Sruti Bala explains: "The gestures of participation in performance . . . indicate possibilities for configuring civic participation in public spaces in unexpected ways, putting less emphasis on direct opposition and instead seeking a variety of modes of resisting co-optation, through unsolicited, vicarious or delicate gestures of participation."[31] Bala shows the necessity of audience participation in art whose concept of "gesture" enables a multiplicity of engagement of "unsolicited" or "vicarious" social and political critique. As such, the inherent spatial contradictions of *Dahil Sa'yo* intersect with an immersive performance via live karaoke with the hotel's Filipinx staff that open up avenues of unanticipated and temporary connection and destabilize settler-colonial liberal relations.

In addition to the exhibit's multilayered resonances, Ara Feducia used her Instagram platform to publicize the installation, which further amplifies the embedded personal stakes of her work. For example, Feducia posted on April 18, 2018, the day of the exhibit's opening, and included a photo of herself dressed in the hotel's housekeeping uniform standing next to a vacuum in a Surfjack hallway. Even further, the caption plays with her creative lyrics for "Dahil Sa'yo":

> For a short window, the hospitality team at @thesurfjack shared their work life. This installation for @contacthawaii is dedicated to all the hard working immigrant workers, predominantly Filipino, working in Waikiki. Dahil Sa'yo (Because of You)
>
> Dahil Sa'yo our beds are made.
> Dahil Sa'yo our toilets are cleaned.
> Dahil Sa'yo our trash is picked up.
> Dahil Sa'yo your family thrives.
> Dahil Sa'yo this tourism industry survives . . .
> Salamat po! [thank you][32]

The post further enhances the exhibit, even if only to a limited audience, as Feducia creates her own lyrics to the chorus in *Dahil Sa'yo*. For instance, the original song's second stanza states, "Dahil sa iyo, nais kong mabuhay/ Dahil sa iyo, hanggang mamatay" ("Because of you, I yearn to be alive, Because of you, 'til death (you) must realize"). Feducia plays with the repetition of the phrase "Because of you" and uses the casual relation to emphasize the necessity of Filipinx labor. Reiterating the conjunctive "because" with the plural pronoun "our," she distinguishes the speaker from the Filipinx workers, identified by the second person singular pronoun "you." Placed in conversation, the "our" is the beneficiary of the hospitality workers' daily labor. Critically, the second person "you" focuses on how "your family thrives," although "exists" or "gets by" might be a more accurate description of most of these workers. The line "this tourism industry survives" creates distance from the immediate Filipinx family to the perpetuation of tourism. Here, the jarring transition from a Filipinx family's survival to the perceived survival of an industry at large effectively reveals how Feducia puts pressure on the interlocking mechanisms of extractive labor conditions placed on Filipinx migrants and the invisibility of their service upholding tourism.

Dahil Sa'yo's immersive experience expands beyond the confines of two nights in penthouse 1038, into social media as Feducia's post reveals and further extends the possibility of sociality and awareness of Filipinx service labor by building audience and follower participation. Relying on a disruption of perceived tourist hotel space and audience participation, *Dahil Sa'yo* does not simply inform viewers of the quotidian tasks of hospitality staff; it also combines their service with the outlet of karaoke as an opportunity for fun, relaxation, and enjoyment. In the interstices of play and work, *Dahil Sa'yo* produces an alternative space that maintains both a critique of the invisibility of hospitality Filipinx labor and asserts the necessity of quotidian social relations.

ALOHA AS COLLECTIVE OCEANIC VULNERABILITY IN PARADISE

While *Dahil Sa'yo* inventively uses audience participation to raise questions about the invisibility of labor in the service industry, Kahakauwila's short story "This Is Paradise" centers on Micronesian hotel workers and imagines a more direct connection between minority groups. The story explicitly addresses socioeconomic and racial hierarchies in Hawai'i and how COFA migrants are situated within and between the categories of Kanaka 'Ōiwi and "locals." Kahakauwila expands her narrative by interweaving three groups of women who collectively witness a white tourist, Susan, who is presumed to be sexually assaulted and ends up being killed by an unidentified man with prison tattoos. In critiquing the tourism industry as a settler-colonial apparatus, "This Is Paradise" centers on Susan's body as the site of touristic and gendered violence that affects all three groups of women in the story. In enacting the fantasies of paradise through Susan's vacation and death, Kahakauwila provides a dual critique of the tourist industry. First the story demonstrates how migrant COFA labor, as noncitizens, contributes to the hospitality industry while alluding to the ongoing anti-Micronesian sentiments present in Hawai'i. Second, the story simultaneously reckons with the inherent gendered violences of tourism and settler colonialism while suggesting a collective sociality instigated by the Micronesian housekeepers. These Micronesian women, as the unseen infrastructure of hospitality, operate as the central observers to the quotidian intimacies of tourism and the routinized expectations to perform, sanitize, and promote the experience of paradise; instead, they perform the Oceanic practice of care, or Kanaka 'Ōiwi–aligned concept of aloha.

Kahakauwila utilizes the first-person plural "we" throughout her short story for each group of women, but notably exclusively uses it for the Micronesian hotel workers, who are never individualized or identified by name. By emphasizing the collective existence of Micronesian migrants, Kahakauwila refuses to disaggregate the women, which can be read both as a rejection of an American idealization of individual agency and as a centering of connected Pacific Indigeneity as always embedded with the community, land, and ocean. Vince Diaz and Kehāulani Kauanui invoke the centrality of place for Pacific Islanders: "The land and sea constitute our genealogies and, not surprisingly, they lie at the heart of the varied movements to restore native sovereignty and self-determinations."[33] This sense of rootedness is further illustrated in Tongan scholar Konai Thaman's assertion that "indigenous wisdom is about the connectedness and interrelatedness of all things and all people."[34] These framings of Oceanic knowledges as grounded in the interconnections of land, sea, and kinship give credence to why Kahakauwila's Micronesian women operate exclusively as one voice. Without indication of where these women live or who these women are, besides documenting their hospitality work, Kahakauwila emphasizes their self-reference as "We, the women of House-keeping."[35] In this assertion of the group name "women of Housekeeping," the collective is defined exclusively by their gendered function of labor in the tourist industry. Even further, the first-person plural "we" is contrasted to the capitalization of "Housekeeping" as a proper noun, which establishes a second collective and perhaps signifies the broader category of hotel house-keeping in Hawai'i. Kahakauwila eventually references the various homes of the "women of Housekeeping" as "Pohnpei or Yap or Kosrae."[36] Through this sharing of information, the collective references multiple home islands within the Federated States of Micronesia but evades specific identification, which further bolsters the idea of a collective.

Kahakauwila's subtle references to militarism emerge in the required surveillance the hotel institutes for the housekeeping staff as a purported response to terrorism. Situated as part of regular work standards, the inherent contradiction of enforcing rules for hospitality staff—especially those from Micronesia, whose existence is inextricable from US militarism—to assess and report on potential threats, comes across as rightfully laughable. Even more so, the expectation that Micronesian migrants are held responsible for securing visitor and hotel safety exposes what Inderpal Grewal names as the permanent emergency of the neoliberal security state, where "nor-mative citizens become empowered to take responsibility for maintaining the imperial security state."[37] However, Micronesian migrants take on the role of "normative citizens," even as they occupy a noncitizen status. This highlights the incommensurability of the legacies of nuclear testing and military occupation in Micronesia and the Pacific with the ongoing need to shore up and protect the neoliberal security state in Hawai'i through the policing of hotel guests. Clearly, paradise in this context is "not a generic or static term—it specifically refers to an idea of passivity and penetrability engendered by imperialism as an alibi for domination" and secured through utilizing everyday individuals.[38] The women of housekeeping reveal their un-certainties about reporting suspicious activity and explain, "The last rule was created to fight terrorism, though we wonder what kind of terrorists would stay in Waikīkī. In fact, we don't entirely understand this rule or trust it. It seems designed only to make trouble for us."[39] In articulating both confusion over terrorists on vacation and the ways in which reporting on guests could be precarious for the workers, Kahakauwila exposes their vulnerability as noncitizens who are asked to assess guest behavior. In the hotel's rules of arbitrating which crimes are considered threats to the nation-state and the safety of the business, the Micronesian housekeepers ironically become the mediators of violence.

In conveying how the tourist industry also operates as a function of the security settler state through multiple types of subject surveillance, "This Is Paradise" situates each group of women as observers and partial witnesses to Susan's assault and murder. While the scattered awareness of Susan elicits judgments and comments from the two other groups of women, the Micronesian housekeepers, who empathetically frame her as comparable to their daughters, initiate a protective circle around her semi-naked body. In performing what they see as a maternal act of care, the Micronesian women step in as pseudo-mother figures for Susan. Kahakauwila writes:

> We form a circle around her, protecting her even though she is beyond our protection . . . she is older than even our eldest girls, and, on any other day, we could have called her *haole,* foreigner, a white woman independent and capable of caring for herself . . . this girl is a child. She is helpless. She is in need of a mother, and that's a job at which we are experts.[40]

This collective acknowledgment of care indicates the priority of Susan's exposed body over even their jobs, as the women refuse multiple times to go back inside the hotel. The perpetual state of vulnerability as noncitizens is juxtaposed with Susan's naked corpse and allows for the housekeepers to become maternal figures, as "All us mothers are here."[41] This ending suggests a call to a collective of mothers that extends beyond the indeterminate number of workers and evokes the possibility of genealogical invocation of maternal presence. Building off the interconnectedness of Oceanic relations, to state not only that "We are here," but that "All us mothers are here" invites acknowledgement of Pacific cosmology, in Māori through Papatūānuku (mother), in Samoan through Papa 'ele (the mother), for Hawaiians through

Papahānaumoku (earth mother), or in Tahitian through Papatuʻoi (the Earth-mother).[42] "Mother" in this instance also evokes nonhuman entities and could be a call to the Micronesian women's various ancestral homes of Yap, Kosrae, or Pohnpei.[43] Still, Christopher Patterson's evocative reading of this scene capitalizes on how "their matronly identity speaks to their function of care and affection" where "the maids' encircling is understood as a mournful act that erases Susan's sexuality and adventurous attitude."[44] Situated through reckoning with the gendered comparison between the Micronesian maids and Susan's tourist and American sexuality, Patterson highlights the imbrication of moral policing of transnational domestic workers, who must perform nonlibidinal "matronly" roles to secure their positions. Understood through this framework, then, as securing both their own sexuality and a policing of the possibilities of hotel guest threats, the Micronesian maids acquiesce to the expectations of the neoliberal security state by functioning as a surveillance apparatus for the tourist industry. However, the refusal for the housekeepers to return to work by continuing their vigil over Susan indicates, even if still intertwined in the gendered demands of migrant labor, a shift in the precariousness of their positions as workers. Instead, the invocation of "All us mothers" protects and bears witness to Susan's passing as ritual grounded in Oceanic connectivity.

The story is ironically titled "This Is Paradise," a drunken refrain stated by Susan and overheard by the professional group of women the night of her murder. Still, it is within Wakīkī or "paradise" that the Micronesian housekeeping staff emerge as visible agents of care and protection. Arguably their act of protection actually embodies Kanaka ʻŌiwi forms of "aloha," which Mary Kawena Pukui defines as "love, affection, compassion, mercy, sympathy, pity, kindness, sentiment, grace, charity."[45] Stephanie Teves elaborates on Indigenous understandings of aloha, as opposed to the capitalization of the concept through tourism: "Aloha thus meant kindness and sharing, especially in the family or ʻohana setting where people are welcomed and all is shared, with the understanding that people gather to provide mutual helpfulness for collective benefit."[46] While the Micronesian maids emerge out of different and specific Pacific Islander cultures and genealogies, the suggestion that their actions to protect Susan evoke a noncommodified form of aloha provides an alternative to the settler state's promotion of Kanaka

'Ōiwi culture. As Noʻu Revilla and Jamaica Osorio explain, "Aloha is a living Indigenous practice that ably straddles sexuality, sovereignty, and kinship" but it is "gratuitously sold as exotic love ... [and] American colonialism uses aloha as an alibi; tourism uses aloha as commodity."[47] In rejecting aloha as purely commodity or exotic love, the dual circles created by the Micronesian women and the local surfers gesture toward at least a performance of a more reciprocal, communal, and Kanaka 'Ōiwi iteration of aloha that contradicts the various extractive structures of tourism.

Given the indeterminate outcomes for both The Surfjack's Filipinx hospitality workers and the three groups of women in "This Is Paradise," a lingering question is how the vulnerability of hotel labor and the quotidian acts of escape function within tourism. While *Dahil Sa'yo* plays with participatory performance by optimizing a penthouse space and calling in both the artist and audience, the possible existence of undocumented workers emerges only through a gesture on Feducia's Instagram post. To read the figure of undocumented Filipinx onto *Dahil Sa'yo* requires an immersion in the exhibit, where artist, hotel staff, and audience interact, sing, and create social relations. While *Dahil Sa'yo* provides temporary release and connection to the material conditions of Filipinx hospitality workers, "This Is Paradise" amplifies how Micronesian maids have become the catalyst for other local Hawai'i women to reflect on how the tourist industry operates through gendered violence. The group of Micronesian maids evoke Pacific Indigeneity through their collective voice and care of Susan's body, even if their actions mirror gendered stereotypes about transpacific domestic workers. By shifting the practice of aloha from tourism and the settler state's dilution of the concept (as premised on multicultural belonging and "our so-called kindness toward one another"), the maids' act of mourning and protection might be read as a gesture of how "aloha is judicious and collaborative, and in its intergenerational practice—even quietly, in order to survive—aloha embraces vulnerability."[48] Vulnerability, as an intergenerational function of aloha, can be read in the seemingly small act of the Micronesian housekeepers not only refusing to leave Susan's body exposed but also refusing to return to work. Resisting the daily requirement of labor can be read as a small gesture toward decolonial solidarity with Kanaka 'Ōiwi, as the Micronesian women call upon their maternal genealogies as protectors. "This Is Paradise" asserts the collective vulnerability of migrant laborers who hold a spectrum of non-citizenship status; their performative gesture and community reflect on the pervasive conditions created through settler colonialism and perpetuated through the tourist industry.

CODA: THE GLOBAL PANDEMIC AND HALTING HAWAI'I TOURISM

The ongoing global pandemic from COVID-19 forced a critical awareness of Hawai'i's dependence on tourism and produced catastrophic effects on the hospitality sector during the subsequent suspension of visitors to the islands in March 2020.[49] With unemployment at a high of 22.3 percent in April 2020 (dropping to 9.3 percent by February 2021, yet remaining the highest in the United States), the impact on the service and hospitality sector of tourism makes clear the disturbing reality of the settler state's reliance on visitors and the commodification of Hawai'i as a vacation, an experience, and a life-style.[50] While the dominant Hawai'i labor union, Unite Here Local 5, which represents over twelve thousand hospitality, health care, and food service workers, raised awareness of the damage resulting from both the pausing of the tourist industry and the pandemic itself, the organization also focused on the process of unemployment, proposed to hotel employers proper safety measures of workers, and provided access to essential resources. As multiple news outlets on the continent reported, the contradictory notion of "essential workers" and undocumented laborers (10.5 million, according to Pew research) reveals the impossibility for communities disproportionately required to work during a health crisis and yet ineligible for federal relief or protections from deportation.[51] As Maurizio Guerrero has noted, "Undocumented essential workers were not even considered in the $2.5 trillion relief package approved by Congress and, except in California, have not received financial aid from state or local governments. . . . Additionally, they are being detained and deported."[52] The glaring recognition of legible, viable, and worthy subjects imbued with legal citizenship sharply contrasts with the government's framing of essential workers in agriculture, meat-processing factories, and retail grocery stores.

In other words, the exclusion from federal aid, the necessity of survival to continue working, and the imminent threat of deportation unmasks the extreme contradictions for undocumented peoples under COVID-19. Rendering control of precarious subjects through disease control and essential service work in 2020–21 simply illuminates the established conditions of existence for undocumented communities in Hawai'i before the shutdown of the tourist industry. What COVID-19's pausing of tourism makes clearer for Filipinx and Micronesian migrant laborers is the inescapable imbrication of settler colonialism, imperialism, militarism, and the ongoing presence of undocumented and unaccounted labor, as well as the vulnerability of "essential" workers. Consequently, innovative and immersive cultural texts like *Dahil Sa'yo* and "This Is Paradise" make visible the overlapping logics that produce, organize, and perpetuate the imaginative labor required for Hawai'i's tourism industry. Through the figure of the undocumented, the Feducias and Kahakauwila assert how the daily routine lives of Filipinx and Micronesian workers produce everyday opportunities for sociality and joy and an Oceanic call to maternal solidarity. They posit how this everyday sociality unmasks, even briefly, the necessary presence of undocumented and migrant labor to uphold the conditions of tourism yet carve out spaces of connection and collectivity.

NOTES

1. Hawai'i Tourism Authority, "Hawai'i Visitors Statistics Released for 2019," January, 29, 2020, https://www.hawaiitourismauthority.org/news/news-releases/2020/hawai-i-visitor-statistics-released-for-2019.

2. Hawai'i Department of Business, Economic Development & Tourism, Research & Economic Analysis Divison, "Hawaii Working Population: An Analysis by Industry 2012–2016," April 2019, https://files.hawaii.gov/dbedt/economic/reports/Hawaii_Workforce_Report_2018.pdf.

3. US Bureau of Labor Statistics, "May 2019 State Occupational Employment and Wage Estimates Hawaii," March 31, 2020, https://www.bls.gov/oes/current/oes_hi.htm.

4. "Hawaii Senate Approves Sanctuary Bill," *Hawaii News Now*, March 12, 2019, https://www.hawaiinewsnow.com/2019/03/12/hawaii-senate-approves-immigrant-sanctuary-bill/.

5. Migration Policy Institute, "Profile of the Unauthorized Population: Hawaii," accessed May 24, 2020, https://www.migrationpolicy.org/data/unauthorized-immigrant-population/state/HI.

6. Hawaiʻi Department of Business, Economic Development & Tourism, Research & Economic Analysis Divison, "COFA Migrants in Hawaii," February 2020, 12, https://files.hawaii.gov/dbedt/economic/reports/COFA_Migrants_in_Hawaii_Final.pdf.

7. This does not seek to use "aloha" as a metonym for Micronesian-specific concepts, but instead signifies the possibilities of a maternal Oceanic collective mode of care.

8. Vernadette Gonzalez, *Securing Paradise: Tourism and Militarism in Hawaiʻi and the Philippines* (Durham, NC: Duke University Press, 2013) 8.

9. See Sha Ongelungel's Twitter/X hashtag thread #beingmicronesian.

10. Lisa Lowe, *The Intimacies of Four Continents* (Durham, NC: Duke University Press, 2015), 137.

11. Lowe, *Intimacies*, 137.

12. Grace Hong, *The Ruptures of American Capital* (Minneapolis: University of Minnesota Press, 2006), xxiv.

13. Hawaiʻi Tourism Authority, "Go Hawaii: Hawaii Travel Information," accessed January 24, 2021, https://www.gohawaii.com/.

14. Haunani-Kay Trask, *From a Native Daughter: Colonialism and Sovereignty in Hawaiʻi* (Honolulu: University of Hawaiʻi Press, 1999), 140.

15. Stephanie Nohelani Teves, "Aloha State Apparatuses," *American Quarterly* 67, no. 3 (September 2015).

16. Patrick Wolfe, "Settler Colonialism and the Elimination of the Native," *Journal of Genocide Research* 8 (2006): 388.

17. Ron Takaki most notably asserts the making of Asian immigrants as "strangers from a different shore" who create belonging and community through hard work, especially in Hawaiʻi, without accounting for Indigenous peoples. *Strangers from a Different Shore: A History of Asian Americans* (Boston: Little, Brown, 1998).

18. Candace Fujikane and Jonathan Okamura, eds., *Asian Settler Colonialism: From Local Governance to the Habits of Everyday Life in Hawaiʻi* (Honolulu: University of Hawaiʻi Press, 2008), 3.

19. Byrd, *Transit*, xxxiv–xxxv.

20. Dean Saranillio, *Unsustainable Empire* (Durham, NC: Duke University Press), 18.

21. Teresia Teaiwa, "bikinis and other s/pacific n/oceans," *Contemporary Pacific* 6, no. 1 (Spring 1994): 89.

22. Keola Davis, "The Compact of Free Association: A Trend of Many Failures" (Master's thesis, University of Hawaiʻi, 2012), 3.

23. Rebecca Hogue, "Decolonial Memory and Nuclear Migration in Albert Wendt's *Black Rainbow*," *Modern Fiction Studies* 66, no. 2 (Summer 2020): 327.

24. Rhacel Salazar Parreñas, "Migrant Filipina Domestic Workers and the International Division of Reproductive Labor," *Gender and Society* 14, no. 1 (August 2000): 576.

25. Rhacel Salazar Parreñas, "Permanent and Transitional Guest Workers: Varia-

tions of Partial Citizenship Among Migrant Filipina Domestic Workers in the Diaspora," in *Race, Ethnicity and Welfare States: An American Dilemma?*, ed. Pauli Kettunen (Cheltenham: Edward Elgar, 2015), 593, ProQuest Ebook Central.

26. Parreñas, "Permanent and Transitional Guest Workers," 206.

27. Puʻuhonua Society, "Contact Hawaiʻi 2018," accessed December 28, 2020, http://www.contacthawaii.com.

28. Website of Ara Laylo, accessed January 27, 2021, https://aralaylo.com/portfolio/dahilsayo/.

29. Josephine Machon, *Immersive Theatres: Intimacy and Immediacy in Contemporary Performance* (Basingstoke, UK: Palgrave Macmillan, 2013), 142.

30. Website of the Surfjack Hotel, accessed January 12, 2021, http://www.Surfjack.com.

31. Bala Sruti, *The Gestures of Participatory Art* (Manchester: Manchester University Press, 2018), 19.

32. Ara Laylo (aralaylo), "For a short window, the hospitality team at @thesurfjack shared their work life," Instagram, 17 April 2018, https://www.instagram.com/p/BhsR_BOBXSA/?igshid=1lhldu6owrcat.

33. Vince Diaz and Kēhaulani Kauanui, "Native Pacific Culutral Studies on the Edge," *Contemporary Pacific* 13, no. 2 (2001): 3, 18.

34. Konai Thanan, "Decolonizing Pacific Studies: Indigenous Perspectives, Knowledge, and Wisdom in Higher Education," *Contemporary Pacific* 15 (2003): 12.

35. Kristiana Kahakauwila, *This Is Paradise: Stories* (London: Hogawarth, 2018), 11.

36. Kahakauwila, 14.

37. Michel Foucault, *The Birth of Biopolitics*, ed. Michel Senellart, trans. Graham Burchell (New York: Picador, 2004), 73; Inderpal Grewal, *Saving the Security State: Exceptional Citizens in Twenty-First-Century America* (Durham, NC: Duke University Press, 2018), 18.

38. Gonzalez, *Securing Paradise*, 7.

39. Kahakauwila, *This Is Paradise*, 13.

40. Christopher Patterson, "Matronly Maids and Willful Women: Migrant Domestic Workers in the Plural," in *The Subject(s) of Human Rights: Crises, Violations, and Asian/American Critique*, ed. Cathy Shlund-Vials, Guy Pierre Beauregard, Hsiu-chuan Lee, and Madeleine Thien (Philadelphia: Temple University Press, 2020), 121; Kahakauwila, *This Is Paradise*, 19.

41. Kahakauwila, *This Is Paradise*, 19.

42. Rawiri Taonui, "Te Haerenga Waka: Polynesian Origins, Migrations and Navigation" (Master's thesis, University of Auckland, 1994), 24.

43. See works by Craig Santos Perez and Kathy Jetñil-Kijiner.

44. Patterson, "Matronly Maids and Willful Women," 121–22.

45. Mary Kawena Pukui and Samuel H. Elbert, *Hawaiian Dictionary* (Honolulu: University of Hawai'i Press, 1986).

46. Teves, "Aloha State Apparatuses," 707.

47. No'u Revilla and Jamaica Heolimeleikalani Osorio, "Aloha Is Deoccupied Love," in *Detours: A Decolonial Guide to Hawai'i*, ed. Hōkulani Aikau and Vernadette Gonazlez (Durham, NC: Duke University Press, 2019), 126.

48. Teves, "Aloha State," 710; Revilla and Osorio, "Aloha Is Deoccupied," 129.

49. Lauren Johnson, "Hawaii's Message to Tourists: Please Do Not Come Here Right Now," *CNN*, April 9, 2020, https://www.cnn.com/travel/article/hawaii-urges-tourists-to-stay-home-trnd/index.html.

50. "Hawaii's Unemployment Rate Jumps to 22.3% under Pandemic," *Hawaii News Now*, May 22, 2020, https://www.hawaiinewsnow.com/2020/05/22/hawaiis-unemployment-rate-jumps-amid-pandemic/; "Hawaii's Unemployment Rate Remains Highest in the Nation," *Hawaii News Now*, February 2, 2021, https://www.hawaiinewsnow.com/2021/02/02/hawaiis-unemployment-rate-remains-highest-nation/.

51. Saket Soni and Marielena Hincapie, "What We Owe Undocumented Workers during COVID-19," *CNN*, May 6, 2020, https://edition.cnn.com/2020/05/06/opinions/undocumented-immigrant-resilience-workers-covid-19-soni-hincapie/index.htm l.

52. Maurizio Guerrero, "Thousands of Essential Workers Are at Risk for Deportation," *In These Times*, May 15, 2020, http://inthesetimes.com/working/entry/22528/essential-worker-deportation-immigrant-undocumented-daca/.

2 PARADOXICAL AFFECT

Cross-Strait Intimacy in the Taiwan Teahouse

I-TING CHEN

Based in Taipei, mainland Chinese hostess Xiaomei works at the erotic teahouse and runs her own two-bed massage parlor simultaneously. One evening in January 2020, following dinner with a part-time hostess at her massage parlor, Xiaomei said, "I was like, you cursed mainlanders. I was like, [but] you always date mainlanders!" According to Xiaomei, her Taiwanese boyfriend has been dating mainland Chinese women since his last relationship. However, he often cursed mainlanders (大陸人) in Xiaomei's presence. The ambivalent attitude of Xiaomei's Taiwanese boyfriend toward mainland Chinese people sheds light on a prevalent emotional paradox across the Taiwan Strait, which is unpacked in this chapter.

How does the transpacific as an analytical framework help us understand the paradoxical affect manifested in how Xiaomei's boyfriend desires yet despises mainlanders? In other words, how can we understand cross-strait relations between Taiwan and mainland China through an examination of intimate encounters between mainland Chinese women and Taiwanese men? To examine such paradoxical affect in the context of cross-strait intimacy, this chapter discusses three examples: Xiaomei's trajectories of mobility; karaoke singing performance in the teahouse; and cross-strait intimacy between Xiaoping and her veteran husband, Old Man. Through ethnographic work in the leisure space, including a massage parlor and erotic teahouses in Taipei, this chapter unpacks everyday conversation and activities among mainland Chinese migrant women and their Taiwanese clients, friends, and partners, highlighting the often-overlooked intimate side of the paradoxical feelings in Taiwan-mainland relations.

The term "cross-strait intimacy" intends to complicate the often taken-for-granted antagonistic and hostile attitudes of Taiwanese toward mainland Chinese residents in Taiwan. Emphasizing cross-strait intimacy allows for a more nuanced understanding of media discourse, daily conversations, and activities involving cross-strait imaginations. The outbreak of the COVID-19 virus in Taipei in May 2021 and subsequent discussion in the public arena demonstrated the paradoxical feelings about mainland Chinese residents and their relatives living in Taiwan. Mainland Chinese migrants were portrayed not only as "outsiders" but also as potential virus carriers, as discussions connecting the virus to China (Wuhan) were circulated on various media platforms.[1] The xenophobic-cum-Sinophobic sentiment escalated in May 2021, after an outbreak in Wanhua teahouses in Taipei. The erotic tea parlors and teahouses are known to have a significant number of mainland Chinese employees, mostly working as hostesses. The first outbreak of cases was detected among a group of pilots who landed in Taipei in April 2021. The virus soon spread throughout Taipei and other New Taipei cities within the nearest circle of the airport. By May, employees in Wanhua district teahouses, drinking parlors, and karaoke shops were confirmed to have contracted the virus. "Wanhua virus" became a popularly circulated term in media reportage.[2] Subsequently, the clients and the hostesses in Wanhua teahouses became the target of the media's prying camera. Such media representation exposed to the public intimate interactions and everyday encounters between clients and hostesses within the erotic space. For example, the story about one teahouse client nicknamed "King of Tea" (茶裏王) by the media was revealed. According to reportage, before testing positive King of Tea had frequented a Wanhua teahouse for twenty-six days in a row.[3] The enthusiastic visits, despite the rise in the number of people continuing to contract the virus, earned him the unintended title.[4] With accumulated fear for the Wanhua district and of the virus, three groups were reported by local television channel SET as the "potential loopholes" in prevention practices against the virus: migrant workers, wanted criminals, and employees of the Eight Special Businesses (八大/特種行業).[5] The Wanhua cluster intensified COVID-19 shaming and discrimination against participants and employees in the area, making the hostesses in the Wanhua teahouse, who are both migrants and employees in the sex industry, the target of social anxiety in relation to their gender and their ethnic and national backgrounds.

Intimacies in sex commerce were not only highly sexualized but also demonized during the pandemic, which can be observed in the discussion of "links between people" (人與人的連結) by the Taiwanese government. During one press conference in June 2021, Chen Shih-chung (陳時中), the minister of health and welfare, alluded to interactions between a client and teahouse hostesses, stating that they had "links between people," which was later interpreted by the media as intimate interactions in the hostess teahouses.[6] By doing so, the authorities implied a connection between sexual and intimate services provided in the teahouse and virus transmission. Wanhua teahouses were then accused of having problems in hygiene, while their migrant hostesses were subjected to derogative portrayal, even by their loved ones. In May and June, concerned about the hostesses' health, I sent them messages to check-in. On June 1 I chatted with Jade, a Vietnamese hostess who worked in one of the Wanhua teahouses that had a few COVID-19 cases. During our call, Jade told me that she felt nothing different physically, since she was staying at home every day after most of the teahouses were temporarily shut down. However, Jade described her husband's concern, and how he acted as though she were a ghost when she went home the day that Wanhua reported two confirmed cases, both teahouse hostesses. Feeling slightly helpless, Jade told me how ironic her husband's cautious behaviors were, given that he is normally "the dirty one." Derogatory portrayals of the hostesses continued to circulate in different online and offline spaces. For example, a netizen commented on a YouTube video about erotic dancers in a Wanhua district KTV (karaoke) establishment: "How on earth will someone wear a mask when she doesn't even wear a bra?" (奶罩都沒戴的 地方 怎麼可能戴口罩).[7] I have discussed elsewhere that some terms, such as "mainland chicken" (daluji 大陸雞) and "mainland little sister" (dalumei 大陸妹), referring to mainland Chinese migrant workers in the teahouses and used by Taiwanese forum netizens during the pandemic, signaled many citizens' prolonged antagonistic sentiment against communism following the Chinese Civil War.

This current discussion investigates cross-strait politics through a trans-pacific and inter-Asia perspective, following the work of scholars like Petrus Liu, Lily Wong, and Kuan-Hsing Chen.[8] Kuan-Hsing Chen sheds light on this historical background, when the "us-other" division among two groups of people, *benshengren* (people of the province) and *waishengren* (people from outer provinces), was formed. The division between these two Han groups is defined by the time each arrived in Taiwan: the benshengren are people who arrived before the Chinese Civil War in 1945, while the waishengren migrated between 1945 and 1949, with the Nationalist Party (the Kuomintang, or KMT). Shaped by different memories of imperialism, colonialism, and the war, including the Cold War and the Chinese Civil War, the languages, classes, genders, and ethnic experiences greatly determined how benshengren and waishengren are similar as much as they are different, contributing to the earlier stage of the paradoxical affect across the Taiwan Strait during the pandemic. This historical and political environment not only rendered the "great reconciliation" impossible;[9] it also contributed to the prolongation of the paradoxical affect of cross-strait relations. After the lifting of martial law and enactment of cross-strait exchange in the late 1980s, Taiwanese society saw new migration from mainland China to Taiwan through cross-strait marriage. At this stage the state's participation in the anti–human trafficking campaign led by the United Nations and the United States shaped the experiences of this new generation of mainland Chinese migrants in Taiwan and continued to inform the paradox of cross-strait intimacy. On the one hand, cross-strait intimacy serves as a framework for understanding identity (trans)formation, including benshengren vis-à-vis waishengren and Taiwanese vis-à-vis mainlander. On the other hand, it complicates identity (trans)formation by paying attention to transpacific movements, namely cross-strait marriage, cross-strait sexual labor, and the advocacy of US and Cold War feminisms in Asia.

THE HISTORY OF WARS ON INTIMACY AND COMMUNISM

The migration from mainland China to Taiwan after the enactment of cross-strait exchange in 1987 coincided with various state agendas and social events. The concern that mainland migrant women may conduct "sham marriage, actually prostitution" as a way to migrate to Taiwan illuminates the role these women and their reproductive labor as wives and sex workers played in shaping cross-strait intimacy after 1987.[10] Their roles as wives and potential sex workers simultaneously stirred fear and desire of multiple images in the public space, such as *dalumei* (mainland little girl 大陸妹), "pink army for gold-digging," "communist spies," and "life-long Red Guards," all of which pose a threat to Taiwan's national and economic security.[11] Ideological antagonisms manifest their power through featuring the opponents as the "evil" and "primitive other" in the production of cultural artifacts and knowledges.[12] Scholars have noted the co-production of feminism and the cold war ideology during the Cold War period, depicting the ways the circulation of feminism, led by the United States and the United Nations (UN), contributed to the US Cold War project.[13] Helen Laville notes the use of women, identified as "Cold War warriors," in this ideological antagonism; concepts such as the "status of women" and "equality" were emphasized to highlight the superiority of the US political system.[14] Combined with the mediation of the UN, the US project of anticommunism was translated into the global task of eliminating authoritarianism and patriarchy.[15] In Taiwan, the US feminist project was facilitated by joining the US- and UN-led global ranking system, which targeted human trafficking and the UN project of gender mainstreaming. Together these led to a series of global legalizations, including the Sexual Assault Crime Prevention Act and the Domestic Violence Prevention Act in 1997 and 1998 in Taiwan.[16]

Taiwan's "sex wars" in 1997 further illuminate the global influence of the US project of feminism and sex work in Asia. When licensed prostitution was abolished in Taipei in the late 1990s, sex workers took to the streets to fight for their right to work.[17] Disagreeing with each other's stances on the movement, the feminists involved formed different camps—a split the media would later deem "family division" (*jiabian*, 家變).[18] Naifei Ding historicizes Taiwan's sex wars in relation to the US sex wars in the 1980s between the pro-pornography/pro–sex work and the anti-pornography campaigns.[19] Ding argues that part of the consequence of this US sex war was the exportation to other countries of an anti–sex work ideology—which commonly conflates sex work with human trafficking—through the work of nongovernmental organizations (NGOs) and the United Nations. US feminism was exported as a "superior model" for women's status around the world.[20] The impact of the internationalization of US feminism as the superior model for women's status globally demonstrates how the debate on sex work in Taiwan needs to be contextualized in line with the formation of the Pacific, drawing attention to the "geohistorical currents of colonial and imperial power dynamics" described in the introduction of this book.

The internationalization of the US feminist discourse to maintain global anticommunist sentiment created what Ding describes as a moment of "sign system change."[21] Paying attention to the historical relations between the global cultural production of the "Chinese" sex worker and China's role in the international arena, Lily Wong examined how sex workers operate as a trope of "politico-affective engagements" in the Pacific.[22] The inter-Asia and transpacific framework by which the abovementioned scholars historicized political and affective feelings encompassing Taiwan, mainland China, Asia more broadly, and the United States is further examined in the context of cross-strait intimacy. I ask how the historical dyad of anticommunism and antiprostitution in Taiwan can serve as a transpacific framework for better understanding of the "cold-sex-war" warriors: the mainland Chinese hostesses whose work, intimacy, and cross-strait mobility afford material and emotional attachments in relation to the sign system change and the paradoxical affect. In other words, as the history of the Cold War and Taiwan's sex wars continues to shape popular sentiment, cross-strait intimacy under such geopolitical and historical conditions requires further examination.[23]

The following relates a conversation I had with a teahouse client, Boss Tian, during an interview in a small drinking parlor. His words illustrate how the paradox of cross-strait intimacy functions to mediate everyday feelings in the field of erotic and entertaining spaces. In late January 2020 the spread of the COVID virus, particularly in China's Wuhan city, had already caught people's attention in Taipei. The interview, which I originally arranged in order to understand the teahouse culture's idea of "return the table" (還檯), turned out to revolve around the virus, the mainland hostesses, and their shrewd business strategies, which "infected" other Taiwanese hostesses in the intimate business.

During our interview the owner of the drinking parlor came to check in on us. He was wearing a mask, which caught our attention, as no one else was wearing one at the time, despite the circulating messages about the new type of virus. Sensing our unintended curiosity over his mask, the owner explained that he had just caught a cold. This seemingly irrelevant episode prompted Boss Tian to incorporate the term "virus" to describe the mainland hostesses who arguably initiated the shrewd practice of "return the table" (還檯) in the teahouse ten years ago.[24] Soon other hostesses started to follow the same practice. Boss Tian's understanding contrasted with observations by Ling, another Vietnamese hostess, who believed that return the table has been a universal practice, despite the national and ethnic background of the hostesses. Despite the contradiction, the way Boss Tian expressed his personal feelings about the mainland hostesses is paradoxical, hence needs further examination. Echoing the attitude of Xiaomei's Taiwanese boyfriend mentioned earlier, Boss Tian despised the mainland hostesses as much as he desired them. When he commented on the mainland hostesses' "influence" on other hostesses in the teahouses, he said: "[The non-mainland Chinese hostesses] are all infected. Just like the SARS in Wuhan, [they] are all infected." Highlighting the irresistible, if not fatal charm of mainland hostesses, Boss Tian explained further:

> About ten years ago, the clients [started to] follow mainland women's rules. Why? Because the mainland Chinese hostesses are good at acting affectionately (hui sajiao, 會撒嬌), cheating on men and fleecing men. However, [they] *are only after your money*. To acquire your money, she does whatever it takes . . . she's like, "Well, since I know you are a client, I will sleep with you, so that you will come to patronise (pengchang, 捧場) me the next day. Well, the condition is: [if] there are thirty women in the teahouse, you must call all of them [to join the table]. Well, then, my sacrifice is like, to have sex with you." [As for] the cost, one has to spend NTD$ 10,000 to NTD$ 20,000 [to patronise all] (Interview with Boss Tian, 2020, January; emphasis added)

Boss Tian regarded the mainland hostesses as women who would "sacrifice" themselves by having sex with their clients in exchange for, not so much their own benefits, but a profit to be shared among all thirty hostesses in the teahouse. "To patronize all" (全捧, *quan peng*) describes this situation: a client pays more than thirty times the usual table fee and tip to patronize all the hostesses in the same teahouse, just to please one hostess. Boss Tian then confessed how he used to be that "foolish client" who would do the same for the hostesses he adored. When I finished asking the questions related to the teahouse culture, Boss Tian shared with me an anecdote of an instance between him and two mainland hostesses who fought with each other over his attention. The paradoxical affect manifested in Boss Tian's confession and in his comments related to his cross-strait encounters with the mainland hostesses invites key questions: How do the entangled sentiments of anticommunism and antiprostitution shape the everyday lives of the mainland Chinese hostesses and the Taiwanese clients in the erotic teahouses in Taipei? How do the politics of the Cold War and the Taiwan sex wars help us comprehend a "Cold War structure of feeling" that generates both fear and affection for people across the Taiwan Strait?[25] What does such intimacy reveal about the complexity of cross-strait relations, beyond state establishments and nationalist discourses? To address these questions, we must examine their daily encounters with an understanding of the hostesses' mobility, memories, song performances, and intimacies across and beyond the Taiwan Strait.[26]

RESEARCH METHODS

The findings are based on my fieldwork between 2018 and 2020 in a teahouse in Taipei called Golden Phoenix (Jinfenghuang, 金鳳凰). I became acquainted with the teahouse hostess Xiaomei in 2015 when I undertook a writing project on the sex industry in Taiwan as an editor of an independent media organization. Later, through Xiaomei's introduction, I came to know other mainland Chinese hostesses. The teahouse Golden Phoenix, Xiaomei's two-bed massage parlor, and the nearby districts are where the ethnographic work was conducted for my doctoral dissertation. From 2018 to 2020 I visited Golden Phoenix for a total period of seven months. My role as a researcher was mixed with my other roles in the field. Sometimes I was Xiaomei's helper and occasionally looked after her massage parlor when she was too busy entertaining her clients. I was also a friend and a helper to the group of other mainland Chinese hostesses at Golden Phoenix. I was known by participants in the district as "the youngest," "little sister" (妹妹), "the one who writes thesis" (寫論文的), "the one from Hong Kong," and "the doctor" (博士).

Registered as a restaurant (*xiaochi dian*, 小吃店) in 1978, Golden Phoenix later became a "drinking shop" (*yinjiu dian*, 飲酒店). However, the hostesses and clients usually call them "tea parlors or teahouses" (*chashi* 茶室 or *chadian* 茶店).

XIAOMEI: THE WOMAN WHO CROSSES BORDERS

Xiaomei's mobility in crossing various borders and pursuing an ideal life is shaped by her experience as a woman running her own business. As an individual in her early sixties, Xiaomei is a very popular hostess in Golden Phoenix. She not only maintained good relationships with her clients and fellow hostesses in the teahouse district, but also expanded her business by running a two-bed massage parlor nearby. Despite the success Xiaomei once described to me as an "empire she conquered on her own" (我一手打下來的江山), she was reluctant to discuss her early business ventures. She considered it too "shameful" to recount.

Xiaomei was born in the mid-1950s, the youngest child in her immediate family. Soon after her birth China encountered the Great Leap Forward and the subsequent economic disaster that lasted from 1959 to 1961. The view of women born and raised in the Mao era was greatly mediated by the political campaign, national discourse, class struggle, and (counter) revolutionary depictions made by the Chinese Communist Party (CCP).[27] Xiaomei remembered that her parents underwent economic hardship when she was born. Xiaomei's mother was the "second wife," being "sold" to her father, who was a Republican official in China until the second Sino-Japanese War. In the later political campaign, Xiaomei's father was deemed a person with "counterrevolutionary antecedents." While Xiaomei is not particularly interested in recounting the economic and political hardships of her family, her memory of her mother is livelier. Xiaomei, not without pride, described to me how attractive her mother was. When her father visited the local villagers, he spotted and immediately adored Xiaomei's mother, "the prettiest woman in the village." He then purchased her from Xiaomei's grandfather. Her mother, the second wife, gave birth to six children and Xiaomei is the youngest. In the 1990s, after Xiaomei's husband died, she bought a house for her son and decided to leave for Taiwan. First she visited Taiwan through a senior relative, where she met her Taiwanese ex-husband, who Xiaomei now refers to as "my divorced husband" (我那個離婚的老公). Later, she migrated to Taiwan through cross-strait marriage.

Long before migrating to Taiwan, Xiaomei had moved back and forth between the countryside where her family resided and the city where her older sisters resettled after marriage. Crossing the boundary between city and countryside life, Xiaomei's journeys started when she turned fourteen. At first she visited the city occasionally to help look after her sisters' children, but she also needed to work in the field in her hometown, a small village nearby, to earn work points. When she turned twenty Xiaomei, through her sister's introduction, married a man whose family was from the city too. Xiaomei moved to the city to live with her husband and gave birth to a son in the late 1970s. However, the husband and his regulated salary as a worker at a state-owned factory did not promise the future Xiaomei had envisioned, one that would enable her pursuits in a nation undergoing economic transformation in the late 1970s and early 1980s. Xiaomei decided to pursue a better economic future by refusing to work at the factory and started trading commodities. She traveled to cities in Guangdong province to purchase small commodities, including shoes and clothes, to sell in the city where she resided.

The memory of Xiaomei's trip to Guangdong recalls for her a time full of tears, sweat, and bitterness. Taking the train to Guangdong province in itself was, at the time, a struggle. She cannot forget how unhygienic the train was, when she squeezed in the space under the sleeping berth or outside the toilet on the train. She endured the toilet's smell and mosquitoes, which did not miss biting one spot on her legs. Meanwhile, the newly established market economy did not welcome female businessowners the same way it did her male counterparts. Xiaomei remembers the threats they encountered during the trip, including male intruders and potential thieves. She recalls that people would sit together in a circle to protect their cargoes from being stolen. Notwithstanding the bitterness, this early business venture established Xiaomei's later ambition and determination in crafting a better future by her own hands.

Xiaomei's mobility questions the symbolic border that divides rural and urban areas, as well as family and market. Such division is enhanced by not only state policies that "spectralize" the rural but also a sense of shame that inscribe in women's memories that act of "going out" and "leaving home."[28] Xiaomei does not recall her participation in this "crossing" with a sense of pride; instead, her narrative is full of feelings of shame, danger, and bitterness.

Similar feelings have been discussed by Hairon Yan. Women who left home and worked as domestic workers in other people's households in the city during the transition period from the Maoist to the post-Maoist era were seen as "transgressors of the proper subject position of rural woman as defined by ideologically espoused heroic agricultural labor, and they reinvoked the specter of the past through domestic service."[29] They were not the ideal "iron girls" expected to devote themselves to agricultural production, nor were they the "good women" who stayed in their own families in the village.[30] Xiaomei, in order to pursue business opportunities, was a business owner on the one hand and a "transgressor" on the other. Yet, she has not stopped moving since then.

THE MAINLAND HOSTESS GANG IN THE TEAHOUSE

Despite being called "mainlander" (大陸人) or "dalumei" (大陸妹) by clients and Taiwanese hostesses in the teahouses and drinking parlors in the same district, Xiaomei transitioned from her previous occupation as a professional masseuse in a touristy and commercial massage parlor to her current job as a hostess, which enabled her to become self-employed.[31] Xiaomei has established her reputation in the teahouse district. In the meantime, her influence over the mainland gang in the teahouse, where many of the mainland hostesses were recruited either by Xiaomei or her fellow villagers, raised the constant concern of another figure of power, the Taiwanese accountant of Golden Phoenix. The antagonistic yet intimate relationship between Xiaomei and the accountant (in terms of daily interaction and the intertwined business model), as well as the mainland hostess gang versus Taiwanese hostesses, is illuminated in the description that follows.

In the teahouse there were more than fifty women who worked at different times, depending on their shifts. The teahouse relied largely on the income from the clients who frequently visited the teahouse to spend time with their acquainted hostesses. The teahouse does not pay the hostesses; rather, it provides space and equipment for the gatherings among clients and hostesses, which demonstrates a unique dynamic in the space. The teahouse earns more profits if the hostesses can attract more clients. In other words, the teahouse needs popular hostesses to support its business, while the hostesses rely on their collaboration with the management and other hostesses to boost their own income. Besides this business model, which binds all parties together, arguments and disagreements happen from time to time.

There are two accountants in Golden Phoenix who together manage the teahouse, which runs twenty-four hours. The older and senior accountant established her power by managing the money and the administrative work in the teahouse as well as a personal connection to the boss lady, the owner of the teahouse. Her power is further manifested by the loyal support from the Taiwanese crew, including the junior accountant, the hostesses, and a helper known as "young master" (少爺). The accountant decides whether a new hostess will have a key to a locker in the teahouse, based on her observation of the hostess's performance, loyalty, and ability.

Even though the accountant seemed to hold great power in the space, Xiaomei is often considered by her clients the "real boss" of the teahouse, due to her great business skills and wide clientele. Knowing that the clients are attracted to "fresh faces," Xiaomei has recruited fellow villagers from her hometown to refresh the crew and keep the business going. Moreover, the accountant endures the fact that Xiaomei often invites her clients to her personal massage parlor for meals or a massage session following their visits at the teashop and she does not consider it the "conflict of interest." The peaceful relationship between Xiaomei and the accountant once became antagonistic because Xiaomei recruited a friend, Bobo, who was on a tourist visa, to briefly work at the teahouse and earn some pocket money.[32] On the final day of her part-time hostess experience, the accountant suddenly threw her out, claiming that Bobo's visa status would cause the teahouse trouble. Xiaomei was furious and had to temporarily shelter Bobo in her massage parlor. Although the incident itself did not directly target Xiaomei or Bobo, the alleged intention was to protect the property of the teahouse from possible legal issues. However, it was comprehended by Xiaomei and Bobo as racist treatment targeting the new mainland hostess, who the accountant did not appreciate. In Xiaomei's massage parlor, Xiaomei and I listened to Bobo talked about how embarrassed she felt when the accountant yelled at her and rushed her out in front of everyone in the teahouse. Trying to console her, Xiaomei shared her own experience with us. After she resided in Taiwan, because of her visa status she was not allowed to work legally in the first two years of her marriage, and it took her half a year to locate a cleaning job at a private household. One day, after Xiaomei finished her cleaning, the female employer offered her some secondhand shoes and asked Xiaomei to try them on and see whether they fit. Xiaomei found the offer extremely offensive, as the employer intended to give her the old shoes as payment for her labor that day:

> She thinks we mainlanders who came to Taiwan are all too poor. [She] provided shoes as payment. Alas. [I] could not find any jobs for more than six months. No one hired me. The reason they provided was all because I did not have a work permit. For two years without a work permit, I had suffered enough. So what? Nothing to feel embarrassed about. (Xiaomei, Participant observation, 2019 July)

The mainland-Taiwan division has shaped how people of both sides understand and explain their entangled life in the same community. Another conversation with Xiaomei unpacks the issues of identity, subjectivity, and a sense of belonging under the cross-strait conditions.

XIAOMEI'S VOICE: AM I NOT THE SAME AS YOU?

On August 1, 2019, China's Ministry of Culture and Tourism suspended a visa program that enables tourists from forty-seven cities in mainland China to travel individually to Taiwan due to rising cross-strait tensions. The decision directly affected Xiaomei, as one of her business strategies was to recruit new hostesses from mainland China visiting Taiwan on tourist visas. Under such circumstances, the 2020 presidential election slogan proposed by the KMT candidate Han Kuo-Yu, promoting cross-strait exchange, caught Xiaomei's attention. Two days before the election, I found Xiaomei watching the live broadcast of Han Kuo-Yu's presidential campaign on YouTube.[33] Using her mobile phone to stream the broadcast, Xiaomei sat in front of one of the two massage beds in her massage parlor with her phone on a phone stand on the bed. I joined her and we watched the rally together. Han's supporters enthusiastically waved the Republic of China (ROC) flag and chanted the campaign slogan. The KMT campaign marketed "economic development" between mainland China and Taiwan as a counter to the pro-independence message of the opponent candidate representing the Democratic Progressive Party (DPP). Apart from Xiaomei, other mainland hostesses I know also supported Han, for they believed he would improve cross-strait relations and bring more profit. Xiaomei believed that Han "is very good at business" (他很會做生意啦). She commented: "He will make two places one family (兩岸一家親), [people from] this side . . . go there to do business [while people from] that side . . . come here to do business. [We] make money if [we] do business, or else what do we eat?"[34] Hoping to "change the current situation," Xiaomei, like other mainland hostesses, is passionate about her right to vote.

This political moment and passion seemed to trigger Xiaomei's memory, as she then shared a past encounter with me. After chanting "Get elected! Get elected!" (凍蒜! 凍蒜!) along with the hosts, Xiaomei suddenly said, while her eyes still stared at the screen of her phone, "Go back to mainland China, they said to me." She was referring to a conflict that happened between her and a former colleague in a commercial massage parlor that catered mostly to tourists. The masseur charged a client lower than the market price. Since the market price was an amount agreed upon by all the massage workers in the parlor, Xiaomei told him not to do this, as it would affect the official price and eventually cut income from other people's business. Irritated, the masseur said, "Go back to your country! You mainlander!" (你是大陸人滾回去!). With rage, Xiaomei showed her Taiwanese ID card and asked, "The-Republic-of-China, am I not the same as you? How dare you humiliate me?" (中華民國, 不是跟你一樣嗎? 你還罵我?). Xiaomei threatened to sue the masseur if he didn't apologize to her. He then apologized. Later, after Xiaomei told me this story, I was curious about how she identifies herself: more as Taiwanese or as mainland Chinese? Her answer was "half [mainlander] and half [Taiwanese]" (我是一半一半啦).

THE IN-BETWEEN SUBJECT

Working as a hostess in the erotic teahouse, Xiaomei is popular among her male clients and friends. However, her boyfriend, whom she nicknamed "Anata" (阿娜答), is the only person who qualifies as her boyfriend. Xiaomei gets excited when she shares with me sweet details about their relationship. "This is the first time that I am in love; I have never felt like this before. I had no idea what love is." Among other economic and emotional reasons, one key boyfriend qualification that Anata has is that "he does not have a wife." Unlike other clients who have come in contact with Xiaomei in the context of the teahouse—usually married men between fifty and eighty years old—Anata had been divorced. Xiaomei's resistance to seriously dating a married man also reveals the nature of her role as a hostess: developing romantic plays with men despite their marital status. Outside the teahouse, Xiaomei refuses to carry the shame imposed on her occupation, such as the media reportage and forum discussions that amplified the connection between mainland Chinese hostesses, and COVID-19 virus, and whores, discussed at the beginning of this chapter.[35] This refusal immediately challenges the way women who work in sex commerce are positioned as "not-yet feminist subjects" in the context of Taiwan's sex wars of the late 1990s.[36] At work, Xiaomei's professional performance and ambivalent relationships with her clients effectively place her as an "intruder" and "outsider" who threatens the power and resource of another woman, namely the wife, in her "uterine family."[37] In the meantime, Xiaomei's ethnic and national ambiguity triggers anxiety for Taiwanese like the masseur who suggested Xiaomei should "go back" to her country. By doing so, he positioned Xiaomei as the "not-quite not-yet national subject" who, even with Taiwanese citizenship, is not able to integrate into the ranks of "free citizens." At that moment of their encounter, Xiaomei not only embodied the shame projected onto migrant sex workers who transgress geographical and ideological boundaries; she also carries the particular shame of being a *mainland Chinese* migrant woman imagined in relation to her "origin" country: red China ruled by the CCP.

The cross-strait experiences of mainland migrant women further demonstrate how sentiments of anti-prostitution and anticommunism not only persist but are intertwined within the Pacific. Such entangled imaginations echo the fears of communism discussed in research on confrontations between Taiwanese veterans and their mainland Chinese wives.[38] The mainland wife Sun Xiangdong was accused by her veteran husband of being a communist spy who "wished me to die sooner so that she could take the house."[39] The husband, Lao Wei, then requested that the state send his wife back to mainland China, as it would "rid the people of harm and the country of evil" (為民除害、為國除奸).

Such imaginations of cross-strait migrant women as "communist spies" who are "inherently corrupt" frame these women as not-quite subjects in both national and feminist terms. What's more, the fear and hostility are backed by state policies. As the Taiwanese state monitors the "authenticity" of cross-strait marriage, it has the power to decide whether or not a spouse should be granted Taiwanese citizenship. The assumption is that only when the mainland Chinese spouse learns to be a good wife will she become a civilized Taiwanese citizen who deserves citizenship.

This affective device links Taiwan and mainland China in an antagonistic yet intimate way, combining anti-communist sentiments with gender and sex-based shaming. It is arguably what Xiaomei's Taiwanese coworker wielded when he told her to "go back to China." While Xiaomei responded defiantly by displaying her Taiwanese ID card and asking, "Am I not the same as you?," she also identified herself as "half (mainland Chinese) and half (Taiwanese)." In so doing, she not only denies the positional superiority occupied by a Taiwanese citizen (identifying as an "in-between [half and half] subject"); she also questions the very subject positioning that reinforces hierarchies between "bad" and "good" women.

SINGING AND RESISTANCE: CALL ME BIG SISTER (JIE, 姐)

Voices of mainland Chinese hostesses are often replaced by mainstream discourses, which frequently approach sex-related industries through dichotomized frameworks of victimization and criminalization. Bitter stories and xenophobic narratives occupy media reportage, obscuring migrant women's agency in their everyday lives. An example would be the video "[A Salty and Wet Piece] The Wild Orgies in a Wanhua Tea Parlor; All Naked; Rubbing and Cheering!" which was recorded and posted online by a former member of parliament Tung Chung-Yen (A-tung, 童仲彥).[40] The video shows hostesses performing erotic dances in a KTV room in the Wanhua district. The purple and blue lighting, deafening stereo music, and intimate interactions when a dancer invites a client to rub her breasts, offer voyeuristic pleasures to the viewer. It is presented as if the former parliament member, A-tung, had revealed "the real Wanhua." The viewers have no idea who these people are or the context in which they labor. Such portrayals contribute to the image of there being a "Wanhua virus"; it suggests that the Wanhua teahouses and tea parlors are hidden threats to society.

A similar scene occurred in a KTV box in the Pink Moon drinking parlor.[41]

When I was invited by a client to join his karaoke party, the hostesses were singing the song "What the Hell's So Great About You" (Ni niu sheme niu, 你牛什麼牛), a popular tune that mainland Chinese hostesses often sing to entertain their clients.[42] The singing and dancing performance is recorded in my fieldnotes:

Pink Moon was located in a deteriorating old building next to a grocery store. When we were waiting for the lift, I found that there were six CCTV cameras on the wall, though I was not sure if they were all functioning. The stairs opposite the lift were extremely narrow. The lift stopped on the 7th floor, and I followed Boss Ho into a KTV box named "Emerald." Unlike the karaoke rooms in Golden Phoenix, the KTV box here was more like the ones in high-end erotic KTVs or nightclubs—each box was equipped with disco lighting, stereo systems, and a huge digital screen. There was enough space for the hostesses and clients to sing and dance together in between the screen and the U-shaped sofa. In this box there sat three clients and two hostesses. Apart from Boss Ho, a hostess sat next to a young client, who I was told was Boss Ho's cousin. There was another client called Brother Wu, who was only a bit older than Boss Ho. Sitting next to him was a hostess who had dyed her hair light brown. She wore glasses, a tight green top, and a pair of denim mini shorts. Like in other tea parlors, hostesses do business as a group and usually with fellow sisters from the same city in mainland China. The hostess, like the others here, was from Fujian province. Brother Wu was singing with one hostess while the cousin and the hostess were dicing for drinks.

After around twenty minutes I excused myself from the party and went back to Golden Phoenix to see how business was going for the other hostesses. When I came back to Emerald after another thirty minutes, there was a hostess sitting next to Boss Ho. She was prepared to sing the song "What the Hell's So Great About You." This was the first time I heard this song. It was impossible not to notice how the song lit up the atmosphere in the room. The thrust of electronic instruments from the song caught everyone's attention. It was as if we were all ready to shake our bodies to the beat. While one hostess was slightly moving her body, the other two hostesses performed erotic dance moves in front of the room. The song had turned the KTV box into a rave party. The singer repeated the lyrics "What the hell's so great about you" many times. I was intrigued by the hostess when she pointed at Boss Ho's nose while singing "What the hell's so great about you," as if she were scolding him seriously. However, no one seemed to be offended by the idea of the song, and quite the opposite, everyone seemed cheerful and delighted with the dramatic performance. As they approached the song's climax, the two hostesses danced more passionately: one hostess leaned towards another as she sexily squatted down; the other shook her body to coordinate with the former. After the hostess finished the song, another hostess changed the disco lighting back to the usual dim light. She then left the room.[43]

"What the Hell's So Great About You" was released in 2014 from the album of the same title, performed by singer Tang Gu.[44] The song portrays a woman scolding someone who fools her in his game of love and money. In the first part of the song the heroine accuses the person who seduces, mistreats, and fools her by saying, "Big sister's true heart cannot be easily fooled" (姐的真心怎能隨便拍拖). Four sets of refrain follow, each beginning with the repeated question "What the hell's so great about you?" By replacing the first person "I" with "big/older sister" (jie, 姐) in the line "Big sister's happiness is merely that true devotion" (姐的幸福只是那真心擁有), the performer demonstrates her seniority over the person to whom she sings. What's more, the phrase "What the hell's so great about you?" (你牛什麼牛) is widely used in mainland China. The usage of niu can be linked to that of niu-bi (牛逼), which literally means cow and vagina. Referring to someone as niu-bi is complimenting someone, sometimes in a satirical way, depending on context. I translate Ni niu sheme niu as "What the hell's so great about you" to show the tone of mockery when complimenting someone who believes themselves to be great (niu) despite not living up to that image. By repeating "What the hell's so great about you," the person who sings the tune becomes the subject who, through questioning and denying the "greatness" of the other person, ridicules their presumed superiority. Following the repeated lines of refrain, the tune continues with a series of statements that destabilize symbols of power and challenge presumptions about the big sister, including the materialistic image (e.g., "Your money won't buy big sister's freedom" and "You have never thought about how big sister feels"). For the hostesses, singing is a way to make a living by entertaining the clients. However, it can also offer openings to scold, question, talk back to, and deny the "betrayed lover" who "never thought about how big sister feels." Songs can further illuminate imaginations of "cross-strait intimacy."

CROSS-STRAIT INTIMACY

Cross-strait marriage, like other types of marriage, institutionalizes and legalizes intimate connections. Marriage can thus be arranged to cater to the exchange of various needs. The arranged marriage between Xiaoping, a part-time mainland hostess, and her Taiwanese veteran husband, whom she called Old Man (老頭子), provided grounds for mutual support and largely transformed the couple's given circumstances. At the time of Xiaoping and Old Man's marriage, they were both dealing with challenging living conditions. In China, Xiaoping moved with one of her two daughters from the countryside to a major city, after divorcing her first husband who had cheated on her. Soon enough, the challenges of urban life became clear: no matter how hard she worked, her income would barely allow her to make rent and pay her daughters' education fees. To improve their life quality, Xiaoping decided to go to Taiwan through marriage migration in the early 2000s.

Xiaoping met Old Man through mutual friends. At the time, Old Man was already seventy-eight years old. Like other elderly veterans, Old Man was not considered a good marriage candidate for local women in Taiwan. Xiaoping told me Old Man spent all his savings building houses for his relatives in mainland China, some of whom he barely knew—this is how he "lost everything" by, ironically, providing for family across the strait. When he and Xiaoping met, Old Man requested that Xiaoping take care of him for the few years he had left to live. They did not have any sexual interactions, Xiaoping said. In return, Old Man promised to help Xiaoping come to Taiwan and become a Taiwanese citizen.

The forty-year age gap explains why Xiaoping calls him "Old Man." When she told me their story, Xiaoping was very proud that, after he passed away, she was able to fulfill his wishes and put his remains in the "best place" in a national military cemetery on Wuzhi Mountain (五指山). The seemingly "not so romantic" marriage arrangement between Xiaoping and Old Man worked to transform their given circumstances and created the possibility for cross-strait intimacy and the building of a shared future.

Intimate encounters among people from Taiwan, mainland China, and Hong Kong have been widely discussed in the literature.[45] Cross-strait marriage between younger mainland Chinese women and older Taiwanese husbands, often veterans retired from the national army, is also commonly discussed.[46] However, it is not as visible in the public discussion as in the literature, and research on the representation of the cross-strait marriage between mainland wives and Taiwanese husbands is also limited.[47] A small piece can be added to the puzzle by examining ideas of happiness, marriage, and the history of cross-strait relations as represented in popular songs, such as "1949."

PURSUING HAPPINESS IN THIS RUTHLESS WORLD

Popular songs have become a unique medium that affords an analysis of cross-strait intimacy, portraying imaginations of shared lives and love beyond the Taiwan Strait. Male-female and Minnanese-Mandarin duets have been written to cater to the needs of those in cross-strait communities who sing in two languages. Some Minnanese-Mandarin duet songs that are popularly sung by participants in the teahouse are "Only for You" (今生只為你) and "Tears of Fallen Flowers" (落花淚). Songwriter Zhang Yanqing (張燕清) is well known for his Minnanese songs written for prestigious singers such as Chen Ying-git (陳盈潔) and Shen Wen Cheng (沈文程) in Taiwan. Zhang has also written a handful of songs depicting cross-strait intimacy: "Love in Shanghai" (上海之戀) portrays a cross-strait romance between a Taiwanese man who falls in love with a mainland Chinese woman when visiting Shanghai; "Love Across the Taiwan Strait" (兩岸情) illustrates the tale of a male migrant in Taiwan who misses his lover in mainland China. In the duet titled "1949," Zhang portrays an encounter between a KMT veteran and a benshengren young woman.[48]

Starting with the sound of snare drums, "1949" is set during the Chinese Civil War. The male performer sings in Mandarin in a deep and sad tone.

As depicted in the lines "A man who left his hometown and lost everything because of warfare" (一個離鄉背景的人 面對戰火沒了一切) and "Being able to have your love—this life is with no regrets" (能夠擁有你的愛 今生無悔), the male character considers himself "incomplete" after losing everything during the war; the woman's love is the hope that enables him to live "with no regrets." On the other hand, she is the "flower waiting for spring" who longs for his support and nurturing, as well as a sincere wedding: "Long for your support—give me a sincere wedding" (望你裁培 會凍乎阮一個真心的婚禮). At the song's close they commit to completing each other, as the "February butterfly" and the "waisheng wife."

Imaginations of happiness and mutual support are at the heart of the song's depiction of cross-strait intimacy, showing how romantic ideas coexist with living strategies. The duo structure of the Cold War and the Chinese Civil War deeply affected people's everyday lives. The island established the Veterans Affairs Council in 1954, which dealt with social unsettlement after a great number of veterans retired from the army and immediately faced unemployment for their lack of other professional skills.[49] By the 1980s these veterans became the "old and single" class in society.[50] This history is reflected in the song "1949," as the voice of the veteran expresses sentiments of "unhappiness" and feeling "incomplete" for having "lost everything" during the war.[51]

While in the song the young woman's love becomes the veteran's only hope, it is not without strategic expectations and considerations of livelihood. Hope for a future is only possible through mutual support: he becomes her "February butterfly" and she becomes his "waisheng wife."[52] This "exchange" cannot be equated to simple economic gains, as is often presumed through the dichotomization of romantic love (reproduction) and transactional sex (recreation). Rather, it should be contextualized through the subjects' given circumstances and socioeconomic conditions. In a similar light, Xiaoping and Old Man—a caregiver and a citizenship patron—found a way to redefine and negotiate the hierarchical structure of the "ruthless world" and the "hopeless society" amid the ruins of the Cold War in East Asia.

CONCLUSION

The affective structures of anticommunism and antiprostitution shape migrant hostesses' everyday lives in the context of Taiwan and across the Taiwan Strait. The hostesses' business strategies, singing performances, and self-narration amplify their frequently muted voices. This examination moves beyond long-standing discourses over cold sex wars and traces, and focuses on the paradoxical affect of cross-strait intimacy. Through the everyday life and work experiences of the hostesses and their Taiwanese clients and friends, this discussion unpacks historically and geopolitically the reasons why the imaginations of cross-strait intimacy have been rendered invisible in the public sphere in Taiwan society and international media. The hierarchical positioning of the mainland migrant subjects in relation to their intertwined backgrounds of gender, nationality, ethnicity, and class is also in question. The hostesses' refusal, resistance, and rearticulation relating to subjectivity suggest a nondichotomous understanding of their roles in the Taiwan teahouse and beyond. The ideas of nation, gendered labor, and subjectivity are often obscured by the invisible and yet powerful framework through which our knowledge is not only produced but also "intimated."[53] The investigation of "cross-strait intimacy" and its paradoxical affect can serve as a starting point for challenging the hidden "either-or" logic in grasping mainland Chinese migrant women's lived experience in Taiwan.

NOTES

1. For more on the circulation of the term "Wuhan virus" during the COVID-19 pandemic in Taiwan and its "war logic," see the detailed discussion in Chien-ting Lin, "In Times of War and Love," *Inter-Asia Cultural Studies* 21, no. 4 (2020): 575–86.

2. Shelley Shan, "COVID-19: 'Wanhua Virus' Headline Sparks Outrage," *Taipei Times*, June 3, 2021.

3. Liu Mingxiu [劉修銘], "Nationwide Level 3 Epidemic Alert in Taiwan: Keelung Elderly Living Alone Becomes the 'King of Tea' Who Tested Positive after 26 Consecutive Days Visiting Wanhua Teahouse by Train" [全台三級警戒: 基隆獨居老人成「茶裏王」連續26天搭火車去萬華茶室確診], *Mirror Media*, June 23, 2021.

4. According to Taiwan's Center for Disease Control and Prevention, in May the island saw on average four hundred to five hundred new and retroactively added cases per day.

5. Huang Chia-wei [黃家緯], "Let's Fight Epidemic Prevention! Is Normal Life Possible Next Month? Scholars Revealed: 800,000 Wanted Criminals, Special Vice Industries and Migrant Workers Might Become Loopholes of Epidemic Prevention" [全民防疫動起來! 下個月也很難回到正常生活? 學者曝: 通緝犯.特種行業.逃逸移工 這80萬人恐淪破口], SETN.com, June 3, 2021.

6. Tim Culpan, "Sexy Tea, the Lion King and Taiwan's Lost Innocence: Covid Complacency and Rebellious Retirees Have Seen the Bubble Burst on One of the Pandemic's Great Success Stories," *Bloomberg Opinion*, June 3, 2021.

7. Tung Chung-Yen [童仲彥], "A Salty and Wet Piece: The Wild Orgies in a Wanhua Tea Parlour; All Naked; Rubbing and Cheering!" [鹹溼片 萬華茶室酒池肉林 一絲不掛 摩蹭吆喝], YouTube, June 4, 2021 (00:00–00:50).

8. See Kuan-Hsing Chen, *Asia as Method: Toward Deimperialization* (Durham, NC: Duke University Press, 2010), chaps. 1, 3, 4.

9. Chen, chap. 3.

10. See Sara L. Friedman, *Exceptional States: Chinese Immigrants and Taiwanese Sovereignty* (Oakland: University of California Press, 2015), 60.

11. For more on the idea of the mainland little girl, see Mayfair Mei-hui Yang, *Spaces of Their Own: Women's Public Sphere in Transnational China* (Minneapolis: University of Minnesota Press, 1999), 290. For more on the pink army for gold-digging, see Mei-Hua Chen, "The 'Fake Marriage' Test in Taiwan: Gender, Sexuality, and Border Control," *Cross-Currents: East Asian History and Culture Review E-Journal* 15 (June 2015): 88. And for more on communist spies and life-long Red Guards, see Antonia Chao, "Rethinking Nationalism Through Intimate Relationships: Conflicts in Cross-Strait Marriages," *Taiwan Sociology* 16 (December 2008): 98.

12. See Petrus Liu, "Cold War as Method," *Prism* 16, no. 2 (2019): 408–31; Hsunhui Tseng, "National Imagination and the Construction of 'the Other' During the 1950s in Taiwan: A Conception of Sexuality," *Hong Kong Journal of Social Sciences* 18 (Winter 2000): 85–112; and Yi-hung Liu, "The World Comes to Iowa in the Cold War: International Writing Program and the Translation of Mao Zedong," *American Quarterly* 69, no. 3 (2017): 611–31.

13. See relevant discussions in Suzy Kim, "Cold War Feminisms in East Asia," *positions: east asia critique* 28, no. 3 (2020): 501–16; Tani Barlow, "International Feminism of the Future," *Signs* 25, no. 4 (2000): 1099–1105; Naifei Ding, "In the Eye of International Feminism: Cold Sex Wars in Taiwan," *Economic and Political Weekly* 1, no. 17 (2015): 60; and Helen Laville, *Cold War Women: The International Activities of American Women's Organisations* (Manchester: Manchester University Press, 2002).

14. See Laville, *Cold War Women*, 115.

15. Ding, "In the Eye of International Feminism."

16. I-ting Chen, "Cold War Intimacy Beyond the Taiwan Strait: Sexual Labour and Chinese Modernities in the Teahouse" (PhD diss., Lingnan University, 2020), 6.

17. Ding, "In the Eye of International Feminism."

18. Ding, 57.

19. Ding, 57.

20. An example would be the ranking system and the TIP (Trafficking in Persons) Report, which aims at evaluating each country's human trafficking circumstances.

21. Ding, "In the Eye of International Feminism," 60.

22. See introduction in Lily Wong, *Transpacific Attachments: Sex Work, Media Networks, and Affective Histories of Chineseness* (Columbia University Press, 2018), 5.

23. Ding, "In the Eye of International Feminism," 60.

24. In the teahouse, when a hostess asks her clients to invite more of her fellow hostesses to join a table, the latter is expected to do the same the next time to return the favor. This is known as "return the table," a set of practices aimed at encouraging the clients to pay more so that the hostesses can earn more. From some clients' perspective, like Boss Tian, the business ethics of return the table force them to pay a lot more. They are expected to invite ten hostesses instead of one so as to give the hostess "face." This culture is detailed in my dissertation, "Cold War Intimacy Beyond the Taiwan Strait" (2020).

25. Liu, "Cold War as Method," 411. Also see Chen, *Asia as Method*.

26. My research methods involve both textual analysis and ethnography. In particular, I analyze popular songs circulated across the strait that reflect the experiences of the mainland hostesses and the clients. This work centers the hostesses' subjectivity by detailing their experiences and memories about crossing the border and their longings and sometimes anger.

27. Naihua Zhang, "In a World Together Yet Apart: Urban and Rural Women Coming of Age in the Seventies," in *Some of Us: Chinese Women Growing Up in the Mao Era. New Brunswick*, ed. Zhong Xueping, Zheng Wang, and Di Bai (New Brunswick, NJ: Rutgers University Press, 2001), 1–26.

28. Hairong Yan, "Specialization of the Rural: Reinterpreting the Labor Mobility of Rural Young Women in Post-Mao China," *American Ethnologist* 30, no. 4 (November 2003): 578–96.

29. Yan, 582.

30. Yan, 581.

31. A hostess is not an employee of the teahouse; rather she is a business partner with the teahouse owner. Hostesses can change to another teahouse anytime they wish, and sometimes they do so when they have bad relationships with other hostesses in the same teahouse. Hostesses' income includes tips directly from the clients and basic table service fees. Aside from tips and the fixed table fees for hostesses, clients also pay a fixed amount of money for the tea and snacks provided by the teahouse.

32. This was just before the People's Republic of China government decided to ban citizens' applications for tourist visas to Taiwan beginning August 1, 2019, as a form of

economic sanction in response to the political tension between the PRC government and Taiwan's Tsai administration.

33. The recording of Han's campaign in Taipei can be watched here: https://www.youtube.com/watch?v=RLStELDdZPc (accessed October 11, 2020).

34. Participant observation (2020), 1.

35. My thanks to Lily Wong, Christopher B. Patterson, and Chien-ting Lin for reading and editing this chapter, as well as providing feedback and emotional support, and their patience for my slow progress during the revision period. I also would like to express my gratitude to the precious feedback given by reviewers of this book, which helped clarify and connect this chapter to the whole book during the revision period. This chapter would not be as polished without the final editing by Ann Baker for UW Press.

36. Naifei Ding, "Feminist Knots: Sex and Domestic Work in the Shadow of the Bondmaid-Concubine," *Inter-Asia Cultural Studies* 3 (2002): 455.

37. Margery Wolf, "Uterine Families and the Women's Community," in *Women and the Family in Rural Taiwan* (Stanford, CA: Stanford University Press, 1972), 33.

38. Chao, "Rethinking Nationalism."

39. Quoted in Chao's interview with the husband. See Chao, "Rethinking Nationalism," 113 (author's translation).

40. Chung-Yen [童仲彥] Tung, "A Salty and Wet Piece—The Wild Orgies in a Wanhua Tea Parlour; All Naked; Rubbing and Cheering! [鹹溼片 萬華茶室酒池肉林 絲不掛 摩蹭吆喝], YouTube, June 4, 2021.

41. The fieldnotes were recorded in Chinese and later translated. Some revisions to that translation are made for the sake of clarity.

42. Gu Tang [唐古], "What the Hell's So Great About You (Ni Niu Shenme Niu)" [你牛什麼牛], https://www.youtube.com/watch?v=bBaSJb8K-Mw.

43. Fieldnotes revised in June 2021.

44. Gu, "What the Hell's So Great About You."

45. To list a few: Suowei Xiao, *Desire and Dignity: Class, Gender and Intimacy in Transitional China* [慾望與尊嚴: 轉型期中國的階層, 性別與親密關係] (Beijing: Social Sciences Academic Press, 2018); Antonia Chao, "Transnational Maternal Citizenship: Changing Moral Economy on State Margins," *Taiwanese Journal of Sociology* 44 (June 2010): 155–212; Mei-Hua Chen, "The 'Fake Marriage' Test in Taiwan: Gender, Sexuality, and Border Control," *Cross-Currents: East Asian History and Culture Review* 15 (June 2015): 82–107; Mei-Hua Chen, "Sexualized Border Control: The Investigation of 'Phony Marriages' and the Exclusion of Chinese Migrants/Sex Workers," *Taiwan Sociology* 19 (June 2010): 55–105; Ko-lin Chin, *Going Down to the Sea: Chinese Sex Workers Abroad* (Chiang Mai, Thailand: Silkworm, 2014); Tiantian Zheng, *Red Lights: The Lives of Sex Workers in Postsocialist China* (Minneapolis: University of Minnesota Press, 2009); and Yang, *Spaces of Their Own.*

46. Chao, "Rethinking Nationalism."

47. Relevant discussions can be found in Maoshan Huang [黃茂善], "Out of Place: Quasi-Taipei People, Under the Eave, and Sinophone Literature" [鄉關何處: 準台北人, 屋簷下 與華語語系文學], *Taiwan: A Cultural Studies Quarterly* [文化研究季刊], 2019, 16649–66; I-ting Chen, "The Cold-War Structure of Feeling: Revisiting the Discourse of "Dalumei" (Mainland Little Sister) in Taiwan," in *Asia in the Old and New Cold Wars: Ideologies, Narratives, and Lived Experiences*, ed. Kenneth Paul Tan (Singapore: Palgrave Macmillan, 2023), 127–56.

48. In "1949" the veteran sings in Mandarin while the young woman sings in Minnanese. See Yanqing Zhang [張燕清] and Dai Meijun [戴梅君], "1949," https://www.youtube.com/watch?v=JUQGZpCR5-w.

49. Chao, "Rethinking Nationalism," 132–34.

50. Chao, 99.

51. For readings on how sentiments of "happiness" relate to conceptions of "social norms and ideals," see Sara Ahmed, *The Promise of Happiness* (Durham, NC: Duke University Press, 2010), 11.

52. Kuan-Hsing Chen has a similar reading of support shared between lower-class waishengren and benshengren in his analysis of the film *Banana Paradise* (1989) in *Asia as Method*.

53. Regarding the use of "to intimate": I adapt the usage to highlight the process by which, in the context of Asia, knowledge is not only produced by but also imagined, appropriated, desired, and selectively embodied in everyday life.

3 THE ARTS OF EMOTIONAL AUTOMATION

Empathy Machines and Asian "Victims"
in Virtual Reality

Y-DANG TROEUNG AND CHRISTOPHER B. PATTERSON

The crises of refugee displacement worldwide since the "War on Terror" has frequently been referenced as a "failure of empathy" on the part of nation-states and publics to open their borders to those seeking asylum. In the lead-up to the 2008 presidential election in the United States, Barack and Michelle Obama sought to address the violences of the War on Terror and the refugee "crisis" by commenting in numerous speeches from 2006 to 2008 that "we should talk more about our empathy deficit—the ability to put ourselves in someone else's shoes; to see the world through those who are different from us."[1] Founded in 2002 in the immediate aftermath of 9/11, Canada's nationally televised "battle of the books" competition, the CBC's *Canada Reads*, has increasingly spotlighted novels by or about refugees as books that will "move readers to feel, think and act." More recently, in the 2010s, Big Tech firms like Facebook and Google have begun to adapt this rhetoric, routinely making the case that their live networking software combats terrorism and hatred with empathy and understanding. In Mark Zuckerberg's first ever address "to a stadium full of people" in 2011, he delivered his company's new mandate after taking "a month" to "travel around the world and reflect: "A lot of the founding principles of Facebook are that if people have access to more information and can be more connected then that will hopefully make the world better, will make it so that people will have more empathy, can develop and maintain more relationships, they'll have more understanding."[2] Zuckerberg's faith that social networking can generate empathy by "giving voice" to the voiceless was repeated in his 2020 appearances in the US House Judiciary hearings on antitrust, and in 2014 when Facebook purchased Oculus, a virtual reality headset that would help pave the way for the "new wave" of virtual reality games that focus on the lives of precarious migrants, many of whom were displaced by the very War on Terror that empathy rhetoric was deployed to disavow.

This chapter explores how the push for empathy for precarious migrants has fueled new convergences between the humanitarian sector and the IT industry through the production of what has come to be known as gamic and virtual reality "empathy machines." The term "empathy machine," coined by Roger Ebert in 2005 to describe how films can enable audiences to "live somebody else's life for a while," has been repopularized as the key byline to sell virtual reality (VR) devices, lending experiential forms of learning to understanding the plight of global warming, poverty, and mass migrancy.[3] In 2015, the VR filmmaker Chris Milk gave the now-famous TED Talk titled "How Virtual Reality Can Create the Ultimate Empathy Machine," describing how his VR film *Clouds Over Sidra*, about Syrian refugees, poised audiences "to combat apathy and elicit empathy from our fickle, oversaturated millennial minds."[4] As the first in a series of VR short films funded by the United Nations to highlight humanitarian crises, *Clouds Over Sidra* represented a new standard in promotions for humanitarian intervention (UNICEF claimed that *Clouds Over Sidra* doubled the likelihood for street-level donations). Narrated by a twelve-year-old Syrian refugee named Sidra, the film takes viewers on a virtual tour of the Za'atari camp in Jordan, home at the time to over eighty-four thousand Syrian refugees. The film's co-directors, Gabo Arora and Barry Pousman, learned while filming that their use of 360-degree VR cameras meant that their own presence had to be removed from every filming space (see fig. 3.1). By making bedrooms, facilities, basketball courts, and bakeries entirely visible through the 360 cameras, the film thus makes the film's actual filmmakers entirely absent in these spaces. *Clouds Over Sidra*, like other humanitarian VR films following it, thus gives the impression that the subject, Sidra, is narrating her own story independent of other parties—in this case, the English-speaking men from the Global North who, after a few days of filming, left with an entire terabyte of footage to re-stitch and edit down to seven and a half minutes.[5]

Since the release of *Clouds Over Sidra* in 2015, "VR fever" has taken hold

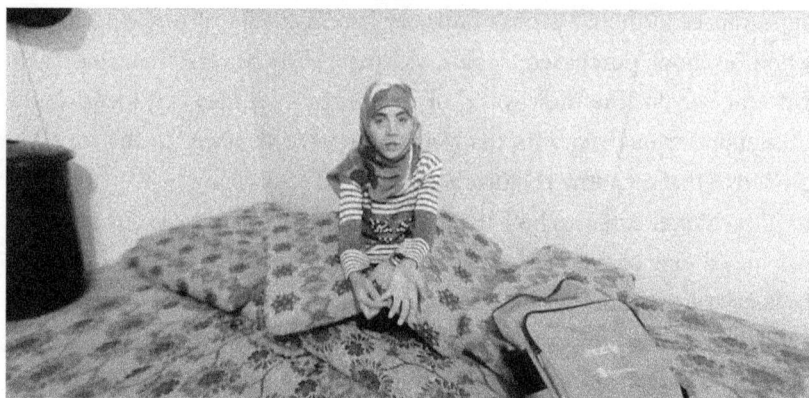

FIG. 3.1. Sidra talks to the camera in her bedroom in *Clouds Over Sidra* (2014). If the viewer looks around the room, they will not see another person (Within). Source: Film still from *Clouds Over Sidra* (2014), Youtube.com, accessed January 5, 2022, https:// youtu.be/mUosdCQsMkM?si=lYKvfgEp37iPSYrH.

among nongovernmental organizations (NGOs), with VR projects funded by Amnesty International, the Clinton Foundation, Greenpeace, and Planned Parenthood.[6] In a strange twist from traditional forms of refugee narration in films, novels, and memoirs, Milk describes the power of VR in providing humanity not to refugees, but to the audience: "It's a machine, but through this machine we become more compassionate. . . . We become more empathetic. We become more connected. And ultimately, we become more human." Milk's conflation of empathy automation with liberal conceptions of "the human" speaks to the mainstream discourse of empathy in the context of US permanent war and the need to disavow imperial violence by showing empathy and care to the victims of war—in turn allowing the nation to remain "human" despite causing so much *inhumane* violence. Indeed, the "second wave" of VR headsets beginning in the 2010s emerged from Big Tech companies who themselves faced criticism for being extensions of imperial and exploitative capitalist projects: the Oculus Rift from Facebook, PlayStation VR from Sony, and smart phone–based platforms like Google Cardboard and Samsung Gear VR. By using onsite locations and 360 cameras that enable viewers to shift their gaze, VR films were promoted as a form of hyperrealism whose authenticity manifests in their seeming lack of dictatorial direction and in their central subjects of refugees and other displaced peoples. In 2017 the renowned film auteur Alejandro González Iñárritu released his first VR film, *Carne y Arena* (*Flesh and Sand*, in English), which follows the experience of Central American refugees fleeing north. That same year, the award-winning novelist Khaled Hosseini partnered with the United Nations High Commissioner for Refugees to produce *Sea Prayer: A 360 Illustrated Film* (2017), about the death of Alan Kurdi, the three-year-old Syrian boy who drowned at sea while attempting to reach Greece in 2015. These VR films and others like them are sponsored by major donation-based NGOs that send volunteers to the Global South, such as Friends of Refugees and Geneva International Centre for Humanitarian Demining. As media scholars Luke Buckmaster and Brian Yecies remind us, even these few VR films offer "a small taste of what is (and will be) possible in the so-called age of digital transformation."[7] Given the wide-ranging impact of VR onto humanitarian infrastructure, the debates concerning empathy in VR trace the various meanings that those in North America and Europe attach to distanced human suffering, and the aesthetic forms such suffering can take.

VR has shifted modes of refugee storytelling by outsourcing stories from the written or spoken voices of refugees themselves to the VR experiences of the refugee camps and border struggles. Rather than see VR as merely exploitative or beneficial, we understand its affective emanation as part of a larger media ecosystem that attempts to represent victimized others. In so doing we view VR's branding as an empathy machine as part of a broader marketing rhetoric used by media marketing firms to establish certain art objects as "empathy experiences" during times of war and imperial violence. Thus, questions concerning empathy within VR often dissolve into decisions about which art objects can generate the most empathy, with little regard for the structural forms of injustice, global capitalism, and imperial war that produce precarious populations in the first place. While companies have sought to endow virtual reality as an empathy machine, some journalists, scholars, and writers have noted the forms of exploitation and "poverty porn" aesthetics that seem more pronounced in VR than in other mediums.[8] Yet many popular articles that push back against the valorizing of VR in turn attempt to revalorize traditional modes for producing empathy for refugees, such as documentary films, novels, and memoirs, though these mediums too have been criticized widely among scholars. How might we understand VR as an emerging empathy machine within a longer history of empathy machines and a present affective field within the context of US "permanent war"?

We nestle our analyses within the frameworks of transpacific studies, critical game studies, and critical refugee studies to explore how empathy functions as an imagined affective relation to precarious migrants and refugees. Within these fields, scholars, critics, and artists have urged reflection and historical understanding in the rush for empathetic refugee identification. The Asian American game designer and writer Robert Yang has likened games labeled as empathy machines to forms of "refugee tourism," arguing that the rhetoric of this industry "asks us to endorse technology without questioning the politics of its construction or who profits from it."⁹ These "VR appropriation machines," Yang asserts, "are fundamentally about mining the experiences of suffering people to enrich the self-image of VR users." Similarly, Ruha Benjamin has noted how pervasive empathy discourses have become within virtual reality projects led by Zuckerberg in partnership with organizations like the Red Cross, where virtual reality has become an extension of what bell hooks called "eating the other."¹⁰ Or, as Wendy Hui Kyong Chun bluntly quipped in a talk on the ethics of virtual reality, "If you're walking in someone else's shoes, then you've stolen their shoes."¹¹

Transpacific studies offers a framing to complicate the binary divisions and unevenness that accentuate the desire to empathize with particular humanitarian subjects (refugees) and not others (precarious migrants, "illegal immigrants," Black and Indigenous peoples). The divisions between Global North and Global South, East and West, Developed and Undeveloped, Immigrant and Refugee are, as Nikhil Pal Singh has written, symptomatic of the United States' desire to separate the "outer wars" of atrocity and human rights subjects from the "inner wars" of riot and identity politics.¹² This separation has been evident in the construction of the human rights subject who, as Crystal Parikh argues, "has largely been imagined as a latently American one—always already, that is, American in character and desires."¹³ In response to Parikh's claim, Guy Beauregard, Cathy J. Schlund-Vials, and Hsiu-chuan Lee have argued for the need for more "diversity of geographical imaginings" that can "reckon with distinct and uneven forms of 'contact' in specific sites in Asia and the Pacific."¹⁴ A transpacific framing here can bring out the particularity of thinking through critical refugee studies alongside (rather than under the umbrella of) Asian American studies. We thus understand transpacific studies as a broad framework that can account for the racial, national, and historical differences among refugee and migrant populations without positing America as the inevitable place of settlement, such as the wayward paths taken by Vietnamese, Cambodian, and Laotian refugees, the diasporic movement of Filipina workers in the Middle East and Asia, or the exploitation and violence that emerges near US military bases globally. Transpacific studies also need not defer to the *human* element of "human rights" as a reference for mobilization. Instead, as Lisa Lowe writes, we can conceive of "'other humanities' within the received genealogy of 'the human.'"[15]

To explore how precarious migrancy has been shaped by discourses of empathy in the context of US imperial projects, we follow Yến Lê Espiritu's use of the transpacific framing to conceptualize "'the refugee' as a site of transpacific critique, whose emergence exposes the linked processes of colonization, militarization, and forced displacement."[16] We thus use both "precarious migrant" and "refugee" to refer to migrant peoples whose categories of legal identification are themselves precarious and subject to state recognition and biopolitical evaluation. We then move to critically juxtapose discourses of refugee empathy in literature that appeared soon after the Vietnam War alongside discourses of empathy in video games and VR that appear soon after the War on Terror. We then consider emerging discourses of empathy in VR through Ken Liu's 2018 short story "Byzantine Empathy," about two VR makers with divergent political interests who remake precarious migrant populations as "refugees" or "terrorists" through the emotional automation of VR. We end by playing through Gina Kim's 2017 VR film *Bloodless*, about the 1992 murder of a Korean female sex worker perpetrated by a US soldier stationed near the South Korean city of Dongducheon. We ask how Kim's film can imagine uses for VR that are not directed at gaining an audience's empathy, but rather on speculating upon the multiple and unseen impacts of imperial violence past, present, and future.

ON EMPATHY

This is love as empathy: I love you, and imagine not only
that I can feel how you feel, but that I could feel your pain for you.

Sara Ahmed | *The Cultural Politics of Emotion*

The valorization of VR as an empathy machine by Big Tech companies has been followed by journalists and scholars who reject VR as a medium capable of empathetic relations. Such rejection has often led to idealizing traditional forms of refugee narration that are also curated, edited, and published by first-world markets: the memoir, the ethnic novel, and the documentary lens. In a 2017 article in *The Atlantic*, the Canadian American popular psychologist Paul Bloom criticized the idea of VR as an empathy machine by comparing VR to books and memoirs, which "enable you to experience the most private experiences of others, both by triggering your own memories and by extending your imagination in radical ways . . . when it comes to understanding the lives of others, nothing else comes close."[17] Indeed, widespread criticism of virtual reality as empathy machines often stop short by merely offering alternative mediums that have also been critiqued for the same reasons (such as "emblematic victim" performances in memoirs like Le Ly Hayslip's *When Heaven and Earth Changed Places*[18]). Similarly, Pooja Rangan and others have criticized the empathy rhetoric of documentary films that seek an authentic voice to be valued by humanitarian projects but are made by white and/or Western directors who implicitly demand performances of victimization. Rajan refuses and reveals the humanitarian gaze of documentary films like *Born into Brothels*, which "invents the very disenfranchised humanity that it claims to redeem."[19]

Critiques of empathy in virtual reality often use a few VR games and companies to represent an entire medium, giving legitimacy to more traditional (but just as problematic) forms of representation that claim to "give voice" and "humanize" precarious subjects. Like many memoirs and documentaries, often the harrowing experiences of refugees are emphasized as a means of revealing their humanity, thus producing refugees as the distinct others to the comforts of modernity (as if those refugees themselves never knew such comforts). As Tina Chen and Cathy Schlund-Vials write, refugees are a consistent "other" within our contemporary "backdrop of perpetual war, ceaseless conflict, and cataclysmic genocide."[20] Put broadly, refugees today are defined by precariousness, "a condition of profound insecurity and an indeterminate geopolitical state."[21] But what effect, then, does "empathy" and "humanization" serve for the precarious subject? How does empathy operate to lend credibility to the way an entire medium like VR is branded or to lend cultural capital to audiences themselves?

Discourses around empathy in VR ripple from wider discourses of empathy and compassion as critiqued by Sara Ahmed and Lauren Berlant in 2004. Ahmed writes that "empathy sustains the very difference that it may seek to overcome," while Berlant similarly argues that empathy re-creates relations defined by distance and cultivates compassion only for "those lacking the foundations for belonging where we live."[22] Translated from the German *Einfühlung* ("in-feeling"), empathy denotes a form of sympathy that still presumes distance, but also assumes "the power of projecting one's personality into the object of contemplation."[23] Empathy operates as what Berlant calls a "humanizing emotion," meant to humanize an object (a distanced victim) not by evoking an antiracist form of "the human" but by including one individual or group into an already-exclusionary definition of the human rooted in the legacies of colonial modernity, or what Sylvia Wynter calls the "'genre' of 'Man.'"[24] As Marjorie Gerber writes, by presuming that humanization is made possible only by seeing the self in the other, empathy becomes a "matter of personal agency and individual emotion," such that the humanization of the victim—the act of welcoming the other into "the human"—has the effect of increasing the humanity of the viewer, as "a person who displays empathy is, it appears, to be congratulated for having fine feelings."[25] While empathy brings the precarious "victim" into the realm of the human, it also grants greater levels of humanity to the viewer based on aesthetic appreciation, cultural capital, and possession of resources. Moral responses generated through empathy are thus predicated upon the victim's willingness to perform in the place of (Einfühlung) the implied first-world audience of donors and policymakers in ways that reinforce humanization.

Through a transpacific framing of empathy and precarious migrancy, we find it crucial to include in our analyses critical works on Filipina migrant workers, whose status rarely falls under the category of "refugee" but are termed as exploited and vulnerable migrant laborers. Neferti Tadiar writes that the Filipina migrant worker's claiming of empathy through a commodified victim identity may not in itself be "a politically debilitating thing," but can offer means of "subjective activity and therefore immanent agency."[26] Though claims of empathy, for Tadiar, can offer alternatives to political silencing, they are also dependent upon "the commodity form of personhood," where "the gaze of empathy is thus the gaze of equivalence, a form of looking that makes the world into images of one's experiences as objects of consumption."[27] Whether in literature, film, or videogames, narratives of precarious victims have acted as generators of empathy and compassion by reducing "others" to commodified identities that function as intellectual property. The roles expected from precarious migrants in humanitarian narratives is thus akin to the roles expected by ethnic affective laborers who are subjected to what Jan Padios calls "emotional extraction," or "the transfer of emotional resources from one individual or group to another."[28] While audiences absorb the emotions of a humanized other, the process of emotional extraction, for Padios, simultaneously produces a particular form of knowledge production: "emotion knowledge" found in the statistics and predictions that help determine how precarious migrants will behave and thus inform how best to control them.

In the empathy machines of literature, film, and VR, emotional extraction commodifies precarious subjects, leading the viewer into emotions of pain and gratitude within a circulating expectation that precarious migrants perform their pain in ways that make their emotion extractable, so that their pain can reinforce the humanity (rather than the violent *inhumanity*) of the imperial nation. Indeed, Padios's concept of emotional extraction is useful to consider in the context of precarious migrants more broadly. It reverses the focus of feeling from the victims of imperial violence to instead understanding how the process of emotional extraction in new media like VR has subsumed precarious peoples into "emotional automation," where the affective desires to witness pain and gain empathy shift from direct accounts by victims (through novels, talk shows, memoirs) to *simulations* of precarity that focus less on narration and more on the subjective experience of space, sight, and practice (moving through a refugee camp, gazing around a warzone, "playing" the everyday actions of a migrant worker).

In VR, reality is not virtual so much as automated—automating the processes meant to provide humanity, not merely to the precarious migrant, but to the viewers themselves. As Yến Lê Espiritu, Mimi Nguyen, Y-Dang Troeung, and other critical refugee studies scholars have argued, traditional forms of refugee representation often presume the precarious migrant (figured as "refugee") will take on sometimes exhausting performances of "gratitude," "luckiness," "hard work," and "suffering."[29] Within these forms, the refugee's story is shaped into a model minority narrative that celebrates the subject's assimilation and attainment of the American Dream, while eliding the imperial conditions of war that produced the refugee's displacement. Espiritu calls this narrative commodification the "good refugee narrative" that enables the United States, as the lauded site of *good refuge*, to rebrand itself from military aggressor into benevolent rescuer.[30] Espiritu urges scholars to remain suspicious of such instrumentalization of refugee narratives while also being "attentive to refugees as 'intentionalized beings' who possess and enact their own politics as they emerge out of the ruins of war and its aftermath."[31]

Rather than nuancing the refugee's complex personhood as an intentionalized being, VR's automation of refugee empathy tends to spectacularize the refugee's ruination from war and its aftermath. VR tends to carry an altogether different schema, not of refugee narratives but of refugee "sensations": the shock of discovering the dead or diseased body, the dread of feeling trapped within a space (institution, camp, wreckage), the frisson of anxiety in not knowing what could happen next, all while feeling strapped and blindfolded by the VR headset. In the next section, we hope to clarify the modes of empathy-making in VR by juxtaposing VR with ethnic literature. Through this comparison, we emphasize how automated experiences of VR produce not affective forms of empathy and compassion but immediate, visceral sensations of pain, fear, dread, and aggravation, which viewers are then encouraged to interpret as direct experiences of refugee vulnerability. This method of critical juxtaposition—not of spaces but of disciplinary domains—allows us to see the larger politics of representation across mediums and historical contexts.[32]

THE ASIAN "VICTIM" IN ETHNIC LITERARY PRODUCTION

The ethnic literary project has always been a humanist project in which nonwhite writers must prove they are human beings who feel pain.

Cathy Park Hong | *Minor Feelings: An Asian American Reckoning*

Not long before virtual reality and video games came along, representations of Asian peoples were often generated through literary-based empathy machines, producing a trope of Asian victimization or what Jinah Kim calls "the ritualistic production of the Asian body as one in pain and in need of rescue."[33] As Cathy Park Hong points out in *Minor Feelings: An Asian American Reckoning*, this production of Asians as all-feeling victims has continued to be manufactured through institutions of literary aesthetic control, such as in her own MFA writing program at the University of Iowa, whose workshops created a "wall of condescension" around "racial politics" and encouraged her to believe that "writing about my Asian identity was juvenile."[34] For Hong, the "Asian body," like many marginalized identities, is rarely given complex mental interiorization, so that even when ethnic autobiographies are released to the public, their narratives are often reduced to mere feelings of victimhood meant for absorption (or extraction) by white audiences. For Hong the presumption that one can prove one's humanity by writing one's pain leads publishers and interviewers to exploit the author's tragic life stories through myopic summaries and reviews. Hong writes of Ocean Vuong's lauded 2019 novel, *On Earth We're Briefly Gorgeous*, that "media ignored Vuong's queer identity because it didn't fit into their image of the tragic Vietnamese refugee," and rather asked Vuong "to rehearse his shattering experiences of refugee impoverishment and the salvation he found in poetry."[35] Even a novel that seeks to capture the violence and afterlife of the Vietnam War can be reinterpreted and marketed to an individualized "libretto of hurt" that is "welded into a single American myth of individual triumph."[36]

Hong's critiques of ethnic literature echo author Nam Le's self-reflexive exploration of his own "ethnic literature" in his 2008 short story, "Love and Honour and Pity and Pride and Compassion and Sacrifice," a fictionalized account of Le's experience at the same Iowa Writers' Workshop. Le's story poses a split common in MFA prose-oriented workshops between "universal" (white) writers and "ethnicized" writers of color who could be accused of exploiting their own histories. "Ethnic literature's hot," says one of Le's writing instructors; "You have to ask yourself, what makes me stand out?" says two visiting literary agents, "your *background* and *life experience*"; "You could *totally* exploit the Vietnamese thing," says another student.[37] Hong and Le attended the Iowa Writers' Workshop at the same time (2004–5), yet had distinctly different experiences that attest to the different genre expectations of poetry and prose, where poetry is often beset by an institutionalized avant-garde tradition that rewards the "quietist minority poets who assuage quasi-white liberal guilt rather than challenge it."[38] In contrast, the ethnicized prose writer has been encouraged to hew to their own marginalization. In Le's story the fictionalized Le takes advantage of his background by writing his MFA thesis around the story of his father, a refugee and child victim of the 1968 massacre at Mỹ Lai that was carried out by US soldiers. As Donald Goellnicht has pointed out, Le's story "reframes the stakes of the debate in terms of ethical representation by turning full attention to the Vietnamese refugee."[39] The stakes shift, given that the father—the victimized subject of emotional extraction—was only made a "victim" by the audience's own imperialist nation-state. As Nikhil Singh and Simeon Man have argued, contemporary wars in Iraq and Afghanistan are part of a broader "permanent war in U.S. culture," which began in the 1950s with the Korean War and continued through the Vietnam War, which "set into motion a range of military and economic activities across the Pacific."[40] Within the current era of permanent war, the atrocities of the Vietnam War perpetrated by American soldiers cannot so easily be appropriated into affective entertainment. By writing a story about a fictionalized self who is writing a biographical story about his father (titled "ETHNIC STORY"), Le puts readers into "the paradoxical position of operating inside the work of a creative writer, Nam Le, whose performative act of writing itself bespeaks a faith in language."[41] The story thus assays the limitations of narrative and language in representing both the victim and the critique of victimization, revealing how the process of writing, marketing, and publishing stories exploits the victims of US war while having little impact on the contemporary cultures of US permanent war.

We read Nam Le's and Cathy Park Hong's texts as dissections of the empathy machines within Asian American literature, which, as Betsy Huang writes, is characterized by "myopic readerly presumptions that cast all Asian American fiction as forms of life writing."[42] As Jodi Melamed has argued, these readerly presumptions have been widely ingrained in American media and scholarship due to the United States' reliance on stories by refugees—particularly those displaced by "communism" or "terrorism"—to legitimize US permanent war.[43] Media saturation of life stories, particularly from Asian and Arab authors, has prompted literary responses throughout the history of Asian American literature, beginning at least with Maxine Hong Kingston's 1976 book *The Woman Warrior: Memoirs of a Girlhood among Ghosts*. Infamously, Kingston's book was initially billed as autobiography, even though myth and imagination played heavy roles in the novel. This autobiographical branding helped make the book the most widely taught text in US universities at the time, yet it also invited controversy from some Chinese American groups and writers like Frank Chin.[44] Lan Cao's 1997 novel *Monkey Bridge*, the first novel to be published by a Vietnamese American, seems to directly respond to Kingston's novel in its telling of a typical immigrant victim autobiography that we later discover (along with the protagonist) is in fact based on the lies told by the narrator's mother to hide the violences of French and American imperialism, what the mother calls in her suicide note an "act of sacrifice" meant to give her daughter "a new beginning."[45] As Troeung has previously argued, Asian North American novels like Cao's reveals how much of the ideological work produced by ethnic autobiography can be compared to the same ideological goals of forced confessions characteristic of communist regimes in the former Indochina.[46] Viet Nguyen's Pulitzer Prize–winning novel *The Sympathizer* makes this comparison unavoidable, as the novel takes the form of a fictional communist confession that also happens to take on all the expected tropes of an American immigrant autobiography.[47] More recently, Ocean Vuong's 2019 novel, *On Earth We're Briefly Gorgeous*, wrestles with the politics of autobiography, as its initial excerpts in the *New Yorker* published in 2016 and 2017 were clearly meant to be read as nonfiction. Though branded as a novel, the book's circumstances and narrator are sometimes indistinguishable from Vuong's own life. Indeed, the book's self-made brand of "novel" failed to affect its reception, as even the Filipina American writer Jia Tolentino categorized the book as "an immigrant novel and a work of autofiction."[48]

The debates in Asian American studies over the merits and imperial collaborations of ethnic autobiographies have been trenchant and ongoing, leading scholars like Stephen Hong Sohn to ask that educators teaching Asian American novels adopt "reading practices that move away from an autobiographical or autoethnographic impulse attuned to authorial ancestry."[49] As Viet Thanh Nguyen similarly argues, because ethnic texts are so often marketed as ways to satisfy a minority population's "urge for self-representation and self-determination," the genre tag of "ethnic" becomes appropriated as a sign "of the ethnic speaking of and for the ethnic population."[50] While the problems of memoir and autobiography continue to dominate discussions in Asian American studies, in mainstream literary discourses ethnic novels are still heralded as a more authentic form of empathetic recognition that is today being challenged by digital media like video games and VR. As the speculative fiction author Ken Liu has argued, the democratization of digital and social media has shifted the landscape from literary expressions of particular tragic life-stories to the digitized "attention economy," where international NGOs seeking funding must compete ruthlessly for attention, and in so doing normalize the emotional extraction of precarious peoples the world over, whose images, spaces, and visceral experiences can "put a face and a name onto some abstract vision of suffering."[51] How does empathy operate within discourses of video games and virtual reality? How does digital media attempt to service empathy for precarious migrants within a competitive attention economy? How have the demands for empathy machines also erased the structural, imperial, and psychological positions of the viewers living in a culture of permanent war?

EMPATHY GAMES

By putting emphasis and value on experiential learning, virtual reality discourses have grown out of similar marketing discourses of empathy in video games. In games, the shift toward "empathy games" began in the early 2010s, when more "indie" artists began to appear on the platform Steam and "personal games," like *Depression Quest* (Zoë Quinn, 2013), and games about queer and marginalized people, like *Gone Home* (Fullbright, 2013) and *Bury Me, My Love* (The Alternative, 2018)—the latter a game about refugees of the Syrian civil war—became more accepted into the mainstream. The popularity of these and other indie games focused on singular stories led many game companies to shift their marketing rhetoric away from seeing games as frivolous objects of fun to experiences of empathy. As inheritors of classic arcade games and pinball arcades, video games, in the 2010s, for the first time began to overlap widely with the affective territory of literature in its ongoing marketing rhetoric of compassion and empathy.

The increasingly pervasive rhetoric of empathy in games, as Bonnie Ruberg puts it, describes "the purported ability of video games to allow players to experience the feelings of others—with a focus on those who are seen as diverse or disadvantaged."[52] Ruberg follows the stringent critiques of empathy by marginalized game designers and journalists, who see the rise of empathy games as an attempt to cater to a heteronormative mainstream and to appropriate an author's or designer's life as a "novelty destination" that reflects a "kind of embodied colonialism."[53] While Ruberg's critiques are indeed warranted, the designers included in her study remain settled in first-world spaces and their work does not seek to elicit a specific moral response in the form of funding, donations, or an increased awareness of a humanitarian atrocity, as is the case in many video games and VR experiences that fall under the banner of empathy game. In contrast, games concerning the plight of refugees and other precarious victims carry few qualms with these problematic aspects of empathy, as their primary goal has been to cater to first-world donors. Empathy games like *Salaam* (2020), about South Sudanese refugees fleeing war (and developed by a South Sudanese refugee), and *1979 Revolution: Black Friday* (2016), about the violences of the Iranian Revolution, have entirely different aims and representational stakes than the so-called empathy games by first-world queer and trans developers who dispute this term. Building upon the critiques of empathy games by Ruberg, Yang, and others, we consider here how companies have branded VR as a more idealized version of the empathy game while simultaneously disavowing the associations of video games with violence and war.

The first wave of VR headsets began in the early 1990s, when VR was being hyped as an ideal form of a video game's ability to "immerse" the player into another world. While "immersion," as coined in Janet Murray's *Hamlet on the Holodeck* (1997), has been seen as a formal characterization of video games, even Murray herself saw immersion in games "as a desired experience, not as an a priori phenomenon."[54] The first wave of VR technology thus appeared as a formal innovation toward this desired experience, offering a utopian post-identity realm as "the technology of miracles and dreams" that could provide "hope for the next century" with its "glimpses of heaven."[55] These techno-utopian dreams of VR were short-lived due to the commercial failure of VR technology (Sega's 1991 Sega VR headset, Nintendo's Virtual Boy in 1995), as well as the discursive political shift that identified video games as generators of violence following the release of *Mortal Kombat* in 1992 and the shooting at Columbine High School in 1999. As Richard King and David Leonard have pointed out, the "utopian discourses" of virtual reality in the 1990s were waylaid by the role of video games in the War on Terror and drone warfare, revealing the utopian discourse of VR as "a delusion of the powerful, those able to detach virtual geographies from material reality."[56]

When considering the recent second wave of VR in 2016 and 2017, it is pivotal to keep in mind that its contemporary operating discourses of empathy are often blanket statements that attempt to brand a new medium by borrowing heavily from how games and literature have been valued, particularly during an era of permanent war that has created unprecedented numbers of precarious migrants. Even so, both video games and VR challenge traditional media by being presented as a superior means of generating empathy. Though virtual reality projects can include the narrative and voice of victims, their main form of obtaining empathy is rather by automating the affective processes of emotional extraction and highlighting the seemingly authentic simulation of "walking in their shoes."

To better understand the politicized forms of emotional extraction in VR's second wave, we turn to Ken Liu's short story "Byzantine Empathy," published in 2018 and written shortly after the media began branding VR as empathy machines. Taking up many of the issues surrounding VR in reference to war and refuge, Liu's story follows two former university roommates, Jianwen and Sophia, who both use the emotional engagements of VR in the service of opposing political ideals. As the executive director of the NGO Refugees Without Borders, Sophia hopes to use VR as a medium to serve US interests, much in the vein of Facebook and other NGOs. Jianwen hopes to use VR to establish a new form of mass funding that bypasses the use of NGOs or government oversight that dictates which populations are most deserving of empathy. Jianwen's mission is tied to her belief that VR can break away from imperial forms of intervention, as she tells Sophia, "I had hoped that by stripping away context and background, by exposing the senses to the rawness of pain and suffering, virtual reality would be able to prevent all of us from rationalizing away our empathy. In agony, there is no race, no creed, none of the walls that divide us and subdivide us. When you're immersed in the experience of the victims, all of us are in Muertien, in Yemen, in the heart of darkness that the Great Powers feed on."[57] For Jianwen, VR represents a superior form of empathy generation that falls into the arguments of what Robert Yang calls the "empathy machine apologists," who believe VR allows an "embodied" and "transparent immediacy" that can "obliterate political divisions."[58] Indeed, while Jianwen encapsulates the empathy machine apologists who see VR as transcending differences in race, creed, and nation, Sophia shows how this medium can be easily manipulated for her own gain, as she takes her own VR camera to a warzone in order to be brutally attacked by precarious migrants, thus turning the "refugees" produced by Jianwen's VR empathy machine into "terrorists" produced by her own VR empathy machine. The result of Sophia's venture is a VR experience that reinforces first-world prejudices: "A defenseless American woman, the head of a charity dedicated to helping refugees, is brutalized by ethnic Han Chinese rebels armed with guns."[59] The equalizing ideals of VR are turned on their head, as multiple empathy machines attempt to rewrite a migrant population while the visual cues of race and terror are amplified by the decontextualized empathy-machine to provide a racialized backdrop that can rebrand a precarious population among categories of refugee, migrant, rebel, and terrorist. By taking advantage of VR's mode of emotional automation, Sophia proves that VR can be just as easily manipulated as any other traditional empathy machine.

Liu's story thinks through the problems of empathy in new media writ large, where virtual reality experiences are not dangerous because they place players "in someone else's shoes," but because these experiences' seeming lack of context and authorial direction insists that viewers take what they absorb as "real:" as unedited and unadulterated truth. The medium's nuances and complex interactive experiences, then, require a visual and interactive literacy that players have had little to no chance to cultivate. For Takeo Rivera, video games "exceed the Aristotelian empathy with the protagonist of drama," as they replace the subject on screen with the viewer themselves, which in effect erases the body.[60] This excess of empathy can be read as "even more empathy," or "ultimate empathy," but only in respect of the player's understanding of the situation being represented in the VR experience. Indeed, sensations of fear, anxiety, and tenderness do not suddenly become empathetic in VR; rather, they are merely amplified by the enclosing apparatus of the VR headset. The sensorial engagements felt in games are thus interpreted through the discourses that exist outside of it, even as those interpretations may be totally irrelevant to the sensations themselves.[61] For Steve Swink, the embodied experience of VR should not be characterized as empathetic emotions but as feelings of disorientation and the anxiety of losing one's "proprioception," that is, an "awareness of the position of his or her own body in space."[62] Indeed, sensations of anxiety and vulnerability are foundational to experiences of VR as a medium that quite literally blindfolds a person to their immediate surroundings—sensations that can easily be politicized and narrativized into "feeling like a refugee." In Liu's story, Jianwen and Sophia do not represent different possibilities of VR's future, but rather different political positions that seek to automate feelings of empathy by evacuating the sensations of VR from any alternative affective meanings. Liu's story thus attempts to dissolve the emotional automation of VR by showing how its sensorial engagements and presumptions of "reality" can be easily manipulated to express divergent political interests and to repurpose precarious populations as refugees, migrants, rebels, and terrorists.

GINA KIM'S *BLOODLESS*

By comparing discourses of empathy in VR with those in ethnic literature, we can see VR not as a more problematic or less-authentic empathy machine, but as a *particular kind* of empathy machine, one that automates processes of emotional extraction through the sensations of the VR apparatus and by claiming to represent the lived experience of an atrocity without the mediation of an author, director, or the questionable (and labor-intensive) performance of the victim herself. Yet in restricting the sensations of VR to discourses of empathy, the process of emotional automation in VR requires that players forgo their ability to subjectively imagine the lives of others, or what the artist and scholar Adrian Piper calls "our capacity to envision what is possible in addition to what is actual."[63] Similarly, the scholar Annie Bares discusses the "moral imagination" as a crucial component in empathetic relations, as imagination can "bridg[e] the gap between oneself and a stranger," which is not grounded in data and exactitude but in "the knowledge of incommensurable differences."[64] These theories of imagination contend that empathy depends less on authenticity and more on the capacity of the audience to imagine another's pain without reducing that pain to something they can claim as an empathetic object separate from the past, present, or future of imperial violence.

To understand the possibilities of imagination in VR, we turn to Gina Kim's 2017 VR film *Bloodless* ("Dongducheon" in Korean), winner of the Best VR Story Award at the 74th Venice Film Festival. In using VR to tell the story of a Korean sex worker raped and murdered by an American GI, Kim refuses to reconstruct the scene of abuse or to even name the victim. Instead, the film provides an immersive experience of touring the present-day red light district of Dongducheon while the sex worker in question haunts the player, asking them to bear witness to the *aftermath* of her death rather than the death itself. Through the speculative figure of the ghost and the present space of Dongducheon—a red light district bordering Camp Casey US military base—Kim's film uses VR technology to express speculation rather than exactitude, and, in doing so, makes inescapably present the uncanny presence of US empire within the space of unspeakable and unseen violence.

Bloodless opens to a dingy alleyway bordering a freeway. The viewer might gaze around to see a black dog sniffing around a concrete slab or drawings of sunflowers on the freeway wall. The screen goes black and it may take some time for the viewer to spot text in both Korean and English: "US servicemen have been stationed in South Korea since the 1950s. US military bases have occupied as much as 17.7 percent of the country's habitable land. They have also produced 96 camp towns offering prostitution for servicemen, involving one million women. This space exists between two countries, and outside the protection of laws." When the viewer reappears below the highway's bridge near clothing stores and shuttered-up food stands, it is unclear if this is even the same highway or the same city. The viewer is displaced again

FIG. 3.2. Production still from Gina Kim's *Bloodless* (2017).
Source: *Bloodless* (2017). Photo from Kim's website.

next to an overhead sign that reads "Dongducheon Special Tourism Zone for Foreigners." The alley fades dark as the pink and purple lights turn on for the night crowd. Two men in military garb exit a club, whose only visible name is "MUS" in bright red letters.

After repositioning throughout the alley, the viewer hears the click-clack of a woman in heels: the ghost. At first she is only heard, then she is seen from behind, wearing all black (see fig. 3.2). Depending upon where the viewer is looking, she might be missed as she walks past. The cutting camera follows her until she stands in front of the camera, staring at the viewer with a slit of light lancing across a portion of her face. *If* the viewer looks at her at this moment (they could instead be looking at the green lights, the alley, the sky, discarded trash) they would see a penetrating gaze—one that might transform the viewer's voyeuristic position into that of a figure within the film (perhaps a client). The film cuts to a decrepit room littered with beer bottles, a floor mat, a floral blanket, a mirror, and a hanging white towel. A red viscous substance oozes out of the blanket; it may take the viewer some time to realize that there is a body underneath. For a full two minutes the blood slowly creeps along the floor. Glass breaks and a pair of legs balance awkwardly atop the oozing blood.

Though *Bloodless* contains intertitles providing some history and context, these are very sparse compared to ethnic novels, memoirs, documentaries, or other VR films like *Clouds Over Sidra*. The film's use of familiar spaces of tourism might leave the viewer with a feverish impulse to learn more—a tendency ripe for the age of internet sleuthing (on Dongducheon's google-maps typography one can find that the club identified as "MUS" in the film is "MUSTANG," located at 426–37 Bosan-dong; sitting nearby are American flags). In conceding control of the 360 camera to the player, *Bloodless* approaches its subjects with a peripatetic disorientation that sees things as merely happening—dogs sniff, people chat, a woman walks. The viewer has no authoritative role in knowing the details of these happenings as feelings of disorientation are punctuated by the consistent anxiety that something more significant is happening out of their view (a dog disappears, a woman appears). Though we have watched the film repeatedly, the disorientations of the first viewing—the loss of the black dog, the mysterious club names, the unknowable woman/ghost—are the most memorable. Little about the VR experience here seems to shout empathy, or even anger, but rather exudes a distinct yearning for all the unknowns. If it is empathy, perhaps it is a type summoned forth in the afterglow of speculation.

The use of speculation rather than authenticity is one of Gina Kim's motivations to experiment with VR rather than traditional filmmaking (she had previously made five feature films). As Kim says in interviews, the story of the murdered sex worker had been gestating within her artistic mind for two decades since the event took place in 1992, yet traditional narratives offered few ways to represent the event without also exploiting it. As Kim says, "What drew me to this new medium (Virtual Reality) is the possibility of 'empathy without exploitation.'"[65] Though VR has been taken up as an experiential medium, Kim's film produces an experience that does not claim the pain of an event as "the horror of being murdered or being sexually assaulted," but rather as an experience of witnessing, lingering, dwelling, and speculating, "just to be there, with her, with genuine sympathy and empathy."[66] This "genuine sympathy and empathy" that Kim seeks through VR is not the same as the empathy machine; it envisions VR as a medium that, as Sara Ahmed writes, can conjure "an ethics of responding to pain" that "involves being open to being affected by that which one *cannot* know or feel."[67]

Bloodless suggests that the more virtual reality and other empathy discourses claim authentic, unmediated access to someone's suffering, the more a viewer's imagination is taken away from the experience. *Bloodless* does not seek to create empathy through what Adrian Piper calls a self-centered level of visceral response.[68] At no point is the viewer asked to feel the same as the precarious subject in her moments of abuse. The viewer instead plays not as subject but as observer and even client, sustaining a state of self-awareness that, for Piper, "requires an imaginative involvement with the other's inner state because we must modally imagine to ourselves what that state must be."[69] Here the victim's role is not in narrating her own "authentic voice," edited and catered to a white audience, but instead manifests through visual, spatial, and performance cues that do not direct the audience's sympathies so much as push the audience to speculate upon the past, present, and future. One drawback to this method, as seen in Liu's story "Byzantine Empathy," is that the reliance on visual signifiers with little narration can sometimes lead racial signifiers (rather than histories) to play a heavy-handed role in VR, as players are meant to take more meaning from visual cues than from dialogue or intertitles explaining context. While the Dongducheon red light district has historically exploited Korean comfort women and sex workers, most of the contemporary adult entertainment parlors featured in *Bloodless* in fact host migrant sex workers, mostly Filipina or Russian migrants on entertainment visas, whose precarity leaves them more vulnerable to abuse and lack of state protection.[70] As *Bloodless* is meant to be the first in a trilogy (the second, *Tearless*, was released in 2021), the speculation it encourages also leaves room for nations and peoples not being represented.

CONCLUSION: GOTTA FEEL 'EM ALL

Ken Liu's story "Byzantine Empathy" makes no attempt to answer the problems of VR that it poses. Rather than ending with a clear "winner" in its argument between VR as a utopian form of empathy (Jianwen) vs. VR as an exploitable tool for US empire (Sophia), the story ends with a series of chatroom messages by VR players who are merely looking for "a new game." Jianwen's visions of VR as an empathy machine with "no race, no creed," has a close bearing to the utopian visions of VR in the 1990s as a space of post-identity immersion, except that here the space of nonidentity (the genderless and raceless identity) is replaced by the migrant in their most extreme moments of precarity. Indeed, as Liu's ending suggests, VR's discursive shift to empathy is both a marketing gimmick to automate experiences of empathy in an era of permanent war as well as a reiteration of past humanistic projects that have sought to use the "rescue" of distant others to disavow the (racial, gendered) violences of the nation-state at home. Liu's story thus points not to the victimized subjects, but to the audience's constant demand for a new game, that is, a new process of emotional automation that follows a Pokémon logic of "gotta feel 'em all," where the pain of every victimized identity is emotionally extracted to create an all-knowing liberal human subject who has "caught" all emotional knowledge of victimized others, who understands the entire gamut of pain and suffering, and who has thus superseded every particular experience of suffering to attain a universal "humanist" perspective.

Both literature and virtual reality participate within "collectible" modes of universality. VR merely appears as the latest optimized form for extracting precarious experiences, offering virtual experiential excursions and impacting players on the visceral level of sensation and touch. At the same time, VR films like *Bloodless* unsettle this collectible form by refusing to present the victim as a knowable subject. Even her name or the name of the perpetrator do not appear anywhere in the film, refusing the viewer's desire to catalog, possess, and extract. The film's lack of information pressures audiences to use the larger media ecosystem to learn more—to see these areas on a digital map or seek out books and films about "comfort women," like Grace M. Cho's *Haunting the Korean Diaspora* (2008) or Laura Kang's *Traffic in Asian Women* (2019), or Ko-Woon Lee's documentary film *Host Nation* (2016), which uses interviews of contemporary migrant sex workers from the Philippines working in the sex parlors of Dongducheon. In its refusal to reveal, narrate, or extract emotion, *Bloodless* asks viewers not to see the film as an empathy-generating machine, but rather to see the precarious subject as a being generated by US permanent war, a figure whose future need not be a reiteration of the past.

As a relatively new medium, VR has yet to be understood through concepts that emerge from actually playing VR games. Perhaps the question is not Does VR help us feel empathy?, but rather *How* can VR help us understand what we mean by empathy? Or, as Liu asks, why do we need people's lives to be "humanized" or "empathized with" in order to see them as human in the first place?[71] One possible form of empathy that is particular to a VR experience, as Anna Anthropy has written, is the type of "empathy that comes from frustration," from not knowing the subjects one sees, of feeling no intimacy with them as an outsider or gawker, of realizing one's complicity with the war machines that produced these subjects, of being led to fail in one's understanding, over and over again.[72] As Liu's and Kim's works show, the possibility of empathy in VR is not in automating experiences of pain and suffering, but in understanding the shared ground between "us" and "them," whose distance is too vast to ever be knowable, though one can make some effort to imagine it.

NOTES

1. Jeffrey L. Sammons and Wolfgang Mieder, *"Yes We Can": Barack Obama's Proverbial Rhetoric* 6 (Lausanne, Switzerland: Peter Lang, 2009), 31.

2. "Zuckerberg Friends BYU," *Y Magazine*, summer 2011.

3. Roger Ebert, "Ebert's Walk of Fame Remarks," RogerEbert.com, June 2005.

4. Chris Milk, "How Virtual Reality Can Create the Ultimate Empathy Machine," Talk at TED 2015.

5. Jacqwi Campbell, "VR Creator—Barry Pousman (*Clouds Over Sidra*, UN Media Specialist)," Medium.com, accessed March 7, 2016, https://medium.com/cinenation -show/vr-creator-series-barry-pousman-57febb93d191.

6. For more on the discourse of VR and empathy, see popular articles in *Wired* (Streep) and *The Atlantic* (Bloom), and on NPR (Sydell).

7. Luke Buckmaster and Brian Yecies, "Docu-Reality and Empathy in *Bloodless* (2017): A Manifesto for Transnational Virtual Reality Cinema," in *Asia-Pacific Film Co-Productions: Theory, Industry and Aesthetics*, ed. Wendy Su and Dal Yong Jin (New York: Routledge, 2019), 275.

8. See Paul Bloom's "It's Ridiculous to Use Virtual Reality to Empathize with Refugees," *The Atlantic*, February 3, 2017, https://www.theatlantic.com/technology/archive /2017/02/virtual-reality-wont-make-you-more-empathetic/515511/.

9. Robert Yang, "'If You Walk in Someone Else's Shoes, Then You've Taken Their Shoes': Empathy Machines as Appropriation Machines," *Radiator 2 Design Blog*, 2017.

10. Ruha Benjamin, *Race After Technology: Abolitionist Tools for the New Jim Code* (Hoboken, NJ: John Wiley & Sons, 2019), 155.

11. Prashast Thapan, "We Went to the Weird Reality Symposium to Find the Limits of Virtual Reality," Vice.com, 2017, accessed January 2021.

12. Nikhil Pal Singh, *Race and America's Long War* (Berkeley: University of California Press, 2017), 31.

13. Crystal Parikh, *Writing Human Rights: The Political Imaginaries of Writers of Color* (Minneapolis: University of Minnesota Press, 2017), 3.

14. Cathy Schlund-Vials, Guy Beauregard, and Hsiu-chuan Lee, "Introduction: The Subject(s) of Human Rights; Recalibrating Asian/American Critique," in *The Subject (s) of Human Rights: Crises, Violations, and Asian/American Critique*, ed. Cathy Schlund-Vials, Guy Beauregard, and Hsiu-chuan Lee (Philadelphia: Temple University Press, 2019), 4–6.

15. Lisa Lowe, *The Intimacies of Four Continents* (Durham, NC: Duke University Press, 2015), 208.

16. Yến Lê Espiritu, "Critical Refugee Studies and Native Pacific Studies: a Transpacific Critique," *American Quarterly* 69, no. 3 (2017): 483–84.

17. Bloom, "It's Ridiculous."

18. Viet Thanh Nguyen, "Representing Reconciliation: Le Ly Hayslip and the Victimized Body," *positions: east asia cultures critique* 5, no. 2 (1997): 605–42.

19. Pooja Rangan, *Immediations: The Humanitarian Impulse in Documentary* (Durham, NC: Duke University Press, 2017), 1.

20. Tina Chen and Cathy J. Schlund-Vials, "On the Subject(s) of Displacement," *Verge: Studies in Global Asias* 6, no. 1 (2020): iii.

21. Chen and Schlund-Vials, iii.

22. Sara Ahmed, *Cultural Politics of Emotion* (Edinburgh: Edinburgh University Press, 2014), 30; Lauren Berlant, "Introduction: Compassion (and Withholding)," in *Compassion: The Culture and Politics of an Emotion*, ed. Lauren Berlant (New York: Routledge, 2014), 3.

23. Marjorie Gerber, "Compassion," in *Compassion: The Culture and Politics of an Emotion*, ed. Lauren Berlant (New York: Routledge, 2014), 24.

24. As Wynter writes, "'Race' is really a code-word for 'genre.' Our issue is not the issue of 'race.' Our issue is the issue of the genre of 'Man.' It is this issue of the 'genre' of 'Man' that causes all the '-isms.'" See Sylvia Wynter and Greg Thomas, "ProudFlesh Inter/Views Sylvia Wynter," *PROUD FLESH: A New Afrikan Journal of Culture, Politics & Consciousness* 4 (2006): 1–36.

25. Gerber, "Compassion," 24.

26. Neferti Tadiar, "Filipinas 'Living in a Time of War,'" in *Body Politics: Essays on Cultural Representations of Women's Bodies*, ed. Maria Josephine Barrios and Odine De Guzman (Manila: UP Center for Women's Studies, 2002), 310.

27. Tadiar, 315.

28. Jan M. Padios, "Mining the Mind: Emotional Extraction, Productivity, and Predictability in the Twenty-First Century," *Cultural Studies* 31, no. 2–3 (2017): 207.

29. See Yến Lê Espiritu, *Body Counts: The Vietnam War and Militarized Refugees* (Oakland: University of California Press, 2014); Vinh Nguyen, Thy Phu, and Y-Dang Troeung, "Refugee Compassion and the Politics of Embodied Storytelling: A Critical Conversation," *a/b: Auto/Biography Studies* 33, no. 2 (2018): 441–45.

30. Espiritu, *Body Counts*, 10.

31. Espiritu, 11.

32. Espiritu calls "critical juxtaposing" "the bringing together of seemingly different and disconnected events, communities, histories, and spaces to illuminate what would otherwise not be visible about the contours, contents, and afterlives of war and empire." See Espiritu, "Critical Refugee Studies," 486.

33. Jinah Kim, *Postcolonial Grief: The Afterlives of the Pacific Wars in the Americas* (Durham, NC: Duke University Press, 2019), 2.

34. For a longer inquiry into the imperial dimensions of the Iowa writing workshop, see Mark McGurl, *The Program Era: Postwar Fiction and the Rise of Creative Writing*; Eric Bennett, *Workshops of Empire: Stegner, Engle, and American Creative Writing during the Cold War*; Christopher B. Patterson, "The Programmatic, the Problematic, and the Radical Racial Tradition (Or, On Being Stamped," in *Creative Writing Scholars on the Publishing Trade: Practice, Praxis, Print*, ed. Marshall Moore and Sam Meekings (New York: Routledge, 2021); and Cathy Park Hong, *Minor Feelings: An Asian American Reckoning* (New York: One World, 2020), 17.

35. Hong, *Minor Feelings*, 42.

36. Hong, 42.

37. Nam Le, *The Boat* (New York: Alfred A. Knopf, 2008), 9.

38. Cathy Park Hong, "Delusions of Whiteness in the Avant-Garde," *Lana Turner* 7 (2014).

39. Donald C. Goellnicht, "'Ethnic Literature's Hot': Asian American Literature, Refugee Cosmopolitanism, and Nam Le's 'The Boat,'" *Journal of Asian American Studies* 15, no. 2 (2012): 201.

40. Simeon Man, *Soldiering through Empire: Race and the Making of the Decolonizing Pacific* (Oakland: University of California Press, 2018), 8.

41. Goellnicht, "'Ethnic Literature's Hot,'" 205.

42. Betsy Huang, *Contesting Genres in Contemporary Asian American Fiction* (New York: Springer, 2010), 7.

43. Jodi Melamed, *Represent and Destroy: Rationalizing Violence in the New Racial Capitalism* (Minneapolis: University of Minnesota Press, 2011).

44. For more on the controversy over *Woman Warrior*, see Christopher B. Patterson, "Diaspora and Its Others: *The Woman Warrior* and Southeast Asian Diasporic Lit-

erature," in *Critical Insights: The Woman Warrior*, ed. Linda Trinh Moser and Kathryn West (Hackensack, NJ: Salem, 2016), 158–72.

45. Lan Cao, *Monkey Bridge* (London: Penguin, 1998), 253.

46. Y-Dang Troeung, "Between Forced Confession and Ethnic Autobiography," in *Research Methodologies for Auto/biography Studies*, ed. Ashley Barnwell and Kate Douglas (New York: Routledge, 2019), 220–27.

47. Yogita Goyal, "Un-American: Refugees and the Vietnam War," *PMLA* 133, no. 2 (2018): 378. According to Goyal, Nguyen himself has sought to distance his work from the immigrant autobiographical novel and states that "*The Sympathizer* is a war novel rather than an immigrant story" (378).

48. Jia Tolentino, "Ocean Vuong's Life Sentences," *New Yorker*, June 10 and 17, 2019.

49. Stephen Hong Sohn, *Racial Asymmetries: Asian American Fictional Worlds* (New York: New York University Press, 2014), 3.

50. Viet Thanh Nguyen, *Nothing Ever Dies: Vietnam and the Memory of War* (Cambridge, MA: Harvard University Press, 2016), 209.

51. Rob Wolf, "Ken Liu: The Hidden Girl and Other Stories," *New Books in Science Fiction and Fantasy* (podcast), March 2020.

52. Bonnie Ruberg, "Empathy and Its Alternatives: Deconstructing the Rhetoric of 'Empathy' in Video Games," *Communication, Culture and Critique* 1, no. 13 (March 2020): 54–71.

53. See Mattie Brice, "Empathy Machine," mattiebrice.com, June 30, 2016; Naomi Clark and M. Kopas, "Queering Human-Game Relations: Exploring Queer Mechanics and Play," *First Person Scholar*, February 2015; Robert Yang, "'If You Walk in Someone Else's Shoes, Then You've Taken Their Shoes': Empathy Machines as Appropriation Machines," *Radiator 2 Design* blog, 2017; and Ruberg, "Empathy and Its Alternatives," 8.

54. Brendan Keogh, *A Play of Bodies: How We Perceive Videogames* (Cambridge, MA: MIT Press, 2018), 880.

55. Barrie Sherman and Phil Judkins, *Glimpses of Heaven, Visions of Hell: Virtual Reality and Its Implications* (London: Hodder & Stoughton, 1992), 134.

56. Richard King and David J. Leonard, "Wargames as a New Frontier: Securing American Empire in Virtual Space," in *Joystick Soldiers: The Politics of Play in Military Video Games*, ed. Nina Huntemann and Matthew Thomas Payne (New York: Routledge, 2010), 92.

57. Ken Liu, "Byzantine Empathy," *BreakerMag*, September 2018.

58. Yang, "If You Walk in Someone Else's Shoes."

59. Liu, "Byzantine Empathy," *Lightspeed Magazine* 125 (October 2020), https://www.lightspeedmagazine.com/fiction/byzantine-empathy/.

60. Takeo Rivera, "Do Asians Dream of Electric Shrieks? Techno-Orientalism and Erotohistoriographic Masochism in Eidos Montreal's *Deus Ex: Human Revolution*," *Amerasia Journal* 40, no. 2 (2014): 69.

61. Keogh, *A Play of Bodies*.

62. Steve Swink, *Game Feel: A Game Designer's Guide to Virtual Sensation* (Boca Raton, FL: CRC, 2008), 26.

63. Adrian M. S. Piper, "Impartiality, Compassion, and Modal Imagination," *Ethics* 101, no. 4 (1991): 726.

64. Annie Bares, "'Each Unbearable Day': Narrative Ruthlessness and Environmental and Reproductive Injustice in Jesmyn Ward's *Salvage the Bones*," *MELUS* 44, no. 3 (2019): 22. For more on the concept of "moral imagination," see David Bromwich, *Moral Imagination: Essays* (Princeton, NJ: Princeton University Press, 2014).

65. Dal Yong Jin, "*Final Recipe* as a Pan-Asian Co-Production Film: Interview with Director Gina Kim," in *Asia-Pacific Film Co-Productions: Theory, Industry and Aesthetics*, ed. Wendy Su and Dal Yong Jin (New York: Routledge, 2019), 298.

66. YoukYung Lee, "Director Turns to Virtual Reality to Tastefully Show Tragedy," *Taiwan News*, October 1, 2017.

67. Ahmed, *The Cultural Politics of Emotion*, 30 (emphasis added).

68. Piper, "Impartiality, Compassion, and Modal Imagination," 731.

69. Piper, 737.

70. Sealing Cheng, *On the Move for Love: Migrant Entertainers and the U.S. Military in South Korea* (Philadelphia: University of Pennsylvania Press, 2010), 105.

71. Wolf, "Ken Liu."

72. Ben Kuchera, "Dys4ia Tackles Gender Politics, Sense of Self, and Personal Growth . . . on Newgrounds," *Penny Arcade Report*, 2012.

PART TWO GRAFTING THE PACIFIC

4 APPREHENDING FILIPINO AMERICA

JOSEN MASANGKAY DIAZ

What, if anything, can the transpacific lend to the study of Filipino America? Recent discourse about the study of the Philippines and Filipinos troubles the state of Filipino and Filipino American studies. Following such provocations, I point to the ways that the conceptualization of "Filipino America" as a transpacific configuration highlights the myriad social and political conditions that constitute its position as a US racial formation. The transpacific ties Filipino America to, as the editors of this volume describe, "the entanglements among ongoing settler-colonial practices, inter-Asia modernization, militarized global capitalism, as well as migrant and Indigenous navigations that challenge the disciplinization of knowledge."[1] The transpacific is an epistemological project that presents Filipino America as a problem of knowledge.

In a 2014 exploration of the "roots and routes" of the Filipino intellectual, Caroline Hau contextualized contemporary debates about the epistemic authority that mediates the study of the Philippines. Hau addresses the responses to Reynaldo Ileto's 2001 assessment of American scholarship about the Philippines, where he critiqued the Orientalist underpinnings of much study of the Philippines. In the chapter Hau poses a series of questions: "What social location is capable of generating more reliable knowledge? What is the scope of this privilege? How is this privilege justified? What other perspectives need to be factored in to generate more reliable knowledge? How can such knowledge be rendered accessible to others? Does one gain better perspective simply by occupying a given social location? To ask these questions is to demand more intellectual work rather than to suspend it."[2] On the one hand, Hau names the conditions by which scholars study and write about the Philippines. At the same time, such questions insist upon a more incisive exploration of the link between subjectivity and knowledge production and the legacies of Orientalism and colonialism that underpin it. In their introduction to the 2016 anthology *Filipino Studies: Palimpsests of Nation and Diaspora*, Martin Manalansan and Augusto Espiritu wrestle with some of Hau's quandaries by addressing the tensions between Philippine, Filipino, and Filipino American studies, arguing that the collection aims to move "beyond identity and invisibility questions, to think more capaciously about cultural production, social justice, transformation, structural politics, historical passages, and collective actions."[3] Indeed, the anthology's authors investigate a range of subjects, from the overlapping colonialisms that materialized in the Philippines at the turn of the twentieth century, to migration and labor across Europe and Asia, to the seemingly unlikely relations and affinities that Filipinos form across race, class, and gender through this movement.

Writing in 2012, Denise Cruz identified "transpacific femininities" as those that are "influenced by the contact between the Philippines, the United States, Spain, and Japan."[4] For Cruz, the transpacific does not simply denote spatial location; it also signifies critical moments of shift and transformation.[5] The figure of the transpacific Filipina reveals the tangled dynamics of nationalism and nationhood. Additionally, in their 2014 work, J. Francisco Benitez and Laurie Sears bring area studies and Asian American studies into critical dialogue, insisting upon a study of Filipinos and Indonesians that "recognizes the contradictions and strategic essentialisms of raced and gendered identities [that] can uncover the ruptures and flows of people and stories. It can also interrupt how people and stories accrue value and privilege in the nodes of power and knowledge differentially organized in an imperial field."[6] In their analysis of the ways that "mobile subjects" complicate the bounds of area studies and American ethnic studies scholarship, Benitez and Sears emphasize a transpacific study of movement and migration that underscores the ways that race and gender shift within the social and political conditions of distinct locations.

While these studies may not rest comfortably within "Filipino American studies" writ large, they do interrogate location, positionality, subjectivity, and knowledge production in ways that challenge the epistemological category of Filipino America as a stable, bounded formation and reveal a set of transpacific relations. I follow their lead by arguing that the transpacific as an analytic can apprehend Filipino America and lay bare the politics that constitute its cohesion and invocation. To apprehend Filpino America is to locate and seize it, to interrogate its constitution and usage, to "resist racialized regimes of knowledge that comfortably rest upon colonial-imperialist compartmentalization of areas, nations, people, and disciplines."[7] The advent of Filipino America as a discourse of US racial belonging and citizenship emerged in the 1970s and 1980s. Its rise can be attributed to the circumstances and conflicts of that time, particularly the rise of Filipino immigration to the United States, which followed the passage of the Immigration and Nationality Act of 1965 (the Hart-Celler Act), as well as the antiracist social movements that coalesced in cities such as Seattle, San Francisco, Los Angeles, Chicago, and New York. Much recent scholarship highlights the transnationality of these social movements, which effectively tied anti-labor and anti-immigrant US legislation to the legacy of US imperialism in the Philippines.[8] Indeed, Filipino organizing in the United States during the period focused on building power against the US-supported dictatorship of Ferdinand Marcos, articulating the regime as a collaboration between Philippine and US state governments that enacted a distinct kind of violence against women, the poor, and various kinds of radicals. The Marcos dictatorship lasted for over two decades, from 1965 to 1986. When Marcos declared martial law in 1972, he justified the executive order as a strategy for squashing growing leftist and communist insurgency in the country. By the time martial law was lifted in 1981, Marcos had developed what he described as the "new society," a juridico-political framework that focused on development and signaled the Philippines' arrival to a modern world of nations.

While Filipino and Filipino American studies often render the Marcos dictatorship as an object of study in and of itself, the dictatorship also offers avenues for interrogating the discursive formation of Filipino America as postcolonial subjectivity. Rather than assume Filipino America as a coherent racial formation, it can be considered a nexus of cold war modernity whose cohesion is always undone by a transpacific geopolitics that betrays the intricate workings of overlapping empires, authoritarian governments, and multidirectional circuits of capitalist exchange. The incisiveness of the transpacific analytic lies in its capacity to illuminate the ways that nations and peoples who were once deemed the object of colonial governance became the subject of a global remaking under the terms of new cold war sovereignties.[9] The term "cold war" is here differentiated from the Cold War to move away from, as Lisa Yoneyama instructs, the "eventness" of the period and to focus instead on the politics of integration and transformation that structured the imperialist struggles of the decades that followed the Second World War.[10] This politics was shaped by the persistence of postcolonial nationalisms, the unevenness of postwar reconstruction, continuing US militarization, and the insidiousness of liberal international governance.

Three distinct readings will aid in apprehending Filipino America in a way that illuminates its transpacific constitution. The cultural objects analyzed here may be well known to scholars of Filipino and Filipino American studies, and in many ways they are part of the very archive that has constituted this understanding. The song, photograph, and novel are dialectical formations whose contradictions must be repaired in order to unearth the logics of their solidity. I am interested in the instances wherein the texts' solidity or completeness gives way to dissonances and incongruencies and point to the conditions of their production. In other words, the objects themselves are legible only to the extent of the validity of the epistemological frames that hold them, and their undoing makes visible the mechanisms that tether them together. To apprehend these objects is to trace the fissures that betray this cohesion and to consider the means by which the objects themselves help uncover a politics of subjectivity and knowledge and dictatorship and colonialism. It illuminates the possibilities they hold for grappling with the legacies and continuities of dictatorship and imperial war. Rather than employ the transpacific to reveal unfound knowledge, the transpacific helps disentangle the objects and subjects from the practice of knowledge. It presents another way of reading (for) Filipino America that attends to its myriad entanglements and a study of identity that leads to a more expansive politics.[11]

ON DICTATORSHIP

The study of dictatorship elucidates both the ongoing US control of its territories and former colonies and the ways that the legacies of overlapping empires transcend the historicity of the colonial century through modes of national and transnational state governance. In addition to ruling by executive order, suspending the writ of habeas corpus, and censoring and controlling the press, the Marcos regime tortured, killed, and disappeared its critics. When Marcos declared martial law over the Philippines in 1972, he promised to establish order over the chaos created by leftist and communist insurrection. With the US war in Vietnam raging throughout Southeast Asia, Marcos, like many of his predecessors, maintained his support for the war and for the US counterinsurgency efforts that aimed to quell communist forces throughout Asia. He extended the US lease of the military bases in Olongapo and Subic Bay in the Philippines.[12] At the same time that Marcos was adhering to US geopolitics, his economic policies were promoting ties with the Soviet Union and China. The regime facilitated modernization through international political and financial institutions such as the World Bank, the International Monetary Fund, and the Asian Development Bank. The currency of such nationalism within the context of cold war US geo-politics, however authoritarian, functioned as an acceptable response to the kind of global political order driven by the memories of totalitarian regimes. In other words, Philippine authoritarianism garnered US support because it relied on a liberalism that justified an acceptable amount of violence in contradistinction to the threat of anti-American fascism and communism.

In recent years, Asian and Asian American studies scholars have begun to pay increased attention to the transpacific as a paradigm for investigating colonialism, imperialism, militarization, and globalization. The transpacific makes visible the multiple routes that traverse the Pacific Ocean, bringing into closer proximity peoples of the Pacific, Asia, and the United States. Catherine Ceniza Choy and Judy Tzu-Chun Wu describe a "trans-Pacific framework" as one that "decenters a teleological and nation-centered narrative of U.S. exceptionalism" and "encourages us to reimagine the migration of people, both coerced and voluntary, across the vast waters and the lands of the Pacific, and to explore persistent and new connections that migrants create within their homelands and with diasporic communities."[13] In this way, transpacific studies, according to Janet Hoskins and Viet Thanh Nguyen, threads together the discourses between Asian American studies, American studies, and area studies to produce more incisive analyses of their interconnections while also delineating their limitations. After World War II the rise of area studies institutionalized Orientalist conceptions of the non-Western decolonizing world. It also weaponized this scholarship in the service of geopolitical containment and capitalist expansion. While area studies often privileges static conceptions of place to produce uncritical scholarship about the "rest" (of the West), American studies often replicates an exceptionalist logic that relies upon US knowledge production to interrogate US and transnational politics. Asian American studies, on the other hand, often focuses on the study of Asian American subjects through a unidirectional approach to migration that, while increasingly tending toward transnational processes, is also often rooted in US epistemologies.[14]

More than considering the "Pacific," "Asia," and "America" simultaneously, the utility of the transpacific lies in its ability to challenge the assumptions of their juxtaposition and interrogate the social formations that become visible at their intersections.[15] Rather than create a composite picture of different disciplinary investments, the transpacific is a method for untangling the politics that constitutes these boundaries, unpacking the systems of knowledge that render categories legible.[16] While the transpacific as analytic has offered ways to study connection and movement that precedes World War II, it is important to underscore the postwar period as particularly significant for constructing a distinct transpacific framework. After World War II, the US-led reorganization of the globe materialized through the rehabilitation of "enemy" nations as well as through the consolidation of its former colonies and outposts during postwar reconstruction. Naoki Sakai and Hyon Joo Yoo argue that the "United States gave license to create the Japanese nation by renewing its vision of East Asia as a spatialization of the Cold War ideology."[17] The US rehabilitation of Japan generally, and its demilitarization and restructuring more specifically, mediated the United States' parallel reconstitution of countries such as South Korea and Taiwan through support for military dictatorships and counterinsurgency campaigns. In the Philippines and Guam the formation of postcolonial national governments transformed these nations from colonial wards into junior military partners to the United States. In such cases, the transpacific points not only to the circuits that bind these connected locales together but articulates the modes by which *ideas* of the Pacific, Asia, and America cohere, shift, and change in the historical and political imagination of the United States.[18] Moreover, in his transpacific analysis, Chien-ting Lin insists upon a critical dialogue between inter-Asia cultural studies and an Asian American political critique, to investigate "the suppressed histories of the Cold War formations in Asia and the Pacific [that] render legible the obscured intimacies among transnational migrant workers across the national divides."[19] Following Lin, it is precisely these transpacific social formations that disrupt rigid, national conceptualizations of subjectivity, especially those rooted in US discourses and formations of race.

As much as Marcos's nationalist politics were based on reform and modernization, they also deployed a decolonial rhetoric of revolution.[20] Central to Marcos's vision of development, not unlike other dictatorial regimes in Asia and throughout the world during the period, was the reinvigoration of a nationalist politics that promoted a new postcolonial subjectivity. Much of Marcos's vision for a new society centered upon the idea of a "new Filipino." Indeed, Marcos's justification of martial law as a state of exception sought to guard the inviolability of this new Filipino subject, who would simultaneously ignite a radical departure from colonial mendicancy and garner international political recognition. For Marcos, the new Filipino represented a distinct kind of raciality: unlike the subservient Filipino of the past century, the new Filipino was better suited to traversing the landscape of the postcolonial present. In other words, the renewal of Filipino subjectivity away from its colonial ontology promoted the Filipino as a hybrid of East and West: nondeferential, unprecedented, and singular. This articulation of past subjectivity mirrored the regime's insistence on an inter-Asia modernization that propounded a cold war Asianness organized under a politics of collaboration and capitalist integration. Marcos advanced this ethnic nationalism through a postcolonial logic buttressed by a new global order that was triangulated as US imperial hegemony, the reconstruction and rehabilitation of postwar Asia, and the modernization of former colonies, or, in other words, "ethnic nationalisms that had previously been abhorred by colonial masters."[21] The emergence of this new subjectivity reflected the ways that the administration was able to consolidate the discourses, energies, and lifeworlds of decolonial movements into the propagation of a new postcolonial and globally recognizable racial subject, while it also violently suppressed antistate and anticolonial resistance struggles.[22]

Several scholars have detailed the rise of the Philippines' labor export economy, which facilitates the migration of Filipino migrant laborers to various countries throughout the world. The Filipino labor migrant has become the emblematic configuration of Philippine modernization. The phenomenon of Filipino labor export has characterized the Philippines' political economy for some time, but it traces its origins to Marcos's development programs. The Marcos regime's proclamation of a new Filipino subjectivity provided a language for bringing the labor of migrant workers into the discourse of modernization. Both *of* the nation and *outside* the nation, the Filipino labor migrant is the expression of national sovereignty and postwar global interconnection. As scholars Robyn Rodriguez, Anna Guevarra, Rolando Tolentino, and Rhacel Parreñas have incisively shown, the Filipina woman has embodied nationalist discourses that imagine and laud the Filipino labor migrant. While the Filipino labor migrant illustrates the inextricability of postcolonial national modernity and neoliberal exchange, it is often Filipina labor that bears the burden of the work and the exploitative violence that is often attached to that work.

Marcos's articulations of the new Filipino emerged alongside the rise of a distinct kind of diasporic Filipino social formation in the United States. The idea of the post-1965 Filipino American emerged precisely from the transpacific cold war politics that mediated the Philippine nationalism of the 1970s and 1980s. The rise of the term "Filipino America," to name a distinct kind of post-1965 diasporic social formation, was simultaneously a product of the social movements that sparked this recognition and the liberal US reforms that sought to contain them. Yet Filipino America also operates as what Lisa Lowe has described as "the trans-Pacific post 1965 Asian immigrant as an object of knowledge" with a "potential to displace a nationalist epistemology."[23] While the Hart-Celler Act removed national quotas from US immigration law and unintentionally facilitated the immigration of Filipinos and other migrants from Asia and Latin America to the United States, such liberal reform was always mediated by US colonial and imperial policies occurring outside the United States. Within most US historical narratives, the Hart-Celler Act, along with the civil rights reforms that formed the nucleus of 1960s US liberal reform, generated the discourses with which to recognize the US racial subject through the language of liberal multiculturalism.[24] However, it is not simply that this multiculturalism operated as an imperialist optics or as a tactic for luring the Third World into the parameters of global integration. More importantly, the racial subject, conceptualized through the logics of US liberalism and its exceptionalism, legitimized both the wars in Asia as necessary "good wars" and the imperialist and neocolonial policies that continued the violence well after the wars' official ends.[25] Yoneyama's study of narratives of the US "rescue" of Japanese women, for instance, describes the ways that numerous reports constructed narratives of militarized liberation and the reconstruction of Japan based on the progressiveness of American masculinity and the backwardness of Japanese masculinity and the objectification of the Japanese woman.[26] In constructing the Japanese woman in this way, US narratives rehearsed the urgency of the victory over Japan and legitimized the containment of its Asian colonies.

Moreover, Marcos's own construction of the labor export economy mediated this migration. The regime's policies made it inhospitable, sometimes impossible, for some Filipinos, particularly educated Filipinos with more financial means, to remain within the country. Spurred by both the failures of development and the violence of martial law, the figure of the Filipino immigrant to the United States, or the Filipino American, disrupts singular approaches to immigration that conceptualize the immigrant as divorced from other ideas that were circulating during the period and were critical to its formation. The recognition of Filipino America must attend to the regime's policies of subjection as well as to the continuation of US development, militarization, and war in Asia that worked in tandem with such policies.

Filipino America is always already a transpacific formation. It not only makes visible the connections between geographic locations and the circuits of exchange that bind them. Most importantly, it highlights the seemingly disparate histories, politics, discourses, and epistemologies that are central to its recognition. The readings that follow illustrate different renditions of Filipino America beyond the figuration of diasporic identity and illuminate these transpacific connections.

"GOD BLESS THE PHILIPPINES"

In 1987 reporters Ken Kelly and Phil Bronstein, writers for *Playboy* magazine, visited Ferdinand and Imelda Marcos in their Makiki Heights home in Honolulu one year after being deposed from office and exiled to Hawai'i, hoping to discuss the legacy of the Marcos presidency, their lives in exile, and their plans to return to the Philippines. When the interviewers asked her to recall the details of her first public performance, the former first lady, known for her sentimental and melodramatic public performances, described the moment in 1944 when she performed Irving Berlin's anthem, "God Bless America":

> Oh, don't ask me this! It was 1944, and I was singing at a garden party in the MacArthur compound. I sang a song—God Bless the Philippines—and Irving Berlin, who was there, heard me. He came up to me and embraced me and said, "Dear girl, this song is God Bless America!" I said, "No, this is God Bless the Philippines." He said, "I composed this song, and it's God Bless America." I said, "There's no difference, because America and the Philippines are the same." Berlin, according to the interviewers, contested the veracity of Marcos's story, claiming that he "composed the song in 1945, not 1944," and "definitely not" for Mrs. Marcos.[27]

Berlin's denial is unsurprising, given Marcos's bizarre, revisionist recollection of her time as first lady and her unapologetic fabrication of the sequence of events. Even so, Marcos's narrative remains compelling for its rendition of the intimacies that characterize the relationship between the empire and colony. Her improvisation—especially the seeming ease with which she replaced "America" with "the Philippines"—positioned the Philippines as the uncanny remnant of US empire, a persistent if not irritating reminder of the Philippines' centrality to US claims of glory. Berlin penned the song in 1918, near the end of the First World War, and revised the song in 1938, three years before the United States officially entered the Second World War.[28] Although the song imagines America as an idyllic prairie land, innocent and good in its wait to defend its own honor, the United States, by the time Berlin released the song, had become a sprawling empire, squelching anticolonial resistance movements and seizing Spanish territories in the Pacific. Marcos's provocation that America was in fact already the Philippines illustrates the significance of the acquisition and colonization of the Philippines to the very invocation of America.

Marcos's adamant revision, on the other hand, is aspirational, positioning the Philippines within the contours of US nation-building. Performed just two years before the US declaration of Philippine independence, Marcos's changing of the name frames the latter within the historical timeline and the political trajectory of the former, predetermining the shape of Philippine independence and signifying the ultimate success of the US colonial mission over the archipelago. Marcos's conscious misinterpretation of the song, the easy slippage between America and the Philippines, renders the two into shadows of each other: both an uncanny remnant of the other but each integral to the other's coherence, solidity, and invocation. In this way, the stability of each is more a promise, perhaps even a fortified fiction, than a guarantee. What Marcos's narrative ultimately reveals is that the possibility of one has depended upon the existence of the other. The emergence of Berlin's new song "Heaven Watch the Philippines," with its call to God to watch over the country in the post-independence period, sits alongside the original song in Marcos's retelling and signifies a new alliance between the newly sovereign state of the Philippines and its former colonizer. No longer a cheap copy of a song "really meant for America," the emergence of the new song announces the Philippines' arrival within a host of nations pursuing the same historical fate.

Marcos's performance just before the end of World War II reaffirms the importance of the Philippines to the United States' renewal of itself as empire: no longer benevolent colonizer but liberator of the colonized. Marcos's adaptation recalls the Philippines as the Theater of the Pacific, a literal and figurative location that sets the stage for an embroiled battle between competing empires. For example, both the struggle for and the commemoration of Bataan as a key site of transpacific war, as Vernadette Gonzalez has discussed, position the Philippines as a place of imperial interconnection. As the site of Japan's and the United States' victories and defeats in their battle for the Pacific, Bataan staged the rise and fall of both empires. Marcos's own rise to office was aided, in part, by a self-constructed narrative of his heroism against Japan during World War II, particularly his survival of the Bataan Death March and his time as a prisoner of war. Within this elaborate state fiction, Marcos characterized his leadership as able to navigate the delicate interplay between an indebtedness to US rescue and an opposing force to a collaborative politics with Japan. Within this narrative, Japan functions as an easy signifier of the Philippine-US enemy around which the Philippines could structure its postwar alliance. This is to say that the authoritarian regime was buttressed not only by US political and military support but also by the rehabilitation of the Japanese nation: no longer as enemy but as ally whose defeat facilitated the emergence of new nationalisms grounded in the reassertion of victimized masculinities.[29] The materialization of this national Philippine masculinity asserts itself in the Philippines' contribution to the US war in Vietnam, Laos, and Cambodia.[30] Marcos's deployment of military units to these locations and his construction of the Philippine Refugee Processing Center in Bataan became vehicles by which to express sovereignty within the political landscape of the US Cold War.

More than a slip of the tongue, the first lady's words overdetermine the arc of Philippine national history, outlining it within the contours of the US nation-state. At the same time it makes clear the problem of remembering and forgetting: a presentation of U.S. colonialism in the Philippines that remembers Douglas MacArthur's mission of return and rescue but forgets the modes by which US reconstruction organized the modernization of Asia and the Pacific in the aftermaths of war. To apprehend this configuration of "Philippines" for "America" (or Filipino America), then, is to tease out the discursive space that exists between the two. It is, as Leo Ching urges, "to consider the continuities *and* discontinuities, the ruptures *and* permutations of colonial power, and the many ways colonization have [*sic*] become indelibly and inescapably inscribed in the cultures of both the (ex)colonizer and the (ex)colonized."[31] By pointing to the multistate investments and aftermaths of war, Marcos's performance untangles the transpacific from the Philippine-US relation. More than a faulty rendition of a song really meant for America, the first lady's appropriation of the song redraws the boundaries of the Philippines and the United States and reveals the necessary violences needed to make the song a commemoration of US empire.

PEOPLE, POWER

In 1986, just one year before a disgraced Imelda Marcos sat with Kelly and Bronstein in Honolulu, *Manila Times* photojournalist Pete Reyes captured a striking photograph of Sister Porfiria Ocariza and Sister Teresita Burias kneeling next to each other, the former defiantly praying the rosary while the latter stares at something beyond the photograph's frame.[32] The image finds them, either by trial or circumstance, between an army tank in the foreground and a massive group of protesters in the background. An assortment of people are haphazardly scattered across the image. A faceless soldier's weaponry, a machine-gun equipped with a seemingly endless cache of bullets, encloses most of the bottom half of the picture. The photograph centers Ocariza and Burias, whose looks of surprise and concern, as well as their act of prayer, sharply contrast the cold power of the soldier's rifle. The photograph, which has come to signify the exceptionality of the People Power Revolution that ousted the Ferdinand Marcos dictatorship after its twenty-one-year reign, tells more than the story of the people's resistance against the autocrat alone. It is also a portrait of Filipino subjectivity and its story of becoming.

Several decades later, recalling the moment captured by the photograph, Sister Ocariza remembered, "'I said, 'Lord forgive me for all my sins and even the offenses of our Filipino people.' If really the tanks would crush us, at least the two of us . . . kill us sisters, not the people because we [did not] want bloodshed. I love my country."[33] Ocariza's statement here, with its request to a divine power to absolve "the offenses of our Filipino people," suggests a Filipino subjectivity born from the salvation of revolution, signaling an emergence made possible only through the desperate circumstances of dictatorship. Ocariza's explanation, that the success of the revolution was equal parts martyrdom, patriotism, and an act of God, points to the confluence of forces at work in this expression of revolution: a combination of extreme power and extreme faith that constitutes both the authoritarian state and the resistance that always stirs within it. Another way to say this is that the revolution tells the story of the struggle to give name to the Filipino people, disarticulating it from its various overdeterminations, and the photograph reveals the extent to which the "Filipino people" comes to signify a historical experience that defies simplification even as it teases it in its invocation.

The People Power Revolution is constituted by intricately woven layers. However, its memorialization within Philippine and US public memory emphasizes the achievement of justice over an aberrational government. The image of the two sisters, among others, has come to represent a bloodless revolt that brought the Filipino people to Manila's Epifanio De Los Santos

Avenue (EDSA) and which, ultimately, forced Marcos into exile. For four days the human masses, along with the president's military generals and leaders of the Catholic Church, denounced Marcos's corruption, rallied behind opposition leader Corazon Aquino, and joined calls for the dictator to relinquish power to democracy. Aquino, the widow of Sen. Benigno Aquino Jr., whose assassination two years before the revolution was attributed to the regime, eventually took office after Marcos's departure. In his own reading of the photograph almost three decades after Reyes captured it, President Benigno Aquino III, the son of Benigno and Corazon Aquino, explained that the image proves that "compassion is the most powerful response to anger; there is no greater weapon than love."[34] As Aquino's comments reveal, postauthoritarian administrations have recuperated the photograph in their effort to commemorate the exceptionality of the movement, to celebrate the fulfillment of liberal governance, and to declare the sanctity of Philippine democracy.

Such postauthoritarian discourse allows the telos of liberal democracy to determine the significance of the image even as it gestures toward other meanings. It situates Ocariza and Burias within a frame of "compassion" and "love," allowing sentimentality to guide the perception of the picture even as it captures a distinct kind of authoritarian violence. The soldier's body and weapon flank the image, making the people visible only insofar as the soldier has moved away long enough for the viewer to witness what his person seeks to hide. A militaristic violence encases the image. Marcos's authoritarian regime was, above all, a military dictatorship. Before the revolution forced the Marcoses to flee the country in exile, Marcos called on the military to blockade and suppress the resistance that was gaining momentum as protestors began congregating along EDSA, bringing Manila traffic to a stop. In the years before the revolution, Marcos's military, filled with the president's loyalists, directed and implemented a system of salvaging. Salvaging was a distinct feature of Marcosian power: a system of disappearance and torture that ensured the violent suppression of resistance to the regime. As Gina Apostol has explained, salvage "was a cross of two words: 'to savage' and to be 'savaje,' which means wild in Spanish, but naughty or abusive in Tagalog. Add to that obscene joke the play on its meaning in English: to redeem, to extract from a wreck."[35] To salvage was to kill, to remove. Its possibility was ever-present, a mode of punishment that awaited those who resisted the regime's power. Salvaging became a modality of definition as much as it served as an instrument of suppression. In its obliteration of dissidents it demanded an abiding citizenry, a nation willing to succumb to ideas of citizenship that the regime had itself constructed.

With Marcos as its commander, the Philippine military accumulated a massive artillery of weapons, much of which the United States supplied in its effort to support the Marcos government and suppress revolts that were gaining strength throughout the country. This movement, led by the various arms of the Communist Party of the Philippines, proved to be one of the most troubling predicaments to face the Philippine government and its allies in Washington. Marcos's ongoing collaborations with the US military fed the long-standing struggle between the Philippine government and the New People's Army (NPA). Marcos's programs for modernization focused much effort on developing the rural areas of the Philippine countryside where the NPA organized, seeking to destabilize the force of communist resistance. The government expanded the national military, growing "from 56,000 to 58,000 in 1972, to about from 223,000 to 236,000 in 1982" and establishing the armed forces as "a partner of the civilian bureaucracy."[36] The regime also extended the US lease of Clark Air Force Base and Subic Bay Naval Base in 1979. The continuation of US militarized occupation of the Philippines materialized alongside the broader US effort to maintain its militaristic stronghold over Asia and the greater Pacific region, attempting to contain any socialist or communist influence from China and the Soviet Union over its former colonies and current territories. The bases structured the political economies of the areas around the needs of the US military in order to fortify its imperialist mission. Sex work in and around the bases coincided with the large-scale feminization of the Philippine economy, or what Vernadette Gonzalez has described as the "familiar positioning of Filipinas as the bodies of service in a transnational age."[37] These military collaborations illuminate the materialization of the cold war in the Philippines, in particular the ways that Marcos manipulated colonial relationships to fortify an authoritarian governmentality.

Yet the revolutionary affect of the image pierces the coherence of the picture by drawing into the frame other periods and struggles that are obfuscated by the photograph but which make themselves known in different ways.[38] While the photo portrays the cold materiality of the soldier's weaponry, it also juxtaposes violence with a belief in the otherworldly. While the shouts of the sisters and of the people surrounding them are only implied by the look on their faces, the viewer might imagine their sounds and reverberations. The portrayal captures a small snapshot of the movement, so the viewer might also envision the mass of people that spill far beyond the photograph. To move beyond the static quality of the captured image is to call forward these moments—the punctum, perhaps—which offer to the figures a certain dynamism.

Where Marcos and his military were deliberate in their suppression of the masses and defined belonging in a new period of Philippine sovereignty, the faith that the photograph captures imagines yet another world called into being by the people's acts of imagination. To recall Reynaldo Ileto's important study of passion and suffering, the residues of a Spanish colonial past emerge in a language of morality and afterlife that provided "lowland Philippine society with a language for articulating its own values, ideals, and even hopes of liberation."[39] As Ileto's work has revealed, this passion and suffering illustrate both the ongoing effects of coloniality as well as the modes of resistance that are fashioned from but which transcend that coloniality. The passion and suffering captured on the sisters' faces reveals the nation's deference to the Church as much as it underscores the dynamic ideology of liberation that has long played a critical role in the Filipino masses' conceptualization of decolonial resistance. Praying the rosary is an act of faith amid and against the logic of totalitarian power: a belief in the unreasonableness of the icon, the ritual, repetition, and the conjuring that stand up against the rationality of the state's calculations of power.[40] Faith expresses a belief in another world—not necessarily a religious one—and is disloyal to the terms that organize the present conditions.[41] While the image affirms the importance of the Church as a testament to the lasting significance of Spanish colonial rule, it also, more importantly, tells the story of a collective that not only gives weight to the Church's infallible authority but also believes in something of the magic of the spiritual realm, a world beyond the one that it has inherited.

As the photograph of this single scene has come to signify the revolution, it also retheorizes and reimagines Filipino subjectivity away from individual self-recognition and self-fulfillment, away from state renditions of citizenship and nationality, and away from a conception of revolution as a singular event enacted for a more democratic nation. Instead, the nuns' call for and toward "the Filipino" is a provocation for another world. It gestures toward an articulation of the force of Filipinos' longings and desires and energies to alter the shape of their lives. In her theorization of the "sorrows of the people," Neferti Tadiar has written that "unleashed, revolutionary passion exceeds the individual persons out of which it flows, manifesting itself on connected planes of a socialized nature—the inflamed, parched field, the burning red sky—and acting as a collective force that forges a revolutionary subject."[42] The photograph demands a different rendition of Filipino subjectivity: not as one that has existed once before but as one whose force is made in its becoming. This "people power" is as much a deliberate resistance against the dictator as it is a reconceptualization of "people" and "power."

The narration of the movement as a proper one relies upon its articulation as a bloodless fight against tyranny that sought to restore democracy. Dominant conceptualizations of the revolution as such obscures both the multiplicity of forces at work in the ignition of the resistance, particularly past and ongoing decades of leftist insurgency, and the extent to which the Philippine state collaborated with the US government to suppress radical movements throughout the Philippines for over a century. Several scholars have described the movement as an "unfinished revolution," given the ineffectiveness of subsequent presidential administrations to radically alter the oligarchic and corrupt structure of Philippine politics. Such a characterization, however pessimistic, emplaces the revolution within the broader history of revolutionary politics in the Philippines, as Ileto writes, in order to situate it as a movement whose beginning and end cannot be historically marked.[43] The photograph captures the palimpsestic quality of coloniality in the Philippines, the ways that the aftereffects and residues of colonialism shift across different historical periods, and the means by which people navigate these legacies. This unfinished revolution unhinges the movement from ownership: belonging to neither historical epoch nor embodying a particular subject formation, people power names an ongoing struggle for democracy.

A FILIPINO AMERICAN NOVEL

While Jessica Hagedorn's 1990 debut novel, *Dogeaters,* has become part of a Filipino American literary canon, the novel reveals a transpacific articulation of the Marcos dictatorship that destabilizes a coherent Filipino American subjectivity and reveals the multidirectionality of any claims to diasporic identity.[44] In other words, despite its absorption within Filipino American or Asian American literature and scholarship, the novel interrogates the very boundaries of Filipino America through its rendition of the dictatorship. *Dogeaters* was published just four years after the EDSA revolution and Marcos's deposal. It offers a complex study of subjectivity, blurring the boundaries between self and community in ways that interrogate the modes by which people come to name themselves and each other. Much has already been said about the novel's importance and form. A novel heralded for its study of immigrant Filipino subjectivity, for the brutalities of martial law, for the legacies of US colonialism and the complexities of urban Manila, it is mentioned here in an effort to highlight what a novel that has often been described as importantly Filipino American tells us about the unwieldiness and incoherence of Filipino America, its formations, and its transpacific constitutions.

The novel theorizes Filipino American subjectivity in ways that attend to the circumstances of Philippine postcoloniality. Addressing the novel's controversial title, Hagedorn explained in an interview that "a lot of Filipinos were upset about the title. The sense of cultural shame came in. I had intended it as a metaphor. I should have fought the whole idea of trying to explain it."[45] A pejorative term some trace to US soldiers' description of Filipinos during the Philippine-American War and to the 1904 St. Louis World's Fair exhibition of Filipinos as dogeating primitives, "dogeater" names a relationship between Filipino and America and describes racial otherness in contradistinction to popular and legal expressions of whiteness.[46] Dean Worcester's collection of photographs of Filipinos from the early US colonial period illuminate this framework of raciality.[47] One particular photograph, an image that depicts a towering Worcester standing next to a nameless Igorot man, illustrates the ways that early renditions of Filipino raciality rested upon the hierarchy between white American subjectivity and Filipino objectivity, that is, between whiteness as the proper subject to which the colonial object must aspire.[48] This relationship buttressed the biological determinism that legitimized colonial discourses of conquest. The designation of the Filipino as dogeater called up Filipino savagery and removed the Filipino from the category of the human, reducing her to her utility within the schema of humanity that underlined US coloniality. Turning the term on its head—or wielding it as "metaphor"—Hagedorn positions the term as an encapsulation of Filipino American raciality as relationality, that is, as a relationship between Filipino and America: less a signification of racial otherness than a declaration of proximity from humanity; not interested in the singularity of racial subjectivity but concerned with the transformation between the racial object to the racial subject. The tensions that Hagedorn describes in the interview—between the metaphor and its transmission—reignite the quandaries described at the beginning of this chapter.

Insofar as *Dogeaters* centers less on the recognition of the Filipino in the United States than with the inextricability between the Philippines and the United States in the postcolonial era, it pays assiduous attention to the gendered and sexualized violence of such postcoloniality needed for managing the terms of Filipino subjectivity. The novel marked a literary departure from earlier texts by Filipino American writers Jose Garcia Villa, Carlos Bulosan, Bienvenido Santos, and N. V. M. Gonzalez, replacing what Denise Cruz has described as a male diasporic longing for homeland born of experiences of racist exclusion with a distinctly postmodern critique.[49] By 1990 the novel's significance was made more palpable by the long-term effects of the Hart-Celler Act. Yet, while it is often heralded as an important Filipino American text, it offers a rendition of Filipino America lacking a proper Filipino American subject. *Dogeaters* addresses not only the distinctiveness of a post-1965 diaspora but especially the terms by which that diaspora is mediated and complicated by the authoritarian violences of the "homeland" as well as the instantiations of US neocolonialism that work in tandem with such violences.

The novel begins in 1956, careens through time and place, and follows Rio as she navigates family drama, history, and the chaos of Manila during the martial law period. At the beginning of the novel Jean Mallat's description of the archipelago's inhabitants presents the omniscient third-person narrative of the anthropologist as an authorial voice. On the following page Rio wields the first-person voice to assume control of the narrative. Yet the narrative periodically leaves Rio to follow an array of other characters—nightclub owners, television show hosts, gossip columnists, the president and the first lady—and finally Joey Sands, who disrupts Rio's coming-of-age story to tell an alternative story of life in Manila's underground. The novel moves across narrative voice, from Rio's and Joey's first-person narrations to a panoptic gossip columnist to William McKinley's benevolent assimilationist proclamations.

Hagedorn frames narrative voice as a site of struggle between the authority of colonial objectivity and the multiplicity of Filipino subjectivities, where the latter makes legible the myriad experiences of life under martial law. Even as Rio and Joey become the clear protagonists of the novel, they disrupt the solidity of the singular account of the Filipino experience by interjecting their stories into each other's narratives. The action moves from Rio's perspective to Joey's story; by novel's end Pucha interjects to declare that her cousin got the story all wrong, and the reader is left to doubt the veracity of Rio's story. The novel's progression through pastiche—a complex array of forms, as Lisa Lowe has written—destabilizes the sanctity of the liberal citizen-subject to allow a multiplicity of voices to claim authority over the narrative.[50] Against the conventional immigrant narrative, wherein the immigrant leaves behind her ethnic and racial difference to become a fully incorporated American citizen, the novel contests the extent to which such a narrative is available to or possible for those for whom difference is made insurmountable.[51] Rio never coheres as a proper immigrant subject in this way, as the solidity of her subjectivity is consistently undone by the persistent and palpable memories of a time and place that she has yet to leave. These memories of Manila render indistinct the historical bounds that demarcate the past from the present in order to invoke other subjectivities that trouble the coherence of Filipino America.

Similarly, Joey consistently troubles the solidity of the Filipino American subject. As his story interrupts Rio's authorial voice, he operates as a spectral presence, the figure made possible by US colonial war who is consistently absented from legibility within the political and discursive spaces of both Philippine society and diasporic Filipino America. As the child of a Filipina sex worker and a Black American soldier, Joey brings into focus the legacies of the Pacific Theater, which brought Manila to the center of a global imperial war. Yet, unlike the ways that Imelda Marcos's song recalls the Pacific Theater as a place of overlapping empires, Joey calls for the ways that the war established new sexual economies in and around US military bases and produced new figurations of race, gender, and sexuality that are rendered in excess of both the nation and the transnational discourses of belonging.[52] Where Joey is desired by mostly foreign patrons in the outskirts of Manila's high society, under martial law his queer Black nonproductivity renders him illegible within the figurations of proper national subjectivity. A Filipino American in its most literal sense, yet unable to subscribe to the privileges of US multicultural citizenship, Joey is also elided by the strictures of post-1965 US diasporic cultural belonging. He illustrates the shape of cold war modernity, bringing into focus the intersection of national sovereignty and postindependence US neocolonialism. By the end of the novel Joey's disappearance from the narrative into the jungle to join a guerilla revolt simultaneously leaves Rio as the remaining narrative voice. This is an alternative rendering of revolution that finds affinity with Reyes's photograph of Ocariza, Burias, and the People Power movement. In both instances the texts refuse to identify the proper subject of revolution, opting instead for an articulation of anticolonial and antiauthoritarian resistance that is both transhistorical and transpacific.

In the end the novel consistently destabilizes Filipino American subjectivity by decentering a Filipino relationship to the United States that is based squarely on a migrant arrival to the colonial metropole and instead rearticulating the United States as a set of political circumstances that functions in myriad ways. Here, Filipino America is no given; rather, it circulates throughout the novel as a presence that challenges the utility of modern subjectivity for advancing the nationalisms that claim it. It functions as a specter of coloniality that materializes into other forms. Hagedorn's Filipino America interrogates the ways that social formations form within and emerge from the dialectical relationship between Philippine postcoloniality and US empire. To this extent, *Dogeaters* unfurls the problem of Filipino American subjectivity. Even as readers usurp the novel as a story *about* Filipino America, its keenness lies in its rejection of the coherency of Filipino America as such. The novel exposes Filipino America as a composite of histories and governmentalities that invest in the comprehension and representation of a particular kind of Filipino American experience. Put differently, the novel speaks to both the limitations of the name Filipino America as the locus of postcolonial recognition and the possibilities that emerge when one decenters Filipino America as a center of political emergence.

Together, these three texts illustrate the tensions, contradictions, and overlappings that constitute Filipino America. This is not an attempt to refuse the materiality of Filipino American social formations nor the specificities of diasporic migration or US racialization. Instead, to apprehend subjectivity is to interrogate the legacies of coloniality for organizing the discourses with which we locate and conceive of ourselves in and of the world. In challenging a politics of recognition and legibility, the transpacific reaches for other coalitions and collectivities.

NOTES

1. Lily Wong, Christopher B. Patterson, and Chien-ting Lin, introduction herein.

2. Caroline Hau, "Privileging Roots and Routes: Filipino Intellectuals and the Contest over Epistemic Power and Authority," *Philippine Studies: Historical and Ethnographical Viewpoints* 62, no. 1 (2014): 51. Also see Reynaldo Ileto, "Orientalism and the Study of Philippine Politics," *Philippine Political Science Journal* 22, no. 45 (2001).

3. Martin F. Manalansan IV and Augusto F. Espiritu, "The Field: Dialogues, Visions, Tensions, and Aspirations," in *Filipino Studies: Palimpsests of Nation and Diaspora*, ed. by Martin F. Manalansan IV and Augusto F. Espiritu (New York: New York University Press, 2016), 8.

4. Denise Cruz, *Transpacific Femininities: The Making of the Modern Filipina* (Durham, NC: Duke University Press, 2012), 6.

5. Cruz, 7–8.

6. J. Francisco Benitez and Laurie Sears, "The Passionate Attachments to Area Studies and Asian American Studies: Subjectivity and Diaspora in the Transpacific," in *Transpacific Studies: Framing an Emerging Field*, ed. Janet Hoskins and Viet Thanh Nguyen (Honolulu: University of Hawaii Press, 2014), 155.

7. Wong, Patterson, and Lin, introduction herein.

8. See Mark John Sanchez, "The Philippines Information Bulletin and the Transnational Anti-Marcos Press," in *Filipino American Transnational Activism*, ed. Robyn Magalit Rodriguez (Leiden: Brill, 2019); Karen Buenavista Hanna, "'Centerwomen' and the 'Fourth Shift': Hidden Figures of Transnational Filipino Activism in Los Angeles, 1972–1992," in *Filipino American Transnational Activism*, ed. Robyn Magalit Rodriguez

(Leiden: Brill, 2019); and Joy Sales, "#NeverAgaintoMartialLaw: Transnational Filipino American Activism in the Shadow of Marcos and Age of Duterte," *Amerasia* 45 (2019).

9. See works by Oscar Campomanes and Neferti Tadiar.

10. Lisa Yoneyama, *Cold War Ruins: Transpacific Critique of American Justice and Japanese War Crimes* (Durham, NC: Duke University Press, 2016).

11. In Lisa Lowe's interview of Angela Davis, Davis discusses "women of color formations" as having the potential to "[base] the identity on politics rather than the politics on identity." See Lowe, *The Politics of Culture in the Shadow of Capital*, ed. Lisa Lowe and David Lloyd (Durham, NC: Duke University Press), 318.

12. See Yến Lê Espiritu, "Militarized Refuge(es)," in *Body Counts: The Vietnam War and Militarized Refugees* (Berkeley: University of California Press, 2014).

13. Catherine Ceniza Choy and Judy Tzu-Chun Wu, "Gendering the Trans-Pacific World," in *Gendering the Transpacific World*, ed. Catherine Ceniza Choy and Judy Tzu-Chun Wu (Leiden: Brill, 2017), 3–4.

14. Janet Hoskins and Viet Thanh Nguyen, "Introduction: Critical Perspectives on an Emerging Field," in *Transpacific Studies: Framing an Emerging Field*, ed. Janet Hoskins and Viet Thanh Nguyen (Honolulu: University of Hawai'i Press, 2014), 16–24.

15. Hoskins and Nguyen, 16–24.

16. Wong, Patterson, and Lin, introduction herein, 5.

17. Naoki Sakai and Hyon Joo Yoo, "Introduction: The Trans-Pacific Imagination," in *The Trans-Pacific Imagination: Rethinking Boundary, Culture, and Society*, ed. Naoki Sakai and Hyon Joo Yoo (Hackensack, NJ: World Scientific, 2012), 26.

18. Walter Mignolo's theorization of coloniality and the making of Latin America is helpful here. It calls attention to the ways that knowledge itself is mediated by a location, language, and history. Theorizing on the colonial formations of the "idea of 'Latin America,'" Mignolo writes that the "geo-politics of knowledge (the local historical grounding of knowledge) goes hand in hand with the body politics of knowledge (i.e., the personal and collective biographical grounding of understanding)." See Mignolo, *The Idea of Latin America* (Malden, MA: Blackwell, 2005), 10.

19. Chien-ting Lin, "Re-Signifying 'Asia' in the Transnational Turn of Asian/American Studies," *Review of International American Studies* 9, no. 2 (2016): 33.

20. Reynaldo Ileto, "'The Unfinished Revolution' in Philippine Political Discourse," *Southeast Asian Studies* 31, no. 1 (1993): 72.

21. Sakai and Yoo, "Introduction," 33.

22. Neferti Tadiar's conceptualization of "life-times" is particularly incisive here. Tadiar writes that troubling dominant discourses of humanity, such as a human rights discourse, is to wrestle "with how the increasingly prevalent deployment of a broader logic of political emancipation to address conditions of disposable life as a matter of expulsion from a juridical (i.e., state-defined and protected legal) humanity may occlude and abet, by naturalizing, the violence of other dominant forms of humanization

in the realm of everyday material social life." See Tadiar, "Life-Times of Becoming Human," *Occasion: Interdisciplinary Studies in the Humanities* 3 (2012): 5.

23. Lisa Lowe, "The Trans-Pacific Migrant and Area Studies" and "Introduction: The Trans-Pacific Imagination," both in *The Trans-Pacific Imagination: Rethinking Boundary, Culture, and Society*, ed. Naoki Sakai and Hyon Joo Yoo (Hackensack, NJ: World Scientific, 2012), 62.

24. See Jodi Melamed, *Represent and Destroy: Rationalizing Violence in the New Racial Capitalism* (Minneapolis: University of Minnesota Press, 2011).

25. See Yến Lê Espiritu, *Body Counts: The Vietnam War and Militarized Refugees* (Berkeley: University of California Press, 2014).

26. Yoneyama writes that "the representation of Japanese women as victims of the male-dominant military state emerged as Washington policymakers anticipated Japan's near defeat. The prewar to postwar transformation of Japanese nationhood was gendered in part because of the need to deploy women as differentiated from Japanese men, who were singularly made to bear the burden of evil [. . .] 'Japanese women' were discursively constituted as passive victims of male-dominant militarism and the devastations of war who were liberated as a result of the nation's defeat and the postwar occupation" ("Liberation Under Siege: U.S. Military Occupation and Japanese Women's Enfranchisement," *American Quarterly* 57, no. 3 [2005]: 892).

27. Ken Kelley and Phil Bronstein, "Playboy Interview: Imelda and Ferdinand Marcos," *Playboy*, August 1987.

28. Find a recording of "God Bless America," at the Library of Congress, https://www.loc.gov/item/ihas.200000007/, accessed December 4, 2018.

29. See Benedict Anderson, "Cacique Democracy in the Philippines: Origins and Dreams," *New Left Review* 169 (1988): 13; and Sakai and Yoo, "Introduction," 9.

30. Of Marcos's decision to send Philippine troops to Vietnam, Simeon Man writes :"In this context, nothing less than Filipino manhood was on the line" (114). Simeon Man, *Soldiering through Empire: Race and the Making of the Decolonizing Pacific* (Oakland: University of California Press, 2018).

31. Leo Ching, "'Give Me Japan and Nothing Else!': Postcoloniality, Identity, and the Traces of Colonialism," *South Atlantic Quarterly* 99, no. 4 (2000): 766.

32. The photograph can be viewed here: https://www.officialgazette.gov.ph/2015/02/25/english-speech-of-president-aquino-at-the-29th-anniversary-of-edsa-revolution/.

33. Simone Orendain, "Philippine Nuns, Priests Say Role in Revolution Affected Their Faith," Global Sisters Report, http://www.globalsistersreport.org/news/spirituality/philippine-nuns-priests-say-role-revolution-affected-their-faith-37656.

34. Aquino's speech addressed the difficulties that continue to plague the nation and its democracy, in particular the conflict in Mindanao.

35. Gina Apostol, "Speaking in Fascism's Tongues," *New York Times*, May 19, 2017.

36. Albert F. Celoza, *Ferdinand Marcos and the Philippines: The Political Economy of Authoritarianism* (Westport, CT: Praeger, 1997): 78–79.

37. Vernadette Gonzalez, "Military Bases, 'Royalty Trips,' and Imperial Modernities: Gendered and Racialized Labor in the Postcolonial Philippines," *Frontiers: A Journal of Women's Studies* 28, vol. 3 (2007): 32.

38. See Tadiar's discussion of the role of sorrow in Neferti Tadiar, *Things Fall Away: Philippine Historical Experience and the Makings of Globalization* (Durham, NC: Duke University Press, 2009).

39. Reynaldo Ileto, *Pasyon and Revolution: Popular Movements in the Philippines* (Quezon City: Ateneo de Manila University Press, 1997), 12.

40. This act of faith lives between the theological and the humanist, where the Marcos regime relied upon conceptualizations of its power as the primordial expression of man's dominance over nature. See Sylvia Wynter, "Unsettling the Coloniality of Being/Power/Truth/Freedom: Towards the Human, After Man, Its Overrepresentation—An Argument," *New Centennial Review* 3, no. 3 (2003): 275.

41. Dierdre de la Cruz's theorization of the iconicity and significance of the Marian figure within Philippine popular movements is noteworthy here. See Cruz, *Mother Figured: Marian Apparitions and the Making of a Filipino Universal* (Chicago: University of Chicago Press, 2015).

42. Tadiar, *Things Fall Away*, 358.

43. Ileto, "The Unfinished Revolution."

44. E. San Juan Jr., "In Search of Filipino Writing: Reclaiming Whose 'America?,'" in *The Ethnic Canon: Histories, Institutions, and Interventions*, ed. David Palumbo-Liu (Minneapolis: University of Minnesota Press, 1995).

45. Ameena Meer, "Jessica Hagedorn by Ameena Meer," *BOMB Magazine*, January 1, 1991, https://bombmagazine.org/articles/1991/01/01/jessica-hagedorn/.

46. See Lucy Mae San Pablo Burns's discussion of the St. Louis World's Fair in Burns, *Puro Arte: Filipinos on the Stages of Empire* (New York: New York University Press, 2013), 25–29.

47. See Nerissa Balce's study of Dean Worcester as "vampire" in Balce, *Body Parts of Empire: Visual Abjection, Filipino Images, and the American Archive* (Ann Arbor: University of Michigan Press, 2016), 152–81.

48. The photograph, titled *Dean Conant Worcester*, is held at the University of Michigan Museum of Anthropology, https://webapps.lsa.umich.edu/umma/exhibits/Worcester%202012/biography.html.

49. Cruz, *Transpacific Femininities*.

50. Lisa Lowe, *Immigrant Acts: On Asian American Cultural Politics* (Durham, NC: Duke University Press, 1996).

51. Against the totalizing conceptualizations of Asian American raciality that are

bound by the conventional immigrant narrative, Lisa Lowe theorizes "heterogeneity" as the "existence of differences and differential relationships within a bounded category" (Lowe, *Immigrant Acts: On Asian American Cultural Politics* [Durham, NC: Duke University Press, 1996], 67).

52. Instructive here is Martin Joseph Ponce's reading of *Dogeaters* in his *Beyond the Nation: Diasporic Filipino Literature and Queer Reading* (New York: New York University Press, 2012).

5 TRANSPACIFIC ARCHIPELAGIC POETICS

Connecting Antibase Activism in Okinawa with Military Buildup Protests in Guåhan

EVYN LÊ ESPIRITU GANDHI

On September 4, 1995, three US servicemen stationed at Camp Hasan in Okinawa raped a twelve-year-old Okinawan girl, sparking a mass mobilization of Okinawan antibase activism. Okinawan women—the spiritual leaders of the community, as expressed in the *unai* belief system—led the fight, critiquing the gendered violence perpetuated by US militarism throughout the Ryukyu archipelago.[1] Such mobilization was but the culmination of a much longer history of Okinawan antibase protests, which originated in 1945, following the construction of Kadena Air Base during the US occupation of Okinawa, and extended through the 1970s, when disaffected Vietnam War soldiers stationed in Okinawa, particularly Black soldiers who faced racism in the military, joined the struggle.[2] Eleven years later, in 2006, Okinawan antibase activists won a significant concession when the United States and Japan signed a bilateral agreement to move US Marine Corps Air Station Futenma from the densely populated city of Ginowan to the coastal district of Henoko and transfer eight thousand marines and their dependents from Okinawa to the US unincorporated territory of Guåhan (Guam).[3]

At first glance this bilateral agreement, entitled "US-Japan Roadmap for Realignment Implementation," seems to have satisfied the multiple stakeholders involved: the United States maintained its military presence in the so-called Asian Pacific, Japan appeased some of its Okinawan citizens' demands, and Guåhan's leaders ostensibly welcomed the influx of marines. In a January 2010 white paper entitled "An Opportunity that Benefits Us All: A Straightforward, Descriptive Paper on Why We Need the Military

Buildup," for example, the Guam Chamber of Commerce argued that the military buildup would increase revenue, generate business and employment opportunities, and expand the island's tourism industry.[4] Then-Democratic congresswoman Madeleine Bordallo added that Guåhan's citizens supported the buildup not only for "economic reasons," but because they also — "more than any other American community" — appreciate their "liberation" and "freedom" and "the sacrifices it will take to preserve that freedom for generations to come."[5] Citing the deep-seated feelings of gratitude felt by many CHamorus toward the US military for liberating Guåhan from Japanese occupation during World War II, Bordallo's statement suggests that Guamanians unequivocally embrace Guåhan's role in the United States' postwar securitization apparatus.[6]

In reality, many Guamanians — particularly CHamoru Indigenous-rights activists — have expressed concern that such a large influx of US marines from Okinawa would accelerate CHamoru land dispossession, damage Guåhan's already fragile ecologies, and increase the gendered violence propagated by the military's presence on the island.[7] In other words, they critique what historian Juliet Nebolon has termed "settler militarism" and I-Kiribati–African American scholar Teresia Teaiwa has called "militourism": the settler-imperial expansion of the US military across Indigenous Pacific islands that in turn facilitates increased settler tourism.[8] Given these Indigenous critiques, I propose that the 2006 bilateral agreement should instead be read through a *transpacific archipelagic framework*. By undisciplining and intimating transpacific and archipelagic perspectives, such a framework both illuminates and calls forth what literary scholar Chadwick Allen terms "trans-Indigenous" relationalities, in order to refute the ways in which the livelihoods of colonized Asian and Pacific Island peoples have been pitted against one another to further Japanese and US interests in the wake of World War II.[9]

An undisciplined transpacific framework centers rather than elides Okinawa's and Guåhan's interconnected histories of Japanese and US imperialism, settler colonialism, and military occupation. Here I invoke Lisa Yoneyama's definition of the transpacific as a "critical methodology" with a particular "decolonial genealogy" — one spanning the geographies of Asia, the Americas, and the Pacific Islands and oriented toward Indigenous self-determination via a critique of both Japanese and US colonial legacies.[10] In 1609 the

Japanese domain of Satsuma invaded Okinawa as part of its larger invasion of the Ryukyu Kingdom. In 1879 Japan annexed the entire Ryukyu archipelago and established the Okinawa Prefecture in order to secure its southern borders, submitting the Ryukyu people to Japanese colonial rule. Guåhan, meanwhile, was colonized first by Spain in 1565 and then by the United States following the Spanish-American War of 1898. The United States separated Guåhan from the rest of the CHamoru-inhabited archipelago, which would become known as the Northern Mariana Islands. During World War II, both Okinawa and Guåhan were strategic sites of military violence, as the United States and Japan fought for domination over Asia and Oceania. After the war both became sites of key US military bases. Following the Organic Act of 1950, CHamorus were granted US citizenship but were denied key constitutional rights, such as the right to congressional representation or the right to vote for president.[11] As of the time of writing, the US military occupies 15 percent of the land in Okinawa and 28 percent of the land in Guåhan, extending colonial legacies into the present.[12]

Archipelagic studies, intimated with transpacific studies, further centers Okinawa-Guåhan relationalities. Yoneyama critiques transpacific studies scholars who singularly focus on global flows between Asia and the Americas, eliding Oceania's vibrant network of political and cultural exchange.[13] This chapter, then, situates Okinawa and Guåhan not through the terms set by Japan and the United States and as articulated in the 2006 bilateral agreement, but as independent island collectives in direct relation to *each other*. An archipelagic framework emphasizes that Okinawa and Guåhan are not only a part of distinct archipelagic formations—the Ryukyus and the Marianas, respectively—but also that they can and should be considered part of a larger transpacific archipelago that spans across nation-state borders dictated by imperial powers.[14] According to Lanny Thompson, "archipe-logics" emphasize "discontinuous connections rather than physical proximity, fluid movements across porous margins rather than delimited borders, and complex spatial networks rather than the oblique horizons of landscapes—in sum, moving islands rather than fixed geographic formations."[15] With its emphasis on movement and relationality, a transpacific archipelagic framework illuminates what Tongan scholar Epeli Hauʻofa calls a "sea of islands," facilitating coalitions across seemingly disjointed struggles.[16]

Central to this transpacific archipelagic framework is the enunciation of Indigeneity. According to Māori scholar Linda Tuhiwai Smith (Ngāti Awa and Ngāti Porou), the term "Indigenous peoples" enables "the collective voices of colonized people to be expressed strategically in the international arena," such that different island communities can "come together, transcending their own colonized contexts and experiences, in order to learn, share, plan, organize and struggle collectively for self-determination on the global and local stages."[17] Indigeneity is articulated differently in Guåhan than in Okinawa: whereas CHamoru activists began to re-identify as *taotao tano* (people of the land) and use the rhetoric of Indigenous rights starting in the 1970s, Okinawan activists, following the 2007 United Nations Declaration on the Rights of Indigenous Peoples, have only recently adopted the term "Indigenous" to characterize their centuries-long struggle against Japanese colonization.[18] Despite these genealogical differences, in the contemporary period, antimilitary activists in both Okinawa and Guåhan have increasingly employed a "logics of indigeneity," critiquing the ways in which US military occupation is predicated on the settler-colonial appropriation of Indigenous lands and waters.[19]

A transpacific archipelagic framework grounded in Indigenous politics would therefore refute the 2006 bilateral agreement's assertion that a transfer of eight thousand marines from Okinawa to Guåhan presents an acceptable solution to Okinawans' antibase protests against gendered military violence. It would instead insist that in order to effectively "demilitarize the currents of empire" across Asia, Oceania, and the Americas, to quote Setsu Shigematsu and Keith L. Camacho, one must understand Okinawans' and CHamorus' struggles as intimately entangled.[20] To that end, it is constructive to highlight the aesthetic strategies used by poets Craig Santos Perez and Collier Nogues to articulate Guåhan and Okinawa and their respective decolonial struggles *in relation*. Whereas Perez's poetry centers CHamoru histories, subjectivities, and politics, Nogues's work simultaneously submerges and reveals the long history of Japanese and US imperialism, settler colonialism, and militarism in Okinawa.

This chapter reads Craig Santos Perez's *from unincorporated territory [guma']* (2014), the third installment in his ongoing series *from unincorporated territory*, alongside Collier Nogues's *The Ground I Stand On Is Not My*

Ground (2015), a book of erasure poems, in order to propose a "transpacific archipelagic poetics": a multi-sited and trans-island writing form that refutes the 2006 bilateral agreement's discursive attempt to pit decolonial struggles in Guåhan and Okinawa against each other. Transpacific archipelagic poetics reorganizes transpacific spheres of influence to facilitate trans-Indigenous coalitions, articulating political entanglements across multiple shores. In their poetry, Perez and Nogues both draw transpacific archipelagic connections between not only Guåhan and Okinawa but also with spaces across the Pacific, such as Hawaiʻi, the Marshall Islands, and Hong Kong. Both writers remix colonial and imperial archives, "critically juxtaposing" different islands of texts to illuminate archipelagic relationalities suppressed by the United States and Japan.[21] Both have engaged each other's poetry: Nogues published an academic article on *from unincorporated territory [guma']* and Perez wrote a blurb for *The Ground I Stand On Is Not My Ground*.[22] Read together, their works illuminate historical and contemporary entanglements between Okinawa and Guåhan.

Previous scholarship on Perez's poetry has largely emphasized how his work refutes colonial and imperial cartographies, instead privileging oceanic epistemologies to recenter Guåhan as a key node of transpacific encounter.[23] Hsuan Hsu, for example, argues that Perez's poetry "addresses specifically geographical problems: how to reinsert Guåhan into the map and voice its history and struggles using the colonizer's language and poetic tradition" and "how to reconnect Guåhan to the larger culture and history of Oceania which has been decimated and submerged through centuries of colonization."[24] In his first book of poetry, *from unincorporated territory [hacha]*, for example, Perez includes what he in later work calls "poemaps": aesthetic groupings of arrows, text (italicized, nonitalicized, bracketed, nonbracketed), lines (curved, straight, solid, dotted), and selectively shaded shapes.[25] One poemap, entitled "*[War: in the Pacific Ocean]*," explicitly links the 1944 US reoccupation of Guåhan to the 1945 US-initiated Battle of Okinawa during World War II via a directional arrow, exemplifying transpacific archipelagic poetics.[26] Perez's scholarly work on Pacific Island literature also enacts cartographic interventions. For example, he offers the term "terripelago" to "foreground territoriality as it conjoins land and sea, islands and continents."[27]

Less scholarly attention has been paid to the poetry of Nogues, an American poet and scholar who grew up on Kadena Air Base in Okinawa, though her work also critically engages transpacific archipelagic cartographies of militarism. For example, "The Ground I Stand On Is Not My Ground" — simultaneously an erasure poem, the title of the book, and its cover art — takes as its source material one of the roughly one hundred maps included in *Illustrations of Reports of General MacArthur Volume 1*, which Nogues found in the National Diet Library of Japan's Digital Collections. Her focus is on plate 104, frame 117, entitled "Enemy Ground Dispositions, General Pacific Area, 30 April 1945." In Nogues' rendition, both Okinawa and Guåhan haunt the image with their absent presence: Guåhan has been consciously erased, while Okinawa has been cropped out of the left side of the frame. Nogues calls attention to how the vibrant Indigenous communities of both Okinawa and Guåhan were rendered *invisible* in the Japanese and US imperial imaginaries, existing only as sites of either enemy advancement or strategic military control during the Pacific War.

Less explored are the hypertextual and intertextual dimensions of Perez's and Nogues's poetry. Notable exceptions include articles by Ann Mai Yee Jansen, who briefly addresses Perez's hypertextual usage of hashtags and URLs in an article on "affinity poetics" — poetics that facilitate cross-oceanic affinities and solidarities — and Huan He, who analyzes Perez's intertextual citation of Theresa Hak Kyun Cha's *Dictee* to posit a "transpacific networked poetics" connecting Korea and Guåhan.[28] Jansen's and He's works posit that hypertextuality and intertextuality are key aesthetic features of what I am calling transpacific archipelagic poetics. Hypertextuality, based on the Greek root "hyper-" to mean above or beyond, resists the isolationist logic of colonial and imperial archives, opening up what Gilles Deleuze and Félix Guattari call "lines of flight" via a turn to the digital.[29] Perez's and Nogues's poetry spans the physical page and the digital web in order to encourage readers' active engagement with their transpacific archipelagic poetics across borders. Intertextuality, meanwhile, rather than pointing elsewhere to the virtual space of the web, links across and between, situating Perez's and Nogues's poetry within a specific literary and historical context. Both writers cite the modernist poet Ezra Pound to locate themselves within a particular avant-garde poetic tradition while also critiquing the ways in which that tradition has been intimately shaped by the racial and gendered history of the Pacific War.[30]

It is important to note that transpacific archipelagic poetics, as a form of anti-imperial and anticolonial praxis, is not isolated to published poetry, but rather has been and continues to be practiced in activist spaces not traditionally understood as "poetic." As scholar-activists such as LisaLinda Natividad, Gwyn Kirk, Camacho, Iwao Uenunten, and Tiara Na'puti have documented, "alliances between Chamorro groups, Okinawan anti-bases activists, and partner organizations in mainland Japan have strengthened opposition to military base expansion in all three places, as organizers stand together in solidarity trying to stop the military from pitting one community against another."[31] Importantly, such efforts also often embody a feminist framework for analyzing gendered military violence. In September 2009, for example, the University of Guam hosted the Seventh International Women's Network Against Militarism conference, where scholars and activists from Okinawa, Japan, the continental United States, the Commonwealth of the Northern Mariana Islands, Australia, the Republic of Belau (Palau), Hawai'i, the Marshall Islands, the Philippines, Puerto Rico, and South Korea shared their work documenting the effects of US bases and military operations on their communities.[32] In June 2017 the organization's ninth conference was hosted in Okinawa. Conference participants documented gendered military violence, forwarded Indigenous-centered analyses, and renewed their insistence that "countries and warring parties utilize conflict mediation and peace negotiations rooted in women-centered and life-affirming principles and visions of justice, genuine security, and sustainability of all life on our planet."[33] Although such political mobilizations exemplify transpacific archipelagic poetics in a different form, they embody many of the aesthetic practices discussed here, such as the hypertextual utilization of Internet websites to increase visibility and facilitate coalition-building as well as the intertextual referencing of shared legacies of World War II. Indeed, this chapter seeks to engage with and contribute to ongoing activist efforts to curb gendered military violence across Asia and Oceania via an analysis of the transpacific archipelagic aesthetics mobilized by Perez and Nogues. As activism inspires poetry, so too does poetry broaden the horizons of what activists can imagine as politically possible.

This chapter ends with a turn to a more recent moment. In September 2019, military buildup projects in Guåhan were halted to divert funding toward the construction of former president Donald Trump's border wall along the southern US border. Such events suggest the need to expand our transpacific archipelagic framework to include the US-Mexico borderlands. Although these borderlands do not constitute a Pacific island in the literal sense, they adjoin the Pacific Ocean. Building on scholarship that has put transpacific studies in conversation with hemispheric studies, I posit that a transpacific archipelagic framework is useful for understanding not only Okinawa and Guåhan but also the US-Mexico borderlands in relation.[34] Just as the demilitarization of Okinawa should not come at the expense of Guåhan, so too should the halt in military buildup in Guåhan not come at the expense of Indigenous nations, whose traditional homelands span the southern US border, or of Central American and South American refugees, who cross such a border fleeing the legacies of US military intervention. Instead, a decolonial politics rooted in transpacific archipelagic poetics critiques what elsewhere I have termed the "transpacific settler-colonial condition," facilitating trans-Indigenous solidarity.[35]

TRANSPACIFIC ARCHIPELAGIC POETICS

HYPERTEXTUALITY

For Craig Santos Perez, a CHamoru poet born in Guåhan and currently living and teaching in the diaspora, "home is an archipelago."[36] In his essay "Guam and Archipelagic American Studies," Perez argues that mapping Guåhan via "complex archipelagic logic" reveals Guåhan to be "more than just a footnote" to studies of US military empire; instead it is a "central node through which to analyze, understand, and critique" US imperial expansion across Asia and Oceania.[37] Perez's methodology for writing *from unincorporated territory [guma']* exemplifies transpacific archipelagic poetics: "I imagine the blank page as an excerpted ocean filled with vast currents, islands of voices, and profound depths. I imagine the poem forming as a map of this excerpted ocean, tracing the topographies of story, memory, genealogy, and culture."[38] One key feature of transpacific archipelagic poetics is hypertextuality: a turn to the digital that renders legible interconnected Indigenous critiques of US militarization across Guåhan and Okinawa.

from unincorporated territory [guma'] is archipelagic in its very organization. Seven poems are interwoven across four sections (or, rather, four "islands"), emerging and submerging in reoccurring segments to form the infrastructure of the book's *guma'*, meaning "house," "home," or "refuge." According to Erin Suzuki, "*[guma']*'s focus on tools, structure, and construction" not only critiques the "cultural and environmental destruction caused by more than three centuries of colonialism," but it also "emphasizes how language and literature," as well as the Internet, "operate as tools that can be used to help rebuild and reconstruct a sense of home '*from*' which Chamorro histories and culture can continue to unfold into the future."[39] The seventh poem, "*ginen* fatal impact statements," most explicitly links Guåhan to Okinawa via the aesthetic practice of hypertextuality. This poem appears six times: twice in each of the first three sections of *from unincorporated territory [guma']*. Like the other poems in Perez's *from unincorporated territory* series, "*ginen* fatal impact statements" begins with the preposition "from," here translated into the CHamoru language and connoting the poem's part of a larger shifting, emergent whole: one island in a larger archipelago of discourse about Guåhan specifically and Oceania more broadly. Like other poems, it is archipelagic in its use of archives, selectively remixing a source text in order to forward a decolonial perspective. In this case the source text consists of the nearly ten thousand public comments submitted in response to the Draft Environmental Impact Statement (DEIS) the US Navy released on November 20, 2009, detailing the ecological effects of the proposed transfer of the eight thousand marines and their dependents from Okinawa to Guåhan. The poem's title asserts that the consequences of military buildup in Guåhan are not only "environmental," but also "fatal," impacting not only the island's ecology but the livelihood of the CHamoru people.

"*ginen* fatal impact statements" bridges the physical and the digital in order to broaden the realm of political engagement spatially, temporally, and affectively, to make way for the enunciation of Indigenous critique. In response to a metaquestion posed in the third segment of "*ginen* fatal impact statements" — "Craig, Is this an experimental translation project?" — Perez self-reflexively explains his methodology in the poem itself: he read the DEIS public comments, which can be found in volume 10 of the Final Environmental Impact Statement (FEIS); posted selections of the DEIS public comments to his Facebook page as status updates; tracked Facebook comments posted in response to these status updates; and then reconfigured this new source material into the resulting poem.[40] In the poem, Facebook comments are typographically distinguished from the original DEIS public comments via indentation, italics, and a dash:

DEIS Public Comment : "I cannot sit back any longer. We, as a whole, need to stop being shoved around, and push back"

— The revolution will not be on Facebook[41]

In both form and content the poem graphically calls attention to its hyper-textual nature, charting transpacific archipelagic connections between the original FEIS and online activist engagement, between the physical page of the poem and the digital "page" of Perez's Facebook, between Okinawa and Guåhan. Neither can exist in isolation; both must be activated in relation for maximum revolutionary potential. Facebook helps to circulate the original FEIS and Indigenous pushback, even as Facebook's CEO Mark Zuckerberg works to dispossess Kanaka Maoli in Hawai'i.[42] A hypertextual aesthetics negotiates these complicated networks of power and resistance.

In "*ginen* fatal impact statements," hypertextuality also facilitates an archi-pelago of affects: the bringing together of a range of emotional responses to the military buildup via the juxtaposition of original DEIS public comments with Perez's Facebook responses. In the poem, the sarcastic—"Buenas. First off, thank you for the false sense of participation created by the comment period. The opportunity to vent, while completely meaningless, is at least very cathartic"—is juxtaposed with the earnest—"I am a 9-year-old girl and I don't want you to do this because I love dolphins and turtles and want them to be here when I have my own kids."[43] The conflicted—"I don't think I am allowed to say that I'm against the military buildup because both of my parents are for the build up [*sic*], and my dad is in the Air Force"—is juxtaposed with the resistant—"Lao pa'go na ha'ane nisisita ta fanachu put i tano'ta, para i famagu'on-ta (Now is the time to stand up for our land for the future of our children)."[44] This complex array of affective responses to the proposed military buildup reflects CHamorus' vexed relationship with the US military, which "liberated" them from Japanese occupation during World War II but also proceeded to appropriate their lands and waters.

Moreover, "*ginen* fatal impact statements" not only voices critiques of the original DEIS public comment format—wherein respondents were given only ninety days to read and respond to the original eleven-thousand-page DEIS, each comment was restricted to 250 characters, and all the comments were then buried in volume 10 of the equally long FEIS—but also enacts a solution, extending the conversation around the proposed military buildup into the digital sphere, past the original ninety-day comment period, and beyond the confines of a bureaucratically mediated response.[45] By transposing the original comments onto first Facebook and then into *from unincorporated territory [guma']*, Perez grants the comments an afterlife of greater visibility and engagement.[46] Facebook users who had not viewed the FEIS were able to read and respond to the DEIS public comments via Perez's posts. The publication of "*ginen* fatal impact statements" in *from unincorporated territory [guma']* archives this interaction, inviting archipelagic repetitions of this hypertextual methodology in other contexts. According to Suzuki, the poem "balances the immediacy of online activism with the longevity of print," constructing a "double archive" that works to "amplify and publicize the concerns about and opposition to the buildup that would otherwise remain effectively buried in a relatively obscure government document that runs into the thousands of pages."[47] In her article on Perez's hypertextual aesthetic practices, Nogues notes that "*ginen* fatal impact statements" "blurs the border between the virtual and physical from both directions, becoming a space that gathers far-flung stakeholders who already consider themselves part of an effective real-world political community, and that also gathers new potential stakeholders, inviting them to join that offline community."[48] Indeed, it is notable that two of the comments that Perez chooses to highlight name Okinawa explicitly, and two others suggest that gendered military violence, which precipitated the protests in Okinawa in the first place, would now increase in Guåhan.[49] In sum, in "*ginen* fatal impact statements," hypertextuality is a key formal strategy for illuminating transpacific archipelagic linkages between the military buildup in Guåhan and antibase activism in Okinawa.

Collier Nogues's four-part poem "Security," featured in her book *The Ground I Stand On Is Not My Ground*, also utilizes hypertextuality to forward a transpacific archipelagic poetics. The book consists of erasure poems of, from, and about Okinawa. In erasure poetry, the poet takes an existing text and erases, blacks out, or otherwise obscures a large portion of the source text to create a wholly new poem from the remnants. Erasure poems "may be used as a means of collaboration, creating a new text from an old one and thereby starting a dialogue between the two, or as a means of confrontation, a challenge to a pre-existing text."[50] According to Nogues, who grew up on Kadena Air Base in Okinawa, the originating question for this project was "How could my mom, just after a divorce, see a safe refuge for the two of us on a nuclear-warhead-storing American military base on a colonized island halfway across the world from our home in Texas?"[51] To answer this question, *The Ground I Stand On Is Not My Ground* selectively erases an imperial archive of texts from the early nineteenth century to the present: Japanese and US military documents, travelogs, political treatises, ethnographic essays, and government memorandums. These texts in turn erased the Indigenous people, land, and culture of Okinawa in their effort to reformulate the island and the larger Ryukyu archipelago as a space of first Japanese and then US securitization before, during, and after the Pacific War. Nogues explains: "I wanted to make the lofty, war-mongering, decision-making texts witness back to themselves about the pain and damage they had helped cause. . . . I wanted to fracture [history]."[52] Similarly, in his blurb for the book, Perez writes that Nogues's poems "express a desire to erase violence," disassembling "the official discourse of empire to articulate a dream for an island of peace."[53] To erase, in this project, is to both call attention to the founding violence of Indigenous erasure as well as refute the imperial archive's totalizing power over representation. Nogues selectively drowns imperial texts in order to make visible a new transpacific archipelago of poetic juxtapositions in the wake of militarization.

"Security" erases an April 1996 congressional transcript of a House subcommittee hearing on Asia and the Pacific entitled "Security in Northeast Asia: From Okinawa to the DMZ." Coinciding with Pres. Bill Clinton's diplomatic visit to Japan and Korea, the hearing alludes to, but never explicitly names, the 1995 rape of the twelve-year-old Okinawan girl that opened this chapter. A QR code included on the poem's printed page directs the reader to an accompanying website for *The Ground I Stand On Is Not My Ground*, where the source material for the erasure poems can be accessed by moving one's "finger (on a touchscreen device) or a mouse (on a conventional computer) from line to line of the poem" in order to make the erased lines of the source text "reappear, then fade out again."[54] Nogues's hypertextual aesthetics thus extend across both the poetry book and virtual website, necessitating a transpacific archipelagic reading practice that holds both the physical and the digital within the same oceanic frame.

"Security" features a first-person "individual observer" who bears witness to the intimate ravages of transpacific securitization: the weaponization of nationalism, the entrenching of borders, and the militarization of everyday civilian life.[55] Part I concludes with a stanza marking the internalization and embodiment of the imperial logics of securitization:

He approaches,

grows larger

as a man of force, his shoulder growing into a point

the arm
into a flag.[56]

What backs this individual "man of force" is an imperial army that demands the transubstantiation of his arm into "a flag," a metonym of militarized securitization. Such a flag symbolizes a threat to Indigenous Okinawan communities who dare to resist such security imperatives.

This poem excerpt is significant for not only what it depicts but also what it erases. A hypertextual turn to the book's website reveals that the congressional hearing source text from which this except emerged actually acknowledges Indigenous protests: "thousands of Okinawan residents" demonstrated against "the US military presence" following the rape of the twelve-year-old Okinawan girl, and Okinawa's governor refused "to renew land leases for US bases" and demanded "the closure of all the island's bases by the year 2015."[57] The source text further reveals that the Clinton administration's decision to "reduce or return 20 percent of the land now occupied by US forces to local landowners in Okinawa" was but a temporary "band-aid approach" that did not adequately address the community's collective anguish or acknowledge that such initiatives would be offset by increases in military personnel to other US bases in Okinawa.[58] Congress, however, ignored Okinawans' complaints, concluding that the administration's decision to keep "forces at current levels" via reshuffling was "the right thing."[59] The United States would replicate the same strategy ten years later, when a renewed call for the demilitarization of Okinawa in 2006 was answered by the proposed transfer of eight thousand marines to Guåhan.

In part IV of "Security" the narrator intones, "I will be the reminder of the war," "I will be the apology."[60] On one level these lines index for the record the antibase activism in Okinawa that would persist after the congressional hearing of 1996, led by women who refused the archival erasure of the Okinawan girl's rape and linked her rape to the larger structural rape of the island's landscape and residents resulting from the ongoing US–Japan Status of Forces Agreement. On another level these lines speak to Nogues's methodology: the "I" here comes to represent the poem itself, the transpacific archipelago of words and phrases that emerge from Nogues's erasure of the original document's textual violence. In other words, the poem itself is a "reminder" of the ongoing war against Okinawan self-determination; the poem itself demands and culls from its source text an "apology." It is only through the aesthetic practice of hypertextuality—this method of writing across the printed poetry book and the digital website—that such an apology becomes legible, broadening the space of decolonial critique.

INTERTEXTUALITY

Whereas hypertextuality points elsewhere (i.e., toward the digital), intertextuality points both inward and toward the past, situating Perez's and Nogues's poetry within a distinct avant-garde tradition that arose alongside the transpacific conflicts of World War II. Both Perez and Nogues cite Ezra Pound's World War II radio speeches, highlighting the ways in which the political fates of Guåhan and Okinawa became entangled during the Pacific War, decades prior to the 2006 US-Japan bilateral agreement. An expatriate American, Pound moved from Great Britain to Italy in 1924, where he embraced Benito Mussolini's fascist government and expressed support for Adolf Hitler. During World War II the Italian government commissioned Pound to create a series of radio broadcasts critiquing the United States, global capitalism, and the Allied Powers. In 1978 these speeches were published in an edited anthology entitled *"Ezra Pound Speaking": Radio Speeches of World War II*, which both Perez and Nogues reference, paying tribute to the avant-garde aesthetics that shape their own transpacific archipelagic poetics while simultaneously critiquing the imperial context from which this tradition emerged.

Perez has credited Pound's *The Cantos* for inspiring the "long poem" format of his *from unincorporated territory* collection.[61] However, Perez's poetry also critiques the ways in which Pound's work is "profoundly tied to Western imperialism."[62] For example, in the epigraph for the first segment of *"ginen* ta(la)ya" —which appears once in each of the four sections of *from unincorporated territory [guma']*—Perez excerpts a World War II radio speech in which Pound proposes that "PEACE in the Pacific" can be secured by "giving Guam to the Japanese in return for one set of color and sound films of the 300 best Noh dramas."[63] Although such a proposition critiques US colonialization of Guåhan by questioning whether possession over Guåhan is worth the United States' war with Japan, it does so by reducing Guåhan to "a few tons of tungsten, with possibly a few family coffins thrown in"—a dehumanizing rhetorical gesture that makes light of the very real hardships that CHamorus suffered under Japanese occupation during World War II. After December 8, 1941, when Japanese forces wrested control of Guåhan from the US Navy and renamed the island Ōmiya-Jima (Great Shrine Island), CHamorus were subjected to forced labor, food shortages, and imposed Japanese language instruction. It wasn't until July 1944 that US forces recaptured Guåhan—an event contradictorily celebrated as "Liberation Day," given the brutality of Japanese occupation, and critiqued as the start of the United States' "Reoccupation," given the postwar period's sharp military buildup on appropriated CHamoru lands.[64]

In this first segment of *"ginen* ta(la)ya," Pound's epigraph is followed by prose poetry stanzas that detail how the US military has continued to render CHamoru bodies disposable, in effect extending Pound's dehumanizing rhetoric into the militarized present. These stanzas—set apart by line breaks, italicized CHamoru prayers, and tildes resembling "an ocean current"[65]— bring together temporally disconnected experiences of militarization: Japan's bombing of Guåhan on December 8, 1941, the attack on the World Trade

Center on September 11, 2001, the first death of a CHamoru soldier in Iraq on December 8, 2003, and Perez's own experience of refusing military recruitment in high school. Taken together, these encounters of CHamoru masculinity with militarization render visible a larger "imperial archipelago."[66]

The title of the poem, *"ginen* ta(la)ya," critiques this state-sponsored premature death of CHamoru youth: *ginen*, meaning "from," reiterates the archipelagic logic of the poem's format ("from" connoting a part of a whole); "ta(la)ya" encapsulates both *tåya'*, meaning "nothing" or "none," and *talaya*, "a circular casting net used for fishing." Whereas *ginen tåya'* both exposes and critiques the error in thinking that CHamorus come "from nothing," and therefore their lives have no value, *ginen talaya* contextualizes the rhetorical force of the poem's concluding lines: "Headline: 'US Territories: / A Recruiter's Paradise: Army Goes Where Fish Are Biting' —."[67] Here CHamorus are compared to fish, seemingly voluntarily caught in the net of US military recruitment. This metaphor, however, does not account for the centuries of Spanish and US colonization of Guåhan that structure CHamorus' gratitude and sense of indebtedness to the US military, which remains one of the largest employers on the island. *Ginen talaya*, in contrast, draws attention to this history of colonization. The modern *talaya* was not traditionally used by CHamorus prior to colonization. Similarly, military recruitment is also a product of colonization. While some believe that the *talaya* was first introduced by the Spaniards, who use a similar casting net called a *tarraya*, others argue that the *talaya* was introduced to Guåhan by the Japanese.[68] This indirect reference to the Japanese occupation of Guåhan in the concluding lines of the poem circles the reader back to its opening epigraph and Pound's proposal that the United States abandon Guåhan to the Japanese. Little did Pound know how valuable Guåhan would become to the United States during the post–World War II period, as a strategic site of military buildup and recruitment. Indeed, by 1947, just one year after the Land Acquisition Act of 1946 enabled the US military to condemn private land, an estimated 1,350 CHamoru families had lost their homes.[69] Today Guåhan manifests "the highest ratio of US military spending and military hardware and land takings from indigenous US populations of any place on Earth."[70]

Like Perez's *"ginen* ta(la)ya," Nogues's two-part erasure poem "Radio Speech" cites Pound to critique the gendered militarization of everyday life.

Whereas "*ginen* ta(la)ya" grapples with the effects of militarism on CHamoru masculinity, "Radio Speech" examines the impact of war on Okinawan domesticity. The poem selectively erases two of Pound's radio speeches, "Last Ditch Democracy" from October 2, 1941, and "On Resuming" from January 29, 1942, calling attention to the military violence Okinawans suffered during World War II. The Battle of Okinawa, for example, was one of the longest and bloodiest battles of the war. On April 1, 1945, US marine and army forces attacked Okinawa, invading the Japanese home islands from the south. Over the course of three months, 149,425 Okinawans were killed, committed suicide, or went missing, resulting in an almost 50-percent decimation of the estimated prewar population of 300,000.[71]

While Perez's critique of Pound's racializing logic is enacted via epigraphic citation and juxtaposition, Nogues's is done by erasure: the selective submerging of Pound's not only racist but also sexist language. In the source text Pound uses feminizing language to ridicule the US and Great Britain's moralism during World War II, which, according to Pound, obfuscated the countries' imperialist desire to open new capitalist markets via military force. Soldiers "were being asked to go out and DIE for gold, for the monopoly of the owners and brokers."[72] In Nogues's poem "Radio Speech," Pound's feminizing language is reformulated to produce a feminist critique of military securitization—how war permeates the so-called private sphere.[73]

"Radio Speech" privileges an unnamed third-person woman's perspective on war, emphasizing how "the carnage" of military violence in Okinawa unwittingly bleeds into the domestic: "a hand/ loom" and "the diapers of the baby."[74] War, in this poem, becomes a site of feminist critique:

She never got ketched up again, she
allus WAS laggin' behind the garden
path, down under the daisies

shuttin' out news
        still trying to HEAR herself.[75]

The poem's protagonist refuses the global capitalist logic of modernization that comes with the militarizing effects of US securitization, choosing instead a temporality of "laggin' behind" in the feminized space of the garden, "shut-tin' out" imperial discourse in order to "HEAR herself" think *for herself*. This "laggin' behind" temporality in turn mirrors the ways in which war itself has lagged behind and outlasted its alleged end date, such that the "future" of peace under military occupation, described in gendered language as "a sort of half trunk full of whitewash," is nothing but war by a different name: "a program of defense, program of / offense—."[76] Indeed, following Japan's defeat in September 1945, the United States occupied Okinawa as part of its military occupation of Japan. Whereas the United States ceded sovereignty back to Japan in 1952, it retained civil administration over Okinawa until 1972. During this period the United States appropriated Okinawans' land to build thirty-two military bases, rendering Okinawa a "virtual colony."[77] According to the poem, to believe that postwar US securitization in Okinawa generates peace is "a weakness of mind in the house"—"house" referencing the intimate domestic space of gendered military violence as well as alluding to the *guma'* in Perez's title.

At the level of structure, "Radio Speech" draws transpacific archipelagic connections between Okinawa and Guåhan: while the erasure poem is set in Okinawa, the source text references "Guam." In his speech entitled "On Resuming," Pound asks sardonically, "So now we [the US] have got pushed out of Guam, and Wake, and I suppose the Philippines, and a 30 years war is in process? Is it? Is a 30 years war what the American citizen thinks will do the most good to the United States of America?"[78] Pound unwittingly critiques the transpacific archipelagic logic of US military intervention across Asia and Oceania—the ways in which military occupation of Guåhan was reproduced not only in Okinawa but also on Wake Island and in the Philippines—even as he does so in a way that demeans these islands and their inhabitants' worth in the eyes of US citizens. In contrast, transpacific archipelagic poetics draws connections between Pacific Island collectives in order to forward decolonial analyses that are attendant to the gendered legacies of World War II.

TRANSPACIFIC ARCHIPELAGIC POETICS
AND THE US-MEXICO BORDERLANDS

Under the 2006 US-Japan bilateral agreement, Okinawa's partial demilitarization came with a simultaneous military buildup in Guåhan. As Natividad and Kirk note, "The military is adept at playing off one community against another as it seeks to control land and resources to support its overriding mission: readiness and global domination."[79] In 2015, in response to successful organizing by activist groups such as Organization of People for Indigenous Rights, i nasion chamoru, We Are Guåhan, Famoksaiyan, and Our Islands Are Sacred, the originally proposed number of military personnel to be transferred was reduced to five thousand marines and thirteen hundred family members, with the move stretched out over thirteen years, starting in 2025.[80] However, as of the time of writing the buildup has yet to be completely halted. Indigenous activism continues in earnest, indexing the urgent need for a transpacific archipelagic poetics that is capable of articulating the intimate entanglements between Okinawa and Guåhan.[81] This chapter has highlighted Perez's and Nogues's usage of hypertextuality and intertextuality to enact such a transpacific archipelagic poetics.

By way of conclusion, I'd like to bring the US-Mexico borderlands into relation with the emergent transpacific archipelago forged between Okinawa and Guåhan. In September 2019 the US Department of Defense announced that eight military buildup projects in Guåhan—including a controversial $50 million live-fire training range to be built on Ritidian Beach, the site of an ancient CHamoru village and the nesting grounds for endangered green sea turtles—would be temporarily suspended in order to divert $275 million to building a $3.6 billion US-Mexico border wall.[82] In response to the news, Jeffrey Hornung, researcher at the RAND Corporation, suggested that this suspension in military funding would also likely delay plans to move the marines and their dependents from Okinawa to Guåhan.[83] But should this delay be considered a victory for antimilitary-buildup activists in Guåhan? While the CHamoru-led Indigenous-rights group Prutehi Litekyan: Save Ritidian celebrated the pause in the controversial live-fire training range's construction, they felt "conflicted about the means in which the pause was achieved because these are two instances of colonial injustice, one impacting the other."[84]

Employing a transpacific archipelagic framework reveals that the divide-and-conquer tactics structuring the 2006 US-Japan bilateral agreement continue to be at play. Just as antibase protests in Okinawa were answered with a solution that came at the expense of Indigenous CHamoru livelihoods, so too have military buildup protests in Guåhan been granted a halt in military construction at the expense of Indigenous nations living across the US-Mexico borderlands, including the Kumeyaay, Pai, Cocopah, O'odham, Yaqui, Apache, and Kickapoo.[85] Tens of thousands of Indigenous peoples, making up thirty-six federally recognized tribal nations, have had their religious ceremonies, work patterns, and everyday mobility further disrupted by the construction of a border wall on what many consider an "imaginary line"—the violent legacy of the 1848 Treaty of Guadalupe Hidalgo and 1853 Gadsden Purchase.[86] The US-Mexico borderlands thus embody another transpacific archipelagic node of trans-Indigenous struggle, connected to Guåhan and Okinawa via circuits of US military violence.

The border wall is designed to halt the northward migration of Central American and South American refugees displaced by decades of US counterinsurgency and military intervention in the Southern Hemisphere. Transpacific archipelagic poetics, therefore, should encompass not only the Pacific Islands, but also the US-Mexico borderlands that adjoin the Pacific Ocean. In his 2020 poem "Teething Borders," Perez enacts such a cartographic intervention through the poem's form and content, forging connections between the Pacific Islands, the US-Mexico borderlands, and other sites of refugee displacement. The free-flowing, single-stanza, fifty-five-line poem sutures together seemingly disjointed geographical locales with the words of a lullaby the two Pacific Islander narrators sing to soothe their teething baby daughter: "Row, row, row / your boat, gently down the stream, / merrily, merrily, merrily, merrily, life is / but a dream."[87] Here, the "stream" of this popular childhood song takes on oceanic dimensions; the "boat" navigates transpacific archipelagic connections between climate refugees displaced by rising sea levels in the Pacific, unaccompanied Central American and South American minors "spit out / from the rotting cavities of America," and Syrian refugees "swallowed by the [Mediterranean] sea's territorial mouth."[88] Oral metaphors link these sites of refugee crossing to the narrators' teething daughter: a juxtaposition manifested in the poem's title, "Teething Borders." The construction of Trump's border wall is compared to the growing of concrete teeth that rise painfully from the gums of the earth, "La Migra's incisors."[89]

Like the other poems already mentioned, "Teething Borders" exhibits intertextuality and hypertextuality. The phrase "teething borders" first appeared in an earlier poem, *"ginen understory: (first teeth),"* in *from unincorporated territory [lukao],* the fourth book in Perez's *from unincorporated territory* series:

> [you] recite the hawaiian alphabet song
> to [neni] \ \ what lullabies echo inside detention
>
> centers and traverse teething borders to soothe
> thousands of youth atop la bestia #unaccompanied / /[90]

Perez's intertextual citation of his own poem is accompanied by the hypertextual invocation of the hashtag #unaccompanied, linking this intimate family scene of Pacific Islander parents comforting a teething daughter to a larger activist movement demanding refuge for unaccompanied migrant minors. "Teething Borders" also includes an intertextual citation of feminist poet Gloria Anzaldúa via a footnote attached to the title, marking the influence of borderlands praxis on Perez's transpacific archipelagic poetics. According to Anzaldúa, the borderlands are "a vague and undetermined place created by the emotional residue of an unnatural boundary" that are "in a constant state of transition."[91] In other words, construction of the US-Mexico border wall and its militarized exclusions are not inevitable. Rejecting the title's pun, "teeming borders," the poem instead centers the domestic space of the lullaby and puts forth a humanitarian response to forced displacement: "where the only documents needed for citizenship / are dreams of sanctuary."[92]

Like Okinawa and Guåhan, the US-Mexico borderlands are a site of gendered military violence, forced displacement, and Indigenous resistance. In response to Japanese and US initiatives to pit antibase activism in Okinawa, military buildup protests in Guåhan, and anti–border wall organizing across the US-Mexico borderlands *against* one another, poets such as Perez and Nogues have enacted a transpacific archipelagic poetics that connects these disparate militarized spaces via the aesthetic practices of hypertextuality and intertextuality. Defying the divisions imposed by teething borders, their poetics instead propose a praxis of "row[ing] your boat": navigating militarized currents to call forth decolonial futures.

NOTES

1. Miyume Tanji, "The Unai Method: The Expansion of Women-Only Groups in the Community of Protest Against Violence and Militarism in Okinawa," *Intersections: Gender, History and Culture in the Asian Context* 13 (August 2006), http://intersections. anu.edu.au/issue13/tanji.html. For more on gendered military violence in the "Pacific Rim," see, for example, Cynthia Enloe, *Bananas, Beaches, and Bases: Making Feminist Sense of International Politics* (Berkeley: University of California Press, 2000), 84–91.

2. Yuichiro Onishi, *Transpacific Antiracism: Afro-Asian Solidarity in 20th Century Black America, Japan, and Okinawa* (New York: New York University Press, 2013), 138–82.

3. This chapter privileges the CHamoru name "Guåhan" but retains the American term "Guam" when referring to a governing body.

4. LisaLinda Natividad and Gwyn Kirk, "Fortress Guam: Resistance to US Military Mega-Buildup," *Asia-Pacific Journal* 8, no. 19 (May 10, 2010), https://apjjf.org/-LisaLinda -Natividad/3356/article.html.

5. Dionesis Tamondong, "Bordallo Addresses Buildup," *Pacific Daily News*, February 17, 2010, quoted in Natividad and Kirk, "Fortress Guam."

6. "Guamanian" refers to all residents of Guam regardless of race or ethnicity, while "CHamoru" (sometimes spelled "Chamorro") refers specifically to the Indigenous people of Guåhan.

7. Tiara R. Na'puti and Michael Lujan Bevacqua, "Militarization and Resistance from Guåhan: Protecting and Defending Pågat," *American Quarterly* 67, no. 3 (September 2015): 837–58; Anumita Kaur, "Prutehi Litekyan to Okinawa Governor: Not All of Guam Supports the Marines' Relocation," *Pacific Daily News*, October 8, 2019, https:// www.desmoinesregister.com/story/news/local/2019/10/08/prutehi-litekyan-guam -denny-tamaki-the-marines/3904543002/.

8. Juliet Nebolon, "'Life Given Straight from the Heart': Settler Militarism, Biopolitics, and Public Health in Hawai'i during World War II," *American Quarterly* 69, no. 1 (March 2017): 25; Teresia Teaiwa, "Reflections on Militourism, US Imperialism, and American Studies," *American Quarterly* 68, no. 3 (September 2016): 847–53.

9. Chadwick Allen, *Trans-Indigenous: Methodologies for Global Native Literary Studies* (Minneapolis: University of Minnesota Press, 2012).

10. Lisa Yoneyama, "Toward a Decolonial Genealogy of the Transpacific," *American Quarterly* 69, no. 3 (September 2017): 472.

11. In 1972 Guåhan was granted a nonvoting delegate to the US House of Representatives.

12. Okinawa Prefectural Government, Washington, DC, Office, "U.S. Military Bases Issues in Okinawa," 2016, http://dc-office.org/basedata; Jon Letman, "Proposed US Military Buildup on Guam Angers Locals Who Liken It to Colonization," August 1, 2016, *The Guardian*, https://www.theguardian.com/us-news/2016/aug/01/guam-us -military-marines-deployment.

13. Yoneyama, "Toward a Decolonial Genealogy," 471, 478.

14. For more on an archipelagic framework, see Evyn Lê Espiritu Gandhi, *Archipelago of Resettlement: Vietnamese Refugee Settlers and Decolonization across Guam and Israel-Palestine* (Oakland: University of California Press, 2022).

15. Lanny Thompson, "Heuristic Geographies: Territories and Area, Islands and Archipelagoes," in *Archipelagic American Studies*, ed. Brian Russell Roberts and Michelle Ann Stephens (Durham, NC: Duke University Press, 2017), 70.

16. Epeli Hau'ofa, "Our Sea of Islands," *Contemporary Pacific* 6, no. 1 (Spring 1994): 148–61.

17. Linda Tuhiwai Smith, *Decolonizing Methodologies: Research and Indigenous Peoples*, 2nd ed. (London: Zed, 2012), 7.

18. Joseph F. Ada, "The Quest for Commonwealth, The Quest for Change," in *Kinalamten Pulitikåt: Siñenten I Chamorro, Issues in Guam's Political Development: The Chamorro Perspective*, ed. Political Status and Education Coordinating Commission (Agaña: Political Status and Education Coordinating Commission, 1996), 200; Keith L. Camacho and Wesley Iwao Ueunten, "Determining Oceania: A Commentary on Indigenous Struggles in Guam and Okinawa," *International Journal of Okinawan Studies* 1, no. 2 (2010): 98–99.

19. Camacho and Ueunten, "Determining Oceania," 86.

20. Setsu Shigematsu and Keith L. Camacho, eds., *Militarized Currents: Toward a Decolonized Future in Asia and the Pacific* (Minneapolis: University of Minnesota Press, 2010), xli.

21. Yến Lê Espiritu, Lisa Lowe, and Lisa Yoneyama, "Transpacific Entanglements," in *Flashpoints for Asian American Studies*, ed. Cathy J. Schlund-Vials (New York: Fordham University Press, 2017), 179.

22. Collier Nogues, "'WITH [OUR] ENTIRE BREATH': The US Military Buildup on Guåhan (Guam) and Craig Santos Perez's Literature of Resistance," *Shima* 12, no. 1 (2018): 21–34.

23. Paul Lai, "Discontiguous States of America: The Paradox of Unincorporation in Craig Santos Perez's Poetics of Chamorro Guam," *Journal of Transnational American Studies* 3, no. 2 (2011): 1–28; Michael Lujan Bevacqua, "The Song Maps of Craig Santos Perez," *Transmotion* 1, no. 1 (n.d.): 84–88; John Carlos Rowe, "'Shades of Paradise': Craig Santos Perez's Transpacific Voyages," in *Archipelagic American Studies*, ed. Brian

Russell Roberts and Michelle Ann Stephens (Durham, NC: Duke University Press, 2017), 213–31; Anne Mai Yee Jansen, "Writing *toward* Action: Mapping an Affinity Poetics in Craig Santos Perez's *from unincorporated territory,*" *NAIS: Journal of the Native American and Indigenous Studies Association* 6, no. 2 (2019): 3–29; Huan He, "'On the Perpetual Motion of Search': The Transpacific Networked Poetics of Craig Santos Perez and Theresa H. K. Cha," *College Literature* 47, no. 1 (Winter 2020): 185–212; Christopher B. Patterson, *Open World Empire: Race, Erotics, and the Global Rise of Video Games* (New York: New York University Press, 2020), 241–44.

24. Hsuan L. Hsu, "Guahan (Guam), Literary Emergence, and the American Pacific in *Homebase* and *from unincorporated territory,*" *American Literary History* 24, no. 2 (Summer 2012): 296–97.

25. Craig Santos Perez, *from unincorporated territory [lukao]* (Oakland, CA: Omnidawn, 2017), 9.

26. Craig Santos Perez, *from unincorporated territory [hacha]* (Kaneohe, HI: TinFish, 2008), 29.

27. Craig Santos Perez, "Transterritorial Currents and the Imperial Terripelago," *American Quarterly* 67, no. 3 (September 2015): 620.

28. Jansen, "Writing *toward* Action," 8, 21; He, "'On the Perpetual Motion of Search.'"

29. Gilles Deleuze and Félix Guattari, *A Thousand Plateaus: Capitalism and Schizophrenia,* trans. Brian Massumi (Minneapolis: University of Minnesota Press, 1987), xvii.

30. For more on Pound and the culture of US imperialism and Cold War neocolonial militarism, see Amie Elizabeth Parry, *Interventions into Modernist Cultures: Poetry from Beyond the Empty Screen* (Durham, NC: Duke University Press, 2007), 113–47. See also Cathy Park Hong, "Delusions of Whiteness in the Avant-Garde," *ARCADE*, 2014, https://arcade.stanford.edu/content/delusions-whiteness-avant-garde.

31. Natividad and Kirk, "Fortress Guam"; Camacho and Ueunten, "Determining Oceania"; Tiara R. Na'puti, "Archipelagic Rhetoric: Remapping the Marianas and Challenging Militarization from 'A Stirring Place,'" *Communication and Critical/Cultural Studies* 16, no. 1 (2019): 17–19.

32. Natividad and Kirk, "Fortress Guam."

33. International Women's Network Against Militarism, "Statement from Okinawa Gathering, June 2017," August 22, 2017, http://iwnam.org/2017/08/22/final-statement-from-okinawa-gathering-june-2017/.

34. For scholarship linking transpacific and hemispheric studies, see, for example, Lok C. D. Siu, *Memories of a Future Home: Diasporic Citizenship of Chinese in Panama* (Stanford, CA: Stanford University Press, 2005); Jason Oliver Chang, *Chino: Anti-Chinese Racism in Mexico, 1880–1940* (Urbana: University of Illinois Press, 2017); and Quynh Nhu Le, *Unsettled Solidarities: Asian and Indigenous Cross-Representations in the Américas* (Philadelphia: Temple University Press, 2019).

35. Evyn Lê Espiritu Gandhi, "Historicizing the Transpacific Settler Colonial Condition: Asian-Indigenous Relations in Shawn Wong's *Homebase* and Viet Thanh Nguyen's *The Sympathizer*," *MELUS* 45, no. 4 (Winter 2020): 50.

36. Perez, *from unincorporated territory [lukao]*, 71.

37. Craig Santos Perez, "Guam and Archipelagic American Studies," in *Archipelagic American Studies*, ed. Brian Russell Roberts and Michelle Ann Stephens (Durham, NC: Duke University Press, 2017), 98.

38. "The Page Transformed: A Conversation with Craig Santos Perez," *Lantern Review Blog*, March 12, 2010, http://www.lanternreview.com/blog/2010/03/12/the-page-transformed-a-conversation-with-craig-santos-perez/.

39. Erin Suzuki, *Ocean Passages: Navigating Pacific Islander and Asian American Literatures* (Philadelphia: Temple University Press, 2021), 182–83.

40. Craig Santos Perez, *from unincorporated territory [guma']* (Richmond, CA: Omnidawn, 2014), 44–45.

41. Perez, 64.

42. AJ+, "Mark Zuckerberg Sued Native Hawaiians for Their Own Land," March 2, 2017, https://youtu.be/W6_RyE6XZiw.

43. Perez, *from unincorporated territory [guma']*, 25, 47.

44. Perez, 27, 66.

45. Perez, 45, 64, 66.

46. Perez, 64, 66.

47. Suzuki, *Ocean Passages*, 186.

48. Nogues, "'WITH [OUR] ENTIRE BREATH,'" 28.

49. Perez, *from unincorporated territory [guma']*, 25, 27, 64.

50. Academy of American Poets, "Erasure," accessed April 4, 2020, https://poets.org/glossary/erasure.

51. "A Conversation between Collier Nogues and Sarah Blake," *Waxwing Literary Journal* 10 (Fall 2016), http://waxwingmag.org/items/issue10/68_Nogues-Blake-A-Conversation.php#top.

52. "A Conversation between Collier Nogues and Sarah Blake."

53. Back cover blurb on Collier Nogues, *The Ground I Stand On Is Not My Ground* (New York: Drunken Boat, 2015).

54. Nogues, "About," accessed April 4, 2020, http://thegroundistandon.com/about/.

55. Nogues, *The Ground I Stand On Is Not My Ground*, 37.

56. Nogues, 36.

57. Nogues, "Security," accessed April 4, 2020, http://thegroundistandon.com/security/security-2/.

58. Nogues, "Security."

59. Nogues, "Security."

60. Nogues, *The Ground I Stand On Is Not My Ground*, 39.

61. "The Page Transformed."

62. Rowe, "'Shades of Paradise,'" 218.

63. Perez, *from unincorporated territory [guma']*, 21.

64. Cecilia C. T. Perez, "A Chamorro Re-Telling of 'Liberation,'" in *Kinalamten Pulitikåt: Siñenten I Chamorro, Issues in Guam's Political Development: The Chamorro Perspective*, ed. Political Status and Education Coordinating Commission (Agaña: Political Status and Education Coordinating Commission, 1996), 74, 76.

65. "The Page Transformed."

66. Lanny Thompson, *Imperial Archipelago: Representation and Rule in the Insular Territories under U.S. Dominion after 1898* (Honolulu: University of Hawai'i Press, 2010).

67. Perez, *from unincorporated territory [guma']*, 23.

68. Guam's Hispanic Heritage, "Word: TALAYA (casting net for fishing)," accessed March 30, 2020, https://www.facebook.com/holaguam/photos/word-talaya-casting-net-for-fishingorigin-spanish-tarraya-the-ancient-chamorros-/322436344548376/; "Ancient CHamoru Fishing Tools," accessed March 30, 2020, https://www.guampedia.com/ancient-chamorro-fishing-tools/.

69. Timothy P. Maga, "The Citizenship Movement in Guam, 1946–1950," *Pacific Historical Review* 53, no. 1 (1984): 71.

70. Catherine Lutz, "US Military Bases on Guam in a Global Perspective," *Asia-Pacific Journal* 30, no. 3 (July 26, 2010), http://apjjf.org/-Catherine-Lutz/3389/article.html.

71. Okinawa Prefecture, "The Cornerstone of Peace: Number of Names Inscribed," accessed March 17, 2020, https://www.pref.okinawa.jp/site/kodomo/heiwadanjo/heiwa/7812.html.

72. Ezra Pound, *"Ezra Pound Speaking": Radio Speeches of World War II*, ed. Leonard William Doob (Westport, CT: Greenwood, 1978), 25; see also "Radio Speech," accessed April 4, 2020, http://thegroundistandon.com/radio-speech/radio-speech-7/.

73. "2 or 20 (second series) questions with Collier Nogues," *rob mclennan's blog*, June 10, 2015, http://robmclennan.blogspot.com/2015/06/12-or-20-second-series-questions-with_10.html.

74. Nogues, *The Ground I Stand On Is Not My Ground*, 45.

75. Nogues, 46.

76. Nogues, 46.

77. Kozue Akibayashi and Suzuyo Takazato, "Okinawa: Women's Struggle for Demilitarization," in *The Bases of Empire: The Global Struggle Against U.S. Military Posts*, ed. Catherine Lutz (New York: New York University Press, 2009), 250.

78. Pound, *Ezra Pound Speaking*, 25.

79. Natividad and Kirk, "Fortress Guam."

80. Nogues, "'WITH [OUR] ENTIRE BREATH,'" 25; Gidget Fuentes, "Navy Signs Off on Plan to Move 5,000 Marines to Guam," *Marine Times*, September 5, 2015,

https://www.marinecorpstimes.com/news/your-marine-corps/2015/09/05/navy-signs
-off-on-plan-to-move-5000-marines-to-guam/.

81. Na'puti and Bevacqua, "Militarization and Resistance."

82. Bruce Lloyd and Johanna Salinas, "Ritidian: Not Here! Protesters Nix Firing
Range Plan," *Pacific Island Times*, October 2, 2017, https://www.pacificislandtimes.com
/single-post/2017/10/03/Ritidian-Not-here-Protesters-nix-firing-range-plan; "Funding
for US Border Wall Being Diverted from Guam Military Projects," *Forces*, September
29, 2019, https://www.forces.net/news/funding-us-border-wall-being-deferred-guam
-military-projects.

83. Quoted in Audrey Mcavoy, "Large Chunk of Border Wall Funding Diverted
from Tiny Guam," *Associated Press*, September 30, 2019, https://www.military.com
/daily-news/2019/09/30/large-chunk-border-wall-funding-diverted-tiny-guam.html.

84. Mcavoy, "Large Chunk."

85. Christina Leza, "How a Border Wall Would Separate Indigenous Communities,"
Pacific Standard, March 19, 2019, https://psmag.com/social-justice/a-border-wall
-would-separate-indigenous-communities.

86. Leza, "How a Border Wall."

87. Craig Santos Perez, *Habitat Threshold* (Oakland, CA: Omnidawn, 2020), 13.

88. Perez, 13.

89. Perez, 14.

90. Perez, *from unincorporated territory [lukao]*, 33.

91. Gloria Anzaldúa, "The Homeland, Aztlán," in *Borderlands/La Frontera* (San
Francisco: Aunt Lute, 1987), 25; Perez, *Habitat Threshold*, 13.

92. Perez, *Habitat Threshold*, 14.

6 FISHERS, CAPTIVES, AND STORYTELLERS IN TAIWAN'S TRANSNATIONAL FISHING INDUSTRY

TZU-HUI CELINA HUNG

REPORTING MISERY ON HIGH SEAS

Taiwan encountered two perturbing cases of violence on offshore fishing boats in the recent decade. In August 2013 six Indonesian fishermen on the *Te Hung Hsing No. 368* were charged with killing their Taiwanese captain and chief engineer; subsequent to their trials, all were sentenced to prison terms of fourteen to twenty-eight years.[1] While news reporters jumped on the deadly captain-crew altercation, the trials also galvanized scrutiny from activists and migrant communities for overlooking longtime labor abuse and for the court's inadequately translated verdict.[2] Two years later, the appalling death of Indonesian migrant fisher Supriyanto on the vessel *Fu Tzu Chun* put Taiwan's Fisheries Agency and the prosecutors of Pingtung County under domestic and international censure for their serious industry oversight, poor human-rights protocols, and haphazard community-interpreting services. Hastening their investigation to produce a perfunctory report stating that Supriyanto died from an untreated knee infection, the prosecutors disregarded evidence indicating prior physical assault and onboard medical negligence; the case was reopened a year later under public pressure and exposed many unflattering problems, particularly illegal brokerage and labor exploitation emboldened by both countries' loose regulations.[3]

These blood-stained stories were neither the first nor the last in the island country's transnational fishing industry. While leading in the world's annual saury and tuna catches, and having the largest number of deep-sea fishing vessels, for decades Taiwan has held a notorious record in its supervision of offshore hiring and other marine practices, including the use of death-wall driftnet in the 1980s; illegal, unreported, and unregulated (IUU) fishing, which led the European Commission into issuing a warning in 2015 and thereby precipitated local reforms in 2017; and, in 2018, an internationally reported incident of onboard abuse of Indonesian crewmembers outside Cape Town, South Africa.[4] In retrospect, the oceanic space on which the island's seafaring industry depends reveals telltale signs of serious material and epistemological contradictions, even as the sea has increasingly become a useful reference point in Taiwan's popular and academic discourses, especially from 2000 onward, in marking its difference from earthbound China.[5] Most evidently, despite Taiwan's growing reliance on Southeast Asian labor migrants since 1990s in a variety of industries, news of workplace violence on- and offshore repeatedly startled the Taiwanese society into uncomfortably confronting their entrenched sociolegal discrimination and ignorance when encountering foreign migrants.[6] Further, when it comes to writing seafaring traditions back into Taiwan history, the public discourse still habitually treats offshore activities in terms of economic yield and geopolitical security while occluding discussions of the sea's actual ecology and real-life shipboard communities. To borrow a phrase from Philip Steinberg, even an interested local rarely "gets wet" or ventures to learn foreign languages and customs when reading stories about migrant fisherfolk on Taiwanese boats.[7]

Ironies run deep in Taiwan's genealogy of seafaring narratives and oceanography. Although the island has long been a busy site of transpacific trade, settlement, and resource extraction—beginning when it caught the eyes of global maritime powers in the seventeenth century—its ocean-themed Sinitic-language writings did not become a noticeable presence until the 1970s, and only since 1990s have writers like Hung-chi Liao, Chin-hsia Liang, Syaman Rapongan, and Dong Nian begun to receive recognition for their stories about littoral ecology and maritime culture.[8] Moreover, while seafaring life and the dynamic between fishers from multinational backgrounds have not escaped these writers' trained eyes, neither have ocean narratives and the fisher figure gained substantial public attention, until local publishers and media coverage in the recent two decades began to take an active interest in reporting on Taiwan's neoliberal relations with the highly racialized and gendered migrants from labor-sending Southeast Asian societies.[9]

The two opening vignettes about migrant fishers highlight the convergence of these public discourses. One need only recall several landmark local publications and collaborative works about Southeast Asian migrants to see that recent news about the fishing industry—especially after the *Te Hung Hsing* tragedy transpired—has contributed to a quickly evolving constellation of multigenre stories about Taiwan's problematic involvement in the transpacific network of gendered and racialized neoliberal capitalism. These include the multilingual magazine *Four-Way Voice* (2006–16); migrant-labor documentaries and photography projects spearheaded by Taiwan International Workers Association (TIWA); *The Reporter*'s investigative reports on the structural problems of Taiwan's offshore fisheries in *Blood and Tears of Fishing Ground* (2017); and the Taiwan Literature Award for Migrants (2014–present), where migrant-fisher stories make repeated appearances.[10] However, in picturing intercommunity encounters in the seafaring space, local Sinitic-language storytellers frequently find themselves challenged by cultural-linguistic barriers, by the difficulties of accessing field sites, by unequal relations with the migrants portrayed, and by how to give voice to mobile experiences that are often ineffable and carefully withheld.

TRANSLATING SEAFARING STORIES ACROSS BARRIERS

This chapter responds to the trends and predicaments existing within transpacific studies by analyzing some recent migrant-fisher stories. It builds on the collective momentum from scholars like Lisa Lowe, Lisa Yoneyama, Janet Hoskins, Viet Nguyen, Denise Cruz, Chih-ming Wang, Christopher Patterson, Lily Wong, Shelley Fishkin, and Yuan Shu et al., among many, to decolonize the often nation- and language-based epistemological impulses within Asian studies, American studies, Asian American studies, and so forth, which, despite their intersecting thematic and methodological concerns, have been conventionally treated as disparate fields.[11] Echoing the call of this volume's editors to problematize and "undiscipline" the ways in which knowledge about the target communities and geocultural areas of these academic fields has been habitually produced and compartmentalized to serve specific imperialist agendas or superficial multiculturalist logic, I turn to an understudied Sinitic-language archive in new-millennial Taiwan to demonstrate the reflexive and "undisciplining" potential of the emerging transpacific framework, especially beyond its better-known American- and Anglophone-centered contexts.[12] Specifically, I analyze migrant-fisher narratives from Taiwan that illuminate the inter-Asia entanglement of seafaring people hailing from differently empowered maritime societies, which at least since the 1990s have based their national developments upon various versions of neoliberal capitalism and in the process have become socioeconomically and in many cases culturally codependent. Reading along with but also against these recent portrayals of multinational migrant seafarers working on Taiwanese boats, I ask how, rather than just broadening the geographic scale of inquiries without also interrogating the epistemological assumptions underlying these Sinitic-language shipboard stories, the *trans-* in transpacific studies functions more importantly as an action word and reminder to scrutinize the manners of intercommunity exchange and rupture in this crisscross seascape. In other words, through the affix trans-, this analysis will emphasize the translational bent existing within both these transpacific seafaring stories and this transpacific analytic perspective. Taiwan's new-millennial seafaring narratives offer a sorely needed testing ground for observing some of the major promises and assumptions in transpacific storytelling, not least because the underrepresented social milieu of multinational fisherfolk challenges local Taiwanese storytellers to practice cultural translation, and not solely on a narrow linguistic register. Practical and conceptual extralinguistic hurdles — like building trust and rapport with multilingual fisherfolk, navigating unspoken harborside rules, avoiding replication of mainstream media's prying eyes, and so on — make sure that these "born-translated" narratives, as Rebecca Walkowitz would call them, are rarely value free; indeed, they are unflattering reminders that Taiwan's transpacific intimacy with neighboring Asian societies is a product of the neoliberal mobilization of gendered and racialized migrant labor.[13] Picturing migrant fisherfolk culture in the context of this highly stratified transnational industry requires border-crossing translational skills, or what the editors of this volume call the "unsettling" and "reimagining" of existing "epistemic (b)orders."[14] I argue that, as such, these translational accounts concretize the transgressive feature of transpacific studies, but since they are written for Taiwan's predominantly Sinitic-language readers, they also risk instrumentalizing foreign migrant figures for tokenistic multicultural consumption by the locals.

Two notable books come to mind. One is *Broken Wings from a Faraway Shore*, published in 2019 by the Taiwan International Workers Association, the country's first nongovernment organization for immigrant and labor rights. The other is *There Is No God: Fishers, Boat Guards, and Those Women*, published in 2018, which combines written and photographic reflections by former photojournalist and news media manager Aming Lee, who lives many downcast midlife years before becoming a minor boat guard at Kaohsiung's Chien-chen Fishing Harbor. Navigating numerous representational challenges, these two works depart from conventional journalism in their personalized tone, narrative emphasis on interpersonal dynamic, and self-reflexive, participatory style. For example, the narrators in both works adopt first-person voices and, in unveiling how migrant seafarers become de facto captives on the open-yet-oppressive boat space, they write about themselves as self-questioning witnesses with emotional investment, as messengers for the migrants, as critics of injustice, and, in the case of *There Is No God*, as fellow workers in the fishing industry. Likewise, the migrant fishers portrayed rarely appear just as passive tokens to validate any self-congratulatory rights discourse; instead, they are active, even mesmeric conversers capable of returning the storytellers' gazes with unyielding authenticity. In reading *Broken Wings*, TIWA's female activist-storytellers use first-person perspectives to picture the migrants and how they juxtapose their written accounts with various visual paratexts to reveal their private thoughts and observations. They write about visiting the migrant workers incarcerated at the Taipei Prison, particularly the six Indonesian inmates from the *Te Hung Hsing* case; to understand the context behind the transnational labor movement they also document fieldtrips to the migrant inmates' home villages in Java. In *There Is No God*, Lee spends nearly four years as a boat guard working alongside the shoreside community of Taiwanese and foreign fishers, agents from fishing companies, police and fellow guards, and other men and women doing odd jobs and small businesses. Documenting the fisherfolk's everyday life without an elevated moralist angle, Lee blends candid, self-deprecating working-class vernaculars with poignant insights about the industry's hidden realities that fly under the radar of mainstream media coverage.

I frame my analysis of these migrant-fisher narratives around major hermeneutic questions generated by the Taiwanese storytellers' Sinitic-language "re-narration," or translation of foreign migrants' hardship in the offshore fishing industry. Mirroring Lawrence Venuti's conceptualization, these translational practices reveal the Taiwanese narrators' active interpretation of their protagonists and expose their own prevailing ideologies, but they also carry obvious power asymmetries and deep ethical implications.[15] As serious attempts to bring marginalized seafaring stories into public view, these recent collections illustrate what James Dawes calls the power of storytelling to occasion debate on justice and rights, even though not all the local narrators discussed here would explicitly self-identify as rights advocates.[16] To be sure, these narrators encounter recurrent self-doubt in their storytelling. Yet it is through these reflexive moments that readers see evidence of vigorous cultural translation. For example, not only do the TIWA activists and Lee acknowledge what Elaine Scarry calls the difficulty of imagining other people; they also take storytelling as a way to disclose and elaborate—if not resolve—their own inner contradictions.[17] In doing so, they experience what Rey Chow describes as a translator's melancholic "narrative consciousness," which urges them to not simply glide over the vast epistemological ocean that, without wetting their clothes, keeps them separated from the reality of the migrant fishers. Rather, in realizing their positional stake, the narrators find ample opportunities to scrutinize their own interpretive limitations, acknowledging that they are narratively soaked in desire-filled transpacific "crosscurrents," as Kale Fajardo would call them.[18] In other words, the transpacific problem of knowledge that makes intercultural storytelling challenging becomes a productive factor that shapes the specific ways in which the narrators picture the otherwise distant and unthinkable spaces of boat, harbor, prison, and tropical home. Rather than presuming to represent the migrants, only to betray this storytelling promise, the narrators in question all appear extremely mindful of their roles both as interpreters with affective stakes and, to borrow again from Chow, as mourners of all the nuanced meanings lost in the stories they set out to understand.[19]

Three intertwined translational issues unfold in this transpacific seafaring space. First, as Paul Gilroy, Édouard Glissant, and Lisa Lowe expound, the boat image offers an oceanic symbol of shared vulnerability among racialized labors under global capitalism.[20] As an intercultural contact zone, the boat and the ocean occupy a murky, liminal position in most territorially defined community imaginations because they expose land dwellers' narrow epistemological view. Fishing vessels are rarely seen from the land, and the diversity of shipboard communities places a high demand on any efforts to translate across languages, ethnicities, citizenships, and so on. These two collections are prime examples of such limitations. The TIWA activists rely heavily on interpreters' assistance while traveling in Indonesia, and their interactions with migrant prisoners are contingent on mutual language proficiencies; likewise, while Lee's inability to speak foreign languages may have saved him from quarrels at work (according to his explanation), it nonetheless leaves readers wondering about the exact mode and extent of his interaction with his migrant cohorts.[21]

The translational quandary and rupture resulting from such spatial symbols leads, next, to questions about accessing the life stories of migrant workers. Public outcries surrounding the fishing industry brought the TIWA representatives to Taipei Prison and Java's north coast; meanwhile, being a boat guard allows Lee to use photography and writing to document his everyday interactions with the Taiwanese and migrant fishers at close range. In effect, while these intercultural storytellers seek out the people in the seafaring community, they also co-create the very "sociality"—as Rita Felski would put it—of this transpacific seascape.[22] More importantly, having the ability to access these field sites suggests not only spatial crossings but also traversals of discursive modalities. As participant-observers of the industry, the narrators often relinquish the veil of a detached third-person voice, entering what Wong describes as a sticky transpacific public sphere where emotions, especially when amplified through mass media, often mobilize people to identify with or act against certain communities.[23] This doubling of detachment and attachment is intensified by the narrators' roles, first as the audience listening to their migrant interlocutors and later as translators who exercise their interpretive lens to renarrate the migrants' life stories for Sinitic-language readers. Feelings of unease ensue, because both the TIWA activists and Lee are acutely sensitive that they do not know everything yet possess enormous creative license.

Such ambivalence for telling their transpacific stories points to the third and most ethically charged dimension of cultural translation, where repelling and enticing emotions intersect to form a troubled crosscurrent. The narrators' concerns with social injustice, as well as their heightened awareness of positional difference, generate specific storytelling strategies that also appear in many contemporary narratives of atrocity. Here I echo Sophia McClennen, Joseph Slaughter, and Yogita Goyal, who emphasize the pivotal role of narrative form in expressing rights and antislavery discourses.[24] Specifically, the two collections combine a strong sense of field knowledge and journalistic rationality with a memoir-like dramatic thrust, thus framing the firsthand accounts of migrant labors explicitly around the narrators' own motivations, gendered perspectives, and temperaments. Sinitic-language readers, on the other hand, interpret these narrators' heavily personalized quests not merely based on their ethnographic, documentary-like language but also through a paratextual abundance of photos, drawings, letters, and maps. These rich paratexts often summon introspective feelings in readers, who may in turn interpret these works as examples of empathy; indeed, such a paratextual storytelling technique helps to craft what Pheng Cheah and Pooja Rangan call the powerful "humanity -effects" out of "inhuman conditions."[25] Enticing as they are, these narrative products often present a sentimental trap.

BROKEN WINGS AND A FARAWAY PRISON

As a product reflecting TIWA's longtime activism, the *Broken Wings* collection is in part made possible by the association's collaboration with the Jakarta-based artist duo Irwan Ahmett and Tita Salina. In 2015 the two artists — known for their interventionist artwork on sociopolitical and humanitarian issues — were invited by the National Taiwan Museum of Fine Arts to participate in the Asian Art Biennale, for which they made two documentary films about Taiwan's Indonesian workers.[26] The first, *Salting the Sea*, captured the emotions of Indonesian families separated by sea and was dedicated to the *Te Hung Hsing*'s six incarcerated fishermen; the second, *Longevity*, was inspired by the story of Yanti, who was imprisoned in Taiwan for killing her former employer but who testified about workplace abuse during her trial.[27] Through the biennale the duo befriended the TIWA activists, who since 2013 have been visiting the Taipei Prison regularly. The two groups subsequently teamed up at a Jakarta forum on migrant labor and again on TIWA's visits to the prisoners' home villages.[28] As the collection shows, the TIWA group made these visits to pursue several goals: to offer help to the prisoners, to bring messages to their faraway families, and to express, beyond standard media sensationalism, the migrants' side of the stories as well as the industry structure that occasions the migrants' workplace misery.

The collection is comprised of twelve migrant portraits, individually written by TIWA's prison visitors from the latter's first-person perspective, set in either Taiwan or Java. Taking centerstage in the book are the six inmates and three acquitted migrants from the *Te Hung Hsing*, the deceased Supriyanto's coworker Sukhirin, and several other migrants imprisoned for other reasons. The TIWA activist-storytellers' position as sympathetic allies is revealed early in the book's epigraph. The quote, taken from the opening of Takiji Kobayashi's classic proletarian seafaring novel *The Crab Cannery Ship*, says: "Buddy, we're off to hell!"[29] As an invitation from "hell," *Broken Wings* takes readers onto the boat, into the prison, and then across the Pacific to Java to see the societal background behind labor migration from contemporary Indonesia. But, as the book's preface maintains, TIWA's witness-bearing storytelling is neither advocating legal exoneration for the migrant prisoners nor extracting confessions from them; rather, it is a first step toward restoring the migrants' ravaged humanity.[30] Wrapped by the preface and an epilogue, in which TIWA activists Shu-ching Chuang and Chun-huai Hsu explain their mission—to spotlight unseen stories and to anticipate concrete action for an improved future—the collection also inserts a list of recorded bloodsheds on Taiwanese fishing boats from 2007 through 2015 and concludes with fifty-two pages of full-size photos.[31] This final photography section visualizes the communities and villages portrayed in the foregoing sections as well as TIWA's protests in 2016 and 2017. Some photographs show the visited migrants and their families, food brought to prison as gifts, calling cards, purchase receipts, letters, and so on. Toward the end of the section are two juxtaposed photos that show how the TIWA visitors act as transporters of the migrant families' transpacific longings and blessings (fig. 6.1): one shows several hairbrushes and toothbrushes backgrounded by a piece of paper that the caption indicates was made by Ahmett and Salina

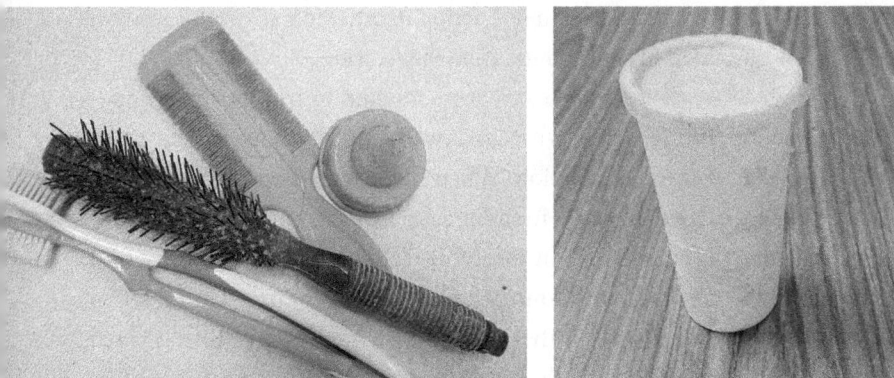

FIG. 6.1. *Left*: Toiletries from Susanto's family members, placed on a piece of paper made from their nails, hair, and shed skin. *Right*: A cup of consecrated water from Yanti's husband, which the TIWA activists deliver to Yanti in prison, to use as food dressing. Source: *Broken Wings from a Faraway Shore* (2019). Photo courtesy of Taiwan International Workers Association.

from the nails, hair, and shedded skin of the Indonesian family of prisoner Susanto; the other displays a cup of consecrated water, brought from Yanti's husband in Indonesia, which the TIWA activists deliver to her during their prison visit, to be used as food dressing.[32]

Besides human portraits, *Broken Wings* incorporates reportage-style commentaries on structural problems—such as the fishing industry's reliance on offshore labor, sociolegal prejudice, and an incarceration system that replicates discrimination, social exclusion, and ethnonationalism in the outside world.[33] However, the TIWA narrators do not assume impartiality or indulge in complacency about their activism; instead, they often discuss fieldwork challenges. For instance, Chuang writes about how their plans to conduct in-depth conversations with the migrants' families were frequently interrupted by "emotional outbursts" and other unforeseen situations, and how they tried to maintain vigilance against "sugarcoating multiculture" with "tearful sentimentalism."[34] Naturally, calling out these challenges will not by itself generate solutions, and Hsu stresses in the epilogue that an important reason the book must close with TIWA's protest photos is to provide "a sample answer we can offer"; to Hsu, how they "imagine the scope of 'us'" and "take action for 'our future'" determines the shape of that future.[35] Cultural imagination must join hands with real action in order to narrow the gap that is often left untreated in sentimental minority stories.

Although *Broken Wings* makes clear its mission to transform imagination into action, it is less clear whether TIWA's fieldtrips have indeed eased the obstacles in cultural translation. When the TIWA group visits two of *Te Hung Hsing*'s acquitted migrants in Indonesia, it seems that the interviewers' wish to connect is clouded by an insoluble feeling of rupture, futility, and unrequitedness. The migrants Yono, who has recently fathered a child, and Hadi, who is soon to board another fishing boat, have both returned home after a dreadful experience in Taiwan. Although Yono receives his visitors with joy, when inquired about his former work on the *Te Hung Hsing*, he replies to all their questions with a simple "I forgot about it."[36] This awkward exchange is followed by a family photo taken by the TIWA visitors, in which Yono and his wife, nursing the infant in her arms, gaze at the camera in an expression that looks friendly yet carefully polite (fig. 6.2). Yono's declared forgetfulness dampens the Taiwanese visitors' desire for further investigation into the tragedy; it also protects him, so to speak, from self-exposure. What should have been a celebration of the family's new baby now appears to befuddle both the narrators and readers' ability to read Yono's undisclosed mind. Following this account, the TIWA visitors accompany Hadi to a local brokerage agency in preparation for embarkation on an outgoing boat. When asked to identify Taiwan on a world map hanging in the agency office, Hadi is "no longer able to point it out."[37] As one of thousands of foreigners who have worked in Taiwan, Hadi's failure to tell it apart from his other employment locations reads like a backhanded satire to Taiwan's nonrecognition of migrant workers. In both cases neither the TIWA group's physical access to the Javan villages nor their prior friendship with the migrants guarantee reciprocity, and much about the *Te Hung Hsing* case remains opaque after their encounters. Just as Wong interprets Sara Ahmed's notion of "dwelling" as an ironic sign of social alienation deeply felt by Taiwan's foreign migrants, we might add that if familiarity and friendship still "dwell" between the migrants and their Taiwanese visitors, their transpacific connection is at best "volatile and reworked."[38] The memory of friendship remains, but so too does the migrants' shipboard trauma.

As Felski suggests, beyond linguistic bartering, translation necessitates

FIG. 6.2. Yono and his wife and baby. Source: *Broken Wings from a Faraway Shore* (2019). Photo courtesy of Taiwan International Workers Association.

navigating social networks; its interpretive function relies on the narrator's firsthand participation and emotional labor. This is where Ahmed's phenomenological study of affect comes in to provide concrete language for understanding intercultural storytelling as an embodied experience of finding one's place.[39] TIWA's narrators enact a series of self-orienting exercises when they enter this volatile transpacific network to tell migrant stories about home, dislocation, and familial ties. One such "homing" exercise, in Ahmed's words, takes place when the TIWA group visits the migrant inmates' Javan villages to witness the latter's home life.[40] Wen Jiang writes in her chapter that the migrant Aji's mother often touches Jiang's face, asking if she is hungry, as though she were her own child.[41] Likewise, on the morning after an exhausting evening arrival at Yanti's home in Blitar, Su-hsiang Chen exclaims with exuberance, "What a beautiful village!" after seeing its "sky-reaching trees, homegrown produce, yard space, vivacious flowers and plants, and dewed leaves"; not only does she "feel warmth and harmony" from conversations with Yanti's mother-in-law, but in writing she also praises the family for looking after Yanti's adoptive parents and a sick neighbor, despite being poor themselves.[42] Here, unlike the confining boat and prison spaces, the migrants' native dwelling spaces in Indonesia are vivacious and loving. While separated by the Pacific, it is as though the migrants are reconnecting with their families through the TIWA visitors.

The second account illustrates how the TIWA narrators devote affective labor to navigating the migrant fishers' life stories, a gesture that can be gleaned from the book's framing strategy. Rather than an all-knowing storytelling position that presumes a victim-savior binary, many chapters in *Broken Wings* orient toward a multi-angled account of interlocked pieces of narration, placing the narrators not outside but within the story, with a mule's-eye view. In her portrayal of Eko and Roro, two Indonesian migrants sentenced for killing another fellow migrant, narrator Ya-ling Yang places herself in this situated role and tries to make sense of her emotional attachment to her subjects.[43] She begins with fragments of direct observations about Eko's appearance, his background, and how he ended up in Taiwan; then, in a reportage-style commentary about the hardship of migrant fishers in general, she incorporates direct quotes from Eko. On the next page, where a photograph of Eko's handwritten letter to Yang is presented, readers realize that her foregoing account is in fact a re-narration of Eko's letter.[44] The letter's paratextual insertion here is a well-timed reminder that the TIWA activists were listeners and readers of their migrant interlocuters—the primary storytellers—before they were translators of these life stories into published forms for the Sinitic-language Taiwanese readership. This shifting narrative angle underscores Yang's process of digesting the story before writing it, and she emphasizes this introspective gesture at the end when she admits having struggled to find expression for her own sorrow regarding the fate of the migrants in the prison.

Of the many chapters in *Broken Wings*, Yu-ching Weng's offers the most alluring yet troubling example of emotional attachment. An impressionable narrator, Weng borrows the melodramatic language of the gangster film genre to construct the persona of the migrant inmate Adi as a fearless outlaw-hero at sea. She writes that "Adi's life is like a movie" and that "as a hero, he is handcrafted by the director."[45] As a heroic character, Adi "summons winds and storms and is known to everyone everywhere"; while his story is "surreal," his heart is "tender and warm." This opening snapshot sets the tone for subsequent passages. Weng expresses "wonder," "surprise," "worry," "bewilderment," and even "envy" at Adi's multilingual ability, like a fascinated fan.[46] Further, her account of Adi's marvelous deeds—as a migrant worker, as a romantic, and as a former gangster who enjoys some small fame in Thailand—makes readers wonder about the effect of her parallel roles as a storyteller and activist, as well as the delicate gender dynamic embedded in her affectionate vocabulary.

A closer examination of Weng's narrative wavers, between her introspective thoughts and her dramatic portrayal of Adi's life-turning episodes, reveals that her account builds heavily on the energy of her private feelings. Rather than discussing the transnational labor system that led Adi to his current situation, Weng dwells primarily on constructing a magnificent character, as if for the silver screen. Adi comes off as a charismatic talker more frequently than as a morose victim; conversely, in Weng's interactions with Adi (except when she solemnly advises him to not commit crimes again in the future), her language is mostly self-questioning and uncertain. Just as she crafts Adi's migrant persona, Weng constructs a deeply attached feeling out of her activist role: for example, she is "unsure" if Adi comprehends her advice and "feels somewhat alienated each time" by her difficulty in matching his crimes with the person who appears to her like a caring brother; she "doesn't quite know what life is like for him before sixteen"; and, when searching information about Adi's favorite band, she listens to the songs he recommends and imagines him as a tender diehard hero who may one day "write a song for his own film" and "surf on a fishing boat bound for Norway."[47] It is ironic and startling to note how little this seafaring fantasy actually says about Adi's current situation and how much empathy Weng's language has projected. Like Lauren Berlant, Goyal takes issue with this sentimental paradox, because the orientation of this emotional appeal, as Weng's writing exemplifies, is concerned not primarily with the captive person's perspective or the "radical transformation of existing social structure" but, instead, with affirming the readers of "their own capacity for empathy."[48] What is circulated here is not a migrant's story but a narrator's preoccupation that takes the place of substantive intercultural exchange.

It would be difficult to miss the narrative's quasi-romantic twist and how Weng prioritizes constructing Adi's heroism over maintaining an impartial position. Weng's surrender of the outsider role in exchange for an emotionally attached one is evident at the closing section, where two photos are juxtaposed (fig. 6.3).[49] On the right is a hand-drawn birthday card from Adi that includes his written well-wishes, suggesting a friendship and affection that otherwise can easily read as romantically enamored. On the left is Adi's pen-and-ink portrait of Weng based on the photo she has given him: Weng wears a short dress, smiles at the camera, and squats girlishly to stroke a cat. Nowhere does Weng comment on these two photos, unlike how text complements photos in most of the book's other chapters. Although readers access Adi's story largely through Weng's interpretive gaze, the warm interaction here between Weng and Adi are open to interpretation. At the same time, while her exalted language risks exoticizing Adi's seafaring life, this same trap gets back at her when she inserts the portrait. Turning Adi into a hero in film, she likewise offers herself as a visual object—captured quite literally under Adi's drawing pen—for readers' consumption and scrutiny.[50]

THERE IS NO GOD AT THE FISHING HARBOR

Whereas *Broken Wings* takes readers to the sites of Taipei Prison and Indonesian villages for a transpacific activist story, Aming Lee's *There Is No God* uses photography and words to opens readers' eyes to Ch'ien-chen Fishing Harbor, the biggest in Kaohsiung and what Lee calls an "open prison without bars," to visualize the toil and everyday emotions of multinational fisherfolk.[51] If the previously described collection illustrates how activist-storytelling works to translate seafaring atrocity across geographic and sociolinguistic barriers in anticipation of change, the latter appears like a brazen satire of this same embedded educational gesture. For TIWA, self-doubt does not invalidate but underscores the affective labor of activist intervention. For Lee, on the other hand, while the blue-collar vernacular knocks mainstream media for instrumentalizing the migrant fisher in order to affirm society's existing prejudice against the entire fishing industry, his self-deprecation further suggests frustration at his own double role as a photographer and insignificant boat guard and failure to wield change.[52] If TIWA's storytelling *trans*-action

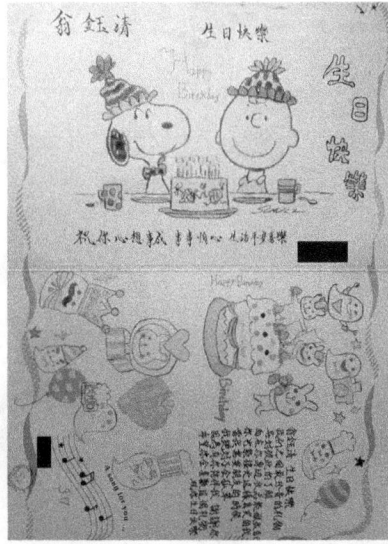

FIG. 6.3. *Left*: Adi's portrait of Weng, based on the photo she provided. *Right*: A hand-drawn birthday card made by Adi. Source: *Broken Wings from a Faraway Shore* (2019). Photo courtesy of Taiwan International Workers Association.

points to an interventionist future, the insider angle of Lee's account seems ambivalent if not downright skeptical about his own participation.

Divided into five parts, *There Is No God* juxtaposes Lee's written reflections with virtuosic photos of harborside culture gathered over four years of participatory observation as a boat guard working year-round on a twenty-four-hour daily wage of a thousand dollars. Featured in his photography are rusted boats, line-patterned anchor chains, wild-caught fish rowed up ashore, and a breathtaking range of portraits of dockside fishers at work or enjoying pastimes, often with a well-silhouetted chiaroscuro effect. The fishers take showers, play soccer, use cellphones, rest in bunkers, smoke, count bills, bicycle, and so on. Some look pensive, some make naughty faces, and most appear to acknowledge Lee's presence with familiarity (fig. 6.4). Out of what most media reportage would headline as a group of strangers, Lee's slice-of-life snapshots go beyond stereotypical images of migrant captives and troublemakers, instead capturing the "vibe" and what Katherine Stewards calls affective "intensities" of ordinary days.[53]

Lee's representational striving for ordinariness and his familiarity with the

FIG. 6.4. Examples of the migrant fishers' pastimes while they are on shore. Source: *There Is No God: Fishers, Boat Guards, and Those Women* (2018). Photo courtesy of China Times Publishing Company.

fishing industry can be seen from various themes included in his book. He laments the industry's extraction of the fishers' "physical labor from the neck down" and the latter's recourse to alcohol to numb physical and emotional pain.[54] He names payment inequalities and other structural ills, as well as the factionalism that permeates daily work between crewmembers of different ranks and nationalities.[55] In portraying his fellow Taiwanese boat guards, he compares their status as "insignificant" domestic workers to that of foreign hires; likening the boat guard's job to those of "watchdogs," "janitors," food distributors, and "pimps," he critiques the media's chase after foreign workers and ironic oblivion to domestic ones.[56] Further, he sees multiculturalism as a product of situational bonding, believing that fishers tend to share a carpe diem philosophy and act like players not because seafaring life dissolves cultural barriers or makes them carefree, but because they see themselves as "floating weeds" at sea.[57] He comments that in an environment where wage earnings determine not just what individual fishers can provide for faraway families but also what sexual and romantic gratification they can get on shore, material yearnings often drive cooperation in acts of pilfering marine catches.[58] It is pragmatic understanding of life's adversities, rather than multiculturalism, that bonds the fisherfolk. Insider knowledge as such is little known to most media workers who, Lee adds, tend to see the community in a flattened master-slave dyad, elevating foreign fishers as perfect victims, overlooking domestic workers' privation, and failing to distinguish between the experiences of different foreigners.[59] As Lee learns from complaints by a group of drunk Taiwanese boat owners, journalists rarely "distinguish between boat companies," "know nothing" about the industry, "mimic the foreigners" by calling their companies "exploiters," and are ignorant that "we, too, are fishers with blood and tears."[60] How Lee judges these drunkards remains unstated, but this passage debunks both Taiwan's notorious seafaring industry and the media's lack of comparable concern about local fisherfolk whose livelihoods also greatly depend on the sea.

Lee's alternative angle is matched by his earthy blue-collar language. Cheng Chang, who writes a foreword for the book, is impressed with Lee's rejection of "abstruse theory" and "stomach-upsetting" moralism and how, instead, he infuses "expletives-filled" details into unabashedly subjective accounts of harborside stories.[61] As Lee explains, his direct observations would not have displayed intensity easily had it not been for his familiarity with working-class social codes: "I grew up in a blue-collar family with two uneducated parents. Even my given name included a vernacular-sounding affix *a-*. So, I thought I would adapt to the job [as a boat-guard] just fine." Dubbing his involvement as the journey of "a dirty-handed photographer at a sunsetting age," Lee satirizes himself for "usurping the name of photography" to energize his torpid life. Through this self-jesting tone he frames his work not in terms of photo-documentary objectivity, "justice," or "humanitarianism," but as "a miscellany of messy thoughts" from "the dregs of society."[62]

Interestingly, self-deprecation lends authority to Lee's firsthand account, and in this aspect *There Is No God* shares with *Broken Wings* a narrative orientation toward introspection: whereas the TIWA storytellers adopt the language of empathy to examine their own limitations, Lee appears repelled by such lofty, respectable emotions. Besides twice inserting photos of himself, toward the end of part 2, Lee places a photo of a defecating dog next to a passage on the same page that mocks himself as a "smart coward" when confronted with injustice.[63] The ironies that exist between Lee's sense of inferiority and what he finds to be an unattainable moral high ground or superhuman capacity to withstand suffering strengthen the weight of his mule's-eye view by placing him squarely within the grassroots community of fellow workers. In the end this satirical bent allows him to explain his interpretive and affective work in powerful yet unorthodox ways: by critiquing frequent occlusion of local fisherfolk and other harborside workers of different genders from the public discourse about Taiwan's fishing industry, Lee challenges readers to rethink the proper protagonists and settings of these transpacific seafaring stories; further, if superficial empathy does not work for Lee in addressing the gaps between storytellers who are emotionally moved and the fisherfolk whose thoughts remain inaccessible, then his strategy for addressing this perennial problem pivots on a radical teardown of a shared language across communities coinhabiting the transpacific open boat.

Part 3 of the book, "Endless Nights," offers a provocative critique of stereotypes in mainstream fisher narratives by reinterpreting gender and sexual politics within the seafaring community through the lens of globalized labor relations. Specifically, Lee portrays women who labor alongside men but whose existence is repeatedly ignored in media coverage. In the chapter

"Vietnamese Chicks," Lee recounts a face-saving fight between two Chinese boatmen over sexual ownership of a young Vietnamese girl whom they both have paid to sleep with and claim to be "my woman."[64] Calling the fight stupid, Lee nonetheless judges the boatmen's buffoonery not in terms of sexism and misogyny: sex, like money, is a commodity that generates fierce competition because it is limited, and though gender, sex, citizenship, and language are common categories to draw community boundaries, these markers are not direct causes of misery within the fishing industry. Rather, commercial sex and its resultant "false feelings of love" are symptoms of a grimmer problem, like the material struggles and labor abuses that both men and women in this business endure.[65] As Lee's story insinuates, gender may be a crucial filter through which the neoliberal global market selects its labor. As such, it makes sense why in popular representations fishers are mostly men and sex workers are mostly women. However, he reminds us, it is money that primarily determines who owns gendered capital and who provides gendered labor.

Lee expands this alternative view on underdiscussed factors affecting the condition of survival within the fishing community through a sketch of Su-chu, who owns a harborside restaurant. As the most popular "local wine girl" and "everyone's sea goddess," Su-chu curses more professionally and jokes more salaciously than the boldest seamen; "manly" in figure and demeanor, Lee jokes, she drinks everything without a fuss and never once throws up. This "bold alacrity" guarantees her survival.[66] On the surface, Lee seems to caricature the woman's masculine self-presentation and unfemininity, but in the context of the harsh male-dominant environment, Lee's account shows that Su-chu's unusual business success depends greatly on her mastery of the fisherfolk's rugged social codes. Like in the example of commercial sex, gender and sex do not translate directly to a person's status; rather, they function as an acute angle for interpreting the existing capital-labor, patron-client dynamic in this trying social field.

While Lee's ethnographic observations provide readers with a rare access to previously untold dockside stories, he encounters serious interpretive and moral dilemmas when personal investment compels him to come out from behind the camera-pen. Although Lee makes daring traversals of social and representational boundaries by becoming the protagonist in his own port-side story, his action turns out to be self-parody. In one such account, Lee discusses a self-employed Taiwanese sex worker whom everyone nicknames "three-hundred-dollar girl" and "mentally disabled," whom Lee once tries to help. Lee ridicules not only his "voyeuristic habit as a former journalist" but also his "rescue" mission: expressing concern, he is consternated not by the woman's work itself but by her lack of means for ensuring safety, her "unreasonably cheap price," and her ignorance about managing earnings and "building public relations."[67] When once he intervenes by raising the price for her to a group of interested migrant clients, he finds that this sudden act only confounds everyone, including the sex worker, into an awkward silence. Although they have once shared what feels to him like a fleeting moment of friendliness—once when the girl talks about her work and dysfunctional family and once when he in return gives her concrete advice—what little heroism Lee may have felt quickly evaporates the next time they meet and she again treats him as a random stranger, withdrawing into her usual oblivious, solitary state.[68]

Lee's awkward intervention suggests a layered self-critique in addition to the obvious voyeuristic male gaze cloaked in his seemingly innocuous role as an insignificant boat guard. By not reciprocating Lee's hope for friendship, the sex worker—whose service to migrant fishers attests to the global chain of labor extraction—seems to symbolically refuse to be accessed and objectified through storytelling. Mirroring Yono's rejection of his TIWA visitors' query in Broken Wings, here the sex worker's uncommunicativeness reminds readers of Scarry's skepticism about what storytelling can accomplish beyond mere cultural consumption.[69] Indeed, it lays bare the intractable gaps met by Taiwan's local storytellers in trying to translate the fisherfolk community's withheld feelings and thoughts. Again echoing Lily Wong: as a figure that easily generates mixed public feelings, the sex worker persona often invites sentimentalist storytelling coated in the language of empathy, moralism, and rights; as such, it shares the unfortunate representational fate of Taiwan's many racialized and gendered foreign labors. Therefore, in placing the sex worker's disquieting story alongside those of the marginalized fisherfolk, Lee broadens the referential scope and reframes the interpretive aim of this transpacific seafaring genre. He judges empathy not as an automatic entryway to intercultural understanding, but as a potential distraction, alibi, and even red herring. As one fellow boat guard sharply puts it, "If things remain the same despite your good will to help, you know there must be an irresolvable issue."[70]

CODA: STORIES FOUND AND LOST
IN THE TRANSPACIFIC SEAFARING TIME-SPACE

The promises and stakes of translation—that is, narration of Taiwan's migrant fisher stories and transpacific seafaring network across multiple barriers—has been analyzed here mostly in spatial terms: how Taiwanese storytellers draw on the spatial images of boat, harbor, prison, tropical village, and seawater to explain the epistemological fissures they seek to mend yet find difficult to bridge. This disconnect underlies the narrative practice of giving voice to minority subjects. However, as Dawes reminds us by way of echoing Theodor Adorno's critique of trauma narratives, these voices may turn out to be "taking voice" as well.[71] Translational barriers are difficult to surmount, because the storytellers are simultaneously "there" and "not really there."[72] The introspective bent in both the examined collections reflects the narrators' heightened awareness of such "psychic friction" but, as Scarry warns, though they possess this reflexive quality, still, it does not cancel the ethical risk of promoting only the "cosmopolitan largess" of storytellers and consumers, even if this type of storytelling is desirable.[73]

Supriyanto's death on the *Fu Tzu Chun* lays bare the gravity of exactly these interpretive challenges. It points to a disturbing pattern of shipboard violence that Taiwanese society has long kept hidden from view. To read Supriyanto's story—indeed, to fathom why and how Taiwan's seafaring industry has perpetuated such violence toward the population of migrant fishers— requires that the storytellers enter this godforsaken boat space and rewind time, not only back to Supriyanto's torturous last few months but also to the preceding years that had led him and many other migrant fishers to this fate. More than a matter of linguistic and cultural translation, a transpacific story that reflects this "psychic friction" is also a product of such spatiotemporal lapses, because oftentimes these shipboard tragedies do not happen within the space of outsiders' immediate view, and oftentimes they extend beyond the lifetime of the deceased to impact their faraway families and loved ones. And yet, navigating these migrant fisher stories inevitably results in narratives about loss, incompletion, and a degree of opacity beyond the spatiotemporal scope of our physical and intellectual reach.

Lee's personal story in "Gazing into the Abyss," the last part of his book, further concretizes this transpacific problem of knowledge production. As an experiment to see "how it feels to be a real migrant fisher," Lee departs for a small town near the coast on Thailand's Phuket Island to take a two-month job as a boat guard for a Taiwanese company.[74] In crossing international borders he brings his book's self-deprecating overtone to a satirical climax. He plunges himself into the darkest corner of a transnational seafaring industry that is not strange to him and yet is new in many ways. Out of eagerness to test the difference between his photographic position and his capacity to live as an object of his own representation, he becomes a migrant boat guard from Taiwan. And, despite "all the books on transnational labor I have read" and the "small fame" he has gained for his photography, he still feels "distressed," "blocked by an unpassable wall," and "lacking something for which I have no name."[75] This mental torment captures the interpretive tenor of spatial and other tangible obstacles he must overcome in order to know what it means to be a real migrant worker.

Lee confesses that this trip offers no deus ex machina for producing a satisfactory story; worse, it makes a scathing satire of his imagined empathy. He dares himself many times: "If I cannot endure what others can, what sort of 'migrant worker' am I?" and "If a migrant fisher can do this, so can I."[76] Yet in learning to withstand anxieties as a newly arrived migrant does, he comes to see the wide gap between his romanticized idea about migrant workers and what living as one actually entails. After escaping his flea-infested room for a villa-style apartment nearby, which he pays for from his Taiwanese bank account and praises as a mini-heaven, he wakes to the epiphany that he cannot pretend to be a migrant worker any longer and that his ordeal is incomparable to that of a real migrant worker who, unlike him, does not foresee an end date to sufferings. The self-parody is comical and sad: despite what he already knows about Taiwan's fisherfolk culture, he does not become a real migrant worker by just traveling to Thailand for an experience. His boat-guarding job here suggests not cosmopolitan connection but rather a rupture that exposes the ludicrousness of his narrative's sentimentality. Indeed, if a short-term trial of flea bites can wear out one's perseverance so quickly, then almost no one can put into words a life of pain, for there is a world of difference, he admits, between exhibiting photography in the gallery and working on a boat loaded with outcries unheard by urban dwellers.[77]

What is lost in these narratives of cultural translation continues outside the text. For Taiwan's transpacific seafaring stories, this means that the trans-action between shipboard workers, narrators, and reader-consumers of this emerging genre form a crisscrossed pattern of storytelling on different platforms and with an extended social life. Lee's book and the subsequent circulation of his photography online and in galleries, such as his solo show in 2020 at the Sin Pink Pier art space, demonstrate this open-ended transpacific network.[78] As migrant fishers and other mobile workers enter public purview through channels beyond news reports, drawing public attention to Taiwan's Southeast Asian locals, it also requires that we scrutinize the concurrent increase of minority narratives that nonetheless replicate Taiwan-centric views. Further, though Lee's photography enters the gallery space and migrant fishers' experiences gain visibility, we should ask whether this recent development facilitates a comparable shift in Taiwan's sociolegal establishment in compensating foreign workers or only serves as a symbolic validation of superficial multiculturalism.

Likewise, TIWA's protest photos in *Broken Wings* remind readers that the collection is merely a midpoint record of ongoing activist work and that many migrant inmates' road home is a very long one. The webpage set up by TIWA's prison visit taskforce, which to date has over two thousand Facebook followings, shows that much of what *Broken Wings* has documented over these years still occur behind prison bars, and the taskforce still posts its prison visit journals and photos, letters, calls for donations, and so on.[79] By December 2020 the inmates visited had increased from *Te Hung Hsing*'s six to a total of thirty-eight, and several migrants had reappeared in online prison visit reports. For example, Agus was finally going home, Wara's mother had died, Mashuri's probation request had been rejected twice, and Yudi talked about his work at the prison factory. Outside public view the prison space continues to house the inmates' unseen transpacific desires and angsts, and with TIWA being their only connection with faraway families, it uncannily symbolizes both the prisoners' volatile kinship ties and an unpredictable future that puts their hearts and minds on trial.

This real-life continuation of transpacific undercurrents also makes an impact on the storytellers themselves: the formal choices made by the narrators reflect not just the manner in which they are touched by the lives of others, despite numerous barriers, but also their own traversals in action and discourse. What their narratives cannot capture, therefore, still performs an interpretive function, precisely because the failure of words and images will be felt as a rupture, or a trench on the seafloor, a place where feelings and thoughts descend at the converging boundaries of two colliding plates. What such underwater collision creates may not emerge atop the water but, having dived in, neither will the storytellers come out clean and dry.

NOTES

1. Anto was sentenced to serve twenty-eight years in the Taipei Prison, Yudi twenty-two years, Iham twenty-two, Susanto twenty-two, Retno seventeen, and Lufin fourteen (TIWA, *Zheyi yixiang: hongde xincun erhao de yigong* (Broken wings in a faraway prison) (Taipei: TIWA, 2019], 6). Also see "Six Indonesians Detained over Taiwanese Fishermen's Deaths," *Focus Taiwan*, August 21, 2013, https://focustaiwan.tw/society /201308210031; and "Taiwan Coast Guard Arrests Indonesian Fishermen," *Tempo*, October 19, 2018, https://en.tempo.co/read/500418/taiwan-coast-guard-arrests -indonesian-fishermen.

2. Dongmu Wu, Ye Xinlu, and Chen Shumin, "Tehongxing sanliubahao diexie: yinniliuyugong rengpan shisi-ershiba nian" (Bloodbath on *Te Hung Hsing*: Six Indonesian migrant fishers still sentenced to fourteen to twenty-eight years), *PTS News Network*, July 29, 2015.

3. Stephanie Chao, "Indonesian Seafarer's Death Highlights Taiwan Interpreter Shortage," *Jakarta Post*, January 24, 2017; Yi-ting Chiang, "*Zaojija, Boxue: xieleiyuchang*" (Falsification and exploitation: Blood and tears in the fisheries), *Reporter*, December 19, 2016; TIWA, *Zheyi yixiang*, 20, 68–72; "Hell on High Waters," *Tempo*, January 10, 2017, https://magz.tempo.co/read/32627/hell-on-high-waters#.

4. Cheng-en Song, "Dangxieleiyuchang yushang guojilaogongbiaozhun, kaipudunjingzhong qiaoxingtaiwanlema" (When international labor standards caught blood and tears in the fisheries: Did Cape Town's warning bell finally wake Taiwan up?), *Reporter*, July 20, 2018; Taiwan Council of Agriculture, "Act for Distant Water Fisheries," January 20, 2017; "Agencies Censured for Lax Management of Taiwan Fishing Ship," *Focus Taiwan*, May 10, 2019, https://focustaiwan.tw/society/201905100013; Nick Aspinwall, "Taiwan's High Seas Fishing Vessels Lost 13 Migrant Fishermen in February," *News Lens*,

March 8, 2019; Sherry Lee, You-en Lin, Yi-ting Chiang, and Han-wen Cheng, *Xielei Yuchang: Kuaguozhiji Taiwanyuanyangyuye zhenxiang* (Blood and tears of fishing ground: Transnational investigation of the truth behind Taiwan's deep-sea fishing industry) (Taipei: Flaneur Culture Lab, 2017), 99–107, 185; "The Rise and Fall of Driftnet Fishing," *Taiwan Today*, July 1, 1992, https://taiwantoday.tw/news.php?unit=29,45 &post=36680#:~:text=Driftnet%20fishing%20quickly%20evolved%20into,the%20 region%20by%20July%201991; TIWA, *Zheyi yixiang*, 10, 184–85; "Jiemi taiwan yuye bazhu" (Secrets of Taiwan's fishing tycoons), *Wealth Magazine*, April 19, 2018.

   5. For critiques of major contradictions in the development of oceanic studies, see Hester Blum, "The Prospect of Oceanic Studies," *PMLA* 125, no. 3 (2010): 670–77; "Introduction: Oceanic Studies," *Atlantic Studies* 10, no. 2 (2013): 151–55; and Philip E. Steinberg, "Of Other Seas: Metaphors and Materialities in Maritime Regions," *Atlantic Studies* 10, no. 2 (2013): 156–69.

   6. Tzu-hui Celina Hung, "Documenting 'Immigrant Brides' in Multicultural Taiwan," in *Asian Video Cultures: In the Penumbra of the Global*, ed. Joshua Neves and Bhaskar Sarkar (New York: Duke University Press, 2017), 159–61.

   7. Steinberg, "Of Other Seas," 158.

   8. Pao-Tsun Tai, *Taiwan de haiyang lishi wenhua* (Oceanic cultures and history of Taiwan) (Taipei: Taiwan Interminds, 2011), 186–90; Shih-Shan Henry Tsai, *Maritime Taiwan: Historical Encounters with the East and the West* (Armonk, NY: M. E. Sharpe, 2009), 19.

   9. This change was due in part to the parallel rise of multiculturalism, Taiwanese identity, and a series of southbound economic policies at the cusp of the new millennium and thereafter. For information about this larger context, see Hung, "Documenting 'Immigrant Brides,'" 158–75.

   10. Susan Chen, dir., *Caihong bale* (Rainbow popcorn) (Taiwan: TIWA, 2012), DVD; Lee et al., *Xielei Yuchang*; Susan Chen, dir., *Tipo gongchang* (Lesbian factory) (Taiwan: TIWA, 2010), DVD; Southeast Asian Migrants, *Hang: Polangerqiu, nifengzhong de ziyou / disanjie yimingongwenxuejiang zuopinji* (Navigation: 2016 Taiwan literature award for migrants) (New Taipei City: Four Way, 2016); TIWA, *Ningshi yixiang: yigong sheyingji* (*Voyage 15840: Photographs by migrant worker*) (Taipei: INK, 2008).

   11. Denise Cruz, "Imagining a Transpacific and Feminist Asian American Archive," *PMLA* 127, no. 2 (2012): 366; Shelley Fisher Fishkin, "Transnational American Studies: Next Steps?," in *Oceanic Archives, Indigenous Epistemology, and Transpacific American Studies*, ed. Otto Heim, Kendall Johnson, and Yuen Shu (Hong Kong: Hong Kong University Press, 2019), 217–38; Janet Hoskins and Viet Than Nguyen, "Introduction: Transpacific Studies: Critical Perspectives on an Emerging Field," in *Transpacific Studies: Framing an Emerging Field*, ed. Janet Hoskins and Viet Than Nguyen (Honolulu: University of Hawai'i Press, 2014), 1–38; Lisa Lowe, "Trans-Pacific Migrant and Area Studies," in *The Trans-Pacific Imagination: Rethinking Boundary, Culture and Society*,

ed. Naoki Sakai and Hyon Joo Yoo (River Edge, NJ: World Scientific , 2012), 61–74; Christopher B. Patterson, *Transitive Cultures: Anglophone Literature of the Transpacific* (New Brunswick, NJ: Rutgers University Press, 2018); Lisa Yoneyama, "Toward a Decolonial Genealogy," *American Quarterly* 69, no. 3 (2017): 471–82; Yuan Shu, Otto Heim, and Kendall Johnson, eds., *Oceanic Archives, Indigenous Epistemology, and Transpacific American Studies* (Hong Kong: Hong Kong University Press, 2019), 16; Chih-ming Wang, "Editorial Introduction: Between Nations and Across the Ocean," *Inter-Asia Cultural Studies* 13, no. 2 (2012): 165–68; Lily Wong, *Transpacific Attachments: Sex Work, Media Networks, and Affective Histories of Chineseness* (New York: Columbia University Press, 2018).

12. See this volume's introduction for a discussion of the "undisciplining" of transpacific studies.

13. Rebecca L. Walkowitz, *Born Translated: The Contemporary Novel in an Age of World Literature* (New York: Columbia University Press, 2017), 1–48.

14. See the introduction herein.

15. Lawrence Venuti, *Contra Instrumentalism: A Translation Polemic* (Lincoln: University of Nebraska Press, 2019), 1–6; Lawrence Venuti, "Translation, Community, Utopia," in *The Princeton Sourcebook in Comparative Literature: From the European Enlightenment to the Global Present*, ed. David Damrosch, Natalie Melas, and Mbongiseni Buthelezi (Princeton, NJ: Princeton University Press, 2009), 366; Lawrence Venuti, *Translation Studies Reader* (London: Routledge, 2012), 5.

16. James Dawes, *That the World May Know: Bearing Witness to Atrocity* (Cambridge, MA: Harvard University Press, 2007), 1–2.

17. Elaine Scarry, "The Difficulty of Imagining Other People," in *For Love of Country?*, ed. Martha Craven Nussbaum and Joshua Cohen (Boston: Beacon, 2002), 98–110.

18. Rey Chow, "Translator, Traitor; Translator, Mourner (Or, Dreaming of Intercultural Equivalence)," *New Literary History* 39, no. 3 (2008): 570; Kale Bantigue Fajardo, "Introduction: Filipino Crosscurrents," in *Filipino Crosscurrents: Oceanographies of Seafaring, Masculinities, and Globalization* (Minneapolis: University of Minnesota Press, 2011), 23.

19. Chow's notion of storytelling here echoes Venuti's formulation of translation as acts of interpretation ("Translator, Traitor," 572–73).

20. Édouard Glissant, *Poetics of Relation*, trans. Betsy Wing (Ann Arbor: University of Michigan Press, 2010), 5–9; Paul Gilroy, *The Black Atlantic: Modernity and Double Consciousness* (Cambridge, MA: Harvard University Press, 1993), 1–40; Lisa Lowe, "The Intimacies of Four Continents," in *Haunted by Empire*, ed. Ann Laura Stoler, Gilbert M. Joseph, and Emily S. Rosenberg (Durham, NC: Duke University Press, 2006), 191–212.

21. Aming Lee, *Zheli meiyou shen: yugong, babasang, he naxie nuren* (There is no god: Fishers, boat guards, and those women) (Taipei: China Times, 2018), 108.

22. Felski uses Bruno Latour's actor-network theory to describe the co-creational dynamic between people, objects, and texts, and she sees this sociality as essential to the work of translation. See Rita Felski, "Comparison and Translation: A Perspective from Actor-Network Theory," *Comparative Literature Studies* 53, no. 4 (2016): 750. See also Bruno Latour, *Reassembling the Social: An Introduction to Actor-Network-Theory* (Oxford: Oxford University Press, 2005).

23. Wong, *Transpacific Attachments*.

24. Sophia McClennen and Joseph Slaughter, "Introducing Human Rights and Literary Forms; Or, the Vehicles and Vocabularies of Human Rights," *Comparative Literature Studies* 46 no.1 (2009): 1–19; Yogita Goyal, *Runaway Genres: The Global Afterlives of Slavery* (New York: New York University Press, 2020), 1–68.

25. Pheng Cheah, *Inhuman Conditions: On Cosmopolitanism and Human Rights* (Cambridge, MA: Harvard University Press, 2009), 10; Pooja Rangan, *Immediations: The Humanitarian Impulse in Documentary* (Durham, NC: Duke University Press, 2017), 2.

26. TIWA, *Zheyi yixiang*, 117–18; "Artists," 2015 Asian Art Biennale, Artist Making Movement, Accessed May 20, 2020.

27. Ahmett and Salina, "Longevity," YouTube video, uploaded October 1, 2015, https://www.youtube.com/watch?v=AfCpAUx9W80; Ahmett and Salina, "Salting the Sea," YouTube video, uploaded October 5, 2015, https://www.youtube.com/watch?v=4Bxs9K7PgKM&list=UUwk5MCcEB090CJocYoWFtTA&index=18.

28. TIWA, *Zheyi yixiang*, 47–48, 118–19.

29. TIWA, 3; Takiji Kobayashi, *The Crab Cannery Ship and Other Novels of Struggle*, trans. Zeljko Cipris, intro. Komori Yoichi (Honolulu: University of Hawai'i Press, 1929), 19.

30. TIWA, *Zheyi yixiang*, 8.

31. TIWA, 26, 74–75, 133–86.

32. TIWA, 180–81.

33. TIWA, 7–8, 79–84.

34. TIWA, 25–26.

35. TIWA, 186.

36. TIWA, 30.

37. TIWA, 35.

38. Sara Ahmed, *Queer Phenomenology: Orientations, Objects, Others* (Durham, NC: Duke University Press, 2006); Wong, *Transpacific Attachments*, 21, 133–34.

39. Ahmed, *Queer Phenomenology*, 8–9.

40. Ahmed, 9.

41. TIWA, *Zheyi yixiang*, 91.

42. TIWA, 121, 123.

43. TIWA, 39–40.

44. TIWA, 38–39.

45. TIWA, 59.

46. TIWA, 59, 61.

47. TIWA, 64–65, 67.

48. Lauren Berlant, "Poor Eliza," *American Literature* 70, no. 3 (1998): 635–68; Goyal, *Runaway Genres*, 52–53.

49. TIWA, *Zheyi yixiang*, 66.

50. Similar examples can be seen in another chapter by Weng and in Ya-ling Yang's account (44, 108–16).

51. Lee, *Zheli meiyou shen*, 118–19.

52. Chih-Wei Huang recounts his impression of Aming Lee's use of masculine, working-class slangs as a habit in social gatherings ("Anye fulang xuying" [Shadows and waves in the dark: Miscellaneous notes on the photography of Aming Lee], *Art Emperor*, July 10, 2020, https://artemperor.tw/focus/3404.

53. Lee, *Zheli meiyou shen*, 252; Kathleen Stewart, *Ordinary Affects* (Durham, NC: Duke University Press, 2007), 3.

54. Lee, *Zheli meiyou shen*, 85, 110, 118–20.

55. Lee, 77, 81–82, 128–33, 139.

56. Lee, 84, 87, 96–109, 142.

57. Lee, 112, 135, 203–4.

58. Lee, 122–24, 205, 210.

59. Lee, 84, 195–99.

60. Lee, 127.

61. Lee, 55.

62. Lee, 75, 65, 206, 252.

63. Lee, 161.

64. Lee, 169.

65. Lee, 166–69.

66. Lee, 190–92.

67. Lee, 172–78.

68. Lee, 175–78.

69. Scarry, "Difficulty of Imagining," 98.

70. Lee, *Zheli meiyou shen*, 178.

71. Dawes, *That the World May Know*, 8.

72. Dawes, 4.

73. Dawes, 3; Scarry, "Difficulty of Imagining," 98.

74. Lee, *Zheli meiyou shen*, 214.

75. Lee, 214.

76. Lee, 228, 231.

77. Lee, 209, 242.

78. Huang, "Anye fulang xuying."

79. TIWA, "Guanzhu yigong shouxingren" (Concerned group for imprisoned migrant workers) Facebook page, accessed May 20, 2020, https://www.facebook.com/groups/385739088281572.

PART THREE UNSETTLING THE PACIFIC

TRANSPACIFIC FEMINIST MOVEMENT

Challenging Japan's Military Sexual Slavery System

KYUNG HEE HA

On December 28, 2015, the White House released a statement by national security advisor Susan E. Rice in which she congratulated the governments of Japan and the Republic of Korea (hereafter, South Korea) on their reaching an agreement on the so-called comfort women issue.[1] The statement reads: "The United States applauds the leaders of the ROK [Republic of Korea] and Japan, two of our most important allies, for having the courage and vision to forge a lasting settlement to this difficult issue. We look forward to deepening our work with both nations on a wide range of regional and global issues, on the basis of mutual interests and shared values, as well as to advancing trilateral security cooperation." The statement was released immediately after a joint press conference in which the foreign ministers of the two countries announced that the "comfort women issue" was resolved "finally and irreversibly."[2] In the previous year, US president Barack Obama hosted the first meeting between South Korea's president, Park Geun-hye, and Japan's prime minister, Shinzo Abe, in The Hague.[3] At the trilateral summit, frictions that had developed in Japan–South Korea relations involving territorial disputes and Japan's wartime atrocities—including the sexual enslavement of women and girls during the World War II—were addressed, in the hope of creating a solid trilateral alliance able to face military threats posed by the People's Republic of China and the Democratic People's Republic of Korea (hereafter, North Korea).[4] The December statement by Rice must be understood in the context of the Obama administration's "Pivot to Asia" strategy.

While the leaders of the United States, Japan, and South Korea had hoped to "irreversibly" settle the issue through the 2015 "agreement," the movement to demand justice for victims continues to grow globally.[5] Specifically in the United States, the first memorial dedicated to the victims of Japan's military sexual slavery system was built in front of the public library in Palisades Park, New Jersey, in 2010. Since then, fifteen similar memorials have been built in North America, including in Toronto, San Francisco, and New York City.[6]

This chapter sheds light on emergent political formations surrounding "comfort women" memorialization and explores challenges and possibilities for a wider framework for historical justice, redress, and decolonization in the transpacific. The analysis focuses on the San Francisco–based Comfort Women Justice Coalition (CWJC) and its campaign to pass the resolution, "Urging the Establishment of a Memorial for 'Comfort Women,'" build a memorial, and move forward the movement to demand justice for Japan's military sexual slaves.[7]

San Francisco is unique among the more than a dozen cities in the United States that host a memorial dedicated to the comfort women. One, the CWJC worked closely with the Kansai Network to Resolve the Comfort Women Issue, a civic group in Osaka, Japan, San Francisco's sister city. A working relationship between people in San Francisco and Osaka enabled the CWJC to counter the narrative of the memorial being "anti-Japan." Two, opposition arose among some local Japanese American community leaders who have spent years in advocating for civil rights and women's rights. These leaders are deeply implicated in the postwar "transpacific complicity" by which Japanese nationalism and US nationalism, both of which are intertwined with imperialism, reinforce each other while turning a blind eye to the war crimes and sexual violence inflicted by both nations.[8] This group's cultural identity and political subjectivity as both *Japanese* and *American* sustained and thrived precisely within the context of transpacific complicity.

The CWJC has been successful in bringing attention to the issue of Japan's military sexual slavery partly through "universalization efforts" that have juxtaposed the comfort women issue with modern-day sex trafficking and with ISIS's systematic use of sexual violence against women as a weapon of war. However, the CWJC has not explicitly named the war crimes and atrocities committed by the US military nor the direct connection between the Japanese military's comfort women and the US military's camp town prostitutes. This is the context in which the transpacific solidarity existing between San Francisco's CWJC and Osaka's Kansai Network, carefully crafted through a shared anticolonial, antiracist, and feminist vision, presents the possibility of a radical politicization of justice that simultaneously challenges US and Japanese military violence.

THE REDRESS MOVEMENT IN THE UNITED STATES

The last few decades witnessed an emerging redress movement for wartime atrocities inflicted by the Japanese military among Asian and Pacific Islander Americans. Around the time Iris Chang's *Rape of Nanking* was published in 1997, some notable Chinese American organizations such as the Global Alliance for Preserving the History of World War II in Asia were established.[9] With regard to military sexual slavery, Korean Americans and other Asian Americans deployed tactics within US juridical venues, legislatures, and communities and on social media to call for formal acknowledgment and legal responsibility from the Japanese government for perpetrating "one of the largest cases of human trafficking in the 20th century."[10] Such efforts in the redress movement resulted in the passage of the 2007 US House of Representatives House Resolution 121 (H. Res. 121) introduced by a Japanese-American congressperson Mike Honda of California's 15th Congressional District.

The recent rise of memorialization of and redress movement for the comfort women in the United States has been documented and discussed by a number of scholars. One newly published anthology, *The Transnational Redress Movement for the Victims of Japanese Military Sexual Slavery*, written by longtime activists and scholars in the United States, South Korea, and Japan, documents an extremely detailed account of the local, national, and global movements for justice for comfort women within the framework of women's rights, human rights, and historical justice.[11] The anthology provides a historical context of democratization and the rise of a women's movement in South Korea in which the redress movement began and gradually gained support. For example, collaboration cultivated among activists and support organizations within Japan and in the more than a dozen home countries of the victims culminated in the Women's International War Crimes Tribunal on Japan's Military Sexual Slavery. The tribunal was held in Tokyo in December 2000 and Emperor Hirohito and other perpetrators were found guilty.

In the latter half of the anthology, the authors offer analyses on the global redress movement and the rise of Japan's denialism to reveal the new set of challenges faced by local and national redress campaigns in the United States.

To explore specific factors that are influential in memorial-building, political scientists Mary M. McCarthy and Linda C. Hasunuma compared and analyzed eleven US cities that had proposed building comfort women memorials. Of the eleven cities they observed, eight successfully built the memorials on public land, while three had completely failed or had to change the location of the memorial due to public opposition.[12] In their analysis, Hasunuma and McCarthy highlighted these factors in determining whether or not the goal of siting a memorial is achieved: relative size of ethnic Korean population, strength of supporting coalition, strength of opposing coalition, and strategy of universalism. The pair found that strength of opposing coalition is not as influential as strength of supporting coalition, the latter whose group identity is typically formed through a universal idea of women's and human rights.

In *The Transnational Redress Movement* anthropologist Tomomi Yamaguchi offers an insightful analysis on Japan's historical revisionism and how it has made its way to the United States since the mid 2000s.[13] Yamaguchi argues that Japan's global campaign to deny wartime atrocities has been a two-wheeled operation, with the Japanese embassy and the Japanese Ministry of Foreign Affairs on one side and grassroots far-right groups on the other. She calls it "Kanmin Ittai no 'Rekishisen'" (The united force of public and private in the "history wars"), whereby the Japanese government and some far-right organizations work closely together to build a united front to fight the "history wars" in the United States.

While these studies describe the historical context in which the comfort women redress movement was born and grew alongside the advancement of women's rights—as well as how it has been met with a united force of denialism by the Japanese government and civic groups locally, nationally, and globally—performance studies scholar Elizabeth W. Son pays particular attention to the process and motivations through which people understand transpacific and intergenerational trauma and memory, and participate in various acts of reckoning, such as memorial-building, protests, tribunal, and theater performances led by Koreans and Korean Americans. Son argues that through these acts, participants actively engage in knowledge production and community formation whose political and cultural implications are complicated. They vary from one's commitment to bringing justice to historical violence to gain visibility and recognition as an ethnic minority that is committed to human rights in their new host country.[14] Similarly, in her book *Traffic in Asian Women*, Laura Hyun Yi Kang criticizes Asian American scholars and activists for distancing themselves from trafficked Asian women, particularly the comfort women victims, placing them in a regressive space and identifying them as an object of disciplinary knowledge while at the same time displacing the issues of US military violence, economic dispossession, and racial exploitation that implicate their Asian American subjectivity.[15] How do Asian and Asian American individuals and organizations negotiate being the racialized other within the redress movement in the US context?

Lisa Yoneyama focuses her analysis on the process through which Asian Americans' efforts employ US juridical and cultural systems to turn the issue into an "American" concern.[16] By Americanizing the Japanese war crimes, Asians and Asian Americans have sought redress for the trauma and memories that have traveled through national boundaries and across generations. Yoneyama warns that this "Americanization of Japanese war crimes" can result in "uphold[ing] American imperialism and its myth of liberation and rehabilitation" if we fail to interrogate the transpacific entanglement of the issue and the structure of impunity under which the myth of American exceptionalism has been sustained.[17]

Do all efforts in memorializing comfort women in the United States inevitably reinforce the image of the United States as righteous arbiter of justice? Does naming Japan as a perpetrator state leave no room to question US atrocities at home and abroad? Yoneyama contends that the process of justice is twofold. She writes:

> On the one hand, the Asian/Americanization of justice can contribute to the obfuscation of past and present America's military and colonial violence. . . . On the other hand, the transnationalization of juridico-historical discourse in U.S. courts, albeit for a brief period, may have inadvertently revealed how profoundly the United States has been implicated in facilitating twentieth-century culture of impunity and how it has subsequently suppressed and silenced the people and nations to

whom it claims to have brought freedom and democracy. The dialectics of memory necessitated by transpacific demands for historical justice may thus effectuate in "un-American" consciousness of disidentification, even as it simultaneously disciplines and assimilates its new subjects into the cohesive National History of the settler-colonial state.[18]

Following these recent scholarship and debates, and Yoneyama's lead in particular, I examine what "transpacific demands for historical justice" look like by focusing my analysis on the San Francisco–based CWJC and transpacific solidarity that incited support to erect the "Women's Column of Strength," a memorial for comfort women. Specifically, this chapter is interested in examining the twofold processes of what Yoneyama calls Asian/Americanization of justice. How does the San Francisco–based CWJC advance its political goals? What kind of challenges and possibilities does it face in its transpacific redress movement?

Analyzing the "transpacific entanglements" between US wars in Asia, US racial capitalism, and US empire-building, groundbreaking works by Yến Lê Espiritu, Lisa Lowe, and Yoneyama have challenged the American exceptionalism that "has rationalized US military and capitalist interventions in Asia and the Pacific Islands as necessary for the 'national security' of the United States and for the humanitarian 'rescue' of Asian peoples."[19] Naoki Sakai further traces the formation of US hegemony in the Asia Pacific region following World War II, when the US occupation administration purposefully preserved certain social orders to effectively create the new global order led by the United States.[20] Focusing on the Japanese case, Sakai discusses how the US administration preserved Hirohito, the supreme commander in chief of the Armed Imperial Forces of Japan, in order to use him as a puppet leader and the symbol of the unity of the Japanese nation.[21] To make this happen the emperor's war and colonial wrongdoing had to be forgiven, which was officially handled by the International Military Tribunal for the Far East (the so-called Tokyo War Crimes Tribunal). Likewise, to maintain cohesion in the nation, the occupation administration allowed the Japanese people to preserve their sense of national tradition and culture. What Sakai calls "the paradox of Japanese nationalism" was developed in the process: the Japanese had to "insist on the separation from and even indifference toward people of neighboring countries in East and Southeast Asia" yet "welcome United States' domination and tend to find their own desires within the scenario of Pax Americana."[22] Sakai argues that Japanese nationalism and US imperial nationalism reinforce each other, creating and perpetuating a transpacific complicity to sustain a cold war governmentality, not only in Japan but also in other parts of Asia under US hegemony.[23] Kuan-Hsing Chen shrewdly describes this complicity when writing that "the United States [had] become the inside of East Asia, and it [was] constitutive of a new East Asian subjectivity."[24] What has been postponed in this structure of transpacific complicity, Sakai argues, is the decolonization of former colonies of the Japanese empire and redress for colonial atrocities, including Japan's military sexual slavery.[25]

This precise structure of transpacific complicity had long been marginalized but then resurfaced in the 1990s, not only in the nations that the Japanese military colonized and occupied but also in the United States. The following analysis employs ethnography and in-depth interviews of CWJC and Kansai Network members and activists in San Francisco and Tokyo, as well as a review of the materials and processes employed in the unanimous passage of the San Francisco board of supervisors' comfort women resolution in 2015.[26] Also examined are various statements released by the CWJC, the Kansai Network, and individuals and groups that opposed the proposed resolution.

BACKGROUND ON THE CWJC AND THE SF MEMORIAL

On September 22, 2018, hundreds of people gathered in St. Mary's Square in San Francisco to celebrate the first anniversary of the establishment of the memorial for the victims and survivors of Japan's military sexual slavery. The memorial, "Women's Column of Strength" (fig. 7.1), was designed by local sculptor Steven Whyte and consists of three girls atop a platform, holding their hands tight, and an older woman standing by herself on the ground nearby. The girls, representing the victims from the Korean Peninsula, China, and the Philippines, are barefoot, signifying the sudden deprivation of their otherwise mundane, ordinary life against their will, and their rigid faces show determination to speak the truth and to fight for redress. The lone statue is

FIG. 7.1. "Women's Column of Strength" memorial in St. Mary's Square, San Francisco. Photo by Kyung Hee Ha.

of Kim Hak-sun, one of the first women to come forward as a former comfort woman, in 1992. Holding her hands together, Kim looks up at the girls and exudes warmth and resilience. Winkles in her face indicate the years of shame, silence, and anger experienced by victims in the post–World War II period. "Women's Column of Strength" is the first memorial built in a major US city; it acknowledges the pain and trauma of victims of Japan's sexual slavery and honors their courage to speak out and bring justice to all victims of wartime sexual slavery.

The resolution urging the establishment of a comfort women memorial was introduced by Eric Mar, District 1 supervisor, and the passage efforts were spearheaded by the Comfort Women Justice Coalition. The CWJC is co-chaired by Lilian Sing and Julie Tang, both of whom were retired judges, and consists of nearly forty different grassroots organizations from various racial, ethnic, cultural, and generational backgrounds.[27] These organizations have close relationships with activists and support groups in their diasporic home countries of South Korea, the Philippines, and Taiwan, which have worked on the issue of Japan's military sexual slavery for many decades. Utilizing these diasporic ties, the CWJC successfully galvanized global support for the campaign. In addition, the majority of the core members of the CWJC are Asians and Asian Americans, many of whom carry memories of Japanese aggression that they themselves or their family members experienced firsthand. These personal memories have led numerous Asian and Asian American members to join in the redress movement. Following unanimous board of supervisors approval, the memorial was unveiled exactly two years later, on September 22, 2017.[28]

DENIALISTS CROSS THE PACIFIC

As in the case of other cities where the comfort women memorials had been built, the effort in San Francisco was met with opposition from Japanese nationals and the *shin issei*, or "new first generation" immigrants from Japan who immigrated to the United States during or after the 1980s.[29] On Saturday, December 13, 2014, Nadeshiko Action, a Japanese rightwing women's group (which also calls itself Japanese Women for Peace and Justice) held a public event at a local community center in Redwood City, California.[30] The event featured the group's president, Yumiko Yamamoto, the former vice president and secretary general of an ultranationalist and far-right political organization, Zaitokukai.[31] Yamamoto aimed to build support among Japanese immigrants for her organization, which denies Japan's military sexual slavery. Yamamoto traveled to the Bay Area and Los Angeles as part of a larger effort to launch an international campaign to "put an end to the lie" about comfort women as sexual slaves.[32]

Learning about this event, Miho Kim, a cofounder of Eclipse Rising, a local group of Koreans from Japan, reached out and mobilized several other groups, including Veterans for Peace, No Nukes Action Committee, United Public Workers for Action, Bay Area Code Pink, Japan-US Feminist Network for Decolonization, and US-China Peoples Friendship Association, to attend a press conference and protest in front of the community center where the Nadeshiko Action event was being held. A dozen protesters gathered and spoke against militarism, historical denialism, and xenophobic racism, holding various picket signs. Yamamoto and her associates approached them and started to ask questions. Insisting that she is not a historian nor interested in any historical debates, Yamamoto seemed relatively calm and confident until she saw one sign being held by a protestor, that said "Stop Racist Attack on Zainichi Korean Community." *Zainichi* Koreans (literally "Korean residents in Japan") are Korean postcolonial exiles and their descendants whose diasporic root is found in Japanese colonization of the Korean Peninsula. Clearly disturbed and somewhat puzzled, Yamamoto exclaimed, "What the . . . !" Why do you know this word, Zainichi? . . . I'd like to say I have never attacked Zainichi Koreans. I am not a racist."[33] She was confused as to why he who is a white American knew the word, Zainichi, which in her mind and probably many others does not apply beyond the Japanese context.

Nadeshiko Action has been active in the United States ever since. In March 2015 it planned to hold panel presentations in New York City at the Japanese American Community Center. When learning the kind of events Nadeshiko Action was planning to hold, the Japanese American Community Center canceled the events, but the organizer managed to find a restaurant to hold the presentations.[34] In March 2016 Nadeshiko Action in New York City, sponsored an event called "Misunderstood Comfort Women" and "Women's Rights under Armed Conflicts: Japan's Approach to Respect Women," as a part of the NGO parallel events being hosted by the Commission on the Status of Women (CSW) to appeal to the United Nations and international organizations regarding the "truth about 'comfort women.'"[35]

In the United States the Japanese denialist efforts around the issue began as early as 2007, when dozens of influential Japanese right-wing politicians, journalists, and scholars, including former prime minister Shinzo Abe, placed a paid advertisement titled "The Facts" on the *Washington Post* (June 24, 2007), to "present historical facts" about "comfort women."[36] Later, denialist organizations such as Nadeshiko Action and the Global Alliance for Historical Truth (GAHT), led by Koichi Mera, started a more grassroots approach for spreading their message to the Japanese-speaking immigrant population in the United States. Mera and other denialist activists, such as Terumi Imamura of True Japan Network and Mariko Okada-Collins from Central Washington University, traveled to San Francisco to testify against the resolution in the public hearings held by the city's board of supervisors in 2015.[37]

LOCAL JAPANESE AMERICANS' OPPOSITION

What was unique about San Francisco was the opposition by a number of local Japanese Americans. Supervisor Eric Mar, who introduced the resolution to call on the erection of a memorial for comfort women, along with other supervisors who cosponsored the resolution and numerous community supporters were "caught off guard" when they learned that prominent Japanese American leaders were opposing the proposed resolution.[38] It was particularly confounding that people like Emily Murase, who served as director of the San Francisco Department on the Status of Women from 2004 to 2020, dissented over the resolution and the building of the memorial in San Francisco.

In 1998 San Francisco became the first city in the world to adopt an ordinance reflecting the principles of the Convention on the Elimination of all Forms of Discrimination Against Women (CEDAW), an international treaty adopted in 1979 by the United Nations General Assembly. In fact, the city's initiative on equality and justice for women of all kinds goes back to 1975, when the Commission on the Status of Women was established "to ensure women and girls equal economic, social, political and educational opportunities throughout the City."[39] Then, in 1994 the permanent Department on the Status of Women was created to carry out the policies of the commission, and Murase served as its director for more than fifteen years. For decades the commission and the department have worked closely with community-based organizations to combat domestic violence and human trafficking, as well as to assure paid parental leave, protection for sex workers, gender pay equity, and violence prevention and intervention.

The Department on the Status of Women does not solely address specific challenges faced by local residents of San Francisco; it also advocates for women and trafficking victims elsewhere. For example, when then-mayor of Osaka Hashimoto Toru made remarks in 2013 claiming the wartime brothels were "necessary" for soldiers, Murase called his statement "very damaging" as it seemed "to justify the exploitation and suffering experienced by the women, some just girls, who were forced into prostitution by the Japanese military during World War II [and] is a flagrant denial of basic human rights. Sex slavery is never 'necessary.'"[40] The San Francisco–Osaka Sister City Association, of which Murase serves on the board, also criticized Hashimoto's statement, stating that his comment "in no way reflects the position of the Association, nor the spirit of the sister city relationship."[41] Subsequently, the San Francisco board of supervisors adopted a resolution that "strongly condemns the attitude and statements of Mayor Toru Hashimoto of Osaka justifying the state-sponsored 'comfort women' system, which forced hundreds of thousands of Asian women into sexual servitude for the Japanese military."[42] The series of protests resulted in the cancellation of Hashimoto's visit to San Francisco.

Given this background, members of the CWJC were surprised to be met with opposition from Murase and other local Japanese American leaders who have worked against violence targeting women and girls and human trafficking—the exact kind of violence suffered by victims of the sexual slavery system that the memorial symbolizes. In addition, the late Janice Mirikitani, a renowned poet and civil rights activist who was incarcerated in a US internment camp as a young girl, shared her concern for the memorial in her letter to the Commission on the Status of Women. Mirikitani emphasized her support for the comfort women redress movement and "it's [sic] goal toward acknowledgement and past and living remembrance of atrocities against the most innocent as spoils of war . . . in this particular case, the Japanese Imperialistic Military."[43] However, she believed that a memorial being part of public debate was "not appropriate" because it would "**engender ill feelings against Japan and by association, Japanese Americans, and perpetuate[s] historical resentment against our country of origins and historical conflicts.**"[44] Although Mirikitani initially agreed to be a part of the comfort women memorial building effort, she later requested to have her name removed because the drafted resolution "feels divisive and singly directed against Japan."[45] Her statement indicates the trauma from mass incarceration during the World War II and the fear that the comfort women memorial naming Japan as a perpetrator nation might help repeat the dark history.

How do we begin to understand the opposition voiced by Japanese Americans who have spent years in advocating for civil rights and women's rights? The narratives by Japanese American community leaders who have publicly expressed their opposition to the comfort women memorial in San Francisco and Mirikitani's letter addressed to the commission on the Status of Women, along with accounts by other opponents cited in scholarly work and mass media, provide a source for close examination.

OPPOSITIONAL NARRATIVES: CONGRUENCE WITH DENIALISM

The narratives put forward by the Japanese American community leaders, none of whom denies the existence of Japanese military's sexual slavery system, are highly congruent with statements employed by ultranationalist Japanese politicians and denialist groups that deny the issue outright, undermine its seriousness, or claim that it has been resolved. Specifically, criticism on "singling out Japan" was voiced by numerous politicians who sponsored the *Washington Post* ad in 2007, along with former Osaka mayor Hashimoto Toru and other grassroots organizations like Nadeshiko Action in more recent years. In addition, the fear of resulting racial violence and systemic discrimination shared by Japanese Americans has been manipulated by Japanese politicians like Sugita Mio and popular magazines like *Shukan Spa*, both of which disseminated a groundless rumor that Japanese residents are being bullied in Glendale, California, due to the presence of a comfort women memorial.[46]

COMFORT WOMEN MEMORIAL "SINGLES OUT" JAPAN

Many local opponents expressed that Japan was unfairly singled out in the wording of the comfort women resolution. In her letter, Mirikitani proposed a memorial that is "not singling out one country, ie [*sic*]. Japan" but is inclusive of "all atrocities against women and children, including modern day sex slavery, trafficking, and genocide against people of color."[47] Likewise, Kathleen Kimura, co-chairwoman of the San Francisco–Osaka Sister City Association, said singling out the country in a statue memorializing sexually enslaved women is "a little bit unfair" as "war is a horrible thing, and war brings out the worst in mankind."[48] Noting that she was not speaking for the Sister City Association, Kimura added, "My objection to all of this is this whole effort has been to single out Japan as the only bad guy."[49] This is the exact narrative shared by Hashimoto Toru, the former Osaka mayor, whose visit to San Francisco was canceled due to his remark calling wartime brothels "necessary" in 2013. Responding to the storm of criticism from domestic and abroad, Hashimoto later explained that he did not "intend to justify [the comfort women system] but various countries at the time had similar schemes." He said that Japan only is being "unduly insulted" and singled out for its wartime sexual enslavement.[50] In their defense of Japan, Mirikitani, Kimura, and Hashimoto claim that other countries have also committed similar acts of violence. Accordingly, they suggest to either remove the word "Japan" or to juxtapose Japan's military sexual slavery with other instances of atrocities in the past and present. This sort of attempt to universalize the war crimes while erasing specificities obfuscates the Japanese state's responsibility, which survivors and supporters have demanded for decades.

INCITING RACISM AGAINST THE JAPANESE COMMUNITY

Another concern expressed by the opponents was that a comfort women memorial that singles out Japan would incite racism against Japan and, by association, Japanese Americans. Mirikitani emphasized in her letter that her major concern was that "**the governmental involvement in this debate continues to engender ill feelings against Japan and by association, Japanese Americans, and perpetuates historical resentment against our country of origins and historical conflicts.**"[51] Mirikitani's sentiment was also expressed by Caryl Ito, a former president of the Commission on the Status of Woman. On September 17, 2015, at a meeting of the Public Safety and Neighborhood Services Committee at San Francisco City Hall, where various opinions were heard about the comfort women resolution, Ito suggested that the proposed resolution could increase the hatred, division, and racism targeting Japanese Americans. As she said, "[Social justice] should never be at the expense of another ethnic group."[52] Mirikitani and Ito remind us of the mass incarceration of 120,000 Japanese and Japanese Americans after Japan's surprise aerial attack on the US naval base at Pearl Harbor in Hawai'i in December 1941. By association, Japanese immigrants and native-born American citizens of Japanese descent were rounded up and sent to internment camps against their will. Recent studies show that this mass incarceration was carried out against people of Japanese descent but not descendants of other "Axis of evil" countries (i.e., Germany or Italy) because anti-Japanese racism had existed well before the Pearl Harbor attack and this racial trauma is passed down to later generations.[53]

Fortunately, there have been no reported incidents targeting Japanese residents in the United States, where more than fifteen comfort women memorials of various kinds of have been installed. However, ultranationalist and homophobic Japanese diet member Sugita Mio raised an issue of Japanese bullying during the Japanese House of Representatives Budget Committee meeting on February 3, 2014. Other lawmakers made a similar claim, that Japanese residents had been targeted in Glendale, California, because a comfort memorial was installed and it incited hatred against Japanese.[54] One popular tabloid magazine, *Shukan Spa!*, devoted two issues to disseminating the false rumors of Japanese bullying. Neither the consulate-general of Japan in Los Angeles nor the local police department has confirmed any reports on bullying to this day.[55] This is but one example where race-based historical trauma shared by many Japanese Americans is maliciously mobilized to make a false claim.

"JAPAN HAS APOLOGIZED MANY TIMES"

When discussing the comfort women issue in Japan and the United States, I have encountered numerous people who argue that Japan has apologized multiple times and paid reparations to the victims. This same narrative is repeated by Japanese American opponents. In her letter, Mirikitani claims that records show that there had been "apologies by several prime ministers of Japan" and that "millions [had been] paid in reparations to the Asian Womens [sic] fund for the comfort women in Korea and China and Phillippines [sic]."[56] Emily Murase of the Department on the Status of Women has reiterated this line of narrative. On September 18, 2015, a comfort women survivor and human right activist Yong Soo Lee, who was visiting from South Korea to testify to the supervisors, had a meeting with Murase and CWJC members. In the meeting Murase insisted that Japan had apologized many times and the issue had already been resolved.[57]

Murase's statement coincides with the official account by the Ministry of

Foreign Affairs of Japan, which says the issue has been "resolved finally and irreversibly" through the "agreement" between Japan and South Korea.[58] It is true that there have been statements, such as the so-called Kono Statement of 1993 and Murayama Statement of 1995, that recognize the involvement of military authorities in the system of sexual slavery and express "sincere apologies" and "deep remorse."[59] It is also true that a quasi-government organization, the Asian Women's Fund (1995 to 2007), provided an apology letter signed by the prime minister along with monetary compensation to the surviving victims.[60] However, to this day the Japanese government has not taken legal responsibility for the enslavement of thousands of women and girls, including investigation of the crimes and persecution of the perpetrators.

Why do these Japanese American women, who have spent years in advocating for women's rights and civil rights, end up narrating similar accounts as those of historical denialists? What does these attempts to defend Japan mean? One way to think about these questions is to understand the role that the Japanese American community and individuals have played in what Naoki Sakai calls "transpacific complicity" between Japanese nationalism and US imperial nationalism. Takashi Fujitani's critical reading of a memorandum authored by Edwin O. Reischauer in September 1942 reveals the wartime foundations of the postwar US-Japan relationship.[61] Merely ten months into the war against Japan, Reischauer had already made a number of strategic propositions for during and after the war, including enlisting Japanese Americans soldiers alongside other people of color to promote the United States as a nonracist nation and to achieve active incorporation of Japan, its emperor, and Japanese Americans into what was imagined to be a new global order led by US hegemony in the postwar period.[62] As early as 1947, at the height of the Cold War, the policies of the US government and the US-led Allied Force that occupied Japan (1945–52) shifted emphasis from the demilitarization and democratization of Japan to economic reconstruction and remilitarization of Japan to fit US Cold War strategies. Commonly known as the "Reverse Course," the shift meant more than building a strategic military alliance between the two nations. It also meant strengthening economic cooperation and deepening cultural understanding by mobilizing ordinary citizens to participate in the broader effort. One example of this civic effort was an initiative that began in 1956 when President Dwight D. Eisenhower proposed a people-to-people citizen diplomacy initiative to create partnerships between communities in the United States and those in other countries through the establishment of "sister cities."[63] Osaka was the first sister city of San Francisco and that relationship began in 1957.[64] Kathleen Kimura, a white American married to a Japanese American, serves as co-chair of the San Francisco–Osaka Sister City Association. Emily Murase, who served as director of the Department on the Status of Women (2004–20), sits on the board of the Sister City Association and is a recipient of the 2021 Japanese Foreign Minister's Commendation after formerly serving as the Northern California regional chair of the US-Japan Council; as the commendation reads, she "devoted herself to strengthening relations and promoting mutual understanding between Japan and the United States."[65] These examples demonstrate the critical role Japanese Americans play in strengthening US-Japan relations where Japanese nationalism and US imperial nationalism reinforce each other. Some of the Japanese American community leaders discussed here are able to maintain their cultural identity and political subjectivity as *Japanese* and as *American* precisely within the context of transpacific complicity. As Naoki Sakai states, transpacific complicity has excused accountability of Emperor Hirohito, war criminals, and the Japanese nation in their wartime and colonial atrocities in the first half of the twentieth century.[66] This transpacific complicity has also turned a blind eye to the war crimes and sexual violence inflicted by the US military in Japan, South Korea, and other parts of the world. When memorial opponents criticized the singling out of Japan they often implied that other nations have also committed a similar crime, but none of them named the United States.

RESPONSES BY THE CWJC

How did the Comfort Women Justice Coalition respond to the opposition and concerns shared by community members? As a start, two Japanese American supporters of the CWJC, the late Peter Kenichi Yamamoto, an award-winning poet and longtime activist, and Grace Shimizu, a Japanese Latin American activist, participated in the Japantown Task Force meeting to have a dialogue with concerned Japanese American community leaders.[67] While the Japanese American leaders did not question the historical validity of the comfort women issue, many expressed their opposition to the proposed memorial because they thought it would be used against Japanese Americans. Meanwhile, the CWJC continued to work closely with Japanese American leaders from Southern California, like Kathy Masaoka and David Monkawa, both of whom were supportive of and involved with the building of the Peace Monument of Glendale, a replica of the original Statue of Peace dedicated to comfort women.[68] The monument was funded and built in 2013 by the Korean American Forum of California, whose executive director, Phyllis Kim, became a secretary of the CWJC.

Additionally, in order to overturn the perception that the memorial is "anti-Japan" in nature and unfairly singling out Japan, it was urgently crucial for the CWJC to work closely with Japanese organizations and activists. Together they appealed to the stakeholders for the resolution that people in Japan are actually supporting the memorialization of comfort women in the United States. As a first transpacific collaborative project, the CWJC carried out the letter campaign in coordination with the Osaka-based Kansai Network.[69] The Kansai Network was founded in 2009 with co-chairs Bang Chungja (second-generation Zainichi Korean woman), Nishimura Sumiko, and Okuda Kazuhiro; the group later became a local chapter of the Japan Nationwide Network for Resolution of Japan's Military "Comfort Women" Issue in 2010.[70] Under the leadership of the Kansai Network, more than twenty civic organizations in Osaka and other cities in Japan sent letters of support to the board of supervisors and the late mayor Edwin Lee, stating that they regard the memorial not as a symbol of Japan bashing but as "the renewed commitment of people and the government of San Francisco to ensure that such violation of human rights and crime against humanity never occur again"; they all "express[ed] [their] unequivocal support" for the resolution.[71] Furthermore, during the public hearing scheduled on September 17, 2015, the CWJC strategically included testimonies by Japanese nationals who supported the memorial.[72]

In the end, though the San Francisco board of supervisors unanimously passed a resolution to build a comfort women memorial in the city and agreed to begin educating the community about stopping human trafficking

of women and girls, the wording of the resolution generated intense negotiations until hours before the vote to address the concerns of it being "anti-Japanese." Supervisors Scott Wiener and Norman Yee suggested inserting
a sentence like "Japan is not the only country that has victimized women."[73]
Accordingly, one sentence was added: "Victimization of women occurred
in other countries, however, it does not in any way excuses the actions of
the Japanese Imperial Army."[74] Other minor changes were also made to the
sentence regarding modern-day human trafficking and the wartime mass
incarceration of Japanese Americans.

After the passing of the resolution, the CWJC continued to work with
different stakeholders—from the Recreation and Parks Department and the
San Francisco Arts Commission to various board supervisors and late Mayor
Lee—to find a site, to raise funds, to choose the design of the memorial,
and to obtain multiple approvals. Another thing that the CWJC was able to
accomplish was to include the comfort women issue alongside the Nanjing
Massacre in China in the tenth grade world history curriculum of California.[75] Transpacific collaborative work between the people of San Francisco
and Osaka also continued and strengthened. In March 2016 Kwangmin
Kim, from the Osaka-based Korea NGO Center, visited San Francisco and
gave a lecture on rising Japanese nationalism and the issue of anti-Korean
hate demonstrations.[76] In November of the same year, members of the CWJC
visited Osaka and Tokyo to participate in the international symposium and
meet the survivors and supporters from South Korea, the Philippines, Indonesia, East Timor, and Japan. In Osaka, the Kansai Network hosted a CWJC
panel discussion event.

Meanwhile, Osaka mayor Yoshimura Hirofumi, Hashimoto's successor,
conveyed his disappointment in five open letters to Mayor Lee, urging the
removal of the comfort women memorial and plaque from public property.[77]
In response to Yoshimura's repeated threat to terminate the sixty-year-long
sister city relationship, citizens of Osaka organized protests and made public
awareness–raising efforts. In November 2017 these groups submitted the petition endorsed by 135 individuals and forty-eight organizations in Japan, such
as women's organizations and labor unions, to Mayor Lee to express their
hope that the "Women's Column of Strength" be approved as a municipal
memorial.[78] In San Francisco the CWJC released a statement in solidarity with

Osaka citizens, urging Yoshimura "to join [our] struggle and to learn not only from the 'Comfort Women' Justice Movement, but also from a long legacy of enlightened human rights movements in Japan led by peoples colonized by Imperial Japan, including the Hisabetsu Buraku ('Untouchables'), Zainichi Korean, Taiwanese, Okinawan, and Ainu communities."[79]

In September 2018 a dozen representatives from Osaka participated in the first anniversary event held to commemorate the placement of the memorial. At this event the Kansai Network was awarded the Certificate of Honor by the San Francisco board of supervisors for its "commitment to the efforts to finding a resolve for the 'Comfort Women' issue and to promote women's human rights by continuing to strengthen the solidarity with the people of San Francisco to fight against historical denialism."[80]

NO MENTION OF THE UNITED STATES AS PERPETRATOR

While the cwjc was successful in erecting the comfort women memorial, having high school students in California start learning about the issue in their world history curriculum, and in strengthening transpacific collaboration with activists and support groups in Osaka, a critique of sexual violence inflicted by the US military on women and girls in Japan, South Korea, and other parts of the world is virtually nonexistent within its official activities. Operating within the US institutional framework and with extensive knowledge on how justice is institutionally legitimized and distributed in the US judicial system, the cwjc rarely names the war crimes and sexual violence inflicted by the US military or shakes transpacific complicity to its foundation as manifested through the opposition force built by Japanese American community leaders. For example, the unanimously passed resolution by the board mentions that other countries also victimized women in the past and human trafficking is a global issue to this day. These points are made to emphasize the relevance of sexual enslavement that occurred in Asia Pacific in the 1930s and 1940s to the contemporary US context, hence the urgency of memorializing these victims in San Francisco. Similarly, the "Joint Statement by SF 'Comfort Women' Justice Coalition and Kansai Network of Osaka" released on October 11, 2018, which criticized Osaka Mayor Yoshimura's threat to terminate the sister city relationship with San Francisco, cites Nadia

Murad as another exemplar of more contemporary sexual violence survivors. Murad is a Yazidi woman who was sexually enslaved by ISIS and received the Nobel Peace Prize in 2018 for her "efforts to end the use of sexual violence as a weapon of war and armed conflict."[81] The joint statement made a clear connection between the comfort women and Murad's suffering, in that "her courage and commitment to speak out echos [sic] that of the 'comfort women.'"[82] A number of statements and speeches have been made by the CWJC members, but none of them explicitly compares comfort women with the victims of sexual violence inflicted by the US military. What is significant is that, as gender studies scholar Lee Na-Young's work reveals, there is a clear continuity of exploitation of local women's sexuality between Japan's military comfort women and the US military's camp town prostitutes in South Korea. While prostitution remained illegal in the United States, US leaders stationed in South Korea used regulated prostitution services in military camp towns with the help of the South Korean government.[83] In establishing the system of controlled prostitution, the US military took over land once used for military bases as well as for licensed prostitution by the Japanese military to serve the same exact purposes.[84] These include areas such as Yongsan and Itaewon, both of which are located in the heart of Seoul. Throughout the Korean and Vietnam Wars, more than a million Korean women have sexually catered to US soldiers in the military camp towns.[85] In 2014, 122 former camp town sex workers sued the South Korean government to seek compensation and damages for this state-run prostitution, and in 2022 the Supreme Court confirmed a lower court ruling that ordered the state to pay each plaintiff between 3 and 7 million won ($2,308–$5,387 USD).[86]

Sexual exploitation by the US military is not only comparable to that of the Japanese military; it is also relational to it, as the former is precisely built upon the latter. Even with these clear connections, neither the opponents nor the proponents of the comfort women memorial explicitly names the United States as a perpetrator state. Is this a testament to US-based comfort women justice movement's limitations to direct its criticism toward its own government, thereby essentially exonerating US military atrocities while also singling out Japan? How can the CWJC challenge a transpacific complicity between Japanese nationalism and US imperial nationalism that has relegated wartime and colonial atrocities?

CHALLENGING TRANSPACIFIC COMPLICITY

In thinking about a possibility of challenging US and Japanese military violence simultaneously, we now turn to postcolonial studies and mixed-race studies scholar Annmaria Shimabuku's concept of "transpacific colonialism," which highlights US and Japanese colonialism not solely as something parallel and comparable but as relational and mutually dependent.[87] Shimabuku focuses her analysis on Okinawa and the controversy around the US military presence, arguing that it is often framed as an issue of conservative versus progressive politics internal to the Japanese state. Consequently, a problem of Japanese colonial domination over Okinawa and the United States–Japan Security Treaty is overlooked. By concealing how colonialism traverses nation-state borders, colonizers are able to contain colonialism within national borders, leading the colonized to seek liberation in the respective nation-state only. Shimabuku writes: "In other words, if the struggle for racial equality focuses *only* on equality within a single nation-state, then Okinawans and American ethnic minorities can never encounter each other as fellow colonized people betrayed by a transpacific colonialism. Instead, they would approach each other only as Japanese and American national subjects."[88] Shimabuku calls for solidarity between the colonized subjects in Japan and the United States to challenge this transpacific colonialism. The collaborative campaigns and activities that members of the CWJC and the Kansai Network have engaged in suggest just this form of solidarity, encountering each other not only as Japanese and Americans but as fellow colonized subjects.

The Kansai Network's co-chair is Bang Chungja, a second-generation Zainichi Korean woman, and its members share an understanding of the comfort women issue at the intersection of patriarchy and Japanese colonialism that underlies their activities. In San Francisco, most of the core multigenerational members of the CWJC are Asian Americans, including Chinese, Japanese, Filipinos, Koreans, Okinawans, and Zainichi Koreans who have organized around the issues of racism, militarism, and women's rights.[89] As Lisa Lowe argues in her seminal work *Immigrant Acts*, the majority of post-1965 Asian immigrants to the United States came from countries that had been disrupted by multiple colonial powers and global capitalism, such as South Korea, the Philippines, and South Vietnam.[90] She writes: "The material legacy of the repressed history of U.S. imperialism in Asia is borne out in the 'return' of Asian immigrants to the imperial center."[91] The pan-Asian nature of CWJC membership is precisely a product of US imperialism and the subsequent "return" of the colonized to the imperial metropole.

The series of San Francisco–Osaka campaigns and activities were carefully planned and executed under the leadership of the CWJC's Zainichi Korean steering committee members Miho Kim and Tomomi Kinukawa. In their coauthored article, Kim and Kinukawa assert that Zainichi Koreans who now reside in the United States are simultaneously (post-)colonial subjects of Japan and a racialized minority of the United States.[92] Importantly, it was not just their linguistic and cultural knowledge in both Japanese and US contexts that played an important role in bridging the cultural gaps between people of Osaka and San Francisco, but also their mutual consciousness of this status. This consciousness helped carefully frame the solidarity, based on an anticolonial, antiracist, feminist vision instead of on universal human rights, which might present the possibility of a radical politicization of justice that does not exceptionalize the United States.

CONCLUSION

This examination of the CWJC's political campaigns and related activities to build a comfort women memorial reveals the possibilities and challenges that transpacific political formations present for historical justice, redress, and decolonization. Building and strengthening the working relationship between peoples of San Francisco and Osaka allowed the CWJC to counter the oppositional narratives of the memorial being "anti-Japan." However, the CWJC did not necessarily address the transpacific complicity of Japanese nationalism and US imperial nationalism or the underlying context in which Japanese American community leaders have maintained their cultural identity and political subjectivity as Japanese and as American. Moreover, by juxtaposing Japan's military sexual slavery against other instances of atrocities both in the past and present, including modern-day sex trafficking and ISIS's systemic sexual violence against women, the CWJC was able to universalize the issue and mobilize support from different communities. However, the war crimes and atrocities committed by the US military as well as the direct connection between the Japanese military's comfort women and the US military's camp town prostitutes were never explicitly mentioned in their official narratives. Nonetheless, and despite these omissions, the solidarity between San Francisco's CWJC and Osaka's Kansai Network suggests a possibility of creating a critical terrain to interrogate and challenge Japanese and US militarism as well as transpacific complicity.

In February 2021 a few core members of the CWJC, along with Okinawan American activists, helped passage of a resolution opposing new US base construction in the Henoko-Oura Bay of Okinawa—the planned relocation site for the US Marine Corps Futenma Air Station by city of Berkeley.[93] The resolution highlights the negative impacts of the construction on "one of the most bio-diverse ecosystems on the planet with over 5,300 species and world-renown coral reef systems" as well as the aggressive and undemocratic imposition by "the Japanese government, in partnership with the U.S. government," despite the overwhelming opposition of local Okinawans.[94] This may be an isolated instance where a US municipal government takes a critical stand against Japanese and the US government's complicity in expanding its military bases. Or it may suggest a possibility where transpacific solidarity is able to simultaneously call out Japanese war crimes and an American race war at home and abroad, both of which have long been pushed aside and made invisible.

NOTES

1. "Statement by National Security Advisor Susan E. Rice on the Republic of Korea-Japan Agreement on 'Comfort Women,'" December 28, 2015, National Archives and Records Administration, https://obamawhitehouse.archives.gov/the-press-office/2015/12/28/statement-national-security-advisor-susan-e-rice-republic-korea-japan.

2. Ministry of Foreign Affairs of Japan, "Announcement by Foreign Ministers of Japan and the Republic of Korea at the Joint Press Occasion," December 28, 2015, https://www.mofa.go.jp/a_o/na/kr/page4e_000364.html.

3. Sheila A. Smith, "The President as Facilitator in Chief," March 26, 2014, Council on Foreign Relations, https://www.cfr.org/blog/president-facilitator-chief.

4. Smith, "The President as Facilitator in Chief."

5. Ministry of Foreign Affairs of Japan, "Announcement by Foreign Ministers of Japan."

6. Tomomi Yamaguchi, "The 'History Wars' and the 'Comfort Woman' Issue: Re-

visionism and the Right-Wing in Contemporary Japan and the U.S.," *Japan Focus: The Asia Pacific Journal* 18, no. 6 (March 15, 2020), https://apjjf.org/2020/6/Yamaguchi.html.

7. San Francisco Board of Supervisors, Resolution No. 342-15, "Urging the Establishment of a Memorial for 'Comfort Women'" (September 22, 2015), https://sfbos.org/ftp/uploadedfiles/bdsupvrs/resolutions15/r0342-15.pdf.

8. Naoki Sakai, "Transpacific Complicity and Comparatist Strategy: Failure in Decolonization and the Rise of Japanese Nationalism," in *Globalizing American Studies*, ed. Brian T. Edwards and Gaonkar Dilip Parameshwar (Chicago: University of Chicago Press, 2010), 240–65.

9. The Global Alliance for Preserving the History of World War II in Asia is a nonprofit, nonpartisan worldwide federation of over forty grassroots organizations founded in 1994 to preserve the historical truth of the Asia-Pacific War (1931–45). For more information, see the group's official website at https://www.global-alliance.net/home.html.

10. Resolution 121 was adopted in the US House of Representatives on July 30, 2007. It reads: "A resolution expressing the sense of the House of Representatives that the Government of Japan should formally acknowledge, apologize, and accept historical responsibility in a clear and unequivocal manner for its Imperial Armed Forces' coercion of young women into sexual slavery, known to the world as "comfort women," during its colonial and wartime occupation of Asia and the Pacific Islands from the 1930s through the duration of World War II." See U.S. Congress website, accessed March 6, 2020, https://www.congress.gov/bill/110th-congress/house-resolution/121/text.

11. Pyong Gap Min, Thomas Chung, and Sejung Sage Yim, *The Transnational Redress Movement for the Victims of Japanese Military Sexual Slavery* (Berlin: De Gruyter Oldenbourg, 2020).

12. Mary M. McCarthy and Linda C. Hasunuma, "Coalition Building and Mobilization: Case Studies of the Comfort Women Memorials in the United States," *Politics, Groups, and Identities* 6, no. 3 (2018): 411–34.

13. Tomomi Yamaguchi, "Kanmin Ittai no 'Rekishisen' no Yukue" [Destination for history wars fought by governments and civilians], in *Umi wo Wataru 'Ianfu' Mondai* ["Comfort Women Issues" Crossing the Ocean], ed. Tomomi Yamaguchi, Nogawa Motokazu, and Tessa Morris-Suzuki (Tokyo: Iwanami Shoten, 2016), 98–136.

14. Elizabeth W. Son, *Embodied Reckonings: "Comfort Women," Performance, and Transpacific Redress* (Ann Arbor: University of Michigan Press, 2018).

15. Laura Hyun Yi Kang, *Traffic in Asian Women* (Durham, NC: Duke University Press, 2020).

16. Lisa Yoneyama, "Traveling Memories, Contagious Justice: Americanization of Japanese War Crimes at the End of the Post-Cold War," *Journal of Asian American Studies* 6, no. 1 (2003): 57–93.

17. Yoneyama, 61.

18. Lisa Yoneyama, *Cold War Ruins: Transpacific Critique of American Justice and Japanese War Crimes* (Durham, NC: Duke University Press, 2016), 173.

19. Yến Lê Espiritu, Lisa Lowe, and Lisa Yoneyama, "Transpacific Entanglements," in *Flashpoints for Asian American Studies*, ed. Cathy J. Schlund-Vials (New York: Fordham University Press, 2017), 176.

20. Sakai, "Transpacific Complicity and Comparatist Strategy."

21. Sakai, 248, 253.

22. Sakai, 244.

23. Sakai, 244–45.

24. Kuan-hsing Chen, *Asia as Method: Toward Deimperialization* (Durham, NC: Duke University Press, 2010), 8.

25. Sakai, "Transpacific Complicity and Comparatist Strategy."

26. San Francisco Board of Supervisors, Resolution No. 342-15, "Urging the Establishment of a Memorial for 'Comfort Women.'"

27. See the list of coalition members at the CWJC's website, accessed March 1, 2023, https://remembercomfortwomen.org/coalition-members-2/.

28. Tomo Hirai, "S.F. Board of Supes Unanimously Passes 'Comfort Women' Memorial Resolution," *Nichi Bei Times* (San Francisco), October 1, 2015, https://www.nichibei.org/2015/10/s-f-board-of-supes-unanimously-passes-comfort-women-memorial-resolution/; CODA WORX, "Comfort Women's Column of Strength," accessed June 1, 2020, https://www.codaworx.com/projects/comfort-women-s-column-of-strength-san-francisco-art-commission/.

29. Emi Koyama, "Japanese Far-Right Activities in the United States and at the United Nations: Conflict and Coordination between Japanese Government and Fringe Groups," in *Japanese Military Sexual Slavery: The Transnational Redress Movement for the Victims*, ed. Pyong Gap Min, Thomas Chung, and Sejung Sage Yim (Munich: De Gruyter Oldenbourg, 2020), 261–72.

30. Nadeshiko Action Japanese Women for Justice and Peace, "Nadeshiko Akushon ni tsuite" [About Nadeshiko action], accessed July 1, 2020, http://nadesiko-action.org/?page_id=323.

31. Zaitokukai's official name is Zainichi Tokken o Yurusanai Shimin no Kai [Association of citizens against the special privileges of the Zainichi], and it has been actively organizing hate speech rallies and parades in urban streets targeting ethnic Koreans and other foreign residents since the early 2000s.

32. Nadeshiko Action Japanese Women for Justice and Peace, "Nadeshiko Akushon ni tsuite."

33. Steve Zeltzer, dir., "US Protest Against Japanese 'Comfort Women' Yumiko Yamamoto Sex Slave Denialists in Redwood City"; the documentary was filmed and edited by Zeltzer, a peace activist based in the San Francisco Bay Area, and published

on YouTube by laborvideo, https://youtu.be/Za-BMvOkzyY?si=jYf4Fn-RCObYRp7B, accessed June 1, 2020.

34. Author email correspondence with Eclipse Rising members, February 27–March 10, 2015.

35. Japan-U.S. Feminist Network for Decolonization, "UN Commission on the Status of Women NGO Parallel Events (2016)," accessed July 1, 2020, http://fendnow.org/encyclopedia/un-commission-on-the-status-of-women-ngo-parallel-events-2016/.

36. Shinzo Abe, "The Facts," *Washington Post*, June 14, 2007.

37. The resolution was introduced on July 21, 2015, by Mar and cosponsored by Supervisors Jane Kim, Malia Cohen, Julie Christensen, Norman Yee, Mark Farrell, David Campos, and John Avalos. See "S.F. Board of Supervisors Considering Comfort Women Monument," *Rafu Shimpo*, August 27, 2015, https://www.rafu.com/2015/08/s-f-board-of-supervisors-considering-comfort-women-monument/.

38. From a handout distributed at the event held at the Zainichi Korean YMCA in Tokyo on November 6, 2016. The author participated in the event as an interpreter and member of Eclipse Rising, one of the member organizations of the CWJC.

39. San Francisco Department on the Status of Women, City and County of San Francisco website, accessed March 1, 2022, https://dosw.org/.

40. "Osaka Mayor's Visit to S.F. Called Off," *Rafu Shimpo* (Los Angeles), June 15, 2013, https://rafu.com/2013/06/osaka-mayors-visit-to-s-f-called-off/.

41. "Osaka Mayor's Visit to S.F. Called Off."

42. San Francisco Board of Supervisors, Resolution No. 218-13, "Condemning Recent Statements by Osaka Mayor Toru Hashimoto," last modified June 18, 2013, https://sfbos.org/ftp/uploadedfiles/bdsupvrs/resolutions13/r0218-13.pdf.

43. Janice Mirikitani, letter addressed to the Commission on the Status of Women, September 3, 2015.

44. Mirikitani letter, September 3, 2015 (bold in original).

45. Mirikitani letter, September 3, 2015.

46. Sugita Mio made a statement that Japanese people in Glendale, California have suffered bullying due to the presence of a comfort women memorial in a public park; see Japanese House of Representatives Budget Committee meeting, February 3, 2014, 17; "Installment of Comfort Women Memorial: Fierce 'Japanese Bullying' in Glendale, U.S." [慰安婦像設置 米グレンデールで起きている凄絶な"日本人イジメ"], *Shukan Spa!*, May 13 and 20, 2014.

47. Mirikitani letter, September 3, 2015.

48. Heather Knight, "Memorialize Wartime Sex Slaves Known as 'Comfort Women,' or Just Move On?" *San Francisco Chronicle*, September 12, 2017, https://www.sfchronicle.com/news/article/Memorialize-wartime-sex-slaves-known-as-12189721.php.

49. Knight, "Memorialize Wartime Sex Slaves?"

50. "Hashimoto Clarifies Remarks on 'Comfort Women' After Flak," *Kyodo News* (Tokyo), May 16, 2013.

51. Mirikitani letter, September 3, 2015 (bold in original).

52. Linda Poon and Alastair Boone, "A 'Comfort Women' Memorial Comes between San Francisco and Osaka," Bloomberg.com, December 4, 2017, https://www.bloomberg.com/news/articles/2017-12-04/a-comfort-women-memorial-comes-between-san-francisco-and-osaka.

53. Jerry Kang, "Thinking through Internment: 12/7 and 9/11," *Berkeley Asian Law Journal* 9 (2002): 195–200; Donna K. Nagata, Jacqueline H. Kim, and Kaidi Wu, "The Japanese American Wartime Incarceration: Examining the Scope of Racial Trauma," *American Psychologist* 74, no. 1 (2019): 36–48.

54. These lawmakers include Sigihara Yoshiko (a former Suginami City Council member), Yoshida Koichiro (a former Tokyo Metropolitan Assembly member and a Nakano City Council member), and Aoyama Shigeharu (a member of the House of Councillors of Japan). For more information, see "Sekaiju de gekika suru Kankokujin shugo no 'hannichi iyagarase' undo" [Anti-Japan harassment movement led by Koreans intensifies globally] *Asagei Plus,* February 27, 2014, https://www.asagei.com/20802; Facebook post on Yoshida Koichiro's page dated January 18, 2014, https://www.facebook.com/koichiro.yoshida.jp/posts/242686089239469; and "The Voice" (radio program), air date May 22, 2014, https://www.youtube.com/watch?v=cVJANvBq9Jk.

55. *Shukan Spa!,* May 13 and 20, 2014.

56. Mirikitani letter, September 3, 2015.

57. Judith Mirkinson, "Building the San Francisco Memorial: Why the Issue of the 'Comfort Women' Is Still Relevant Today?," in *The Transnational Redress Movement for the Victims of Japanese Military Sexual Slavery*, ed. Pyong Gap Min, Thomas R. Chung, and Sejung Sage Yim (Berlin: De Gruyter Oldenbourg 2020), 162.

58. Ministry of Foreign Affairs of Japan, "Japan's Efforts on the Issue of Comfort Women," accessed March 1, 2023, https://www.mofa.go.jp/policy/postwar/page22e_000883.html.

59. Ministry of Foreign Affairs of Japan, "Statement by the Chief Cabinet Secretary," August 4, 1993, https://www.mofa.go.jp/a_o/rp/page25e_000343.html; Ministry of Foreign Affairs of Japan, "Statement by Prime Minister Tomiichi Murayama 'on the Occasion of the 50th Anniversary of the War's End' (15 August 1995)," accessed March 1, 2023, https://www.mofa.go.jp/announce/press/pm/murayama/9508.html.

60. Because survivors in Indonesia were not recognized as victims by their government, the AWF provided a total of 380 million yen to help build elderly care facilities. See Asian Women's Fund, "Ajia josei kikin no kaisan to sonogo" [Dissolution of the Asian Women's Fund and thereafter], accessed March 1, 2023, https://www.awf.or.jp/3/dissolution.html.

61. Takashi Fujitani, "The Reischauer Memo: Mr. Moto, Hirohito, and Japanese American Soldiers," *Critical Asian Studies* 33, no. 3 (2001): 379–402.

62. Fujitani, "The Reischauer Memo."

63. See the website of Sister Cities International (SCI), accessed March 1, 2023, https://sistercities.org/.

64. City of San Francisco, "International Sector Businesses Development," accessed March 1, 2023, https://sf.gov/information/international-sector-businesses-development.

65. Ministry of Foreign Affairs of Japan, "Foreign Minister's Commendation Conferment Ceremony for Dr. Emily Murase," accessed March 1, 2023, https://www.sf.us .emb-japan.go.jp/itpr_en/23_0302.html.

66. Sakai, "Transpacific Complicity and Comparatist Strategy."

67. Education for Social Justice Foundation, "Reflection and Chronology: Eric Mar," accessed March 1, 2023, https://www.e4sjf.org/reflection-and-chronology-eric-mar.html.

68. As members of Nikkei for Civil Rights and Redress (NCRR), both Masaoka and Monkawa have helped to lead a grassroots campaign to win redress for the incarceration of Japanese Americans and educate the general public about the dark history of the United States. Masaoka and Monkawa have also worked closely with Koreans in Japan in their struggle to abolish fingerprinting by the Japanese government.

69. The official name in Japanese is Nihongun 'Ianfu' Mondai Kansai Nettowaku (日本軍『慰安婦』問題・関西ネットワーク).

70. The official name in Japanese is Nihongun 'Ianfu' Mondai Kaiketsu Zenkoku Kodo, also known as Zenkoku Kodo (日本軍『慰安婦』問題解決全国行動).

71. Kansai Network, "Re: Support for Resolution 150764—Urging the Establishment of a Memorial for 'Comfort Women,'" submitted to the mayor and board of supervisors of San Francisco.

72. Tomoki Kinukawa, "The Power of Two-Minute Statements," Japan Multicultural Relief Fund, accessed March 1, 2023, http://relief.jprn.org/two-minute-statements.php.

73. Emily Green, "S.F. Supervisors Call for Memorial to WWII 'Comfort Women,'" *San Francisco Chronicle*, September 22, 2015, https://www.sfgate.com/bayarea/article /S-F-supervisors-call-for-memorial-to-WWII-6522926.php.

74. San Francisco Board of Supervisors, Resolution No. 342-15, "Urging the Establishment of a Memorial for 'Comfort Women.'"

75. California Department of Education, "History–Social Science Framework," accessed March 31, 2023, https://www.cde.ca.gov/ci/hs/cf/hssframework.asp.

76. Kim was chosen to be the first Zainichi Korean person delegate for the International Visitor Leadership Program under the US Department of State. For more information, see Korea NGO Center, "Beikoku Soryojikan kara Ryojira raiho" [Consul and others visit from US Consulate General], accessed July 1, 2020, http://korea-ngo .org/ver3/kokusai/kokusai01.html. Upon completion of the program, Kim stopped by in San Francisco and gave a lecture that Eclipse Rising helped organize for the CWJC.

See the event announcement, Eclipse Rising, "Suppressed Ethnic Diversity, and Multi-cultural Education as Resistance in Osaka, Japan," blog post, February 24, 2016, https://eclipserising.blogspot.com/2016/02/suppressed-ethnic-diversity-and.html?m=0.

77. Osaka City Government, "Open Letter from Mayor Yoshimura to Mayor Lee, September 29, 2017," accessed July 1, 2020, https://warp.ndl.go.jp/info:ndljp/pid /11389901/www.city.osaka.lg.jp/keizaisenryaku/page/0000453324.html. All open letters are found on the Osaka City Government website. In October 2018, despite the grass-roots efforts, Mayor Yoshimura unilaterally declared that the sister city relationship was terminated.

78. Petitions and letters from organizations and people in Osaka and Japan was translated by Eclipse Rising and sent to San Francisco mayor Edwin M. Lee on November 22, 2017 (Japan Time). See Kansai Network, "'Ianfu' Kinenhi no Hitei wa Rekishi to Josei no Jinken Hitei!" [To Deny the 'Comfort Women' Memorial is to Deny History and Women's Human Rights!], posted December 7, 2017, https://www.ianfu-kansai -net.org/cgi-bin/sfs6_diary/sfs6_diary.cgi?action=article&year=2017&month=12&day =07&mynum=167.

79. CWJC, "Statement in Response to Recent Opposition to Our Memorial," December 7, 2017, https://remembercomfortwomen.org/cwjc-statement-on-sf-osaka -controversy/.

80. Kansai Network, "San Furansisuko Homon Hokoku" [Report on visit to San Francisco], accessed July 1, 2020, http://www.ianfu-kansai-net.org/2018/201809.html #20180921.

81. Nobel Foundation, "The Nobel Peace Prize 2018," October 5, 2018, https://www .nobelprize.org/prizes/peace/2018/press-release/.

82. CWJC, "Joint Statement by SF 'Comfort Women' Justice Coalition and Kansai Network of Osaka—Comfort Women Justice Coalition," October 11, 2018, https:// remembercomfortwomen.org/joint-statement-by-sf-comfort-women-justice-coalition -and-kansai-network-of-osaka/.

83. Na-Young Lee, "Nihongun 'Ianfu' to Beigun Kichimura no 'Yokoshu'" [Japanese "comfort women" and US military prostitutes (Yang-gongju) in South Korea], *Ritsu-meikan Studies in Language and Culture* 23, no. 2 (2011): 209–28.

84. Lee, "Nihongun 'Ianfu' to Beigun Kichimura," 213–14.

85. Katherine H. S. Moon, *Sex among Allies: Military Prostitution in U.S.-Korea Relations* (New York: Columbia University Press, 1997), 24–32.

86. Woo-yun Lee, "After 40 Years in US Camptown Sex Trade, S. Korean Woman Rejoices in Court Victory," *The Hankyoreh*, September 30, 2022.

87. Annmaria Shimabuku, "Transpacific Colonialism: An Intimate View of Trans-national Activism in Okinawa," *CR: New Centennial Review* 12, no.1 (2012): 138.

88. Shimabuku, 138 (italics in original).

89. Asian Americans represent the largest "minority" population in San Francisco,

comprising 34.1 percent of the city's population. US Census Bureau, "Hispanic or Latino Origin By Race," Explore Census data, accessed June 1, 2020, https://data .census.gov.

90. Lisa Lowe, *Immigrant Acts: On Asian American Cultural Politics* (Durham, NC: Duke University Press, 1996).

91. Lowe, 16.

92. Miho Kim and Tomomi Kinukawa, "Amerika ni okeru Nihongun 'Ianfu' Mondai" [Japan's military 'comfort women' issue in the United States], *Jinken to Seikatsu* [Human rights and life] 42 (June 2016): 40–43.

93. Peace and Justice Commission, City of Berkeley, "Opposition to New U.S. Base Construction," February 23, 2021, https://berkeleyca.gov/sites/default/files/documents /2021-02-23%20Item%2022%20Opposition%20of%20New%20U.S.%20Base.pdf.

94. Peace and Justice Commission, "Opposition to New U.S. Base Construction."

8 PACIFIC INTERNATIONALISM
Movements for a Nuclear-Free and Independent Pacific
SIMEON MAN

On July 10–20, 1983, the newly independent Pacific island nation of Vanuatu hosted a historic gathering of over 150 people from throughout Oceania, Asia, and the United States, who were brought together by a common desire for a world free of nuclear power and released from colonialism. Arriving at this vision and place took many long roads. On the agenda of the Nuclear Free and Independent Pacific conference were various issues, including the French nuclear tests at Moruroa, the construction of a nuclear power plant in Bataan, Philippines, uranium mining in western Australia and the Black Hills of South Dakota, and more. These spatially disperse activities share a foundation, the delegates insisted, and combatting them required a vision and a strategy that kept their connections in view. Organizers' insistence on the need for decolonization on a world scale led them to adopt The People's Chart for a Nuclear Free and Independent Pacific, which stated: "The political independence of all peoples is fundamental to attaining a Nuclear Free Pacific."[1]

The Nuclear Free and Independent Pacific Conference of 1983 took place at a historical moment marked by global uprisings against nuclear proliferation, environmental degradation, and state racial terror in South Africa, South Korea, the Philippines, and elsewhere. Amid the disasters wrought in the wake of colonialism's formal ends in parts of the world, the idea of a nuclear-free and independent Pacific was offered as a tangible solution. "If suddenly big America falls down, and you think they'll say this part of the world will fall, forget it," the delegate from Samoa, Bernadette Pereira, said. "We can rely on our taro, we rely on our coconut, we rely on our fish, we rely on all the natural resources that we have. . . . They'll survive."[2] The sense that a world without US militarism and colonialism was wholly achievable speaks to this profound moment of internationalism. It also alerts us to other histories unaccounted for, elided, perhaps, by the very visibility of that moment.

This chapter tells of the making of that moment of possibility, when people who had seemingly little to do with one another got together, literally or otherwise, to say that freedom in one place is not possible without freedom elsewhere. Moved first by the stories and memories of the place where they are, they found each other by way of confronting a shared violence that had accrued over the last quarter century, resulting from efforts by the United States and Japan to build a nuclear industry.[3] In the 1950s the two countries "liberated" their colonial territories by subjecting them to new rounds of capitalist integration. Imperialists referred to this as "decolonization," and it entangled the territories anew with each other. The islands of Micronesia, Okinawa, and Diné Territory, among other places, formed the underside of a growing transpacific economy, where uranium mining, nuclear weapons storage and testing, and nuclear fuel processing and waste dumping were concentrated. In the imperial imagination, these were nonproductive spaces that held immense value, in which the land could be creatively destroyed, and where "natives" occupied a perpetually absent presence. This colonial racial economy was buttressed by post-1945 bilateral and international security arrangements that, among other things, legitimated US and Japanese claims to these spaces. For the two once-rival powers, making Asia-Pacific safe for capitalism required sharing in its control. It was a partnership premised on the reassertion of settler-colonial claims past and present and the expansion of US militarism, the two proceeding in tandem, "perpetuating, legitimating, and concealing one another."[4]

The NFIP was the long coming together of anticolonial undercurrents in Oceania and beyond, emerging over several decades in response to the violence of US-led decolonization. It was not simply a variation of the continent-based environmental or antinuclear movements of the 1970s and 1980s, unfolding in a region called the Pacific. As a feminist decolonial project, the NFIP sought to make visible—and to disrupt—the colonial relations of extraction, industrial pollution, and militarized violence that were pivotal to, yet absented from, the making of the "transpacific" as a fantasy of Cold War development.[5] The NFIP was an effort at what Lisa Yoneyama calls "co-conjuring," or the "summoning across time and geographies those specters" of devastation caused by the nuclear industry, whose connections were disavowed and foreclosed by the colonial division of knowledge.[6] It rejected the fictions of "peaceful use" of nuclear energy and the "safety" of its industrial production as wishful words repeatedly expressed by US and Japanese officials to disavow nuclearism's death-dealing effects. The NFIP countered these fictions and called forth a more expansive conception of life by insisting on survival, not safety. Working against a decolonization effort predicated on turning Indigenous lands into sites of extraction and exploitation, the NFIP articulated a vision of global decolonization that centers Native survivance and the persistence of Indigenous modes of relationships.

Writing this history of the NFIP requires an undisciplined approach to the "transpacific" that disrupts its coherence as an object of study. In the US colonial archives, the transpacific emerges with some clarity through the documents of international relations attesting to the promises and perils of the US-Japan alliance. A masculinist regional approach is the foundation of this knowledge production, as it renders the Pacific Islands and Indigenous lands as excess to be incorporated and sites of "wastelanding." A more unruly archive confounds the authority with which the transpacific imperial project is documented. This is the counter-archive of activists' writings, including pamphlets, newsletters, poetry, conference proceedings, and other textual and visual materials scattered in various holdings. This archive presents the transpacific as a problem of knowledge and invites a method of intimating that which had been foreclosed. By its nature this archive tells an incomplete story that reveals other routes imagined and pursued toward a decolonized Pacific.

The Tongan and Fijian writer Epeli Hau'ofa has offered the idea of "our sea of islands" as a way of seeing Oceanic relationships that were long foreclosed by European colonization; it is a framework of liberation from the never-ending violence of the transpacific.[7] The NFIP manifested this decolonial vision, and in the coming together it created something new: a Pacific internationalism that transformed what was imaginable then and for our current moment.

COLONIAL VIOLENCE, ERASURE, AND TRANSPACIFIC RACIAL CAPITALISM

US colonialism in Micronesia began at the dawn of the age of decolonization, in 1947. This temporal disjuncture tells us that Micronesia's significance to the US empire had everything to do with its concealment. The 1947 United Nations Trusteeship Agreement formalized the US administration of the Trust Territory of the Pacific Islands (TTPI), which included all of Micronesia, including the Caroline Islands, the Marshall Islands, and the Mariana Islands (but not Guam, which was already colonized by the United States in 1898). The TTPI was one of eleven such territories included in the UN trusteeship system, all of which were former colonies and territories controlled by the Axis Powers under the League of Nations mandate. As Japan's Pacific mandate, Micronesia had developed extractive industries in sugar, phosphate, copra, and commercial fishing in the 1920s and 1930s, industries that relied on Indigenous workers and migrant workers from throughout the Japanese empire, including Okinawans and Koreans, and that contributed to the rise of Japanese colonial capitalism and settlements in the region.[8] After Japan's defeat in World War II, Micronesia was placed on a path toward self-government and independence, even as many non-Micronesian settlers remained.

In one sense the TTPI tells the story of Micronesia's passage from the colonial era, but as with any narrative of progress, that story is belied by pasts that refuse closure. For one, the swiftness by which the defeated Japanese empire came to reassert its role in the capitalistic development of Micronesia during the US administration reveal the entanglements of US militarism and Japanese capital in the making of the decolonizing Pacific. And elided entirely from this narrative of two empires are other social relations and lifeworlds that existed beyond colonial rule and an insistence on survival that was always present.

One beginning of this story occurred on March 1, 1954, when the United States detonated Castle Bravo, the largest nuclear test ever conducted, on Bikini Atoll in the Marshall Islands. As the Marshallese faced the slow violence from the radiation, the international public learned of the event not through what happened to the Marshallese but through news of the Japanese tuna fishing boat that was showered by radioactive fallout. Media coverage of the boat arriving in Japan with sickened crewmembers and contaminated fish led to widespread public uproar. Fishing ports and markets demanded compensation for their economic losses and adopted resolutions calling for an immediate end to all nuclear tests. Women organized a ban-the-bomb petition drive in Tokyo that gathered twenty million signatures throughout the country. In response, the US government settled with a $2 million ex gratia payment to the Japanese government, "to reassure the Japanese public of US friendship and humanitarian concern."[9]

The striking omission of any mention of the Marshallese as victims of the nuclear blast, as part of the protests, or in the settlement reached is a telling sign. In a sense, the "Bikini incident" of 1954 ushered the beginning of two parallel worlds: a Pacific world marked by a continuous nuclear-colonial violence, of islands rendered uninhabitable, and of Indigenous peoples facing long-term ill health and premature death; and a world shaped by Japan's resurgence as a subempire. These two mirroring worlds formed the backdrop of each other even as their relations were continually elided. The elision of the Marshall Islands in the narratives of the "Bikini incident" is constitutive of Japan's national mythmaking in order to represent Japan as a victim of the first use of nuclear weapons and to disavow Japan's colonial past and wartime aggression, a disavowal that manifested in the failure to properly compensate war victims, including forced laborers and colonial populations. As past and present colonial violences remained unaccounted for, the United States and Japan barreled forward with their postwar alliance, laying the pathway for the US militarization of Japan and Okinawa and elsewhere in Asia and the Pacific.

At this time there were already rumblings of what would become, in another decade or two, unmistakable anticolonial and anti-imperialist eruptions. On May Day 1952 tens of thousands of people in Japan protested the San Francisco Peace Treaty and the Mutual Security Treaty, rejecting a US-Japan peace settlement that all but guaranteed Japan's remilitarization and role in future US wars. A growing antinuclear left mobilized the memory of the atomic destruction of Hiroshima and Nagasaki toward antimilitarist ends, founding the grassroots nuclear disarmament group Japan Council Against

A- and H-Bombs (*Gensuikyo*) in 1955.[10] Okinawa, which remained under US military occupation, experienced in 1954 what appeared to be the opening acts of an anti-American and anti-base resistance that, according to Wendy Matsumura, were actually a far more expansive and deeply rooted struggle over the preservation of place waged by Okinawan women farmers who refused the US military's attempts to quantify the value of their land and lives.[11] The Marshallese people also mobilized quickly after the Bravo test. In April 1954 members of the Marshallese Congress Hold-Over Committee and "100 other interested Marshallese Citizens" petitioned the United Nations, framing their antinuclear demands as "complaints" and a "plea" to immediately end all nuclear testing in the area. Contained in their plea were subversive words about the meaning of land, whose significance likely escaped their audience: "Land means a great deal to the Marshallese. It means more than just a place where you can plant your food crops and build your houses; or a place where you can bury your dead. It is the very life of the people. Take away their land and their spirits go also."[12]

Louder rumblings, such as the "Bloody May Day" in Japan in 1952, were violently suppressed, while quieter ones mostly went unheard, their radicality misrecognized and subsumed by dominant narratives of the Cold War. Across the decolonizing world the restless conspired and fought to maintain their livelihoods. They were not yet internationalized and not yet nodding to or learning from each other as they later would. Instead, this moment hinted at the many signs of what could be and the reactive violence of the US empire to those aspirations. The violence took form as police crackdowns, dispossession, forced removals, and erasures. It also manifested in a sinister counterstrategy that promoted the spread of nuclear power in the decolonizing world and claimed that it could bring people out of the shadows of colonialism and war and into a prosperous life. This counterstrategy was co-conspired between the United States and Japan, and it flew under the banner "peaceful uses of nuclear energy."

Beginning in the early 1950s, Japan's industrial and government leaders had been pursuing the so-called peaceful uses of nuclear energy as a pathway for national economic development. After the Bikini incident they redoubled the effort. A key figure here was Matsutaro Shoriki, a conservative media mogul who was determined to transform national sentiments about nuclear power. In January 1955 Shoriki invited John Jay Hopkins, president of the defense company General Dynamics Corporation, to visit Japan to speak about his concept of an "Atomic Marshall Plan" to construct nuclear power plants throughout the "under-developed" areas of the world. Nuclear power, Hopkins had told Congress the previous year, "has its greatest potential not as a destroyer of cities and nations but as a builder and a savior." This "atomic world" was to Hopkins a new "frontier," a "world of forces invisible, immense, and basic to the life and growth and continuity of all things."[13] This world had been relatively unexplored, and enterprising capitalists the world over wanted to tap its potential. In his invitation to Hopkins, Shoriki wrote: "Eighty million Japanese will feel very grateful and joyous to have you, who pioneered in peaceful use of nuclear energy, to assist in the reconstruction and development of the weak Japanese economy," to benefit "the welfare not only of the Japanese but of one billion Asians."[14]

The US Department of State did not formally endorse Hopkins's Atomic Marshall Plan, but senior officials agreed that promoting the "peaceful uses" of nuclear energy in Japan could serve long-term US objectives in Asia, and they "intended to plug it hard."[15] In November of that year the two countries signed an agreement of cooperation providing US assistance to develop Japan's nuclear industry. The agreement ushered the transnational exchange of technical knowledge and visits with nuclear engineers, industry leaders, and scientists working throughout the United States; it also made available the lease of enriched uranium to Japan as part of President Dwight D. Eisenhower's Atoms for Peace program.[16] By 1957 a complex network of government agencies, research institutes, and basic laws formed the backbone of Japan's growing atomic energy bureaucracy, involving the collaboration of government and private enterprise.[17] That year, at Tokai Village northwest of Tokyo, Japan's first nuclear reactor, with parts built in California by North American Aviation and using uranium mined from Native lands, reached critical stage and marked the beginning of Japan's atomic era.[18]

The story of the rise of Japan's nuclear industry is in many ways a familiar one. The transnational circulation of knowledge and peoples as forms of soft power and the revival of Japan as an industrial engine in East Asia are thematic anchors in Cold War historiography. Yet there is another dimension of this story: the persistent settler colonialism, by which Indigenous lands and peoples rendered as past were mobilized anew. Multiple forms of settler colonialism, sustained by various legal regimes and spanning different geographies across Oceania, Asia, and the Americas, constitute the patchwork of contested Indigenous sovereignties that made possible Cold War development. These geographies of colonialism, moreover, were becoming increasingly integrated and conjured as shared or codependent spaces through interimperial conversations about resource extraction and "wastelanding" practices. In 1955, a Japanese delegation visited with representatives of the US Atomic Energy Commission to discuss methods for extracting uranium in the United States on Native territories, just as the Geological Survey of Japan began sending survey teams to the massif regions of Tottori and Okayama Prefectures and then shortly after discovering uranium deposits at the two locations.[19] The activities that constitute the start and end of the nuclear fuel cycle—uranium mining and radioactive waste disposal—were grounded in and dependent on ongoing colonial structures and claims.

The nuclear destruction of the Marshall Islands cast a shadow over Japan's "peaceful" rehabilitation as a subempire, and this relation was more than a metaphor. In the subsequent decades, as Japan sought greater access to the world's energy supply in order to export nuclear power to the rest of the world, the false binary of peaceful and destructive uses of nuclear energy became inescapably clear. The colonial division of humanity—marking certain bodies as disposable—undergirded transpacific racial capitalism at midcentury and the nuclear industry in particular. Uranium mining, radioactive waste disposal, and other environmentally harmful and life-shortening activities associated with the nuclear industry were spatially organized and directed away from metropolitan areas to Indigenous lands. These lands were not stagnant places but were the subject of endless debates among imperial powers about how to reorganize them and make them functional, that is, how to "free" them from existing colonial structures. In the 1960s and 1970s, as the United States and Japan sought to resolve the crises of colonialism and capitalism, these debates and activities centered on the TTPI.

CRISIS, SECURITY, AND PALAUAN STRUGGLES
AGAINST "PORT PACIFIC"

In October 1968 the legislature of the Marshall Islands passed a historic resolution calling on the United Nations to reconsider the entire basis for the continued US presence in Micronesia. Members wanted to abolish the trusteeship. Speaker Amata Kabua sent a copy of the resolution to the White House with a note to President Lyndon Johnson, stating: "This Resolution is one of the first attempts by the peoples of Micronesia to cry out to the world for help in righting the unjust neo-colonial situation under which we now exist. We believe that it is time the world be made aware of our problems and our struggle."[20] The resolution listed grievances accumulated over the twenty years of US administration, including land dispossessions to make way for the military, underdevelopment of the Micronesian economy, and deprivation of the people's political voice. It was an indictment of US colonialism taken up to the international body, and it would not be the last time to happen.

US colonial administrators had anticipated this crisis, observing "the people in the area are coming to maturity" and the time of the trusteeship was nearing its end.[21] Their solution, however, was not to terminate the relationship with Micronesia but to make it permanent in a different form. The islands, operationalized for weapons testing, weapons storage, and other naval and air activities, was indispensable as a "lifeline to our Asian commitment."[22] Throughout the 1960s the United States sought to bring about this permanent relationship by steadily increasing Micronesians' freedoms to participate in capitalist modes of production. In 1963 a US survey mission recommended programs of "accelerated development" to benefit Micronesians and to guide them "to make an informed and free choice" to associate permanently with the United States.[23] Development and decolonization were to proceed apace as constitutive means of US security. One State Department memo summed up: "The sooner the TTPI is given an opportunity for self-determination, the sooner we will get the answer which will best protect our strategic interests. We will, however, have to offer the Territory sufficiently attractive political and economic terms so that its people will freely choose this relationship."[24]

In 1969 the United States and Micronesia began negotiating the territory's future political status, and as part of the process, the United States reached an agreement with Japan to settle Micronesian World War II damage claims. Micronesians' long-standing demands for war reparations were ignored until responding to them proved politically expedient. Without consulting Micronesians, the two countries pledged to provide $10 million to promote "the welfare of the inhabitants of the Trust Territory." Japan's $5 million payment was earmarked for the purchase of Japanese commodities and services; in exchange Japan secured access rights of Japanese fishing vessels to the ports of Truk and Palau.[25] The settlement partly satisfied Japan's aim to reopen commercial activity in the former mandate. Although Japanese economic activities were largely prohibited by the US administration, by the 1960s a consensus was reached that it "should not be discouraged," as Japanese capital could help stimulate US development programs.[26] In 1969 Japan was working to integrate the periphery economies of Southeast Asia and the Pacific into the world system; the war damage payment to the TTPI was one part of this calculus.

Japanese capital investments in the region accelerated in the 1970s in response to two shocks to the world system. The first, the US defeat in the Vietnam War, spurred Japanese technological assistance and investments in the postwar rebuilding efforts.[27] The second was the global oil crisis resulting from the Arab oil embargo in 1973, which directly resulted in the expansion of Japanese capital in Micronesia. In the early 1970s Japan was the largest supplier of the world's heavy and chemical industrial products, making Japan also the largest importer of the world's crude oil, over 81 percent of which came from the countries that imposed the embargo.[28] The near quadrupling of oil prices in 1973–74 impacted Japan's petrochemical, shipbuilding, and aluminum industries, leading Japanese and US officials to deem the continued flow of foreign oil to Japan to be a matter of national security. In response, the Japanese government proposed to build a crude oil storage facility that could hold a ninety-day supply to buffer future emergencies.[29] The proposed construction project was unprecedented in size and scope, requiring the mobilization of labor and access to a particular land: land that was both situated along existing sea lanes, to facilitate the efficient movement of capital, and that was deemed politically viable and able to absorb the risks of environmental disasters from oil spills with minimal pushback from inhabitants. In 1974 an oil spill off the coast of Okayama Prefecture from a

Mitsubishi refinery combined with the growing environmental movement within Japan starting in the 1960s made clear that any such project needed to be located far from Japan's shores.

Japan ultimately selected Palau as the site for the oil storage facility. Located on an existing tanker line and under the protection of the US military, Palau was an ideal location to pursue such a project to overcome the global recession. The proposal involved Japanese banks and corporations that were products of the colonial world and that remained key players in post–World War II global capitalism: Nissho-Iwai Company, a conglomerate and major manufacturer of steel and heavy machinery, and the Industrial Bank of Japan, which financed steel production and Japan's postwar infrastructure. Both companies were crucial to Japan's postwar prosperity, and both saw the oil crisis as an opportunity to expand their ventures overseas. The proposal also involved the National Iranian Oil Company, one of the largest oil producers in the world, which was committed in continuing a supply of oil to Japan. In April 1974 the three companies commissioned Robert Panero, an American developer experienced in working and thinking with military strategists, to conduct a prefeasibility study for the construction of the oil facility on Palau. Panero gave it a name: Port Pacific. Under his plan it was to become the primary oil storage facility in the western Pacific and the largest supertanker port in the world. Palau and Port Pacific were to become virtually synonymous.[30]

Port Pacific, also called a superport, was estimated to cost $1.8 billion for initial construction. The plan required a cartographic imagining of Palau as terra nullius, empty of inhabitants and severed from the islands and waters around it. The main port was mapped onto the north of the main island, where reefs two to six miles wide enclosed a deepwater anchorage system capable of "handling tankers of up to one million tons." The "largely undeveloped" island of Babeldaob would become home to an oil refinery, petrochemical plants, a thermal power plant, and other harmful infrastructure. With most of Palau's population of fourteen thousand concentrated in the district center of Koror further to the south, the activities of the plants and ports, the planners believed, would meet minimal resistance. The imagined availability of land and water spaces lacking inhabitants, coupled with low taxes and "nearly nonexistent" pollution controls and enforcement procedures, made Palau a dreamworld of energy capitalism.[31]

The Port Pacific project reinforced notions of imperial space and time that alienated Palauans from their land and erased their social worlds. It proceeded from twin assumptions: that Micronesia would remain a part of the United States for the foreseeable future and that Japan would play a role in securing that relationship. It was a triangular outlook shared widely by US policymakers. In 1975 Capt. N. R. Gooding Jr., a senior research fellow at the National War College, wrote a report titled "A Role for Japan in Micronesia," which advocated for increasing Japan's capital investments to strengthen US perpetual claims to the islands. "To many [the notion] may seem repugnant—an increased role for an old enemy in an old battleground," Gooding wrote. "But times change . . . [and] Japan is now in a position to help us."[32] The report waxed nostalgic about the mandate period, when Japan had established sugar and pineapple fields, sugar refineries, canning plants, and an extensive infrastructure serving primarily Japanese settlers, calling it a time "when things were happening." Now, Japanese capital investment could develop the economy once again, help "provide greater satisfaction of Micronesian aspirations and needs" in terms of revenue, jobs, and expertise, and minimize US subsidies, as Micronesians moved toward self-government. In turn, Japan would have access to "a *very* sensitive Micronesian commodity": land on which to build. The report told a narrative of Japanese colonialism in the Pacific that was still unfolding. It was a vision of a shared "settler militarism" in which institutions that were responsible for underwriting Japan's settler-colonial project were invited to assist in the perpetuation of US militarization on the islands.[33]

The ideas spelled out in Gooding's report formed the basis of Ford's New Pacific Doctrine, a post–Vietnam War strategy premised on the US-Japan alliance and the "unimpeded ocean trade and free movement of strategic materials," including oil and the military.[34] Palau and the superport were critical to this vision. In addition to "enhancing the security of oil flowing to our most important Asian ally," Ambassador to Japan James Hodgson told Secretary of State Henry Kissinger that the superport could provide refueling and bunkering facilities for the US Navy.[35] Indeed, the port aligned with the Department of Defense's long-term vision of transforming Palau into a forward base for the navy's new Trident long-range ballistic missile submarine and the use of Ponape and Babeldaob as nuclear storage and training sites.[36]

The many dreams of Port Pacific, however, hinged on one shaky factor: that Palauans would not object to these encroachments and would "not disasso-ciate . . . political[ly] from the US."[37] US officials were nervous to what they knew, deep in their colonizer minds, to be utterly unthinkable, but all signs were pointing otherwise.

Indeed, an organized opposition to the US military was already afoot by this time. In 1972, twenty-nine traditional and elected leaders of Palau issued a joint declaration asserting Palauans' "right to control their land as the basis of Freedom, Justice, and Equality," and they were "unequivocally opposed to the use of land in Palau by the United States military."[38] The proposed superport stoked these existing oppositions. "This project will de-stroy our environment and our culture," High Chief Ibedul Yutaka Gibbons remarked. "Is Palau to become a dumping ground for others' pollution?"[39] Ibedul Gibbons emerged as a visible leader and spokesperson in the fight against the superport, and he strategically mobilized environmental groups to translate Palauans' grievances to the international public. The Pacific Science Association, representing scientists from forty-two countries, condemned the project "on scientific grounds" and called for its termination "because of the potential adverse effects upon the human population and biota of Palau."[40] In a first major victory against the superport, in January 1977 the Environmental Defense Fund, the Natural Resources Defense Council, and the recently formed Save Palau Organization jointly threatened Nissho-Iwai with a lawsuit, forcing the corporation to both give up exclusive development rights and make public the results of its feasibility study, including environ-mental assessment reports.[41]

The two-year span of 1976–77 was a time of widespread political organiz-ing among Palauans against the construction of the superport. In January 1976, timed with the publication of the first exposé about the superport in Palau's daily paper, *Tia Belau*, Ibedul Gibbons formed the Save Palau Or-ganization and commenced an island-wide, village-to-village campaign to educate the people and hear their concerns.[42] Rejecting Panero's paternalistic claim that the superport "will be good for them," Palauans understood its adverse effects on their environment.[43] They asserted counterclaims and di-rected them to the halls of power. In one instance the people of Peleliu Island petitioned the Palau Legislature to reject the plan, threatening secession. In

March 1977 a delegation of five Palauans flew to Washington, DC, to testify at the Senate Committee on Energy and Natural Resources. Given just a few minutes to speak, Ibedul Gibbons presented a petition signed by more than twelve hundred Palauans and said, "The risks of [*sic*] our traditional cultural and social way of life are not worth the small economic benefit that we would gain from the proposed superport."[44] Similar petitions were presented by the Save Palau Organization to the UN Visiting Mission in Koror and by Ibedul Gibbons to the UN Trusteeship Council in New York the previous year.[45]

Although Palauan women were marginalized in these public spaces of protest dominated by men, their absence should not be taken to mean they were not actively contesting and shaping the terms of the struggle. As Rebecca Hogue and Anaïs Maurer have argued, "With a few notable exceptions . . . women were routinely excluded from circles of power during this period."[46] Yet Palauan women continued to mobilize around their influence as traditional caretakers of the land and future generations, and by the mid-1980s they were among the key drivers of the radical feminist vision of the NFIP through their insurgent poetry. In the decade before the flowering of "anti-nuclear poetry as feminist praxis," in the various petitions and demands forwarded against the superport, concerns about the harmful impacts to the land and future generations as signs of Palauan women's assertions can be seen.[47] Indeed, what may seem on the surface to be an "anti-port" struggle, when read deeper indicates a far more radical insistence on the importance of land to Palauan social relations and of women's role in the emerging anticolonial movement.

In appealing to the United Nations, Palauans were insisting that the fight against the superport was no less than a fight against colonialism. They internationalized the struggle at the precise moment Indigenous peoples throughout the world were seeking to gain a seat at the UN, reviving what Nick Estes has called a "radical Indigenous internationalism" that allowed them to "make relatives, so to speak, with those they saw as different, imagining themselves as part of Third World struggles and ideologies."[48] The internationalism spread throughout the Palauan diaspora. In Oʻahu, Hawaiʻi, seasoned activists of antimilitary and anti-eviction struggles formed the Micronesia Support Committee in 1975 to advocate for Micronesian self-determination. The group's monthly publication, *Micronesian Support*

Committee Bulletin, provided crucial coverage of the superport and served as an organizing tool for Palauans in Hawai'i and the United States. In the spring of 1977 thirty-five Palauan students in Susanville and Chico, California, started a campaign to organize Micronesian students throughout the West Coast, including in San Diego and Modesto, California, Twin Falls, Idaho, and Las Vegas, Nevada. One leaflet addressing their "Micronesian brothers and sisters" asked, "Are you tired of what is happening to Micronesia? Are you tired of seeing the islands being exploited? Then now is the time to consolidate and organize!" They formed the Micronesian Student Coalition and circulated a petition calling on students to write home to their friends, families, and politicians to reject the superport. The petition, with 170 signatures, stated: "We strongly believe that the proposed superport will bring ecological disaster to Palau and Micronesia in the form of oil spills and other related problems. In the long run, . . . the Palauan people will lose their self-determination by becoming dependent on the superport and those who manipulate it for their own self-interests."[49]

Environmental destruction, dependency, and dispossession were the terms that propelled anticolonial activism globally in the 1970s. Palauans and activists around the world came to see the struggle against the superport as vital to the broader struggle for the future of the planet and for Indigenous life. In 1976 Ibedul Gibbons appealed to the people of Japan in an open letter published in the *Asahi Shimbun*: "Our future, *beyond the short life-time of your oil line*, depends on the preservation of the reefs, islands, and culture. There is a Japan we would like to be close to, . . . Japan that fights to preserve its fishing ground and soil, Japan that understands it cannot take its neighbor's resources."[50] It was a call to build cross-border alliances and enact a politics of long-term survival against the violence of transpacific capital. In October 1977, as environmental activists in Japan began to mobilize against the superport, the Japan Congress Against A- and H-Bombs (*Gensuikin*) sent a delegation of nuclear survivors and antinuclear activists to meet with Marshallese victims of the US nuclear testing to discuss the possibility of dispatching a Japanese medical survey team, since a similar effort in 1971 had been denied by US officials.[51] Their journey of solidarity reactivated what was possible yet foreclosed in 1954 in the rush to rehabilitate the Japanese subempire.

The year 1979 was a year of revolutions and counterrevolutions. In Palau, following a historic referendum in which voters overwhelmingly rejected "free association" with the United States as the baseline of their political future, 92 percent of the people voted to adopt a "nuclear-free" constitution—the first of its kind in the world—banning the storage, testing, and dumping of nuclear weapons and materials on its lands and waters. On the other side of the globe, the Iranian Revolution had toppled the US-backed Shah and ushered in the Islamic Republic. These nationalist oppositions made the superport finally untenable. The antiport movement, however, proved to be one phase of a protracted struggle, because energy capitalists went on the offensive. In November 1979 industrialists and security strategists in the United States, Japan, and Germany, representing groups including the Heritage Foundation, the Industrial Research Institute of Japan, the Social Science Research Institute of Germany, and Westinghouse Corporation, met in Honolulu to discuss the future of nuclear power. Nuclear power, they argued, could be harnessed to overcome recent threats to the world economy, but developing it required "a coherent counterstrategy" involving a public information campaign and investments in nuclear waste management technologies that could demonstrate a commitment to safety.[52] "Safety" was the operative keyword here. As a function of crisis management, success once again depended on the colonial organization of time and space that rendered particular lifeworlds nonexistent. Armed with the lessons of the antiport struggle, antinuclear activists in the early 1980s fought against the nuclear industry by enacting a more expansive chronopolitics of survival.

INDIGENOUS RESURGENCE

In November 1979 Japan's Science and Technology Agency (STA) announced it would start dumping low-level radioactive waste from its nuclear power plants into the Pacific Ocean. It was to be an experimental phase to demonstrate their commitment to safety in proceeding with the final stage of the nuclear energy production cycle. The waste would be encased inside cement-solidified 55-gallon steel drums and dropped six thousand meters below sea level, at a location determined to be a safe distance from continental shelves, volcanoes, and marine resources southeast of Japan and north of the Mariana Islands. Five to ten thousand steel drums would be dumped during the experimental phase and, at the end of three years, if no leakage was discovered, the STA would begin full-scale dumping of one to two million drums per year.[53] The temporal and spatial boundaries of their safety demonstration did not account for or encompass the oceanic life of Pacific peoples.

Lessons from the antiport struggle had taught Pacific peoples that Japan's scheme to export industrial pollution was part of a globe-spanning project of integrating the decolonizing world under capitalism, and this project was dependent on the reproduction of colonial racism through policies of extraction and development. In the early 1980s this colonial racial capitalist project was known as the "Pan-Pacific Community." The concept was first proposed at the Pacific Basin Economic Council meeting in Los Angeles in 1979 to describe three worlds—the United States and Japan, the "rim" countries of Southeast Asia, and the Pacific Islands—all interconnected by the militarized industrial production chain.[54] Tamaki Ipponmatsu, vice president of the Japan Atomic Industrial Forum, argued for the application of this concept to nuclear energy production to establish a "Pan-Pacific nuclear power community" involving the promotion of nuclear power development abroad and the export of Japanese reactors to several Southeast Asian countries, including Indonesia, Malaysia, the Philippines, and Singapore. The Pan-Pacific nuclear power community embraced new relations of dependency in response to the oil crisis, yet that geography was more expansive than the name implied. "Where does he [Tamaki] think the uranium will come from for the purpose and where does he think the wastes should be disposed?" asked the antinuclear activist Shunji Arakawa.[55]

This question was the fundamental challenge for antinuclear activists in 1980. Especially for the growing antinuclear movements in Japan and the United States, it was a call to broaden the struggle, both spatially and politically, to make global Indigenous decolonization a central organizing framework. At the historic Nuclear Free Pacific Conference in Honolulu on May 10–18, 1980, fifty delegates representing twenty Pacific and Pacific Rim countries gathered to discuss the nuclear-free movements in their countries and regions and endeavored to find common ground. Organizers committed to the difficult work of elevating grassroots movements in Pacific nations and insisted that delegates from the United States, Japan, and other "rim" nations "keep a low profile" and listen. As a result, the conference issued a declaration of self-determination for Pacific peoples as the key to a demilitarized and nuclear-free Pacific.[56] Lopeti Senituli, the delegate from Fiji, remarked on the spirit of internationalism:

> We were literally drawn together by the realisation that if we were to examine the nuclear fuel and nuclear bomb cycles we would emerge with the disconcerting fact that each major stage . . . is being centred in or around areas populated by [indigenous] peoples. Uranium is mined on Australian Aborigines' and American Indians' lands. This uranium is transported via the Pacific Ocean to nuclear reactors erected in areas like the Bataan province in the Philippines or on American Indian soil. Nuclear bombs are being tested on Moruroa and were tested in the past in the Micronesian area. Now they are talking of dumping radioactive waste in the Pacific Ocean.[57]

The nuclear industry had traversed an expansive geography that demanded an equally expansive strategy and vision of liberation in response.

In their resistance, Pacific activists continually made the distinction between safety and survival, seeing one as antithetical to the other. They understood safety as a crisis management strategy produced life-shortening effects for Indigenous peoples, furthering colonial genocide. Elected leaders of ten Pacific nations made this clear during their annual gathering on Guam in August 1980, when they confronted a delegation of four Japanese scientists trying to explain the safety of the dumping plan. Tosiwo Nakamura, speaker of the Palau Legislature, remarked: "The chance that our waters and our fish could become radioactive is unthinkable, bringing back the all-too-real recollection that our fellows on Bikini Atoll still cannot eat their native foods because of radioactive contamination." Long imagined as settled and consigned to the past in Japan's memory, the Bikini incident continued to obstruct Indigenous survival: "Before I am willing to commit the lives and well-being of our citizens and our descendants for the next thousands of years," the Northern Mariana Commonwealth governor Carlos Camacho retorted, "these scientists must refine their methods."[58]

Pacific Islanders' insistence on survival centers an Indigenous way of seeing the world and thus a different understanding of time. It refuses truncated conceptions of life and evokes the notion of regeneration. "Regeneration," Maile Arvin writes, "is acting on the recognition of a responsibility to a people and a place to refuse the settler colonial order of things."[59] In the context of the nuclear industry's assault on Indigenous people's bodies and their relationship to the land, regenerative refusal was powerfully asserted by Pacific women who led the antinuclear struggle. They protested the STA delegation each of the five times the scientists traveled to the Pacific islands in 1980–81. When the scientists arrived in Apia, Western Samoa, a group of women confronted them by marching in the street, some with their children and carrying signs that read "Join the Nuclear Family and have Funny Children," and simply "NO"—powerful words refusing the colonial logics of scientific safety and the imposition of heteropatriarchal forms of kinship.[60]

The antinuclear movement in the Pacific was an Indigenous feminist project linking the violence of energy capitalism to the everyday violence of colonialism. At a meeting in Suva on October 30–November 3, 1980, twenty-nine women delegates articulated an Indigenous feminist vision of women's liberation. The meeting followed the UN Mid-Decade Conference for Women that had concluded in July in Copenhagen and was a direct response to the limitations of its universalist assertions of women's equality. At the Suva meeting, Pacific women responded: "In a world where so many nations have proudly and fiercely cast off the stains of colonialism and economic imperialism, there remains in the Pacific sister islands, including New Caledonia and French Polynesia, who are denied their inalienable right to self-determination, to walk in dignity as free Pacific peoples."[61] The delegates formulated and adopted proposals aimed to translate the general spirit of the UN conference into concrete actions in the Pacific, including a rejection of development programs that prolonged economic dependency and gender discrimination and violence. An effective decolonization strategy, they insisted, had to account for all these things at once and women's role in the process.

Oppositions against the transpacific nuclear industry in the early 1980s gave rise to an international feminist solidarity network connecting Hawai'i, Guåhan, Fiji, Okinawa, and other islands in the Pacific. In October 1980 the grassroots movement Japan Stop the Pollution Export Committee (J-SPEC) invited two CHamorus from the Mariana Islands—Felipe Mendiola, the mayor of Tinian, and David Rosario of the Marianas Alliance Against Nuclear Waste Dumping—on a three-week speaking tour throughout Japan. They engaged with local grassroots movements and shared lessons from their struggles. At a rally in Tokyo, J-SPEC issued a "Pacific Solidarity Resolution" that was adopted by the approximately 750 participants, that read in part: "The people of the Pacific are struggling in their part of the world against joint rule by Japan and the US. We Japanese, Okinawa and Amami people propose here a joint international front to put an end to the ambitions of the Japanese government and capital to rule the Pacific and seize the world nuclear market. With the world as our witness, we pledge to fight the government to the end. Let us rise up together."[62]

In Japan and the United States, antinuclear activists were learning from Indigenous Pacific Islanders about the need to center the question of decolonization in the antinuclear movement; and Pacific Islanders understood the importance of building solidarity with those in Japan and the United States and with colonized peoples around the world. These relations were forged through the literal movements of people, crossing different geographies and connecting multifaceted struggles. In the fall of 1980 four activists who were organizing against the construction of an oil facility in Kin Bay, Okinawa, of a nuclear reprocessing plant in Amami Islands, and of the Narita Airport in Sanrizuka traveled to Palau and Guam. They wanted to learn from the struggles of the Palauan people who had organized against the superport and produced the antinuclear constitution and from the CHamorus who were fighting for political independence and reunification against US imperialism.[63]

The struggle for a decolonized Pacific stretched to the heart of the US settler empire in July 1980, when more than ten thousand people descended at the Black Hills International Survival Gathering in Rapid City, South Dakota. People came together with the shared goal of resisting against the profit motive of energy corporations and to end Native genocide. Darlene Keju of Micronesia Support Committee spoke about the Nuclear Free Pacific movement and anticolonial struggles that had taken place in Micronesia, joining groups including Women of All Red Nations, Black Hills Alliance, and Live Without Trident.[64] Participants discussed alternative technologies and self-sufficiency projects. A Declaration of Dependence on the Land was drafted, which read, in part: "We are the guardians of the land. The future of our children, and of all generations to come, will depend on our efforts today to prevent corporate seizure and abuse of the land. We challenge our concerned sisters and brothers throughout the world to unite with us in the struggle to liberate the land and all people from the economic and political domination of the transnational corporations and the governments that serve them."[65]

Although the Black Hills International Survival Gathering took place far from the islands of the Pacific, it too was part of the making of the nuclear free and independent Pacific. Insistence on survival in a moment of danger transcends colonial borders and calls for the forging of shared pasts. The NFIP was such an invocation: multiple histories spanning multiple places, an internationalist movement that showed what was achievable when people around the globe came together and pointed to the source of their violence, and imagined a world freed from it. This growing sense of possibility prompted US Ambassador to Fiji William Bodde to characterize the NFIP as "the most potentially disruptive development" to US security in the region and called on the US government to "do everything possible to counter this movement."[66] Internationalism provoked a reactive counterinsurgency, manifesting in the increasing foreign economic aid, the subversion of popular democracy, and gendered state violence in Palau, Fiji, Papua New Guinea, West Papua, and elsewhere.[67]

Today the transpacific economy is wielded through massive infrastructural projects such as the Dakota Access Pipeline, Thirty Meter Telescope, and military bases plundering the earth. As state agents are deployed to defend these projects and the flow of global capital, they confront water and land protectors who are moved by the spirit of internationalism that connected earlier struggles. "Our history is our strength," said Madonna Thunder Hawk (Lakota), an American Indian Movement elder, reflecting on her decades of organizing, including during the 1980 Black Hills International Survival Gathering and the more recent #noDAPL struggle. "There is no light at the end of the tunnel for us, because we are land based."[68] The struggles to liberate the land from militarism and capitalism persist, from Okinawa to Guåhan, from the Northern Marianas to Puerto Rico to Hawai'i, and coalesce in the insurgent call "Water is life," which demands a reckoning with our collective pasts toward an unfinished decolonization.

NOTES

1. Conference pamphlet, "For a Nuclear-Free and Independent Pacific, July 10–20, 1983," in Nuclear Disarmament Collection, folder "Readings for Pacific Leaders on the Risks of Nuclear Technology," Graduate Theological Union Archives, Berkeley, CA.

2. Puhipau and Joan Lander of Na Maka o ka 'Aina, prod. and dir., *A Nuclear Free and Independent Pacific*, 1983.

3. I am guided by Ayano Ginoza's theorization of "archipelagic feminism." See Ayano Ginoza, "Archipelagic Feminisms: Critical Interventions into the Gendered Coloniality of Okinawa," *Critical Ethnic Studies Journal* 7, no. 2 (Fall 2021), https://doi.org/10.5749/CES.0702.07.

4. Juliet Nebolon, "'Life Given Straight to the Heart': Settler Militarism, Biopolitics, and Public Health in Hawai'i," *American Quarterly* 69, no. 1 (March 2017): 25.

5. Teresia K. Teaiwa, "Bikinis and Other S/Pacific N/Oceans," *Contemporary Pacific* 6, no. 1 (1994): 87–109; Rebecca H. Hogue and Anaïs Maurer, "Pacific Women's Anti-Nuclear Poetry: Centering Indigenous Knowledges," *International Affairs* 98, no. 4 (2022): 1267–88.

6. Lisa Yoneyama, "Co-Conjuring Nuclear Ghosts," presentation at conference "Transpacific Epistemologies, Settler Colonialism, and Image," University of California, San Diego, March 6, 2023.

7. Epeli Hau'ofa, "Our Sea of Islands," *Contemporary Pacific* 6, no. 1 (1994): 148–61.

8. Wendy Matsumura, *Waiting for the Cool Moon: Anti-Imperialist Struggles in the Heart of Japan's Empire* (Durham, NC: Duke University Press, 2024).

9. Policy statement, "Compensation to Japan for Bikini Atomic Damages," January 3, 1955, box 505, folder 21:52, Country File—Japan, entry 3008-A, General Records Relating to Atomic Energy Matters, 1948–1962, General Records of the Department of State, Record Group 59 (RG 59), National Archives and Records Administration, College Park, MD (hereafter NACP).

10. Toshihiro Higuchi, "An Environmental Origin of Antinuclear Activism in Japan, 1954–1963: The Government, the Grassroots Movement, and the Politics of Risk," *Peace & Change* 33, no. 3 (July 2008): 339–43.

11. Wendy Matsumura, "'Isahama Women Farmers' against Enclosure: A Rejection of the Property-Relation in US-Occupied Okinawa," *positions* 28, no. 3 (2020): 547–74.

12. Petition from the Marshallese People Concerning the Pacific Islands to the United Nations, April 20, 1954, in Nic MaClellan, "Manuscript XLIII: Petition to the United Nations Trusteeship Council from the Marshallese People, 20 April 1954," *Jour-*

nal of Pacific History (December 2023), https://doi.org/10.1080/00223344.2023.2285475.

13. Memorandum, Wayne G. Jackson to Gerard Smith, January 27, 1955, box 505, folder: Country File—Japan, Atomic Development Program, entry 3008-A, General Records Relating to Atomic Energy Matters, 1948–1962, RG 59, NACP; John Jay Hopkins, "The Atomic Revolution," *Congressional Record* 100 (June 2, 1954): A4138.

14. Cable, Matsutaro Shoriki to John Jay Hopkins, January 5, 1955, box 505, folder: Country File—Japan, Atomic Development Program, entry 3008-A, General Records Relating to Atomic Energy Matters, 1948–1962, RG 59, NACP.

15. Letter, Howard L. Parsons to Frank Waring, August 1, 1956, box 506, folder: Country File—Japan, General July–December 1956 (part 1 of 2), entry 3008-A, General Records Relating to Atomic Energy Matters, 1948–1962, RG 59, NACP.

16. Memorandum, Atomic Energy Relations with Japan, December 13, 1956, box 506, folder: Country File— Japan, July–December 1956 (2 of 2), entry 3008-A, General Records Relating to Atomic Energy Matters, 1948–1962, RG 59, NACP.

17. Booklet, "Atomic Energy in Japan," Atomic Energy Commission, 1956, box 506, folder: Country File—Japan, July–December 1956 (2 of 2), entry 3008-A, General Records Relating to Atomic Energy Matters, 1948–1962, RG 59, NACP.

18. Clipping, *Asahi Evening News,* February 1961, fox 508, folder: Country File—Japan, j R&D 1956–1961 (2 of 2), entry 3008-A, General Records Relating to Atomic Energy Matters, 1948–1962, RG 59, NACP.

19. Memo of conversation regarding Atomic Energy Development in Japan, August 29, 1955, box 505, folder: Country File—Japan, Atomic Development Program, entry 3008-A, General Records Relating to Atomic Energy Matters, 1948–1962, RG 59, NACP; Booklet, "Uranium Resources of Japan, Atomic Fuel Corporation, 1960," box 508, folder: Country File—Japan, j R&D 1956–1961 (2 of 2), entry 3008-A, General Records Relating to Atomic Energy Matters, 1948–1962, RG 59, NACP.

20. Marshall Islands Nitijela Resolution No. 71, Fifteenth Regular Session, October 21, 1968, box 22, folder: Trust Territory Pacific Islands 68, entry A1 5421, Bureau of East Asian & Pacific Affairs, Subject Files, Country Director for Australia, New Zealand, & Pacific Islands, RG 59, NACP.

21. Memo, "Future Relationships Within the Area," April 5–7, 1967, box 21, folder: Quadripartite Discussions on the South Pacific Islands, entry A1 5421, Bureau of East Asian & Pacific Affairs, Subject Files, Country Director for Australia, New Zealand, & Pacific Islands, RG 59, NACP.

22. Policy Briefing, "U.S. Role and Policy in the Pacific," box 21, folder: Policy Background Briefing—General, Suva 1968, entry A1 5421, Bureau of East Asian & Pacific Affairs, Subject Files, Country Director for Australia, New Zealand, & Pacific Islands, RG 59, NACP.

23. Solomon Report, reprinted in *The Young Micronesian,* March 1971, box 3, folder:

2A, Catholic Action/Peace Education Center Collection, Manuscript Collections, University of Hawaiʻi at Mānoa Library.

24. Memo, Robert S. Linquist to Samuel D. Berger, Meeting with Under Secretary on the Future of the TTPI, February 27, 1967, box 22, folder: Trust Territory of the Pacific Islands 1968, entry A1 5421, Bureau of East Asian and Pacific Affairs, Subject Files, Country Director for Australia, New Zealand, and Pacific Islands, RG 59, NACP.

25. US House of Representatives, Hearings before the Subcommittee on International Organizations and Movements of the Committee on Foreign Affairs, Micronesian Claims Act of 1971, 92nd Congress, First Session, H.J. Res. 521, April 22, 1971.

26. Report, "General Conclusions Reached at Meeting of Pacific Study Group," November 26–29, 1962, box 21, folder: Quadripartite Discussions on the South Pacific Islands, entry A1 5421, Bureau of East Asian & Pacific Affairs, Subject Files, Director for Australia, New Zealand, & Pacific Islands, RG 59, NACP.

27. Thomas R. H. Havens, *Fire Across the Sea: The Vietnam War and Japan, 1965–1975* (Princeton, NJ: Princeton University Press, 1987), 238.

28. OPEC stands for Organization of Petroleum Exporting Countries. Nile Russell Gooding Jr., "A Role for Japan in Micronesia," Washington DC: National War College, Strategic Research Group, July 21, 1975, 10.

29. Robert Gale, "Palau: Can the Japanese Pull It Off?," *Micronesian Support Committee Bulletin* 2, no. 1 (January 1977), reprinted from *Petroleum News* (December 1976).

30. Robert Gale, "Palau Superport: End of the Sea of Eden?," *Micronesia Support Committee Bulletin* 2, no. 6 (July 1977).

31. Gale, "Palau Superport."

32. Gooding, "A Role for Japan in Micronesia."

33. Nebolon, "'Life Given Straight from the Heart.'"

34. Gooding, "A Role for Japan in Micronesia."

35. Telegram, James Hodgson to Henry Kissinger, August 27, 1975, https://aad.archives.gov/aad/createpdf?rid=46718&dt=2476&dl=1345.

36. Robert Aldridge, "Palau: Secret Trident base," *Micronesian Support Committee Bulletin* 2, no. 2 (February 10, 1977).

37. Hodgson to Kissinger, August 1975.

38. Joint Declaration of the United Leadership of the People of Palau Against the Use of Land in Palau by the United States Military," reprinted in *Micronesian Support Committee Bulletin* (January 1977).

39. Quoted in *Micronesian Support Committee Bulletin* 2, no. 6 (July 1977).

40. *Micronesian Support Committee Bulletin* 2, no. 6 (July 1977).

41. "EDF Threatens Nissho-Iwai with Lawsuit," *Micronesian Support Committee Bulletin* 2, no. 1 (January 1977).

42. Gale, "Palau Superport."

43. "No Time for Palauans at Senate Superport Hearing," *Micronesian Support Committee Bulletin* 2, no. 5 (May 1977).

44. "No Time for Palauans."

45. Gale, "Palau Superport."

46. Hogue and Maurer, "Pacific Women's Anti-Nuclear Poetry," 1275.

47. Hogue and Maurer, 1279.

48. Nick Estes, *Our History Is the Future: Standing Rock versus the Dakota Access Pipeline, and the Long Tradition of Indigenous Resistance* (New York: Verso, 2019), 204.

49. "Student Coalition: Micronesians Organize on the Mainland," *Micronesian Support Committee Bulletin* 2, no. 6 (July 1977).

50. Reprinted in *Micronesian Support Committee Bulletin* 1, no. 10 (October 5, 1976) (emphasis in original).

51. "Japan Bomb Victims Meet Marshallese Counterparts," *Micronesian Support Committee Bulletin* 2, no. 11, (November 1977). Gensuikin was formed in 1965 after splitting from Gensuikyo over a dispute. See Muto Ichiyo, "The Buildup of a Nuclear Armament Capability and the Postwar Statehood of Japan: Fukushima and the Genealogy of Nuclear Bombs and Power Plants," *Inter-Asia Cultural Studies* 14, no. 2 (2013): 188–89.

52. "The Future of Nuclear Power: A Conference Report," Institute for Foreign Policy Analysis, 1980, Pacific Collection, University of Hawaiʻi at Manoa Library.

53. Lorie Eichner, "Face-Off Over Nuclear Dumping in the Pacific," *New Pacific* 5, no. 6 (November–December 1980).

54. Iraphne Childs, "Nuclear Waste Disposal: Regional Options for the Western Pacific," Research Paper no. 34, Center for the Study of Australian-Asian Relations, Griffith University, Nathan, Australia, December 1985.

55. Shunji Arakawa, "Belau: Target of Military and Multinational Oil Interests," *Micronesia Support Committee Bulletin* 6, no. 1 (Spring 1981).

56. Ched Myers, "Toward a Nuclear-Free Pacific: Summary of NFPC/80," folder: Readings for Pacific Leaders on the Risks of Nuclear Technology; Nuclear Disarmament Collection, Graduate Theological Union Archives, Berkeley, CA.

57. *Micronesia Support Committee Bulletin*, winter 1981.

58. "Chamorro Face Off Against STA Scientists in Guam," *New Pacific*, November–December 1980; *Micronesia Support Committee Bulletin,* summer 1980.

59. Maile Arvin, *Possessing Polynesians: The Science of Settler Colonial Whiteness in Hawaiʻi and Oceania* (Durham, NC: Duke University Press, 2019), 21.

60. "Samoa Women Have No Yen for Japanese Nuclear Waste," *New Pacific*, November–December 1980.

61. "A Chorus of Female Voices," *Pacific Islands Monthly*, January 1981.

62. Pamphlet, "Don't Make the Pacific a Nuclear Dumping Ground!" Japan Stop the Pollution Export Committee (J-SPEC)/Jishu-Koza, January 1981.

63. Pamphlet, "Don't Make the Pacific!"

64. "July 1980: Black Hills International Survival Gathering, Rapid City, South Dakota," *Hawaii Network News*, January 1981.

65. See "Black Hills Gathering: People Unite for Survival," accessed January 18, 2024, https://archive.scienceforthepeople.org/vol-12/v12n6/black-hills-gathering/.

66. US Ambassador to Fiji William Bodde, "Nuclear Free Pacific Movement Biggest Threat to US Pacific Policy: Bodde," *Micronesia Support Committee Bulletin*, winter 1981.

67. "Japanese PM Visit Pacific," *Pacific Islands Monthly*, March 1985; Zohl de Ishtar, ed., *Pacific Women Speak Out for Independence and Denuclearisation* (Christchurch, New Zealand: Raven, 1998).

68. Interview with Madonna Thunder Hawk at a virtual screening of the film *Warrior Women*, University of California San Diego, April 23, 2021.

9 TRANSPACIFIC RUPTURE

Neoliberal Relationalities and Economic Violence in the COVID Era

QUYNH H. VO

On a Saturday evening in 2019, the United States' then president, Donald Trump, called former president Jimmy Carter for the first time to express concern about China "getting ahead" of the United States. Carter confirmed Trump's consternation.[1] Trump's agitation over China later unleashed a rampant resurgence of Sinophobic violence and social unrest amid the COVID-19 pandemic. Trump renamed the coronavirus the "China virus" and "Kung flu" and popularized his neologisms on social media.[2] Politicians amplified them. "China has a 5,000 year history of cheating and stealing. Some things will never change," tweeted Sen. Marsha Blackburn on December 3, 2020.[3] The US presidential election in 2020 drew enormous attention toward Vietnamese nationals. Similar to 57 percent of their Vietnamese fellows in the United States, 79 percent of Vietnamese nationals participating in a poll conducted by VnExpress—the leading media platform in Vietnam—expressed their support of Trump's campaign.[4] Joining the chorus of Vietnamese Americans who advocated for Trump's unconventional grip on power and his "hawkish stance on China," a large percentage of Vietnamese nationals amplified their "Trumpism."[5] "If I could die for Mr. Trump to become the President," one Facebook user in Vietnam wrote, "I would be very willing to do so."[6] Driven by anti-China sentiments, many Vietnamese communities in Vietnam and the United States grieved over the downfall of the Trump administration, whose forceful exertion in its policies against China, they believed, was without precedent in US history.

Yet, while many South Vietnamese in the United States who had worked with Americans through the Vietnam War seem to ally with Trump over his anti-China rhetoric, those who stormed Capitol Hill on January 6, 2021, did not represent the entire Vietnamese American community.[7] As Tuan Hoang astutely observes, "Different groups [of Vietnamese Americans] had different reasons for opposing communism, and the degree of opposition varied. In the absence of a large-scale confrontation, there was no consensus about an anticommunist ideology."[8] The fall of Saigon—signaling the end of the Vietnam War, in 1975—shattered the country and displaced hundreds of thousands of Vietnamese to different shores of the world. Since then, Vietnamese nationals and Vietnamese Americans have inhabited asynchronous temporalities and different ideological representations of politics and history. These incompatible positionalities resonate with what Homi Bhabha addresses in his seminal book, *Location of Culture*, where Bhabha questions the absence of productive dialogues and solidarity between the deprived, oppressed communities with shared histories who are torn asunder in their "profoundly antagonistic, conflictual, and even incommensurable" strife.[9]

Tracing these genealogies of contested intimacy and disunity between Vietnamese national and Vietnamese American communities across the Pacific, this assessment aligns with one in the introduction of this anthology, as it "unsettles the liberalizing management of power by accounting for how various fields—and the methods they use for study—have historically affirmed the liberal discourses of multiculturalism and exceptionalism that value socioeconomic success."[10] Engaging "transpacific" as a fluid, messy, volatile, and "undisciplined" space, I propose "transpacific rupture" as a productive prism through which to examine political dynamics of antagonism—of Vietnam–United States–China in particular—not as a new surge of dissensus and belligerence but as waves galvanized through a long history of oppression and resistance. While sharing Vietnamese nationals' anti-China sentiments, Vietnamese Americans who support Trump also echo his rhetoric of racism and anticommunism. Essentializing or reducing a country to one virus or to a rigid entity such as communism is not only insular but also dangerous.[11] Thus, in mobilizing "transpacific rupture" as an analytic, I trouble the ossified, monolithic representations of a country (be it China,

Vietnam, or the United States). The geospatial context and affective mobility of "transpacific rupture" allow us to approach the entanglements between Vietnam, the United States, and China through in-transit and contingent undercurrents that continue to flow into an unknown future.[12]

During their official visits to Vietnam in the decades following the end of the American war in Vietnam, US presidents Bill Clinton, Barack Obama, and Joe Biden have wooed Vietnamese people into believing in the American dream. The US presidents' romantic diplomacy has mesmerized Vietnamese audiences as they suavely weave Vietnamese poetry into their speeches at their exuberant receptions. Clinton, Obama, and Biden have all quoted Nguyen Du, a legendary Vietnamese poet (1765–1820) whose eminent epic poem *Truyện Kiều* (*The Tale of Kiều*) has been incorporated into Vietnam's official educational curricula and taught widely at multiple levels of schools across the nation. *The Tale of Kiều* has been memorized by many Vietnamese generations who have never questioned or examined its underlying message. Written through a lens of patriarchal misogyny and Confucianism, *The Tale of Kiều* chronicles the female protagonist (*Kiều*) who is commodified, downtrodden, and rescued only by men. Representing Vietnamese women as subservient "bitches" devoid of agency, *The Tale of Kiều* alludes to Vietnam as a hapless country that is both savaged and liberated by superpowers.

In the year 2000, during his visit to Vietnam, former US President Bill Clinton addressed a formal gathering at the Presidential Palace. This event took place a quarter-century after the conclusion of the Vietnam War in 1975, and during his speech, he referenced *Truyện Kiều* (The Tale of Kiều): *Sen tàn cúc lại nở hoa / Sầu dài ngày ngắn đông đà sang xuân* (The lotus is withering, daisies blooming / the winter of sorrows is transient, and here comes the spring). As I have interpreted elsewhere, Clinton's poetic speech suggests that the Cold War period has dissolved, like "dying lotus," and the Việt Nam–US relationship has now blossomed like "blooming daisies."

In May 2015, at the National Convention Center in Hanoi, Vietnam, Obama used Nguyen Du's verses to symbolize a new beginning in the US-Vietnam relationship and pledged to embark on a journey together: "Please take from me this token of trust, so we can embark upon our 100-year journey together."[13] Obama impressed millions of Vietnamese people with his powerful speech. With his poignant words, he pleaded for a swift relinquishment of the harrowing past and beckoned the collective yearnings for a collaborative future with his Vietnamese listeners. A significant portion of the population, half the country of 96 million are under age 30.

According to Viet Thanh Nguyen, Vietnam does not extend a hand of reconciliation to the United States without conditions. In his thought-provoking work *Nothing Ever Dies: Vietnam and the Memory of War*, Nguyen posits that the act of compromise or mutual forgiveness between the two nations must be predicated on a quid pro quo: Vietnam will pardon America only on the condition that the latter safeguards Vietnam against China. As he states, "America will forgive Vietnam, so long as Vietnam allows itself to be invested in and permits the use of its territory—land, sea, or air—for America's fight against China."[14] Nguyen argues that Vietnamese nationals' view of Americans solely as a source of financial gain intensifies the bitterness between Vietnamese nationals and those living abroad who may feel disenchanted with such a facile alliance. Since a great many Chinese and Vietnamese have not been able to forget Chinese colonialism in Vietnam, Nguyen asserts that the conflict is ongoing.

Some Vietnamese Americans have flown the defunct South Vietnam flag to convey both a longing for a home that is lost and a stance against communism. To those who carried that flag on Capitol Hill during the January Sixth riot, any reconciliation might seem a bridge too far.[15] Their joining in the riot can be linked back to the historical praxis of the Homeland Restoration Movement and the establishment of the Republic of Vietnam (South Vietnam), which underscored anticommunism as its nationalist and state doctrine. In his article "Remaking the South Vietnamese Past in America," Y Thien Nguyen argues that these political and violent movements fueled Vietnamese Americans during the 1980s, as they saw that the destabilizing violence in Indochina during that time presented an opportunity for former South Vietnamese military operatives to violently overthrow the communist regime.[16] Those who spoke out against this anticommunist ideology were subject to condemnation as traitors, and in some cases even faced death as a consequence. Political tension between Vietnamese nationals and Vietnamese Americans has also been reflected in Vietnamese American literature.

Amid the lingering remnants of a bygone era, Vietnamese Americans seek to purge the residue of a communist system that now exists only as a shadow of history. Upon the departure of the last Americans in 1975, the Vietnamese people were left to bear witness to the arduous struggle of a new regime attempting to rebuild a nation from the ruins of war. Yet in the following decades, Vietnam was ravaged by a planned economy and collective farming that brought devastation to the land. Widespread poverty and social unrest compelled the government to enact a drastic overhaul in 1986 with the advent of the Đổi Mới (Economic reform) program.[17]

Scholars have been polemic against Vietnam's one-party rule, a system many deem a mere imitation of China's political structure.[18] Michael G. Kort, in his book *The Vietnam War Reexamined*, argues that Vietnam remains a communist state in name alone. While the country is still governed by a one-party administration, the socialist economy has undergone a profound transformation into a state capitalist model. Kort maintains that since the collapse of the collective farm system, the Socialist Republic of Vietnam and its administration "are nothing but veils masking a one-party dictatorship ruling over a country with a state-capitalist economy."[19] To put it simply, the communist state that many Vietnamese Americans strive to disrupt has been supplanted by a hybrid capitalist-socialist state since 1986. The government's open-door policy and the dismantling of a centralized economy paved the way for a market-oriented mechanism. In 1995 Vietnam extended a cordial handshake to the United States, ushering in a new area of progress and an unconventional pursuit of the American Dream in Vietnamese fashion.

With a transpacific history in mind, the critical moment—following a US presidential election during a pandemic—offers a unique historical reckoning. Unprecedentedly, the American transition of government seemingly bolstered a transpacific solidarity between Vietnamese nationals and Vietnamese Americans despite their intense antagonism after the end of the Vietnam War in 1975.[20] Despite having fled communist Vietnam, the anti-Chinese Vietnamese Americans who support Trump are in solidarity with Vietnamese nationals, and these transpacific Vietnamese communities reflect deep-seated political animosity and decolonial activism against China. But do Vietnamese nationals and Vietnamese Americans really share these nationalist sentiments? Does this "transpacific solidarity" represent an emerging anti-China movement that was exacerbated by American leaders' racial slurs during the pandemic? This chapter contends that there are enough differences that the "solidarity" is better described as a transpacific rupture, a hostile solidarity between Vietnamese nationals and Vietnamese Americans in the era of COVID-19 combined with Sinophobia. This rupture unfurls asymmetrical realities that are deeply rooted in neoliberal relationalities and the economic violence that is instigated by capitalist empires and their stratagems of economic hegemony in the Pacific and Asia.

The term "transpacific," as Lisa Yoneyama defines it, is associated with geopolitics that unfold existing connections of knowledge and power.[21] While the transpacific can be explained as mobility of people, knowledge, and ideologies across the Pacific Ocean, it can also be used as a conceptual framework to scrutinize flows that map out the genealogy of asymmetrical movements and trouble the fantasies of solidarity. The pandemic's outbreak and contested nationalisms have been exacerbated by Sinophobic sentiments on both sides of the Pacific Ocean. Partnerships that exist in the context of imperial mobility and contested ideologies, which have long facilitated imperial powers' historical erasure and transnational exploitation, engender conflicts and division among marginalized communities. Scrutinizing transpacific rupture as such opens up critical space and decolonial dialogues, allowing a subversive reimagination of Asia and America through arts and literature.

These historical entanglements are represented in an award-winning Vietnamese film by Dang Nhat Minh, *The Town within Reach*, in the Vietnamese patriotic song "My Country Is Calling My Name" (adapted from Nguyen Phan Que Mai's poem of the same name), and in current social media, illuminating the *longue durée* of colonialism, imperialism, and global capitalism. The film *The Town within Reach* takes place during the 1979 Sino-Vietnamese border war and massacre that claimed more than ten thousand lives, both soldiers and civilians, from both sides. From a similar lens, Nguyen Phan Que Mai's poem "My Country Is Calling My Name" sheds light on the countries' historical tension, relating how Chinese vessels have rammed and sunk Vietnamese fishing boats near Paracel Island and the water territories of Vietnam since 2017.[22] Both Dang Nhat Minh and Nguyen Phan Que Mai witnessed their country struggling to defend itself against China's aggression. Their works articulate the contested history and serve as a form of protest. Tracing a transpacific rupture through these cultural productions advances what might be called a praxis of transpacific decoloniality. These texts reimagine the still-present polarization that, despite some alteration, continues to undergird economic partnership, diplomatic normalization, and other militarized scripts. The methodology renders visible the pitfalls of facile coalitions. It compels us to question the founding decolonial perspective as we build toward deeper forms of solidarity for a more just world.

THE TRANSPACIFIC ON AND OFF DANG NHAT MINH'S SCREEN

In his award-winning film *The Town within Reach*, Vietnamese director Dang Nhat Minh shows the insidious erosion of human relations that have taken place beyond historical events. Lauded as one of the most influential films about the Sino-Vietnamese war, *The Town within Reach* revisits the mutual animosity of China and Vietnam that can be traced back to 111 BCE, when the Han Dynasty from China worked to assimilate Vietnam into its empire then subsequently colonized Vietnam for the next thousand years.[23] The specter of Chinese colonialism haunts contemporary Vietnam and deepens the rift between these ideological "bedfellows, strange dreamers."[24] Set in Lang Son, a northern province of Vietnam at the end of the Sino-Vietnamese war in 1979, the film chronicles Vu, a Vietnamese journalist, who is dispatched to Lang Son to report on the town immediately after the Chinese military troops withdrew from the borderline.[25] Amid the shambles, Vu mentally drifts back to the days when he met his first love, Thanh, who lived in that town. They were happily in love until a misunderstanding shattered their union, for which Vu never forgave himself. As such, he incessantly revisits his memories of that time. In his own memoir, *Cinematic Memories*, Dang relates that when he came to Lang Son to shoot the film, the town was in ruins. "People were still scattered in their evacuation places and hadn't returned to their town yet, so we had full control of the scene," Dang recalled, opining that *The Town within Reach* is the best film of his career, vis-à-vis its cinematic quality.[26]

Emerging from the revolutionary generation that experienced French colonialism and the American war in Vietnam, Dang (b. 1938) is nationally recognized as "the People's artist" and an "unrivaled" filmmaker, writer, and journalist. He maintains his paramount position in the contemporary celluloid industry of Vietnam. His original works are still impactful nearly half a century after the Vietnam War ended; the war's aftermath reverberates in Dang's aesthetics of representation. His debut film, *When the Tenth Month Comes*, was the first Vietnamese film to premiere in the West after the Vietnam War.[27] The film garnered numerous international awards and was recognized as "one of the greatest Asian films of all time" by CNN in 2008.[28] His other films include *The Return, Hanoi — Winter 1946*, and *The Girl on the River*. In 2005 Dang traveled to North Carolina and met Fred Whitehurst — a US veteran of the Vietnam War who had found a diary by a Vietnamese doctor, Dang Thuy Tram, when visiting a battlefield hospital that was flattened after the American bomb raids in the early 1970s. After returning to the United States, Fred struggled as he pored over the diary to fathom what his "enemy" had written. Fred then brought the diary to a seminar on the Vietnam War at Texas Tech University. There, the diary was archived and later returned to Dang Thuy Tram's family in Vietnam. When Dang Nhat Minh asked Fred about his impression of the diary, Fred pointed to the poetic lines in it: "And do you ever know / Love has given us wings." This became the inspiration for Dang's film *Don't Burn*, which won several top awards in Vietnam and the audience award at the 2009 Fukuoka Film Festival.[29]

While *The Town within Reach* bears a resemblance to his other cinematic works, this film captures a particular moment of history: the Sino-Vietnamese war in 1979. The film reveals decolonial undercurrents in Vietnam through a historical smokescreen. In his visual articulations Dang unfolds multiple layers of betrayal, a story within a story, as he lets the narrator, Vu, question his own memories and allegiances. In Vu's early days in love with Thanh, he was already agitated and submissive to an invisible power. Even though Vu desired to marry Thanh, he ended up leaving her in Lang Son, where they had shared sweet memories. He moved to Hanoi because his *tổ chức* (organization) was investigating Thanh's father, who had mysteriously disappeared from town one day; the employer was suspicious that Thanh's father had migrated to South Vietnam to work for the American proxy government in power there. As the story unfolds, we learn that Vu's abrupt abandonment of his girlfriend was instigated not only by his *tổ chức* but also by a Chinese neighbor who sold herbal medicine in the neighborhood where Thanh and her mother lived. Whispering between breaths, the Chinese neighbor tells Vu that Thanh's father was a traitor who betrayed the *cách mạng* (Communist revolutionaries) to serve the (capitalist) enemy in South Vietnam. "I already reported this to the local government," he tells Vu. "Let's do the Cultural Revolution! Such a glorious revolution!" Alluding to the Great Proletarian Cultural Revolution led by Mao Zedong, Dang shows the Cultural Revolution to be a destructive force in both China and Vietnam.

The film depicts the powerlessness of young Vietnamese people, who struggle in an ideological morass of unpredictable violence. Characters in the film sink in perils and navigate political turmoil that perpetuates violence. The film shows us flashbacks of Vu and Thanh roaming through Lang Son when this border town was still within China's reach. Newspapers from China glorifying the achievements of the Cultural Revolution in China were regularly distributed to Vietnamese inhabitants in Lang Son. Walking alongside Vu, who was reading a Chinese newspaper, Thanh keeps inquiring into the Cultural Revolution which was in full swing. "Why do they destroy all historic relics?" she asks Vu, who dithers for a moment, then says, "They want to exterminate all old things to create new ones." "But why," Thanh incessantly asks, "does China carry out this bloodshed revolution without anyone ever questioning the agenda behind it?" Vu struggles to figure it out for himself and struggles for the words to explain it.

Viewers are told that Vietnamese people are frightened of another brutal war with China, a war that would destroy the Vietnamese people, land, and rivers all over again. They keep quiet; yet theirs is a suppressed silence, a silence of fear, skepticism, and submission. By zooming his camera in on the intimate conversation between Vu and Thanh, Dang holds space for the unspeakable to work as also a form of resistance. Through filmic representation, Dang creates space for ambivalence that subversively reveals suppressive miseries of colonial subjects who are cognizant of the absolute confines of the country where history is strategically created to fit a designed logic. By foregrounding the voices of such self-constrained subjects as Vu and Thanh, Dang negotiates a liminal space beyond nationalist rhetoric of political allegiances.

The representation of historical liminality in *The Town within Reach* is pathbreaking, as most visual arts during these twilight years of the political rupture between China and Vietnam eschew this topic. Dang had a reason to depart from his peers. Unlike most of his contemporaries who came from humble backgrounds, Dang was born into a privileged family. His father was a prestigious medical doctor whose nationally recognized research on antibiotics saved soldiers from having their limbs amputated. Such prestige was also what allowed him to work in Japan from 1943 to 1950. In their father's absence, Dang and his siblings mostly lived with their mother. In his memoir, Dang notes that he was sent to China for military training and recalls being "brainwashed" with Chinese political doctrines and self-censorship.[30]

Through his visual art, however, Dang makes an aesthetic intervention into national politics. After returning from China, Dang was sponsored by Vietnam's Communist Party to study Russian so he could become an interpreter in the Soviet Union. Returning home, Dang discovered materials for his filmography: the war realities of Vietnam renarrated through the eyes of those who soldiered on through atrocities. His characters, including Vu and Thanh, display a montage of verisimilitudes that shed light on human experiences esthetically. This differentiates Dang's filmography from that of his peers, who are often inclined to portray what is designated as "real" by national rhetoric rather than eschewing its very construction. There is an intimate connection between reality and film, and directors should use their power to disrupt this connection by "contradicting, molding, shaping reality rather than reproducing it."[31] *The Town within Reach* places the characters within the vexed history of the "border war" to address the politics of Vietnam and China; the "border" serves as a metaphor of historical liminality and the site of resistance to nationalisms that break people apart.

Dang's visceral depictions of war exhibit the intense antagonisms that have plagued the violent relationship between China and Vietnam. In an encounter with a Japanese journalist who had also entered the town to cover the aftermath of the Sino-Vietnamese War, Vu reflects on Chinese military training that turns soldiers into heartless murderers:

> How do they become such brutal killers? At first, it appears there are no signs of crime: killing birds, swimming across the Truong Giang River, reading memory books, writing journal articles — all are seemingly innocent activities, yet they serve to desensitize and dehumanize people. It's an ongoing tragedy, years of deception. Mao's hegemony and expansionism, the green beret, the empire of Japan, and German fascism con-

tribute to this environment. Those Chinese soldiers never flinch in the face of monstrous acts, but when they confront themselves, they become cowards. Cowardice is complicity to crime.[32] [author's translation]

The experience of military training tears apart those who are placed on the interstice of history, as it fosters a sense of mutual apprehension and fragments one's relationship with oneself; antagonisms play out *within* each character's self-reflection.

Vu agonizes over his choices. If he persistently pursues his love with Thanh, he will be unable to sustain his career. After the Chinese store owner reports Thanh's father to the local government, Vu leaves the town for his professional survival and promotion. In a letter sent to Vu later, when everything was settled, Thanh reveals that her father did not move southward in Vietnam to work for Americans or the Army of the Republic of Vietnam; he left his family for a clandestine love affair with a woman in the south. The viewers then see Vu wistfully jolted back to his memory of Thanh. He then returns to the Chinese herbal store to retaliate against the insidious owner, only to find a pile of rubble.

Dang shows the relationality of violence and betrayal on and off screen when the Japanese journalist asks Vu, "They [China] used to stand by you. Since when have they turned against you? Where did this betrayal arise from?" The film demystifies the conundrum, unveiling Vu's ruminations on a multitude of betrayals: his comrades against him, his own toward Thanh, and China against Vietnam. Vu says: "There used to be that time of intimacy [between China and Vietnam] but now they [China] chase after greed and become selfish. They could betray anyone, including their dearest people. And this betrayal is the first step to violence and brutality" (my translation). This mutual animosity seeps into the souls of the nations, in both China and Vietnam.

Toward the end of *The Town within Reach*, the Japanese journalist recites a haiku he had not been able to understand until the moment he walked into the bombarded town of Lang Son: "I remember yesterday afternoon / a regiment couldn't frighten me / This afternoon I'm scared of my own shadow." The journalist tells Vu that he now comprehends the poem: "It is a warning. I love human beings," he says. Then a wandering bullet, flying out of the blue, kills him. Falling into Vu's arms, blood surging from his chest, the journalist utters his last words between breaths: "Be vigilant!" Vu holds his foreign colleague in his lap, and his eyes turn somber in misery.

This visual narrative of betrayal represents the splitting of marginalized people who are not only interpolated *into* ideological war but also narrated *by* others. In Vietnam's dominant discourse, China is represented as a stranger and a brother. While the states of Vietnam and China perform fraternal relation and solidarity in public, people who lived through the colonial relations manifest otherwise. This split narrative creates polarized political ideologies and the narrative of betrayal makes visible the nationalist reconfigurations of history as a cultural mastery that is monolithic and secretive. This form of reframing history in the film creates what Homi Bhabha calls the "liminality of the nation-space," providing a productive conceptualization and "narrative authority for marginal voices or minority discourse."[33] *The Town within Reach* suggests that the polarized history of China and Vietnam should be examined through the stories of marginalized people like Vu, Thanh, and the Japanese journalist, to fully question the state and competing Chinese and Vietnamese accounts. Such representation cannot be conceived in a static context that is confined to a particular historical moment; it must be instead approached as a historically mobilized form of transpacific rupture.

Resistance against China runs deep within the Vietnamese nationalist population who lived throughout Vietnam's decolonial and anti-imperial history. Enduring Chinese colonization that lasted a thousand years, Vietnamese people experienced the sanitization of their language, culture, and identities, undergoing what sociologist Orlando Patterson calls "social death": the disposable status of an enslaved country that was unable to decide its own fate.[34] While Patterson deploys the term to describe a dehumanizing society in slavery and the Holocaust, this concept might also speak to Vietnam under Chinese colonial rule, when Vietnamese people and their culture were denigrated and reconstructed in light of Chinese ideologies. The legacy of Chinese colonization is entrenched in the soul of the nation. In *The Town within Reach*, Dang portrays a silent form of resistance through his Vietnamese characters, who faced Chinese expansionism four years after the end of the Vietnam War when China invaded Vietnam on February 17, 1979, and seized the three northern provinces bordering China.

On that same day, at a horse race in Texas, a stout Asian man wearing a dark suit raised a cowboy hat and smiled brightly. That moment was captured and broadcasted worldwide, and eventually becoming a diplomatic emblem. That man was Deng Xiaoping, vice premier of the State Council of the People's Republic of China. Twenty-seven days after the US-China accords were signed, on January 28, 1979, Deng began his official visit to the United States. During the opening-day reception, Deng requested a private meeting with President Jimmy Carter regarding the Vietnam issue. Unlike his predecessors, who had tried to foster a good diplomatic relationship with Vietnam, Deng politically detached himself from Vietnamese leaders before and after the Vietnam War. Amid the political turmoil and escalating conflict between North and South Vietnam, Deng deepened this antagonism by convincing North Vietnam to denigrate political resistance in South Vietnam while also forcing Vietnamese leaders to choose an alliance: Soviet or China.[35] Despite mutual effort at negotiation, Deng ended up breaking the relationship with Vietnam and waged a war "to teach Vietnam a lesson."[36] At least six hundred thousand Chinese troops were then mobilized to carry out a massive sabotage on Vietnamese soil. Even though China lost in the border war with Vietnam, the Chinese military killed tens of thousands of Vietnamese soldiers and civilians. It is this historical legacy, not impulsive animosity, that drives the countries to antagonistic violence.

Since Vietnam regained its independence from China in 1979, the state has struggled to reconcile historical memories and appease social unrest. As Tuong Vu observes, soon after Vietnam exerted its Open Door policy of economic reforms in 1986, it witnessed "political civil society" burgeoning with emerging groups of dissidents—spontaneously formed by former communist officials, disillusioned military officers, and bloggers whose voices are amplified by social media. Seeking an ideological exit, these "fragmented and fragile" forces not only challenge the party's power but fiercely protest against China at the same time.[37] In his critical article "The Party v. the People: Anti-China Nationalism in Contemporary Vietnam," Tuong argues that the ruling Communist Party of Vietnam has lost its legitimacy by allowing the emerging popular nationalist movement in the country to pressure the party to terminate its relationship with Beijing due to the recent skirmish in the South China Sea.[38]

In 1988 the Chinese military attacked Vietnam's Johnson South Reef—Spratly Island—killing unarmed Vietnamese soldiers.[39] The event further fueled anti-China and decolonial movements that have barely ebbed away. The Vietnamese government, however, has hardly brooked any anti-China protests, even those that have led to serious damage of Chinese factories in Vietnam. The government's gesture of tolerance and silence in the face of injustice has been publicly castigated as "impotent" and "cowardly" by Vietnamese nationals and other Vietnamese in the diaspora on social media. These dissident voices are ubiquitous online and have grown beyond the control of the Vietnamese government.

As Benedict Kerkvliet argues in his book *Speaking Out in Vietnam*, since the 1990s, public political criticism has morphed into an eminent force that shapes the political landscape of Vietnam. Gauging the growing public reactionary discourses, Kerkvliet shows how family whispers have turned into widespread criticism over the recent three decades. Drawing on a wide variety of sources that focus on public uprisings in sectors of factory labor, land rights, anti-China sentiment, and democratizing activism, Kerkvliet demonstrates that the public reactionary discourse ranges from condemning corruption among authorities, to pressing the government to free political dissidents, to protests for better working conditions. Instead of repressing this public criticism, Kerkvliet points out, Vietnamese authorities often tolerate such social unrest.[40]

The US presidential election manifested the transformation of Vietnamese public criticism. On social media in recent years, besides talking about Trump, Vietnamese Facebook users have conducted heated conversations about social issues that were deemed taboo a mere decade ago. For example, Vietnamese people were not expected to discuss issues such as Chinese-Vietnamese disputes, US-Vietnam diplomatic complexities, or corruption of government authorities. However, since social media started to blossom in Vietnam (over half of the population, or 46 million, have been active users as of 2019), much can be dissected and exposed online. Vietnamese authorities, while being vigilant, can hardly put down all dissident voices. Though the government often tolerates public criticism, it tends to suppress protests regarding China's belligerence to Vietnamese sovereignty because of the strategic diplomacy issue, which aims to nurture peace with the aggressive neighbor yet expanding military, political, and economic power.

Aligning with Dang Nhat Minh's resistant representation of the vexed relation between China and Vietnam, Vietnamese national poet and novelist Nguyen Phan Que Mai unravels the strangeness and irony of such fraternal relations through her prominent literary works. Author of eleven books (in Vietnamese and English), Nguyen weaves political sensitivity into every piece of her oeuvre. Her recently released novel *The Mountains Sing* (2020)—an international bestseller—has garnered several prestigious awards, including the Dayton Literary Peace Prize (2021), and has been translated into more than fifteen languages. One of her poems was turned into a nationally popular song: "My Country Is Calling My Name." The poem and lyrics call for Vietnamese people to remember the *longue durée* of the country's struggles against invaders. The song has been performed by hundreds of artists across Vietnam in the face of Chinese illegal occupation of the Spratly and Paracel archipelago and control of the water sovereignty of Vietnam:

> I'm listening . . .
> My country is calling my name
> Through the waves of Spratly and Paracel islands
> Rushing to the shore
> The calling of my country echoed
> From the ocean
> Where thunderstorms are raging,
> swallowing my country

The irony is inherent, as the author elides all designations and employs the metaphor of thunderstorms as an allusion to Chinese assaults. In the heat of a decolonial movement that culminated in the Vietnamese government's brutal suppression and imprisonment of dissident voices protesting China's invasion, Nguyen stands by anti-China activists and articulates the suppressed pain of Vietnamese people on the verge of losing their land in the Pacific Ocean.[41] Beyond the aesthetics of solidarity lies another pain of the oppressed. "My Country Is Calling My Name" is an attempt to articulate unspeakable brutality, as Nguyen reminds her Vietnamese fellows of a painful history of the country:

The ocean waves are surging
In the shape of the country
The ocean is severed in pain
My country, oh, my country
has never rested for thousands of years
For our peace, countless people have died,
Their blood flows into ocean waves.
My beloved country, oh, my beloved country. [author's translation]

Using metaphors of ocean waves and thunderstorms, Nguyen troubles the politics of silence that cannot be articulated without the arts. Her awareness of the limitations of history becomes more explicit and retrievable through the aesthetics of violence and pain of the ocean waves and thunderstorms. "My Country Is Calling My Name" is placed in a collectively suppressed anger that frustrates the neocolonial fraternal relation and promises of mutual benefits and the fantasy of equal freedom. If nationalism seems to displace the arts and literature with its fierce enforcement of power and fantasy, artists like Nguyen navigate imaginary spaces beyond such dominant spheres to evoke human pathos and critical activism against artificial and vicious constructions of power. Through her art, oppressed people are liberated, as they collectively fight for freedom; the song compels them to move forward with its evocative lyrics:

Millions of Vietnamese people are muttering: Việt Nam.
Millions of Vietnamese bodies falling down to shield this country

By appealing to the Vietnamese audience's nationalism during this perilous moment of history, Nguyen's poem calls for Vietnamese people's awareness of their fragile fates under double oppressions: the state and China. The state represses collective resistance to injustice, and China proceed in a reckless invasion.

"My Country Is Calling My Name" activates decolonial undercurrents and the transpacific rupture that dates back centuries. The Pacific Ocean has been an irresistible lure for European empires for its "mildness" since the sixteenth century, and it has incessantly flown in the fantasy of multiple empires ever since.[42] In the name of "civilization" and "liberation" of Asia, the French and the Japanese jointly occupied and claimed control over the region during the Pacific War. Both powers established their colonialism in Asia and ended up in a debacle, as the decolonial revolts surged in the Pacific Ocean.[43] But the "Asia-Pacific" was, ironically, a European-American construct that conceals a dream of "Oriental markets" and a desire for an "earthly paradise," as Arif Dirlik observes.[44] The invention of the term Asia-Pacific not only blurs boundaries of the Western Hemisphere as a continent, but it is also misleading, since it overshadows the human activity that undergirds the idea. As Dirlik argues, this "Pacific ideology," which embraces alternative designations of the Pacific basin and the Pacific Rim, is problematic; we should confront this conceptualization by asking "What is Pacific? . . . Whose Pacific? — and when?"[45]

The Transpacific Partnership (TPP, signed 2016) was not simply an agreement signed between twelve countries bordering the Pacific Ocean and the United States to end trade barriers and to create economic partnerships. As the Obama administration articulates it: "With the TPP, we [the Americans] can rewrite the rules of trade to benefit America's middle class. Because if we don't, competitors who don't share our values, like China, will step in to fill that void."[46] The TPP, an ambitious agenda of contested empires, implicates not only economic benefits but also militarized cooperation to maintain national security of the empires, as manifested in China's subsequent and ongoing expansionism and domination in the Pacific, as well as the United States' military tension over the region. With such a contested partnership, the military-industrial complex expands and undergirds only the economic powers in their exploitation of the marginalized countries involved. While all TPP signers agreed on a long-term cooperation, they do not equally benefit from the agreement. The agreement's asymmetrical partnership benefits only superpowers. It projects a form of economic violence for the poor of involved countries. Nonetheless, while many in the Vietnamese community expressed their fervent advocacy for Trump and his anti-China sentiment, Trump's withdrawal from the TPP troubles the Vietnamese and Vietnamese Americans who fear that "Trump's political preeminence" will not contain but will enhance the economic and geostrategic influence of China in the Pacific.

The Pacific Ocean has been ceaselessly flowing in imperial fantasies, embracing within its bed the bodies, bones, and blood of a profusion of refugees, soldiers, heroes, and villains who crossed it for freedom, exploited it as their lucrative pond, shed their blood to preserve the territorial sea of their ancestors, or remapped it for occupation. Rethinking transpacific rupture through the aesthetic representation of Dang Nhat Minh and Nguyen Phan Que Mai in the era of COVID-19 and hostile nationalisms reveals lasting entanglements of colonization, imperialism, and global capitalism. Such historical entanglements resist the dominant rhetoric of comprehensive partnership and other prosperity narratives about the Asia-Pacific that eschew wholesale militarized cooperation, unjust intervention, and neoliberal relationalities of economic violence.

NOTES

1. Emma Hurt, "President Trump Called Former President Jimmy Carter to Talk about China," *NPR*, April 15, 2019, https://www.npr.org/2019/04/15/713495558/president -trump-called-former-president-jimmy-carter-to-talk-about-china.

2. Ken Bredemeier, "Trump: 'I Beat This Crazy, Horrible China Virus,'" Voice of America (VOA), October 11, 2020, https://www.voanews.com/a/2020-usa-votes_ trump-i-beat-crazy-horrible-china-virus/6196998.html.

3. "'Sanctified Sinophobia' and the Role of Christian Nationalism in Anti-Asian Racism: An Interview with Lucas Kwong," *Anxious Bench* (blog), https://www.patheos .com, January 11, 2021, https://www.patheos.com/blogs/anxiousbench/2021/01/sanct ified-sinophobia-and-the-role-of-christian-nationalism-in-anti-asian-racism-an -interview-with-lucas-kwong/.

4. Viet Thanh Nguyen, "There's a Reason the South Vietnamese Flag Flew during the Capitol Riot," *Washington Post*, January 14, 2021, https://www.washingtonpost.com /outlook/2021/01/14/south-vietnam-flag-capitol-riot/; "'Sóng Ảo' Xanh—đỏ Trong Bầu Cử Tổng Thống Mỹ," *VnExpress*, November 3, 2020, https://vnexpress.net/song-ao -xanh-do-trong-bau-cu-tong-thong-my-4186021.html.

5. "Why Do Vietnamese Americans Support Donald Trump?," *Deutsche Welle*, accessed November 13, 2021, https://www.dw.com/en/trump-popular-amongvietnamese -americans/a-55702032.

6. Thuy Dung T. Pham and Quynh T. Truong, "In Vietnam, Many Are Mourning the Downfall of an American Idol," *The Diplomat*, last modified November 12, 2020, https://thediplomat.com/2020/11/in-vietnam-many-are-mourning-the-downfall-of-an -american-idol/.

7. Long Bui, "Why the Flag of South Vietnam Flew at US Capitol Siege," *Yahoo!*, January 12, 2021, https://www.yahoo.com/now/why-flag-south-vietnam-flew -201839699.html.

8. Hoang Tuan, "South Vietnam's Flags at the Capitol Riot," *Asia Sentinel*, last modified January 9, 2020, https://www.asiasentinel.com/p/south-vietnams-flags-at-the -capitol, 53.

9. Homi Bhabha, *The Location of Culture* (London: Routledge, 2004), 2.

10. See this volume's introduction for this discussion.

11. The 2021 shooting of six Asian women in a massage parlor in Atlanta was the consequence of a static and perilous mentality. Likewise, seeing Vietnam as a monolithic, despotic, unchanging nation-state is a parochial, reductive, and detrimental outlook that jeopardizes any peace-making process.

12. Along with the burgeoning of the Internet and the Fourth Industrial Revolution (or "Industry 4.0") that characterize our age, social media like Facebook, Twitter (now X), and other digital platforms prompt the world to complicate and reimagine transpacific rupture in light of multiplicity and versatility that enact changes and relationalities.

13. Barack Obama, "Remarks by President Obama in Address to the People of Vietnam," National Archives and Records Administration, May 24, 2016, https:// obamawhitehouse.archives.gov/the-Press-Office/2016/05/24/Remarks-President -Obama-Address-People-Vietnam.

14. Viet Thanh Nguyen, *Nothing Ever Dies: Vietnam and the Memory of War* (London: Harvard University Press, 2016), 287.

15. However celebratory this nationalist performance may seem, the Trump administration was at the same time trying to deport nine thousand Vietnamese refugees who had committed offenses in the past but had already served their time.

16. Y Thien Nguyen, "(Re)Making the South Vietnamese Past in America," *Journal of Asian American Studies* 21, no. 1 (2018): 68, https://doi.org/10.1353/jaas.2018.0003.

17. Emerging from this twilight period were a capitalist-minded population that included the economic evangelists who benefited from nepotism or intimate relationships with high-ranking leaders of the Communist Party in their (il)legitimate partnerships. This uneven distribution of power and privilege has eroded the socioeconomic equality and exacerbated political discontent.

18. The sociopolitical hegemony that Vietnam and China have consistently maintained frustrate the majority of the intelligentsia as well as progressive populations in these countries, as such a flawed mechanism continues to jeopardize democracy and human rights. Police brutality and censorship are normalized and revolts, violent and nonviolent, for whatever reason are neither encouraged nor suppressed.

19. Michael Kort, *The Vietnam War Reexamined* (Cambridge: Cambridge University Press, 2018), 221–22.

20. The collapse of the (anticommunist) Republic of Vietnam forced hundreds of thousands of South Vietnamese to flee the country for fear of persecution when the communists seized Saigon (in South Vietnam) and reunited the country, establishing the new regime.

21. Lisa Yoneyama, *Cold War Ruins: Transpacific Critique of American Justice and Japanese War Crimes* (Durham, NC: Duke University Press, 2016), 7.

22. For more information about the Sino-Vietnamese strife at Paracel Island, see Bengali Shashank and Bao Uyen Vo Kieu, "Sunken Boats, Stolen Gear: Fishermen Are Prey as China Conquers a Strategic Sea," *Los Angeles Times*, November 12, 2020, https://www.latimes.com/world-nation/story/2020-11-12/china-attacks-fishing-boats -in-conquest-of-south-china-sea; Chau Hoang, "Chinese Ships Attack Vietnamese Fishermen," *Asia News*, July 9, 2017, https://www.asianews.it/news-en/Chinese -ships-attack-Vietnamese-fishermen-41670.html; and Khanh Vu, "Vietnam Protests Beijing's Sinking of South China Sea Boat," *Reuters*, April 4, 2020, https://www.reuters .com/article/us-vietnam-china-southchinasea/vietnam-protests-beijings-sinking-of -south-china-sea-boat-idUSKBN21M072.

23. For more information about the power dynamics and intimacy between China and Vietnam evolving over time, read Khue Dieu Do, "Japanese 'Blood' in the 1979 Sino-Vietnamese Border War," *Journal of Vietnamese Studies* 16, no. 4 (November 1, 2021): 36–67, https://doi.org/10.1525/vs.2021.16.4.36.

24. Do, "Japanese 'Blood.'"

25. In 1979 China launched a bloody war to punish Vietnam for sending army forces to support Cambodia in its fight against the Khmer Rouge (Communist Party of Kampuchea), which was largely funded by China (i.e., Mao Zedong). China claims to have killed and injured fifty-seven thousand Vietnamese troops. Both Vietnam and China, however, have never released a precise record of deaths. Read more about this Sino-Vietnamese border war in J. Mulvenon, "The Limits of Coercive Diplomacy: The 1979 Sino-Vietnamese border war," *Journal of Northeast Asian Studies* 14 (1995): 68–88, https://doi.org/10.1007/BF03023429.

26. Minh N. Dang, "Cinematic Memories," Viet-studies.net, last modified November 27, 2011, http://www.viet-studies.net/DangNhatMinh/DangNhatMinh_HoiKyDien Anh.htm.

27. Festival des Cinémas d'Asie de Vesoul, "When the Tenth Month Comes," August 5, 2016, https://www.cinemas-asie.com/en/archives-en/item/2206-when-the-tenth -month-comes.html.

28. "Pick the Best Asian Films of All Time," *CNN*, accessed November 14, 2021, https://edition.cnn.com/2008/SHOWBIZ/Movies/08/12/asiapacific.top10/index.html.

29. Tuoi Tre, "Đặng Nhật Minh và Sự Nghiệp Điện Ảnh Chưa Có Người Thay Thế," *Quitrent*, March 15, 2018, https://tuoitre.vn/dang-nhat-minh-va-su-nghiep-dien -anh-chua-co-nguoi-thay-the-20180315091925898.htm.

30. Indomemoires, "Dang Nhat Minh," hypotheses.org, accessed November 26, 2021, https://indomemoires.hypotheses.org/tag/dang-nhat-minh.

31. James Monaco, *How to Read a Film: Movies, Media, and Beyond*, 30th ed. (New York: Oxford University Press), 2009.

32. Dang Nhat Minh, dir., *The Town within Reach (1983)*, accessed November 27, 2021. https://www.youtube.com/watch?v=1xEGVWu42Hg.

33. Homi K. Bhabha, *The Location of Culture* (London: Routledge, 2019), 150.

34. Orlando Patterson, *Slavery and Social Death: A Comparative Study* (London: Harvard University Press, 1990).

35. Xiaoming Zhang, "Deng Xiaoping and China's Decision to Go to War with Vietnam," *Journal of Cold War Studies* 12, no. 3 (2010): 3–29, https://muse.jhu.edu/article/392776.

36. Qiang Zhai, *China and the Vietnam Wars, 1950–1975* (Chapel Hill: University of North Carolina Press, 2000), 214.

37. Tuong Vu, "The Party v. the People," *Journal of Vietnamese Studies* 9, no. 4 (December 1, 2014): 33–66, https://doi.org/10.1525/vs.2014.9.4.33.

38. Vu, "The Party v. the People."

39. Joshua Lipes, "Vietnam Marks Anniversary of Naval Clash with China Over Spratly Island Reefs," RFA, last modified March 13, 2018, https://www.rfa.org/english/news/vietnam/anniversary03132018160914.html.

40. Benedict J. Kerkvliet, *Speaking Out in Vietnam: Public Political Criticism in a Communist Party-Ruled Nation* (Ithaca, NY: Cornell University Press, 2019).

41. "Vietnamese Dissidents Who Backed Anti-China Protests Harassed in Prison," Radio Free Asia, May 29, 2014, https://www.rfa.org/english/news/vietnam/harassment-05292014174256.html.

42. Betty Burnett, *Ferdinand Magellan: The First Voyage around the World, Library Edition* (Brilliance Audio, 2009).

43. Chizuru Namba, "The French Colonization and Japanese Occupation of Indochina during the Second World War: Encounters of the French, Japanese, and Vietnamese," *Cross-Currents: East Asian History and Culture Review* 32 (2019): 74.

44. Arif Dirlik, "The Asia-Pacific Idea: Reality and Representation in the Invention of a Regional Structure," *Journal of World History* 3, no. 1 (1992): 55–79, http://www.jstor.org/stable/20078512.

45. Dirlik, "The Asia-Pacific Idea."

46. The White House, "The Trans-Pacific Partnership," n.d., https://obamawhitehouse.archives.gov/issues/economy/trade.

CONTRIBUTORS

I-TING CHEN is lecturer of media, cultural and creative studies at HKU SPACE Community College, Hong Kong. Her research interests include Cold War politics, sexual and intimate labor, migration and mobility, and feminisms in Asia. She is currently working on a book focusing on the intersection of migration, cross-strait relations, gender and sexuality, and teahouse culture in Taiwan. Her articles are published in and accepted by *Cultural Studies and Inter-Asia Cultural Studies.*

LEANNE P. DAY is associate professor in English at the University of Hawaiʻi at Hilo. She recently was the inaugural Daniel K. Inouye postdoctoral fellow at the University of Hawaiʻi at Mānoa. Her research focuses on questions of Indigeneity, Asian immigration, settler colonialism, and US empire in Hawaiʻi through examination of contemporary "local" literature and cultural production. She is currently working on a book manuscript about the genealogy of settler-colonial liberal multiculturalism in Hawaiʻi from the nineteenth century to the present.

JOSEN MASANGKAY DIAZ is associate professor of ethnic studies at the University of San Diego. Her book, *Postcolonial Configurations: Dictatorship, the Racial Cold War, and Filipino America*, analyzes the formation of Filipino American subjectivity at the intersections of colonialism, liberalism, and authoritarianism.

EVYN LÊ ESPIRITU GANDHI is associate professor of Asian American studies at the University of California, Los Angeles. Her work engages critical refugee studies, settler-colonial studies, and transpacific studies. Gandhi is author of *Archipelago of Resettlement: Vietnamese Refugee Settlers and Decolonization across Guam and Israel-Palestine*, which examines what she calls the "refugee settler condition": the vexed positionality of refugee subjects whose very condition of political legibility via citizenship is predicated upon the unjust dispossession of an Indigenous population.

KYUNG HEE HA is assistant professor in the Department of World Languages and Cultures at North Carolina State University. She is a founding member of Eclipse Rising, a San Francisco Bay Area member organization of the "Comfort Women" Justice Coalition, and a member of Kibō no Tane Kikin (KIBOTANE), Seed of Hope Foundation, a Tokyo-based foundation dedicated to educating youths on the comfort women issue. Ha was a founding member of Japan's first intersectionality feminist seminar series for young adults called FemiZemi. Her recent publications appear in *Social Identities: Journal for the Study of Race, Nation and Culture* and in *Japanese American Millennials: Rethinking Generation, Community, and Diversity*. She is currently working on a book project on pro–North Korea schools in Japan in the context of thriving Japanese nationalism and the US-led War on Terror.

TZU-HUI CELINA HUNG is an independent scholar whose research centers on issues about Sinophone culture in the context of globalization, Chinese migration and related sociocultural networks, Anglophone literature, postcolonial Southeast Asian studies, and the discourses of creolization and multiculturalism in contemporary Sinophone societies. She is currently completing a book manuscript that examines multilingual articulations of creolization at the turn of the twentieth century onward, by writers and filmmakers hailing from Southeast Asia with peranakan Chinese and other interconnected backgrounds amid a nexus of sociopolitical and cultural forces.

CHIEN-TING LIN is associate professor in the English Department at National Central University in Taiwan. His research engages medical modernity and biopolitics; studies of empires, militarism, and neocolonialism; transpacific (post) Cold War studies; inter-Asia cultural studies; and critical race, gender, and sexuality studies. He has published his research (in English and Chinese) in *Inter-Asia Cultural Studies, Verge: Studies in Global Asias, Review of International American Studies, Taiwan: A Radical Quarterly in Social Studies,* and *American Quarterly,* among others. He is currently completing a book manuscript that investigates transpacific colonial and neocolonial formations of knowledge production and hierarchies of reproductive labor and life politics within different periods of Taiwan's medical modernization.

SIMEON MAN is associate professor of history at the University of California, San Diego. His research focuses on the politics of race, militarism, and imperialism in Asia and the Pacific in the twentieth century. He is author of *Soldiering through Empire: Race and the Making of the Decolonizing Pacific*. His essays have been published in *American Quarterly, Race & Class, Radical History Review*, and other edited volumes.

CHRISTOPHER B. PATTERSON is associate professor in the Social Justice Institute at the University of British Columbia, where he researches transpacific discourses of literature, video games, and new media through the lens of empire studies, Asian American studies, and queer theory. He is author of *Transitive Cultures: Anglophone Literature of the Transpacific* and *Open World Empire: Race, Erotics, and the Global Rise of Video Games*. He publishes fiction and poetry under his matrilineal name, Kawika Guillermo, including *Stamped: An Anti-Travel Novel* and *Nimrods: a fake-punk self-hurt anti-memoir*.

Y-DANG TROEUNG was an associate professor of English at the University of British Columbia and associate editor of the journal *Canadian Literature: A Quarterly of Criticism Review*. She is author of the books *Refugee Lifeworlds: The Afterlife of the Cold War in Cambodia* and *Landbridge [life in fragments]*.

QUYNH H. VO is professorial lecturer of Asia, Pacific, and diaspora studies at American University. Her research focuses on globalization and Asian literature, Asian American interdisciplinary studies, Vietnamese American literature and culture, and neoliberalism in American transnational literature. She is currently working on a book manuscript on neoliberal peace and transnational kinship in Vietnamese American literature and culture. Her writings (in English and Vietnamese) have appeared in *The Routledge Handbook of Ecofeminism and Literature, Los Angeles Review of Books, diaCRITICS, Journal of Vietnamese Studies, Da Mau, Saigoneer, Peace, Land, Bread*, and other venues. She is co-translator (with Quan Manh Ha) of *Longings: Contemporary Fiction by Vietnamese Women Writers*.

LILY WONG is associate professor of literature as well as of critical race, gender, and culture studies at American University and serves as associate director of AU's Antiracist Research and Policy Center. Her research focuses on the politics of affective labor, racial capitalism, minor-transnational coalitional movements, and media formations of transpacific Chinese, Sinophone, and Asian American communities. She is one of the founding board members of the Society of Sinophone Studies and serves on the advisory board of *Verge: Studies in Global Asias*. She is author of *Transpacific Attachments: Sex Work, Media Networks, and Affective Histories of Chineseness* and is coeditor (with Eric Tang) of "Dimensions of Violence, Resistance, and Becoming: Asian Americans and the 'Opening' of the COVID-Era," a special issue of *Journal of Asian American Studies*.

INDEX

Italicized page numbers refer to figures.

Arora, Gabo, 77
arrivant (term), 35
Arvin, Maile, 11, 242
Asahi Shimbun, 238
Asian/Americanization of justice, 197–98
Asian American literature, 87–88, 124
Asian American studies, 2–3, 10–12, 81, 89, 108, 111–12, 162
Asian Art Biennale, 167
Asian Development Bank, 111
Asian studies, 2–3, 9–10, 111, 162
Asian Women's Fund (1995–2007), 207–8
Asia-Pacific 5, 225, 266–67
Atlantic (magazine), 82
Atomic Marshall Plan, 230
Atoms for Peace, 230
attachments. *See* "transpacific attachments"
Australia, 139, 224, 241
authoritarianism, 1, 5, 16, 54, 109; Philippines, 111, 118–21, 125, 127
automation, 16, 78, 81, 84–85, 91–93, 98–99
avant-garde, 87, 138, 146–47
"Axis of evil," 207

Bahng, Aimee, 5
Bala, Sruti, 38
Bares, Annie, 94
Barker, Holly, 35
Bataan Death March, 117
Battle of Okinawa, 137, 149
battle of the books (competition), 76
Bay Area Code Pink, 201
Beauregard, Guy, 80
Benitez, J. Francisco, 108
Benjamin, Ruha, 80
benshengren ("people of the province"), 53, 69, 75
Berlant, Lauren, 82, 173
Berlin, Irving, 116–17
Bhabha, Homi, 251, 261
Biden, Joe, 252
Big Tech, 76, 78, 82. *See also individual tech companies*

Bikini Incident, 228–29, 241
biopolitics, 2, 81
Blackburn, Marsha, 250
Black Hills Alliance, 243
Black Hills International Survival Gathering, 243
Blackness, 5, 12, 80, 126–27, 133
Black Pacific, framework, 5
Blood and Tears of Fishing Ground (Lee et al.), 162
Bloody May Day, 229
Bloom, Paul, 82
Bobo (Xiaomei's friend), 61
Bodde, William, 244
Bordallo, Madeleine, 134
borders, 145, 238, 244, 258, 261, 266; and border war, 255–56, 259, 262; crossing of, 58–60, 73n26, 140, 163; national, 15, 20; nation-state, 135, 214; and refugees, 76, 79; US-Mexico, 140, 151–54
Born into Brothels (film), 82
Boss Ho, 66–67
Boss Tian, 55–57, 73n24
Brathwaite, Kamau, 35
Broken Wings collection, 164, 167–75, *169, 171, 175, 178, 180, 183*
Bronstein, Phil, 115, 118
Brother Wu, 66
brown boy/rice queen dyad, 14–15
Buckmaster, Luke, 79
Bulosan, Carlos, 125
Burias, Teresita, 118–20, 127
Bury Me, My Love (game), 89
Byrd, Jodi, 35

California, 45, 195, 212, 230; Bay Area, 201, 272; Chico, 238; Glendale, 205, 207, 210, 219n46; Los Angeles, 1, 109, 201, 207, 240; Modesto, 238; Northern, 209; Redwood City, 201; San Diego, 238; San Francisco, 17, 109, 194, 198–99, 201, 203–6, 210–12, 214–15; Southern, 210; Susanville, 238

Camacho, Carlos, 241

Camacho, Keith L., 18–19, 25n44, 136, 139

Cambodia, 13, 81, 118, 269n25

Camp Casey, 94

Camp Hasan, 133

Canada, 76; Toronto, 194

Canada Reads (TV show), 76

Canadian Broadcasting Corporation (CBC), 76

Cao, Lan, 88

capitalism, 16, 112, 225, 232, 244, 254–55, 258, 268n17; energy, 234, 239, 242; and Filipino America, 107, 109, 112–13; global, 147, 149, 166, 214, 267; and hospitality, 31, 34, 41, 43; neoliberal, 162–63; racial, 2, 6, 8, 198, 227–31, 240; and virtual reality, 78–79

Carne y Arena (virtual reality film), 79

Caroline Islands, 227

Carter, Jimmy, 250, 262

cartography, 9, 20, 137–38, 152, 234. *See also* mapping

Castle Bravo (nuclear weapon), 227

Central America, 79, 140, 152

Central Washington University, 203

Cha, Theresa Hak Kyun, 138

Chamorro people, 20, 25n44, 134–36, 139–42, 147–52, 154n3, 154n6; and NFIP, 17, 243

Chang, Iris, 195

Cheah, Pheng, 167

Chen, Mel, 21

Chen, Tina, 5, 9, 14, 23n11, 82

Chen Kuan-Hsing, 18, 24n26, 52, 199

Chen Shen Wen, 69

Chen Shih-chung, 52

Chen Su-Hsiang, 172

Chen Ying-git, 69

Cheng Chang, 177

Chin, Frank, 88

China, 2, 5, 7–8, 21, 92, 111, 121, 193; and comfort women, 199, 207, 211, 214; Guangdong province, 59; Guangzhou, 1; mainland, 50–53, 56–58, 62–69, 71, 161; and Trump, 250–52; and Vietnam,

253–66, 268n18, 269n25; Wuhan, 51, 55–56, 71n1; Xinjiang, 1, 19

Chinese Americans, 88, 195

Chinese Civil War, 15, 52–53, 69–70

Chinese Communist Party (CCP), 58, 64

Chinese Ministry of Culture and Tourism, 62

Ching, Leo, 118

Chin-hsia Liang, 161

Chiokai, Edwin T., 238

Cho, Grace M., 98

Chow, Rey, 165

Choy, Catherine Ceniza, 111

Chuang, Shu-ching, 168–69

Chuh, Kandice, 3

Chun, Wendy Hui Kyong, 80

Chungja, Bang, 210, 214

citizens, normative, 41

citizenship, 52, 73, 109, 150, 153, 166, 179, 241; and Chamorro people, 135; and Filipinos, 109, 121, 123, 126–27; Guåhan's, 134; Japanese American, 206, 208; liberal, 30, 32–33; Marshallese, 211–12; non-, 40–42, 45; Okinawan, 133; Osakan, 211–12; partial, 36; Taiwanese, 64–65, 68, 70

civil rights, 114, 194, 204–5, 208

Clark Air Force Base, Philippines, 121

class, socioeconomic, 53, 58, 71, 108; middle, 266; working, 165, 178, 188n52

Clinton, Bill, 144–45, 252

Clinton Foundation, 78

CNN, 257

Cocopah Nation, 152

cold sex war, 55, 71

Cold War, 5, 13, 121, 199, 225–26, 229–31, 252; and cross-strait relations, 15, 53, 70; and feminism, 53–55, 57; and inter-Asian formations, 4, 7–8, 110–14; modernity, 109, 127; US, 118, 208

collectivity, 47n7, 122–23, 128, 129n18, 146, 265; and aloha concept, 39–44, 45–46; collective action, 17, 108; island collectives, 135–36, 150, 253–54; and transpacific labor, 31 colonialism, 1, 7, 12, 53, 55, 81, 83, 266; anti-, 116, 127–28, 129n18, 139, 195, 215; and cartography, 9, 137; Chinese, 253–58, 261, 263; embodied, 90; Japanese, 17, 135, 217; and nuclear power, 224–31, 232, 234–35, 237–44; overlapping, 108–14; Spanish, 122, 148; transpacific, 18–19, 21, 151, 214; US, 44, 117–18, 121, 124–26, 147; and violence, 197, 199, 209, 213. *See also* imperialism; neocolonialism; settler colonialism

coloniality, 122–23, 125, 127, 128; Mignolo on, 129n18. *See also* decoloniality; post-coloniality

Columbine High School shooting, 91

comfort women, 97–98, 193–207, 209–10, 211–16, 217n10, 219n46

Comfort Women Justice Coalition (CWJC), 17, 194, 200, 209, 212

Commission on the Status of Women (CSW), 202–5

communism, 52–57, 64, 88, 109, 111, 254, 258, 262; anti-, 65, 71, 121, 251, 253, 268n20

Communist Party of the Philippines, 121

Compact of Free Association (COFA), 30–36, 40

compassion, 78, 82–85, 90, 120

complicity, transpacific, 194, 199, 208–9, 212–16

Confucianism, 252

Contact Zone (exhibition), 37

Convention on the Elimination of all Forms of Discrimination Against Women (CE-DAW), 203

counterinsurgency, 111–12, 244

COVID-19 pandemic, 1, 7, 17, 45–46, 51–52, 55, 64, 71n1; violence during, 250, 255, 267

critical game studies, 16, 80

critical refugee studies, 16, 80–81, 85

cross-strait intimacy, 50–53, 55, 57, 60, 65, 68–71

Cruz, Denise, 14, 108, 125, 162

Cruz, Dierdre de la, 131n41

Dahil Sa'yo (art installation), 29–31, 33, 37–39, 44, 46

Dakota Access Pipeline, 244

dalumei ("mainland little sister"), as term, 52, 54, 60

Dang Nhat Minh, 255–61, 264, 267

Dang Thuy Tram, 257

Dawes, James, 165, 181

Declaration of Independence on the Land, 244

Declaration on the Rights of Indigenous Peoples, UN, 136

decoloniality, 5–6, 16–17, 44, 122, 162, 194; genealogy, 24, 134; of Japanese empire, 199, 215; non-Western, 112–13; and nuclear power, 224–27, 229, 232, 240, 242–43, 245; and poetry, 136–37, 140–41, 146, 150, 154; and Vietnam, 254–57, 261, 263–66

Deleuze, Gilles, 138

demilitarization, 112, 136, 140, 146, 151, 208, 241

democracy, 5, 11, 120, 123, 198, 244, 268n18

Democratic People's Republic of Korea. *See* North Korea

Democratic Progressive Party (DPP), 62

democratization, 89, 195, 208, 263

Deng Xiaoping, 262

denialism, 17, 196, 201–9, 212

Denmark: Copenhagen, 242

deportation, 1, 45, 268n15

Depression Quest (game), 89

development, 5, 7–8, 80, 163; Cold War, 225–27, 231–36; economic, 62, 229–30, 239; and Ferdinand Marcos, 113–15, 121; nuclear power, 240, 242, 244

diaspora, 11, 14–15, 18, 81, 140, 201–2, 237, 263; Filipino, 81, 111, 114–15, 124–28

Diaz, Vince, 35, 40

dictatorship, 109–15, 135, 254; Ferdinand Marcos, 119–20, 123–24

Diné Territory, 225

Ding, Naifei, 54–55

Dirlik, Arif, 266

disciplines, academic, 4–6, 24n26, 85, 109, 197–98; and disciplinization, 15, 18, 107; and interdisciplinarity, 2–3, 16–17

discrimination, 51, 161, 169, 205, 242

displacement, 10, 36, 152–53, 251; refugee, 76–77, 79, 81, 85, 88

dispossession, 11, 134, 142, 197, 229, 232, 238

Đổi Mới (Economic reform) program, 254

Domestic Violence Prevention Act, 54

Dong Nian, 161

Draft Environmental Impact Statement (DEIS), 141–43

East, the, 80, 113

East Asia, 1, 7, 70, 112, 199, 230

East Asian Americans, 35

East Timor, 211

Eclipse Rising, 201, 219n38, 221n76

EDSA revolution, 124

Eight Special Businesses, 51

Einfühlung (term), 83

Eisenhower, Dwight D., 209, 230

Eko (Indonesian migrant), 172

emotional extraction, 84, 86–87, 89, 91, 93, 98

empathy, 10, 16, 42, 76–86, 167, 173–74, 178, 180–82; in video games, 89–94, 96–99

empathy games, 89–93, 97

empathy machines, 76–77, 80, 82, 84, 91–92; term, coined by Roger Ebert, 77

entanglements, 57, 107, 110, 225, 227, 267; and cross-strait relationships, 62, 64; inter-Asian, 2, 151, 163; and Okinawa, 136–37, 146, 151; transpacific, 3, 5–6, 8–9, 13–17, 197–98; and Vietnam, 252, 255

Epifanio De Los Santos Avenue (EDSA), 119–20

epistemic asymmetries, 7, 23n11

epistemology, 2–5, 9–10, 13–14, 16–18, 110, 137; and seafaring, 161–65, 181; and transpacific, 107–8; US, 112, 114–15

erasure, 5, 36, 144, 206, 227–31, 235, 255; by empathy machines, 89, 93

erasure poems, 137–38, 144–46, 148–50

erotic dance, 52, 65–67

erotics, 14–15; and teahouses, 50–51, 55, 57, 63

Espiritu, Augusto, 108

Espiritu, Yến Lê, 3, 5–6, 14, 16, 81, 85, 198

essential workers, 1, 45–46

Estes, Nick, 237

ethnicity, 9, 84, 126, 154n6, 166, 201, 214; and cross-strait relations, 51, 53, 56, 64, 71

ethnic literature, 82, 85–89, 93, 96

ethnic studies, 2, 108

ethnography, 50, 57, 73, 144, 167, 179, 199; auto-, 89

Europe, 1, 79, 108, 226, 265–66

European Commission, 161

Environmental Defense Fund, 236

exceptionalism, 3, 111–13, 115, 197–98, 215, 251

expansion, 2, 4, 134, 139, 216, 225; capitalist, 112, 233–34; Chinese, 259, 261, 264, 266

exploitation, 5, 18, 78–79, 84, 86–87, 96–97, 177, 226; labor, 10, 15, 33–39, 81, 114, 160; racial, 2, 197; transnational, 255, 266; of women, 204, 213

extraction, 2, 5, 15, 225–27, 240; emotional, 84, 86–87, 89, 91, 93, 98; labor, 31, 33–35, 37, 39, 44, 177, 180; resource, 19, 161, 231

Facebook, 76–78, 91, 142–43, 183, 250, 263, 268n12

"Facts, The" (advertisement regarding comfort women), 202

Fajardo, Kale, 165

Famoksaiyan, 151

far-right groups, 196, 201. *See also individual groups*

fascism, 111, 146, 259

Federated States of Micronesia, 17, 30, 32–33, 41, 47, 225, 238; investment in, 37; Kosrae, 41, 43; nuclear industry in, 241, 243; Pohnpei, 41, 42, 43, 235; Truk (Chuuk Lagoon), 233; US colonialism in, 227, 232–33, 235; Yap, 41, 43

Feducia, AJ, 29–31, 33–34, 37, 46

Immigration and Nationality Act, US (Hart-
Celler Act, 1965), 109, 114, 125
imperialism, 1–10, 19–20, 117, 147–50, 163,
225, 255–56, 266–67; anti-, 228, 261; and
China, 53, 55; economic, 242; French,
88; and Hawai'i, 41, 46; Japanese, 5, 8,
134–40, 144–45, 199, 212, 227–28, 259;
military, 16–18; and nationalism, 194;
nuclear, 36; overlapping, 109–10, 127;
and the Philippines, 108–11, 113–15, 117,
121, 127; and Port Pacific project, 235;
sub-empires, 13, 21, 228, 231, 238; transpacific, 226, 231; US, 5, 11, 33–37, 81, 87–
89, 197–99, 208–9, 213–15; and violence,
78–79, 84–85, 94; and virtual reality, 92;
Western, 147. *See also* colonialism
i nasion chamoru (group), 151
Indian Ocean, 19
Indigeneity, 2, 5, 11–12, 107; and Chamorro
people, 136; and Hawai'i, 31, 40, 43–44;
and trans-Indigenous coalitions, 137–42
Indigenous Peoples, 17–18, 80; Chamorro,
134, 136, 151–53, 154n6; erasure of, 144–
45, 148; and Hawai'i, 32, 34–35, 47n17;
and Micronesia, 227–28, 230–31, 237–38;
and organizing, 21
Indigenous resurgence, 239–44
Indigenous studies, 3–4
Indochina, 88, 253
Indonesia, 12, 108, 169, 172, 174, 220n60,
240; and fishing, 160–61; Jakarta, 167–
68; Java, 164, 166, 168, 170–71
Industrial Research Institute of Japan, 239
Instagram, 38, 44
institutionalization, 3–4, 6, 68, 87, 112
insurgency, 109, 111–12, 123, 152, 237, 244–45
inter-Asia cultural studies, 2, 7, 24n26, 113
interconnection, 40, 42, 111, 114, 117, 140,
240; historical, 4, 8, 134
internationalism, 17, 225–26, 229, 237, 241, 244
International Military Tribunal for the Far
East, 198
International Monetary Fund, 111

International Women's Network Against
Militarism conference, Seventh (Guam,
2009), 139
internment camps, 204, 206
intimacy, 3, 5–6, 26n54, 53–57, 99, 113, 116,
150; and COFA migrants, 31, 35, 40;
cross-strait, 50–53, 55, 57, 60, 65, 68–71;
and Taiwan, 163; and Vietnam, 251,
258–60, 258n17, 269n23
intimating, 13–21, 75n53, 134–36, 138, 145,
151, 153, 226
Iowa Writers' Workshop, 86–87
Ipponmatsu, Tamaki, 240
Iranian Revolution, 90, 239
Iraq, 87, 148
ISIS, 213
Italy, 146, 207
Ito, Caryl, 206

Jade (hostess), 52
Jansen, Ann Mai Yee, 138
January Sixth Riot, 251, 253
Japan, 2, 7, 32, 108, 112, 115, 137, 259–61;
Armed Imperial Forces of, 198, 217n10;
capital investments of, 233–35; and comfort women, 205–6, 207, 213, 216; and
denialism, 196–97, 201–3, 208–11; Ginowan, 133; and Guam, 134–35, 147–48;
Henoko, 133; Hiroshima, 228; Nagasaki,
228; and nuclear industry, 225–26,
229–31, 238–41, 243; Okinawa, 16–17,
21, 133–46, 149–53, 212–16, 225, 227–29,
242–44; Ōmiya-Jima, 147; Osaka, 17,
194–95, 203–6, 209–12, 215–16, 222n78;
Satsuma, 135; and sexual enslavement,
193–95, 212, 217n10; Tokyo, 195, 199, 211,
228, 230, 243, 272; and World War II,
117–18, 143–44, 206
Japan Atomic Industrial Forum, 240
Japan Council Against A- and H-Bombs
(*Gensuikyo*), 228–29
Japanese American Community Center, 202
Japanese Americans, 11, 35, 203–5, 208, 212;

labor (*continued*)

  exploitation of, 10, 160; export economy of, 115; extraction of, 180; factory, 263; forced, 147, 228; gendered, 41, 71, 179; hospitality, 30, 31–34, 44; legislation opposing, 109; migrant, 15, 40, 43, 84, 108, 114, 161–64, 167–69; native, 25n44; racialized, 166; transnational, 173, 182, 184; undocumented, 34–39, 45–46; war-related, 14. *See also* essential workers; sex work

labor export economy, 113–14

labor unions, 45

Lakota people, 244

Laos, 81, 118; bombing of, 13

Latin America, 17, 114, 129n18, 209

Laville, Helen, 54

Le, Nam, 86–87

Lee, Aming, 164–67, 174–75, 177–80, 182–83

Lee, Edwin, 210–11, 222n77

Lee, Hsiu-chuan, 80

Lee, Ko-Woon, 98

Lee Na-Young, 213

Lee, Yong Soo, 207

legibility, 4, 16, 18, 140, 146; and Filipino America, 110, 112–13, 126, 128; and immigrant labor, 30, 33, 37, 45. *See also* illegibility

Leonard, David, 91

Liao, Hung-chi, 161

liberalism, 78, 110–11, 120; and citizenship, 32–33, 126; and guilt, 87; legal structures of, 30; and multiculturalism, 3, 251; and reform, 114–15; and the security state, 16; and settler-colonialism, 32–33; and subjectivity, 98; subjects of, 13. *See also* neoliberalism

Liberation Day, 147

liminality, 36, 166, 258–59, 261

Ling, 55

Liu, Ken, 89, 92–93, 98–99; "Byzantine Empathy" (short story), 81, 91, 97

Liu, Petrus, 52

Live Without Trident, 243

"Love Across the Taiwan Strait" (song), 69

"Love in Shanghai" (song), 69

Lowe, Lisa, 2–3, 5, 12–14, 19, 33, 81, 198, 214; on Filipino America, 114, 126, 132n51; on seafaring stories, 162, 166

Lufin (migrant prisoner), 184n1

MacArthur, Douglas, 116, 118

Machon, Josephine, 37

"mainland chicken" (term), 52

mainlanders (China), 50, 52–53, 60, 62–63

Malaysia, 240

Manalansan, Martin, IV, 3, 108

Mandarin language, 69, 75

Manila Times, 118

Māori people, 25n44, 42, 136

Mao Zedong, 58, 60, 258–59, 269n25

mapping, 5, 14, 98, 138, 140, 167, 170; re-, 5, 267. *See also* cartography

Mar, Eric, 200, 203, 219n37

Marcos, Ferdinand, 109, 111, 113–22, 124, 130n30

Marcos, Imelda, 115, 118, 127

Mariana Islands, 227, 240, 243; Northern, 135, 139, 244; Tinian, 243

Marianas Alliance Against Nuclear Waste Dumping, 243

Marshallese Congress Hold-Over Committee, 229

Marshallese people, 32, 36, 227–29, 238

Marshall Islands, 30, 137, 139, 231–32; Bikini Atoll, 35–36, 227–29, 241; Enewetak Atoll, 35; Rongelap, 35; Utirik, 35

martial law, 53, 109, 111, 113, 115, 124–27

Masaoka, Kathy, 210, 221n68

masculinity, 115, 118, 149, 179, 188n52, 226

Mashuri (migrant prisoner), 183

Matsumura, Wendy, 229

Maurer, Anaïs, 237

McCarthy, Mary M., 196

McClennen, Sophia, 167

medical modernity. *See* "transpacific medical modernity"

Palauan diaspora, 237
Palauans, 32, 235–38, 243
Palau Legislature, 236, 241
Palumbo-Liu, David, 9
Pan American Airways, 34
Panero, Robert, 234, 236
Pan-Pacific Community (project), 240
Pan-Pacific nuclear power community, 240
Papua New Guinea, 244
paratextuality, 164, 167, 172
Parikh, Crystal, 80
Park Geun-hye, 193
Parreñas, Rhacel, 114
patriarchy, 54, 214, 242, 252
Patterson, Orlando, 261
Pax Americana, 199
Pearl Harbor, attack on, 206–7
People Power Revolution (Philippines), 119, 123, 127
People's Chart for a Nuclear Free and Independent Pacific (NFIP), 224
People's Republic of China (PRC). See China
Pereira, Bernadette, 224
Perez, Craig Santos, 14, 20, 25n44, 136–44, 146–53
Philippine-American War, 13, 124
Philippine independence, 117
Philippine Refugee Processing Center, 118
Philippines, 12–13, 21, 107–9, 115–27, 130n30, 131n41, 139, 150; Bataan, 117–18, 224, 241; colonial history of, 16, 33, 36–37; and CWJC, 199, 201, 211, 214; government in, 111–12; labor from, 30, 32, 113–14; Manila, 119–20, 124–27; and nuclear power, 224, 240–41; Olongapo, 111; Subic Bay, 111, 121
Philippine studies, 107–8
Pink Moon drinking parlor, 65–66
Piper, Adrian, 94, 97
Pivot to Asia (strategy), 193
Planned Parenthood, 78
Playboy, 115
PlayStation VR, 78

"poemaps" (term, Perez), 137
pollution, 20, 126, 225, 234, 240
Polynesia, 11–12, 25, 242. *See also* French Polynesia
Port Pacific project (Palau), 232–39
possession, 11, 20, 83, 98, 147. *See also* dispossession
postcolonial grief, 14
postcoloniality, 8, 109, 112–14, 202, 214; and the Philippines, 124–25, 127–28
postcolonial studies, 2, 214
post-identity immersion, 91, 98
post-transpacific studies, 21
Pound, Ezra, 138, 146–50
Pousman, Barry, 77
poverty, 77, 79, 86, 109, 172, 254, 266
precarity, 7, 31, 33–34, 36, 42, 46; and migrancy, 77, 79–85, 89–93, 97–98
Presidential Palace (Vietnam), 252
primitive other, 54
prisons, 11, 17, 117, 160, 165–74, 181, 183–84, 264. *See also* Taipei Prison
progress, 10, 115, 214, 227, 254, 268n18; national, 15
protests, 7, 119–20, 196, 202, 204, 211, 255, 262–64; against military buildup, 133, 136, 143, 145, 152–53; against nuclear industry, 228, 237, 242; TIWA, 168, 170, 183. *See also* activism
Prutehi Litekyan: Save Ritidian, 151
Puerto Rico, 139, 244
Puʻuhonua Society, 37

QR codes, 144
queer people, 86, 89–90, 127

racial capitalism, 2, 6, 8, 198, 227–31, 240, 274
racial formations, 5, 13, 109
racialization, 5–7, 24, 31, 92, 128, 149, 197, 215; of labor, 1, 11, 30–31, 33–34, 36, 162–63, 165–66, 180
racism, 1, 7, 25n44, 125, 133, 202, 214, 251; anti-, 83, 109, 195, 215; colonial, 11, 240;

supporting, 54; prostitution, 53–57, 64, 71, 94, 194, 204, 213, 216

Shigematsu, Setsu, 18–19, 23, 136

Shimabuku, Annmaria, 214

Shimizu, Grace, 209

shin issei ("new first generation"), 201

Shoriki, Matsutaro, 229–30

Shu, Yuan, 162

Shukan Spa! (magazine), 205, 207

Sing, Lilian, 200

Singapore, 1, 240

Singh, Julietta, 15

Singh, Nikhil Pal, 80, 87

Sinitic language, 161–67, 172

Sino-Japanese War, 58

Sinophobia, 1

Sinophone studies, 2

Sino-Vietnamese War, 255–57, 259, 269, 269nn22–23, 269nn25

Sin Pink Pier art space, 183

Slaughter, Joseph, 167

Smith, Linda Tuhiwai, 136

socialism, 121, 254

Socialist Republic of Vietnam. *See* Vietnam

Social Science Research Institute of Germany, 239

Sohn, Stephen Hong, 89

soldiering, 14–15

soldiers, 119–20, 122, 133, 148–49, 203; US, 81, 87, 124, 126, 213; and Vietnam, 255, 259, 262–63, 266

solidarity, 16, 33, 46, 138–40, 194, 211–12, 214–16, 238; aesthetics of, 262, 264; decolonial, 44; feminist, 242–43; transpacific, 154, 198; between Vietnamese and Vietnamese Americans, 17, 251, 254–56

Somerville, Alice Te Punga, 18–20, 25n44

Son, Elizabeth W., 196

songs, and cross-strait intimacy, 66–68, 69–70

Sony, 78

South Africa, 224; Cape Town, 161

South America, 140, 152

South Asia, 1, 7, 12

South China Seas, 7, 21

South Dakota: Black Hills, 243; Rapid City, 243

Southeast Asia, 7, 111, 161–62, 183, 199, 233, 240, 272

Southern Hemisphere, 152

South Korea, 13, 112, 138–39, 144, 201, 209, 211–12, 224; comfort women in, 193–95, 207–8, 214; Dongducheon, 81, 94–98; Seoul, 213

South Pacific, 1, 12

South Vietnam. *See* Republic of Vietnam

Soviet Union, 111, 121, 259, 262

Spanish-American War, 36, 135

Steinberg, Philip, 161

St. Louis World's Fair, 124

St. Mary's Square (San Francisco), 199–200, 200

Subic Bay Naval Base, Philippines, 111, 121

subjectivity, 10, 62, 71, 73n26, 113, 136, 194, 197; and Filipinos, 108–10, 113–14, 119, 123–28; legibility of, 14–15; political, 209, 215

Su-chu (restaurant owner), 179

Sudan, 90

Sukhirin (Supriyanto's coworker), 168

Sun Xiangdong, 64

Supriyanto (Indonesian migrant), 160, 168, 181

Surfjack Hotel, 29, 38, 44. See also *Dahil Sa'yo*

Susanto (migrant prisoner), 169, 184n1

Suzuki, Erin, 4–5, 141, 143

Swink, Steve, 93

Syria, 77, 79, 152; civil war in, 90

Tadiar, Neferti, 84, 123

Tahitian people, 42

Taipei Prison, 164, 166, 168, 174, 184n1

Taiwan, 21, 112, 201, 212; Fisheries Agency, 160; fisheries in, 16–17, 160–68, 170, 172, 177–78, 180–83, 185n9; Pingtung County, 160; sub empire of, 13; Taipei, 50–51, 54–55, 57; Taiwanese Trump nationalism, 7,

eeship Council, 237; Visiting Mission in Koror, 237

United Public Workers for Action, 201

United States–Japanese Security Treaty, 214

Unite Here Local 5, 45

universalism, 7, 18, 98, 194, 196, 206, 215, 242

University of Guam, 139

University of Iowa, 86

unsettling, 3–4, 7, 9, 15, 33, 70, 163, 251; of methods / forms, 21, 98

Untouchables. *See* Hisabetsu Buraku

uranium mining, 224–25, 230–31, 240–41

US Bureau of Labor Statistics, 31

US Census Bureau survey (2018), 31

US-China Peoples Friendship Association, 201

US Department of Defense, 151, 235

US Department of State, 221n76, 230, 232

US federal government, 1, 45, 193, 232

US House of Representatives: House Judiciary hearings, 77; Resolution 121 (H. Res. 121), 195, 217n10

US-Japan Council, 209

US Marine Corps, 133–34, 136, 141, 146, 149, 151, 216

US-Mexico border, 140, 151–54

US military, opposition to, 136

US military bases, 1, 10, 13, 94, 206, 216, 244; in Philippines, 111, 121, 127; protests against, 133, 136, 139, 143–46, 152–53, 229; and violence, 81, 135, 150. *See also individual bases*

US Navy, 25, 141, 147, 206, 232, 235

US occupation administration, Japan, 198

US permanent war, 78, 80, 87–89, 91, 98

USS *Theodore Roosevelt*, 1

US Supreme Court, 213

Vanuatu, 224

Venice Film Festival: VR Story Award, 94

Venuti, Lawrence, 165, 186n19

veterans, 50, 64, 68–70, 257

Veterans Affairs Council, Taiwan, 70

Veterans for Peace, 201

victimization, 65, 79, 82, 87, 98, 118, 212; Asian, 86–87

victims, 78, 82–84, 90–94, 97–98, 130n26, 173, 177; Asian, 86–89; of Japan's military sexual slavery system, 194–95, 197, 199–200, 203–4, 207–8, 211–13, 220n60; Marshallese, 228, 238

victim-savior binary, 172

video games, 80, 86, 90; empathy in, 81, 84, 89–93; virtual reality, 77, 82, 98

Vietnam, 18, 81, 250, 252, 254–55, 257–62, 264, 268n11; colonialism in, 16, 253, 256; Communist Party of, 259, 262, 268n17; Hanoi, 252, 257; Lang Son, 256–58, 260; relationship with US, 252; Saigon, 251, 268n20; Spratley Island, 263. *See also* Republic of Vietnam

Vietnamese Americans, 17, 88, 250–51, 253–55, 266

Vietnamese nationals, 17, 250–51, 253–55, 263

Vietnamese people, 52, 56, 250–52, 254, 256–58, 262–65; girls, 179; nationalism for, 7, 261; refugees, 81, 86–87, 268

Vietnamization of war, 14

Vietnam War, 13, 86–87, 111, 118, 133, 213, 233, 256; postwar period, 81, 235, 251–52, 261–62

violence, 33, 76, 86, 90, 206, 238, 242; anti-Asian, 1; colonial, 227–31; during COVID, 250, 253, 255, 258–60, 262, 265–67, 268n18; domestic, 203–4; and erasure, 144, 146; and Filipino America, 111, 113–15, 118, 120, 122, 125, 129n22; and fishing, 160–61, 181; gendered, 40, 42, 44, 133–36, 139, 143, 244; histories of, 8; imperial, 11, 78–79, 81, 84, 88, 94; military, 25n44, 149–50, 152–53, 197, 225–26; neocolonial, 24n30; racial, 205; sexual, 17, 194–95, 209, 212–13, 215; state-sanctioned, 1, 10; and video games, 90–91, 98

www.ingramcontent.com/pod-product-compliance
Lightning Source LLC
Chambersburg PA
CBHW020503270326
41926CB00008B/717